Managerial Perspectives on Intelligent Big Data Analytics

Zhaohao Sun
Papua New Guinea University of Technology, Papua New Guinea

A volume in the Advances in Data Mining and
Database Management (ADMDM) Book Series

Published in the United States of America by
    IGI Global
    Engineering Science Reference (an imprint of IGI Global)
    701 E. Chocolate Avenue
    Hershey PA, USA 17033
    Tel: 717-533-8845
    Fax: 717-533-8661
    E-mail: cust@igi-global.com
    Web site: http://www.igi-global.com

Library of Congress Cataloging-in-Publication Data

Names: Sun, Zhaohao, editor.
Title: Managerial perspectives on intelligent big data analytics / Zhaohao
  Sun, editor.
Description: Hershey, PA : Engineering Science Reference, an imprint of IGI
  Global, [2019] | Includes bibliographical references and index.
Identifiers: LCCN 2018022054| ISBN 9781522572770 (hardcover) | ISBN
  9781522572787 (ebook)
Subjects: LCSH: Big data. | Quantitative research. | Industrial
  management--Data processing.
Classification: LCC QA76.9.B45 M35 2019 | DDC 005.7--dc23 LC record available at https://lccn.loc.gov/2018022054

This book is published in the IGI Global book series Advances in Data Mining and Database Management (ADMDM) (ISSN: 2327-1981; eISSN: 2327-199X).

British Cataloguing in Publication Data
A Cataloguing in Publication record for this book is available from the British Library.

For electronic access to this publication, please contact: eresources@igi-global.com.

Advances in Data Mining and Database Management (ADMDM) Book Series

David Taniar
Monash University, Australia

ISSN:2327-1981
EISSN:2327-199X

MISSION

With the large amounts of information available to organizations in today's digital world, there is a need for continual research surrounding emerging methods and tools for collecting, analyzing, and storing data.

The **Advances in Data Mining & Database Management (ADMDM)** series aims to bring together research in information retrieval, data analysis, data warehousing, and related areas in order to become an ideal resource for those working and studying in these fields. IT professionals, software engineers, academicians and upper-level students will find titles within the ADMDM book series particularly useful for staying up-to-date on emerging research, theories, and applications in the fields of data mining and database management.

COVERAGE

- Data Warehousing
- Cluster Analysis
- Database Security
- Web Mining
- Text Mining
- Customer Analytics
- Data Mining
- Data Analysis
- Profiling Practices
- Database Testing

IGI Global is currently accepting manuscripts for publication within this series. To submit a proposal for a volume in this series, please contact our Acquisition Editors at Acquisitions@igi-global.com or visit: http://www.igi-global.com/publish/.

Titles in this Series

For a list of additional titles in this series, please visit: www.igi-global.com/book-series

Optimizing Big Data Management and Industrial Systems With Intelligent Techniques
Sultan Ceren Öner (Istanbul Technical University, Turkey) and Oya H. Yüregir (Çukurova University, Turkey)
Engineering Science Reference • copyright 2019 • 238pp • H/C (ISBN: 9781522551379) • US $205.00 (our price)

Big Data Processing With Hadoop
T. Revathi (Mepco Schlenk Engineering College, India) K. Muneeswaran (Mepco Schlenk Engineering College, India) and M. Blessa Binolin Pepsi (Mepco Schlenk Engineering College, India)
Engineering Science Reference • copyright 2019 • 244pp • H/C (ISBN: 9781522537908) • US $195.00 (our price)

Extracting Knowledge From Opinion Mining
Rashmi Agrawal (Manav Rachna International Institute of Research and Studies, India) and Neha Gupta (Manav Rachna International Institute of Research and Studies, India)
Engineering Science Reference • copyright 2019 • 346pp • H/C (ISBN: 9781522561170) • US $225.00 (our price)

Intelligent Innovations in Multimedia Data Engineering and Management
Siddhartha Bhattacharyya (RCC Institute of Information Technology, India)
Engineering Science Reference • copyright 2019 • 316pp • H/C (ISBN: 9781522571070) • US $225.00 (our price)

Data Clustering and Image Segmentation Through Genetic Algorithms Emerging Research and Opportunities
S. Dash (North Orissa University, India) and B.K. Tripathy (VIT University, India)
Engineering Science Reference • copyright 2019 • 160pp • H/C (ISBN: 9781522563198) • US $165.00 (our price)

Optimization Techniques for Problem Solving in Uncertainty
Surafel Luleseged Tilahun (University of Zululand, South Africa) and Jean Medard T. Ngnotchouye (University of KwaZulu-Natal, South Africa)
Engineering Science Reference • copyright 2018 • 313pp • H/C (ISBN: 9781522550914) • US $195.00 (our price)

Predictive Analysis on Large Data for Actionable Knowledge Emerging Research and Opportunities
Muhammad Usman (Shaheed Zulfikar Ali Bhutto Institute of Science and Technology, Pakistan) and M. Usman (Pakistan Scientific and Technological Information Center (PASTIC), Pakistan)
Information Science Reference • copyright 2018 • 177pp • H/C (ISBN: 9781522550297) • US $135.00 (our price)

Handbook of Research on Big Data Storage and Visualization Techniques
Richard S. Segall (Arkansas State University, USA) and Jeffrey S. Cook (Independent Researcher, USA)
Engineering Science Reference • copyright 2018 • 917pp • H/C (ISBN: 9781522531425) • US $565.00 (our price)

701 East Chocolate Avenue, Hershey, PA 17033, USA
Tel: 717-533-8845 x100 • Fax: 717-533-8661
E-Mail: cust@igi-global.com • www.igi-global.com

Editorial Advisory Board

Table of Contents

Section 1
Foundations of Intelligent Big Data Analytics

Section 2
Technologies for Intelligent Big Data Analytics

Section 3
Applications of Intelligent Big Data Analytics

Detailed Table of Contents

Section 1
Foundations of Intelligent Big Data Analytics

Intelligent big data analytics is an emerging paradigm in the age of big data, analytics, and artificial intelligence (AI). This chapter explores intelligent big data analytics from a managerial perspective. More specifically, it first looks at the age of trinity and argues that intelligent big data analytics is at the center of the age of trinity. This chapter then proposes a managerial framework of intelligent big data analytics, which consists of intelligent big data analytics as a science, technology, system, service, and management for improving business decision making. Then it examines intelligent big data analytics for management taking into account four managerial functions: planning, organizing, leading, and controlling. The proposed approach in this chapter might facilitate the research and development of intelligent big data analytics, big data analytics, business intelligence, artificial intelligence, and data science.

The Fourth Industrial Revolution provides companies with new opportunities, and business picks up allies represented by technologies that can change mechanisms of corporate decision making in corporations. Rapid development of technologies, which allows working more efficiently with information, can lead to the creation of a new system of stakeholder interaction, thanks to better analytics, transparency, and speed of decisions. In this regard, the analyst based on big data with the use of artificial intelligence (AI) is able to significantly affect the quality of decisions. How can the application of AI for analysis of big data be able to influence the decision-making process and to what extent can it influence the system of corporate relationships? To answer this question, the authors will try to describe how transformation of decision-making methodology at the Board of Directors level under the influence of the Fourth Industrial Revolution and the development of AI technologies and big data, and what are the opportunities, limitations, and risks of the decision-making process with AI.

Chapter 3

Nabeel Al-Qirim, United Arab Emirates University, UAE
Kamel Rouibah, Kuwait University, Kuwait
Mohamad Adel Serhani, United Arab Emirates University, UAE
Ali Tarhini, Sultan Qaboos University, Oman
Ashraf Khalil, United Arab Emirates University, UAE
Mahmoud Maqableh, The University of Jordan, Jordan
Marton Gergely, United Arab Emirates University, UAE

This chapter investigates the strategic adoption of big data (BD) and analytics (BDA) in organizations. BD represents a large and complex phenomenon which spans different disciplines. BD research is fraught with many challenges. This research develops BD adoption model that could aid organizations in assessing the strategic importance of BD to gain different advantages including gaining a competitive advantage. BD is considered a radical technology and realizing its advantages in organizations is challenged with many factors. The research attempts to outline the different aspects of BD highlighting different contributions, implications and recommendations.

Chapter 4

Kenneth David Strang, Multinations Research, USA
Zhaohao Sun, Papua New Guinea University of Technology, Papua New Guinea

This chapter discusses several fundamental and managerial controversies associated with artificial intelligence and big data analytics which will be of interest to quantitative professionals and practitioners in the fields of computing, e-commerce, e-business services, and e-government. The authors utilized the systems thinking technique within an action research framework. They used this approach because their ideology was pragmatic, the problem at hand, was complex and institutional (healthcare discipline), and they needed to understand the problems from both a practitioner and a nonhuman technology process viewpoint. They used the literature review along with practitioner interviews collected at a big data conference. Although they found many problems, they considered these to be already encompassed into the big data five V's (volume, velocity, variety, value, veracity). Interestingly, they uncovered three new insights about the hidden healthcare artificial intelligence and big data analytics risks; then they proposed solutions for each of these problems.

Section 2
Technologies for Intelligent Big Data Analytics

Chapter 5

Mihai Horia Zaharia, "Gheorghe Asachi" Technical University, Romania

Big data has a great potential in improving the efficiency of most of the specific information society instruments. Yet, because it uses the newly introduced cloud technology support, it may need continuous improvements especially in the security assurance area. In this chapter, a possible solution based on the intelligent agent paradigm in securing the big data infrastructure is presented. This approach will also require some changes at the general strategy level. The main accent is on using big data techniques and tools to ensure data security. Unfortunately, due to some security-related issues at the global level, the business environment must increase the amount of resources driven to this area.

Chapter 6
Vardan Mkrttchian, HHH University, Australia
Leyla Gamidullaeva, Penza State University, Russia
Svetlana Panasenko, Plekhanov Russian University of Economics, Russia

The authors in this chapter show the essence, dignity, current state, and development prospects of avatar-based management using blockchain technology for improving implementation of economic solutions in the digital economy of Russia. The purpose of this chapter is not to review the existing published work on avatar-based models for policy advice, but to try an assessment of the merits and problems of avatar-based models as a solid basis for economic policy advice that is mainly based on the work and experience within the recently finished projects Triple H Avatar, an avatar-based software platform for HHH University, Sydney, Australia. The agenda of this project was to develop an avatar-based closed model with strong empirical grounding and micro-foundations that provides a uniform platform to address issues in different areas of digital economic and creating new tools to improve blockchain technology using the intelligent visualization techniques for big data analytic.

Chapter 7
Paul John Blayney, University of Sydney, Australia
Zhaohao Sun, Papua New Guinea University of Technology, Papua New Guinea

Can big data research be effectively conducted using spreadsheet software (i.e., Microsoft Excel)? While a definitive response might be closer to "no" rather than "yes," this question cannot be unequivocally answered. As spreadsheet scholars, the authors' inclination is to answer in the positive. To this regard, the chapter looks at how Excel can be used in conjunction with other software and analytical techniques in big data research. This chapter also argues where and how to use spreadsheet software to conduct big data research. A focal argument of this chapter is that the key behind big data driven research is data cleansing and big data driven small data analysis. The proposed approach in this chapter might facilitate the research and development of intelligent big data analytics, big data analytics, and business intelligence.

Chapter 8
Veena Gadad, Rashtreeya Vidyalaya College of Engineering, India
Sowmyarani C. N., Rashtreeya Vidyalaya College of Engineering, India

As a result of increased usage of internet, a huge amount of data is collected from variety of sources like surveys, census, and sensors in internet of things. This resultant data is coined as big data and analysis of this leads to major decision making. Since the collected data is in raw form, it is difficult to understand inherent properties and it becomes just a liability if not analyzed, summarized, and visualized. Although text can be used to articulate the relation between facts and to explain the findings, presenting it in the form of tables and graphs conveys information effectively. Presentation of data using tools to create visual images in order to gain more insights into data is called as data visualization. Data analysis is processing and interpretation of data to discover useful information and to deduce certain inferences based on the values. This chapter concerns usage of R tool and understanding its effectiveness for data analysis and intelligent data visualization by experimenting on data set obtained from University of California Irvine Machine Learning Repository.

Section 3
Applications of Intelligent Big Data Analytics

Chapter 9
Andrew Stranieri, Federation University, Australia
Venki Balasubramanian, Federation University, Australia

Remote patient monitoring involves the collection of data from wearable sensors that typically requires analysis in real time. The real-time analysis of data streaming continuously to a server challenges data mining algorithms that have mostly been developed for static data residing in central repositories. Remote patient monitoring also generates huge data sets that present storage and management problems. Although virtual records of every health event throughout an individual's lifespan known as the electronic health record are rapidly emerging, few electronic records accommodate data from continuous remote patient monitoring. These factors combine to make data analytics with continuous patient data very challenging. In this chapter, benefits for data analytics inherent in the use of standards for clinical concepts for remote patient monitoring is presented. The openEHR standard that describes the way in which concepts are used in clinical practice is well suited to be adopted as the standard required to record meta-data about remote monitoring. The claim is advanced that this is likely to facilitate meaningful real time analyses with big remote patient monitoring data. The point is made by drawing on a case study involving the transmission of patient vital sign data collected from wearable sensors in an Indian hospital.

Chapter 10
Mark Wallis, Bond University, Australia
Kuldeep Kumar, Bond University, Australia
Adrian Gepp, Bond University, Australia

Credit ratings are an important metric for business managers and a contributor to economic growth. Forecasting such ratings might be a suitable application of big data analytics. As machine learning is one of the foundations of intelligent big data analytics, this chapter presents a comparative analysis of traditional statistical models and popular machine learning models for the prediction of Moody's long-term corporate debt ratings. Machine learning techniques such as artificial neural networks, support vector machines, and random forests generally outperformed their traditional counterparts in terms of both overall accuracy and the Kappa statistic. The parametric models may be hindered by missing variables and restrictive assumptions about the underlying distributions in the data. This chapter reveals the relative effectiveness of non-parametric big data analytics to model a complex process that frequently arises in business, specifically determining credit ratings.

Chapter 11

Indivar Mishra, KIIT University, India
Ritwik Bandyopadhyay, KIIT University, India
Sourish Ghosh, KIIT University, India
Aleena Swetapadma, KIIT University, India

Considering the growing applications of big data analytics in the various fields such as healthcare, finance, e-commerce, and web services, it is essential to continuously develop techniques useful for big data. Among various techniques used for big data analytics, regression analysis is very important. In this chapter, an attempt is made to take a detailed look into some of the main regression algorithms and their origin that are used for big data analytics. In this study, some of very famous works related to regression along with some latest research are analyzed. Regression is the process of deducing a predictive model for real-world information based on verified information that is already received. It is used for making predictions, optimizing solutions to complex problems, and understands trends in large and big data analytics. The goal of this study is to promote and facilitate a better understanding of regression algorithms that are in use in the real world for big data analytics.

Chapter 12

Ionica Oncioiu, Titu Maiorescu University, Romania
Anca Gabriela Petrescu, Valahia University, Romania
Diana Andreea Mândricel, Titu Maiorescu University, Romania
Ana Maria Ifrim, Titu Maiorescu University, Romania

Taking into consideration the competitive market, the protection of information infrastructure for a company means competitive advantage. The protected information along with risk analysis are the underlying decision making in the company: either development, positioning on new markets, expansion on emerging markets, exit markets, or acquisitions. At the same time, the protection of information together with operational business intelligence systems are the keys for the decisions of CEOs. Implementing appropriate security measures to counter threats such as attacks can be blocked, or its effects can be mitigated. In this context, this chapter intends to be a thorough reflection on the awareness of potential threats and vulnerabilities, as well as a preoccupation towards cooperation in countering them with well-established rules and mechanisms created at a national and organizational level. The results are relevant to better understand how the actors involved in information and communication technologies could develop new models of information systems and risk management strategies.

Chapter 13

Sherif H. Kamel, The American University in Cairo, Egypt
Iman Megahed, The American University in Cairo, Egypt
Heba Atteya, The American University in Cairo, Egypt

In today's ever-changing global environment, the higher education industry is facing many diversified and evolving challenges and its landscape is becoming more competitive, dynamic, and complex. To proactively operate in such a changing and complicated environment, innovation, creativity, information, and knowledge represent key competitive edges that need to be introduced, cultivated, and managed effectively. The American University in Cairo (AUC) is a leading institution of higher education in the Middle East North Africa (MENA) region that recognized early on the power of knowledge and the need for a paradigm shift in management that capitalizes on innovative information and communication technologies. Accordingly, the university embarked on an ambitious journey as the first higher education institution in Egypt to build a state-of-the-art business intelligence (BI) platform that would support proactive, informed decision-making as a distinctive and sustainable competitive advantage.

This chapter treats the movement that marks, affects, and transforms any part of business and society. It is about big data that is creating, and the value generating that companies, startups, and entrepreneurs have to derive through sophisticated methods and advanced tools. This chapter suggests that analytics can be of crucial importance for business and entrepreneurial practices if correctly aligned with business process needs and can also lead to significant improvement of their performance and quality of the decisions they make. So, the main purpose of this chapter are exploring why small business, entrepreneur, and startups have to use data analytics and how they can integrate, operationally, analytics methods to extract value and create new opportunities.

Preface

We are living in an age of trinity: big data, analytics and artificial intelligence. Big data, analytics and artificial intelligence are at the frontier for revolutionizing our work, life, business, management and organization as well as healthcare, finance, e-commerce and web services. Intelligent big data analytics is at the core of this age of trinity, and becomes disruptive technology for healthcare, web services, service computing, cloud computing and social computing. However, many fundamental, technological and managerial issues in developing and applying intelligent big data analytics remain open. For example, what is the foundation of intelligent big data analytics? What are the characteristics of the age of trinity? How can apply intelligent big data analytics to improve healthcare, mobile commerce, web services and digital transformation? What is the impact of intelligent big data analytics on business and management as well as decision making? How should intelligent big data analytics be classified? What are the real big characteristics of big data? This book will address these issues by exploring the cutting-edge theory, technologies and methodologies of intelligent big data analytics based on the ten big characteristics of big data, and emphasize integration of artificial intelligence, business intelligence, digital transformation and intelligent big data analytics from a perspective of computing, service and management. This book also provides applications of the proposed theory, technologies and methodologies of intelligent big data analytics to e-SMACS (electronic, social, mobile, analytics, cloud and service) commerce and services, healthcare, digital transformation including the Internet of things, sharing economy, and Industry 4.0 or the 4th digital revolution in the real world. The proposed approaches will facilitate research and development of big data analytics, intelligent analytics, data science, artificial intelligence, digital transformation, e-business and web service, service computing, cloud computing and social computing.

Intelligent big data analytics is science and technology about collecting, organizing and analyzing big data to discover and visualize patterns, knowledge, and intelligence as well as other information within the big data based on artificial intelligence and intelligent systems. Intelligent big data analytics at least includes big data, intelligent data analysis, intelligent data warehousing, intelligent data mining, intelligent statistical modelling, intelligent machine learning, intelligent visualization and intelligent optimization and their intelligent integration. Currently, intelligent big data analytics can be classified into intelligent big data diagnostic analytics, big data descriptive analytics, big data predictive analytics and big data prescriptive analytics. All these mentioned should be improved through theoretical, technological, and methodological development in order to meet the global and social demands from different organizations or individuals for intelligent big data analytics with applications.

Foundations in this book mainly include core foundations and supporting foundations. The core foundations include intelligent data warehouses, intelligent data mining, intelligent statistical modelling, machine learning, intelligent visualization and optimization. The supporting foundations include mathematics and statistics, computing such as intelligent computing and cognitive computing, data computing including data science, artificial intelligence and optimization, domain sciences including business and management science.

Technologies in this book include intelligent technology, computational technology, web technology and Internet technology, social networking technology, cloud technology, management technology as well as big data technology, to name a few.

Applications in this book cover all the applications and case studies of intelligent big data analytics in e-commerce, social networking, big data, digital transformation, SMACS computing, healthcare and other real-world problem solving.

In order develop this book, we released the Call for Book Chapter (CFP) (https://www.igi-global. com/publish/call-for-papers/call-details/3134). The CFP includes the following topics as a realization of above-mentioned vision and a part of the book's basic structure.

Section 1: Foundations of intelligent big data analytics. Topics includes fundamental concepts, models/architectures, frameworks/schemes or foundations for planning, designing, building, operating or evaluating, managing intelligent big data analytics.

Section 2: Technologies for intelligent big data analytics. Topics includes technologies for developing intelligent big data analytics.

Section 3: Applications of intelligent big data analytics. Topics include cases and applications for using foundations and technologies in Section 1 and 2 for planning, designing, building, managing and operating or evaluating intelligent big data analytics in the various domains such as digital transformation, SMACS computing, commerce and services, financial services, legal services, healthcare services, educational services, and military services taking into account intelligent diagnostic, descriptive, predictive and prescriptive big data analytics.

Section 4: Emerging technologies and applications for intelligent big data analytics. Topics include emerging technologies, methodologies, and applications for intelligent big data analytics.

It is certainly impossible for a book to cover each of the listed topics in the CFP, although the editor has tried to do his best to use various media and also the official websites such as wikiCFP (http://www.wikicfp.com), aisworld@lists.aisnet.org, BISC group (bisc-group@eecs.berkeley.edu), and irma-1@irma-international.org to attract contributions from scholars worldwide. Based on the review reports of double-blinded peer reviews, 14 book chapters are selected and published in this book, each of them aligns with one or few of the mentioned topics.

SECTION 1: FOUNDATIONS OF INTELLIGENT BIG DATA ANALYTICS

Section 1 consists of four chapters as follows.

Chapter 1, contributed by Zhaohao Sun, titled "Intelligent Big Data Analytics: A Managerial Perspective," explores intelligent big data analytics from a managerial perspective. More specifically, it first looks at the age of trinity and argues that intelligent big data analytics is at the center of the age of trinity.

This chapter then proposes a managerial framework of intelligent big data analytics, which consists of intelligent big data analytics as a science, technology, system, service and management for improving business decision making. Then it examines intelligent big data analytics for management taking into account four managerial functions: planning, organising, leading and controlling. Finally, this chapter examines theoretical, technical and social implications of the research.

Chapter 2, contributed by Maria Nikishova and Mikhail E. Kuznetsov, titled as "Is Artificial Intelligence a New Dawn or Challenge for Corporate Decision Making?", argues that the big data analysis with the use of artificial intelligence can significantly affect the quality of decisions. In order to address the research questions: How can the application of artificial intelligence for analysis of big data be able to influence the decision-making process and to what extent can it influence the system of corporate relationships? this chapter looks at how decision-making methodology is transformed at the Board of Directors level under the influence of the Fourth Industrial Revolution and the development of artificial intelligence technologies and big data, and what are the opportunities, limitations and risks decision-making process with artificial intelligence.

Chapter 3, contributed by Nabeel Al-Qirim and Kamel Rouibah, titled "The Strategic Adoption of Big Data in Organizations," investigates the strategic adoption of big data and analytics in organizations. This research presents a big data adoption model that aims to aid organizations in assessing the strategic importance of big data to gain different advantages including gaining a competitive advantage. This chapter also outlines the different aspects of big data with highlighting different contributions, implications and recommendations.

Chapter 4, contributed by Kenneth Strang and Zhaohao Sun, titled "Managerial Controversies in Artificial Intelligence and Big Data Analytics," discusses several fundamental and managerial controversies associated with artificial intelligence and big data analytics. The chapter utilizes the systems thinking technique within an action research framework. It also uses the literature review along with practitioner interviews collected at a big data conference. This chapter uncovers three new insights about the hidden healthcare artificial intelligence and big data analytics risks and proposes solutions for each of these problems. The approach proposed in this chapter will be of interest to quantitative professionals and practitioners in the fields of computing, e-commerce, e-business services, and e-government.

SECTION 2: TECHNOLOGIES FOR INTELLIGENT BIG DATA ANALYTICS

Section 2 consists of four chapters as follows.

Chapter 5, contributed by Mihai Zaharia, titled "Using Intelligent Agents Paradigm in Big Data Security Risks Mitigation," presents a solution for securing the big data infrastructure based on the intelligent agent paradigm. This approach requires some changes at the general strategy level. The main objective of this research is to use big data techniques and tools to ensure data security. This chapter also shows that the business environment must increase the amount of resources driven to this area, due to some security related issues at the global level.

Chapter 6, contributed by Vardan Mkrttchian, Leyla Gamidullaeva and Svetlana Panasenko, titled "Optimizing and Enhancing Digital Marketing Techniques in Intellectual Big Data Analytics," shows the essence, dignity, current state and development prospects of avatar-based management using blockchain technology for improving implementation of economic solutions in digital economy of Russia. The purpose of this chapter is to assess the merits and problems of avatar-based models as a solid basis for economic policy advice that is mainly based on the work and experience within the recently finished projects Triple H Avatar, an Avatar-based Software Platform for HHH University, Sydney, Australia. This project aims to develop an avatar-based closed model with strong empirical grounding and micro foundations that provides a uniform platform to address issues in different areas of digital economic and creating new tools to improve blockchain technology using the intelligent visualization techniques for big data analytics.

Chapter 7, contributed by Paul Blayney and Zhaohao Sun, titled as "Using Excel and Excel VBA for Preliminary Analysis in Big Data Research," looks at how Excel can be used in conjunction with other software and analytical techniques in big data research. This chapter also discusses where and how can use spreadsheet software to conduct big data research. A focal argument of this chapter is that the key behind big data driven research is data cleansing and big data driven small data analysis.

Chapter 8, contributed by Veena Gadad and C. N. Sowmyarani, titled "Census Data Analysis and Visualization Using R Tool: A Case Study," defines data visualization as presentation of data using tools to create visual imagines in order to gain more insights into data, and data analysis as the processing and interpretation of data to discover useful information and to deduce certain inference based on the value. This chapter looks at usage of R tool and understanding its effectiveness for data analysis and intelligent data visualization by experimenting on data set obtained from University of California Irvine Machine Learning Repository.

SECTION 3: APPLICATIONS OF INTELLIGENT BIG DATA ANALYTICS

Section 3 consists of six chapters as follows.

Chapter 9, contributed by Andrew Stranieri and Venki Balasubramanian, titled "Remote Patient Monitoring for Healthcare: A Big Challenge for Big Data," considers remote patient monitoring (RPM) involving the collection of data from wearable sensors that typically requires analysis in real time. This chapter demonstrates that standards for clinical concepts for remote patient monitoring can facilitate stream mining and integration of RPM into electronic health records. The research of this chapter shows that the open EHR standard that describes the way in which concepts are used in clinical practice is well suited to be adopted as the standard required to record meta-data about remote monitoring.

Chapter 10, contributed by Mark Wallis, Kuldeep Kumar, and Adrian Gepp, titled "Credit Rating Forecasting Using Machine Learning Techniques," considers machine learning as one of the foundations of intelligent big data analytics, and presents a comparative analysis of traditional statistical models and popular machine learning models for the prediction of Moody's long term corporate debt ratings. The research shows that machine learning techniques such as artificial neural networks, support vector machines and random forests generally outperformed their traditional counterparts in terms of both overall accuracy and the Kappa statistic. The parametric models may be hindered by missing variables and restrictive assumptions about the underlying distributions in the data. This chapter reveals the relative effectiveness of non-parametric big data analytics to model a complex process that frequently arises in business, specifically determining credit ratings.

Chapter 11, contributed by Indivar Mishra, et al., titled "Analysis of Cutting Edge Regression Algorithms Used for Data Analysis," demonstrates that it is essential to continuously develop techniques useful for big data, taking into account the growing applications of big data analytics in the various fields. Regression analysis is very important among various techniques for big data analytics. This chapter looks into some of the main regression algorithms and their origins that are used for big data analytics. The research aims to facilitate a better understanding of regression algorithms for big data analytics.

Chapter 12, contributed by Ionica Oncioiu, et al., titled "Proactive Information Security Strategy for a Secure Business Environment," intends to be a thorough reflection on the awareness of potential threats and vulnerabilities, as well as a preoccupation towards cooperation in countering them with well-established rules and mechanisms created at a national and organizational level. The research results might facilitate to better understand how the actors involved in information and communication technologies could develop new models of information systems and risk management strategies.

Chapter 13, contributed by Sherif H. Kamel, Iman Megahed, and Heba Atteya, titled "The Impact of Creating a Business Intelligence Platform on Higher Education: The Case of the American University in Cairo," demonstrates that the American University in Cairo (AUC) is a leading institution of higher education in the Middle East North Africa (MENA) region that recognized early on the power of knowledge and the need for a paradigm shift in management that capitalizes on innovative information and communication technologies. Accordingly, the university, embarked on an ambitious journey, as the first higher education institution in Egypt, to build a state-of-the-art business intelligence platform that would support proactive, informed decision-making as a distinctive and sustainable competitive advantage.

Chapter 14, contributed by Soraya Sedkaoui and Mounia Khelfaoui, titled "Building an Analytics Culture to Boost a Data-Driven Entrepreneur's Business Model," addresses two significant issues: why does small business, entrepreneur, and start-ups have to use data analytics? how can they operationally integrate analytics methods to extract value and create new opportunities? This chapter demonstrates that analytics can be of crucial importance for business and entrepreneurial practices, and can also lead to significant improvement of their performance and quality of the decision making.

Big data and big data analytics have become the important frontier for innovation, research and development. Big data analytics has big market opportunities. For example, the researcher of IDC forecasts that big data and analytics-related services marketing in Asia/Pacific (Excluding Japan) region will grow from US$3.8 billion in 2016 to US$7.0 billion in 2019 at a 16.3% CAGR (compound annual growth rate). Big data and its emerging technologies including big data analytics have been not only making big changes in the way the business operate but also making traditional data analytics and business analytics bring new big opportunities for academia and enterprises.

Intelligent big data analytics is an emerging big data technology, and is becoming a mainstream market adopted broadly across industries, organizations, and geographic regions and among individuals to facilitate big data-driven decision making for business and individual to achieve desired business outcomes.

This book is the first book on "Intelligent big data analytics" and focuses on intelligent big data analytics in the age of trinity: the age of big data, the age of analytics, the age of artificial intelligence. This book titled *Managerial Perspectives on Intelligent Big Data Analytics* is the first book to reveal the cutting-edge theory, technologies, methodologies and applications of intelligent big data analytics in the age of trinity in an integrated way. This is also the first book demonstrating that intelligent big data analytics is an important enabler for developing big data analytics, smart analytics, intelligent analytics, digital transformation, business, management, governance and services in the age of trinity.

This book's primary aim is to convey the foundations, technologies, thoughts, and methods of intelligent big data analytics with applications to scientists, engineers, educators and university students, business, service and management professionals, policy makers and decision makers and others who have interest in intelligent big data analytics, artificial intelligence, digital transformation, SMACS computing, commerce and service as well as data science. Primary audiences for this book are undergraduate, postgraduate students and variety of professionals in the fields of big data, data science, analytics, artificial intelligence, computing, commerce, business, services, management and government. The variety of readers in the fields of government, consulting, business and trade as well as the readers from all the social strata can also be benefited from this book to improve understanding of the cutting-edge theory, technologies, methodologies and applications of intelligent big data analytics in the age of trinity.

Zhaohao Sun
Papua New Guinea University of Technology, Papua New Guinea

Acknowledgment

The publication of this book reflects the wisdom and perseverance of many researchers and friends worldwide. I would like to express my sincere gratitude to all the members of editorial board committee for their erudite comments and guidance. I heartily thank all the contributors for their time and submission of manuscripts, they have made this book possible and transformed our initiative to reality. I would also like to thank all the contributors who have submitted book chapter proposals, drafts, ideas to this book. My special thanks go to the international team of reviewers for reviewing the book chapters and submitting review reports selflessly, timely and professionally. I have to express sincere thanks to PNG University of Technology, Federation University Australia and Hebei University of Science and Technology for their excellent research environment that I have used to develop my ideas, books and research papers effectively. My heartily thanks also go to researchers who access WikiCFP, ResearchGate, and IS World, IRMA and BISC and care for our CFP. My sincerest thanks go to my good friend at IGI-Global, Ms Jordan Tepper, who has given me outstanding and continuous support through the book development process. Finally, I would like to express my deep appreciation for the support and encouragement of my wife, Dr Yanxia (Monica) Huo. Without her lasting support and patience, authoring and editing this book would not have been possible.

Section 1
Foundations of Intelligent Big Data Analytics

Chapter 1
Intelligent Big Data Analytics:
A Managerial Perspective

Zhaohao Sun

ⓘ https://orcid.org/0000-0003-0780-3271

Papua New Guinea University of Technology, Papua New Guinea

ABSTRACT

Intelligent big data analytics is an emerging paradigm in the age of big data, analytics, and artificial intelligence (AI). This chapter explores intelligent big data analytics from a managerial perspective. More specifically, it first looks at the age of trinity and argues that intelligent big data analytics is at the center of the age of trinity. This chapter then proposes a managerial framework of intelligent big data analytics, which consists of intelligent big data analytics as a science, technology, system, service, and management for improving business decision making. Then it examines intelligent big data analytics for management taking into account four managerial functions: planning, organizing, leading, and controlling. The proposed approach in this chapter might facilitate the research and development of intelligent big data analytics, big data analytics, business intelligence, artificial intelligence, and data science.

INTRODUCTION

Big data and big data analytics have become the important frontier for innovation, research and development (Chen & Zhang, 2014) (Laney & Jain, 2017). Big data analytics has big market opportunities. For example, IDC forecasts that big data and analytics-related services marketing in Asia/Pacific (Excluding Japan) region will grow from US$3.8 billion in 2016 to US$7.0 billion in 2019 at a 16.3% CAGR (compound annual growth rate) (Roche, 2016). Big data and its emerging technologies including big data analytics have been not only making big changes in the way the business operates but also making traditional data analytics and business analytics bring forth new big opportunities for academia and enterprises (Sun, Sun, & Strang, 2016, Sun, Strang, & Yearwood, 2014; Sun, Zou, & Strang, 2015; McAfee & Brynjolfsson, 2012).

DOI: 10.4018/978-1-5225-7277-0.ch001

Artificial intelligence (AI) is becoming a core business and analytic competency to transform business processes, reconfigure workforces, optimize infrastructure and blend industries (Laney & Jain, 2017). Gartner predicts that 30% of new revenue growth from industry-specific solutions will include AI technology by 2021 (Laney & Jain, 2017).

Intelligent big data analytics is an emerging science and technology based on AI, and is becoming a mainstream market adopted broadly across industries, organizations, and geographic regions and among individuals to facilitate decision making for business and individual to achieve desired business outcomes (Laney & Jain, 2017) (Sun, Sun, & Strang, 2018) (Howson, Sallam, & Richa, 2018). However, the following issues have not been drawn significant attention in both academia and industries.

- What is the foundation of intelligent big data analytics?
- What is a managerial perspective on intelligent big data analytics?

This chapter will address these two research questions through exploring intelligent big data analytics from a managerial perspective. The first key contribution of this paper is to propose that intelligent big data analytics is at the center of the age of trinity. The second key contribution of this paper is to present a managerial framework of intelligent big data analytics. The framework demonstrates intelligent big data analytics as a science, technology, system, service and management. The third key contribution of this paper is to examine intelligent big data analytics for management as intelligent big data analytics for planning, organizing, leading and controlling.

The remainder of this chapter is organized as follows: Section 2 explores the age of trinity: age of big data, the age of analytics, and the age of AI, and shows that intelligent big data analytics is at the center in the age of trinity. Section 3 proposes a managerial framework of intelligent big data analytics. Section 4 discusses intelligent big data analytics as a management. Sections 5 and 6 provides discussion and implications as well as future research directions of this research. The final section ends this chapter with some concluding remarks and future research directions.

AN AGE OF TRINITY: BIG DATA, ANALYTICS, AND ARTIFICIAL INTELLIGENCE

This section first briefly overviews the age of big data, the age of analytics, and the age of AI, and then looks at the age of trinity and shows that intelligent big data analytics plays a central role in the age of trinity.

The Age of Big Data

The age of big data can be dated back to 2001. At that time, Doug Laney of the META Group (now Gartner) uses 3 Ds: data volume, data velocity, and data variety to represent the characteristics of data management in e-commerce (Laney, 2001). McKinsey Global Institute claims big data as the next frontier for innovation, competition, and productivity (McKinsey, 2011), which plays a catalytic role in the coming of the age of big data. The age of big data has officially arrived in 2012 (Lohr, 2012 February 11), because of the US Government's announcement of "Big Data" Initiative (Weiss & Zgorski, 2012). At that time, the 3 Ds had been changed into 3 Vs (volume, velocity, and variety) which have been explained as three characteristics of big data (McAfee & Brynjolfsson, 2012) (McKinsey, 2011). The age of big data has drawn significant attention in the academia, industry and government since then. The Chinese government also announced its national initiative on big data in 2015 (Sun Z., 2018). The initial 3Vs have been evolved to 10 Bigs to represent the 10 big characteristics of big data in order to meet the ever-increasing global and social demands (Sun Z., 2018). These 10 Bigs consists of big volume, big velocity, big variety, big veracity, big analytics, big infrastructure, big service, big market, big value, and big intelligence. We are in the age of big data, and enjoy these 10 Bigs of big data such as big service and big market. For example, 2.2 billion people are enjoying the Facebook commerce and services monthly (Wikipedia, 2018). More than 1 billion people are enjoying the WeChat services and free call worldwide (Wikipedia, 2018). Smart phones have become an indispensable part of our human brains to read, to speak, to write, to listen and to do business. It is possible to use Google searches, Facebook posts and Twitter messages to measure the behaviour and sentiment of every netizen in fine detail (Lohr, 2012 February 11).

The Age of Analytics

Analytics was first in scholar publication in 1936 (Semanticscholar.org). Analytics is "the scientific process of transforming data into insight for making better decisions" (Wang, 2012). Data analytics can be considered as data-driven discoveries of knowledge, intelligence and communications (Delena & Demirkanb, 2013). More generally, data analytics is a science and technology about analyzing, examining, summarizing, acquiring intelligence, and drawing conclusions from data to learn, describe and predict something (Sun, Strang, & Yearwood, 2014) (Gandomi & Haider, 2015). Data analytics has been in academia and industry for a long time although it has not become a disruptive technology until recently (Holsapplea, Lee-Postb, & Pakath, 2014) (Davis, 2014).

The age of analytics has started with the release of "The age of analytics: Competing in a data-driven world" by McKinsey Global Institute in 2016 (Henke & Bughin, 2016). We are in the age of analytics, and enjoy the analytics as a service (Delena & Demirkanb, 2013) (Sun & Yearwood, 20014) (Laney & Jain, 2017) and big data analytics as a service (Sun Z., 2018). For example, Google Analytics provides services like Google map to billions of people worldwide. Clarivate analytics is the largest academic quality publication database to provide subscription services to academia and industry. Tableau, Python and R as software have been used widely to develop big data analytics services. A popular analytics service is that one can enjoy the health analytics service provided by various smart phones in a real-world mode. Big Data and analytics are increasingly critical elements across most industries, business functions and IT disciplines. They are creating unlimited business value possibilities, based on the research of Gartner (Laney & Jain, 2017).

The Age of Artificial intelligence

The age of Artificial intelligence (AI) can go back to 1950 when Alan Turing published his seminal paper titled 'Computing Machinery and Intelligence' (Turing, 1950). AI was first coined by John McCarthy in 1955, defined as the "science and engineering of making intelligent machines" (Wang, 2012). It aims to imitate, extend, augment, automate intelligent behaviors of human being using computing machinery (Russell & Norvig, 2010). In the past six decades, researchers and developers have been working on intelligence of machines (Wang, 2012), neural networks, machine learning and translation (Laney &

Jain, 2017), natural language processing, machine translation, expert systems, knowledge base systems, fuzzy logic and systems, genetic algorithms and so on under the flagship of AI (Russell & Norvig, 2010).

The age of AI has officially arrived in 2013 (John, 2013). The significant success and global concern of market-driven AI is another reason for the coming of the age of AI. Autonomous vehicles, advanced vision systems, virtual customer assistants, smart personal agents and natural language processing are all the advanced technology of market-driven AI (Laney & Jain, 2017). Google and Baidu Driverless cars running on the road in USA and China symbolizes the significant progress of market-driven AI. Smart phones as intelligent products provide health analytics, weather, shopping and travel services to one wherever and whenever one is.

Intelligent Big Data Analytics at the Center of the Age of Trinity

Based on the discussion of previous sections, we have been living in the age of big data (Tsai, Lai, Chao, & Vasilakos, 2015), the age of analytics and the age of AI. Therefore, we are living in an age of trinity that integrates big data, analytics and AI, as shown as in Figure 1.

Big data, analytics and AI and their integration are at the frontier for revolutionizing our work, life, business, management and organization as well as healthcare, finance, e-commerce and web services (Henke & Bughin, 2016) (Lohr, 2012 February 11) (John, 2013) (Sun, Strang, & Yearwood, 2014).

Big data has not very big value without big data analytics, just as oil without the significant progress of petrochemical industry. However, the commercial value of big data becomes bigger and bigger with the processing, deep processing, smart processing, intelligent processing of big data. Big data analytics is behind processing, deep processing, second time processing, multi-processing .... of big data. Therefore, big data analytics is more important than big data, and intelligent big data analytics is at the core of this age of trinity, and becomes disruptive technology for the age of trinity in terms of healthcare, web services, service computing, cloud computing and social networking computing (Laney & Jain, 2017). AI-derived business value is forecasted to increase to $US3.9 trillion in 2022 from $US1.2 trillion of 2018 (Pettey & van der Meulen, 2018), 325% jump! Intelligent big data analytics is an enabler for effective management and decision making in the age of trinity.

Figure 1. An age of trinity: big data, analytics and AI

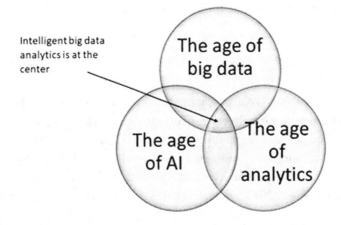

It should be noted that Gartner uses advanced analytics to analyze AI, big data and analytics and their impacts (Laney & Jain, 2017). With the further development of the age of trinity, intelligent analytics or smart analytics might be the choice for representing either advanced analytics or intelligent big data analytics, because the general customers hope to use the simple concept to cover what they perceive just as smart phone rather than intelligent phone is accepted in the world.

A MANAGERIAL FRAMEWORK OF INTELLIGENT BIG DATA ANALYTICS

A managerial framework of intelligent big data analytics consists of intelligent big data analytics as a science and technology, intelligent system, service and management for improving business decision making, as shown in Figure 2.

This section will examine each of them in terms of goals, processes for support decision making of business process and organization.

Intelligent Big Data Analytics as a Science and Technology

Like mathematics, intelligent big data analytics (IBA) is science and technology about collecting, organizing and analyzing big data to discover patterns, knowledge, and intelligence within the big data based on AI, and domain-specific mathematical and analytical models (Holsapplea, Lee-Postb, & Pakath, 2014)(Sun, Sun, & Strang, 2018) (Chen, Chiang, & Storey, 2012) (Davis, 2014). Currently, IBA can be classified into intelligent big data descriptive analytics, big data predictive analytics and big data prescriptive analytics (Sun, Sun, & Strang, 2018), as mentioned in the previous section. All these

Figure 2. A managerial framework of intelligent big data analytics

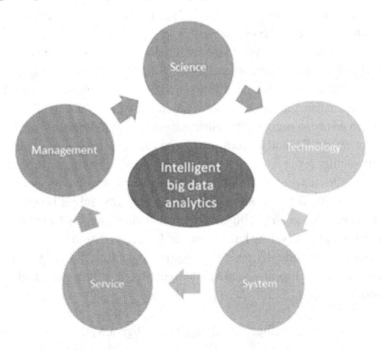

mentioned should be improved through theoretical, technological, and methodological development in order to meet the global and social demands from different parties or individuals for intelligent big data analytics with applications.

Foundations of IBA consists of core foundations and supporting foundations. The core foundations include intelligent data warehousing, intelligent data mining, intelligent statistical modelling, machine learning including deep learning (Al-Jarrah, Yoo, Muhaidat, & Karagiannidis, 2015), intelligent visualization and optimization (Sun, Sun, & Strang, 2018). The supporting foundations include mathematics and statistics including descriptive and predicative statistical methods (Davis, 2014), computing and data science, AI and optimization, domain sciences including business and management science (Sun & Wang, 2017).

Technologies of IBA include intelligent technology, computational technology, web technology and Internet technology, social networking technology, cloud technology, and management technology, to name a few (Laney & Jain, 2017). Gartner predicts that half of IT organizations will apply IBA or advanced analytics in application development to improve application quality and deliver speed (Laney & Jain, 2017).

Intelligent Big Data Analytics as a System

Intelligent systems (IS) encompasses the principles, methodologies, techniques and processes of applying AI to real world problem solving (Schalkoff, 2011). An IS is a system that can imitate, and/or automate intelligent behaviors of human beings and solve problems that were heretofore solved by humans through generating representations, inference procedures, and learning strategies (Schalkoff, 2011) (p. 2). Intelligent systems are built based on the following intelligent techniques: Knowledge representation (Schalkoff, 2011), expert systems and knowledge-based systems (Moutinho, Rita, & Li, 2006), case-based reasoning (CBR) (Sun & Finnie, 2004), genetic algorithms, swarm intelligence (Schalkoff, 2011), neural networks, fuzzy logic, intelligent agents and multiagent systems (Russell & Norvig, 2010), data mining and knowledge discovery from databases (KDD), decision support systems (DSS), and knowledge management (Moutinho, Rita, & Li, 2006), to name a few.

Intelligent big data analytics is designed into intelligent systems and embedded in intelligent systems. This is an application form of intelligent big data analytics as an intelligent system in specific and system in general. There are a number of intelligent big data analytics as an intelligent system in smart mobile phones, in airplane, in supermarket, even in a driverless car. Intelligent big data analytics as an intelligent system has been accepted by business, market, finance, banking, healthcare and other industries in the age of trinity. Recently, Woolworths and Coles, K market in Australia have used intelligent machines with intelligent big data analytics. One scans what buying at supermarket and pays the bill there by clicks. No sales assistants work there anymore. Unmanned stores have become more and more in China nationwide. At Airports, one can check-in using IDS and get boarding card automatedly.

Intelligent big data analytics as an intelligent system can aid managers by extracting useful patterns of information, capturing and discovering knowledge, and generating solutions to problems encountered in decision making, delegating authority and assigning responsibility (Sun & Firmin, 2012).

The relationships among intelligent systems, intelligent big data analytics, and intelligent analytics as follows can be summarized as

Intelligent Big Data Analytics $\subset$ intelligent analytics $\subset$ Intelligent Systems.

Intelligent Big Data Analytics as a Service

Analytics as a service is relatively new (Delena & Demirkanb, 2013) (Sun & Yearwood, 2014). Big data analytics as a service is an extended form of analytics as a service (Sun, Sun, & Strang, 2018). Big data analytics as a service has been evolved into intelligent big data analytics as a service in the age of trinity. Intelligent big data analytics as a service has been revolutionizing people's work, life and thinking with the healthy development service-centered society (Sun & Yearwood, 20014) (Sun, Sun, & Strang, 2018). Currently, many enjoy intelligent big data analytics services in terms of living, studying, working, moving and socializing. For example, when one drives from one city to a corner of another city, the GPS navigation services can guide the car to arrive the destination optimally. The automation of driving (Vardi, 2016) armed with intelligent big data analytics will make everyone enjoy wonderful driving service from one place to a corner of another city easily, safely and optimally even if he can sleep, enjoy the online chat, and watch movies in the car, until his car arrives the destination and tells him "You have reached your destination, my darling".

Figure 3 is an intelligent big data analytics service-oriented architecture (IASOA), based on the big data analytics SOA proposed in (Sun, Strang, & Yearwood, 2014) (Sun, Zou, & Strang, 2015). In this architecture, intelligent big data analytics service provider, intelligent big analytics service requestor, intelligent big data analytics service broker are three main players.

In Figure 3, intelligent big data analytics service requestors include organizations, governments and all level business decision makers such as CEO and CFO as well as managers (Sun, Strang, & Yearwood, 2014). Intelligent big data analytics service requestors also include business information systems and e-commerce systems. Intelligent big data analytics service requestors require big data analytics services including information analytics services, knowledge analytics services, organization analytics services, intelligent business analytics services, market analytics services to provide knowledge patterns and information (Coronel & Morris, 2015) for decision making in the form of figures or tables or reports (Kauffman, Srivastava, & Vayghan, 2012). More generally, intelligent big data analytics service requestors include people who like to make decisions based on analytical reports provided by big data analytics service provider (Sun, Strang, & Yearwood, 2014). Therefore, a person with smartphone receiving intelligent analytics services like GPS information is also an intelligent big data analytics service requestor (Delena & Demirkanb, 2013; Sun, Zou, & Strang, 2015; Sun, Sun, & Strang, 2018).

Intelligent big data analytics service brokers are all the entities that facilitate the development of intelligent big data analytics services, which include popular presses, traditional media and social media, consulting companies, scholars and university students, and so on (Sun, Strang, & Yearwood, 2014). All these use a variety of methods and techniques to improve intelligent big data analytics services (Sun, Strang, & Yearwood, 2014). McKinsey (http://www.mckinsey.com/) and Gartner as intelligent big data analytics service brokers have played an important role in pushing intelligent big data analytics in businesses and enterprises.

Intelligent big data analytics service providers include analytics developers, analytics vendors, analytics systems or software and other intermediaries that can provide intelligent analytics services. For example, Tableau as a software developer has been promoting intelligent big data analytics (Tableau, 2015). Google is not only a search engine provider, Google Analytics (http://www.google.com/analytics/) is also an intelligent big data analytics service provider. Mobile App Analytics (http://www.google.com/analytics/mobile/), a part of Google Analytics, is also a mobile big data analytics services provider that helps the smartphone customers to discover new and relevant users through traffic sources reports.

Figure 3. An IASOA

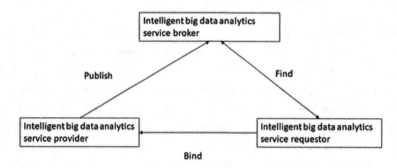

INTELLIGENT BIG DATA ANALYTICS AS A MANAGEMENT

Management is the process of manager's coordinating and overseeing the work activities of others so that their activities are completed (Robbins, Bergman, Stagg, & Coulter, 2012). There are three levels of management: operational management, tactical management, and strategic management, which correspond to activities of operational managers, middle managers and top managers of organizations respectively (Robbins, Bergman, Stagg, & Coulter, 2012) (pp. 14-19). The main management functions or activities of a manager consist of planning, organizing, leading and controlling (Terry, 1968) (p.133) (Robbins, Bergman, Stagg, & Coulter, 2012) (pp.14-19). Intelligent big data analytics as a management can be briefly represented as:

Intelligent big data analytics as a management = Management of intelligent big data analytics + intelligent big data analytics for management (1)

The following subsections will look at management of intelligent big data analytics and intelligent big data analytics for management to some detail.

Management of Intelligent Big Data Analytics

There are many methods and techniques that are useful for managing intelligent big data analytics, for example, data management, information management, and knowledge management (Sun & Firmin, 2012). These have played a significant role in big data analytics as an intelligent system, because data, information, and knowledge are the foundation for intelligent systems and big data analytics (Sun & Finnie, 2004), as shown in Figure 4. Data management (Laudon & Laudon, 2014), information management (Laudon & Laudon, 2014), knowledge management (KM) (Sun & Finnie, 2005) are well-known in either information systems (Chaffey, 2009) or intelligent systems (Turban & Volonino, 2011). We do not go into each of them, owing to space limitation. For detail see other references such as (Sun & Finnie, 2004) and (Chaffey & White, 2011).

Figure 4. A model of management for intelligent big data analytics

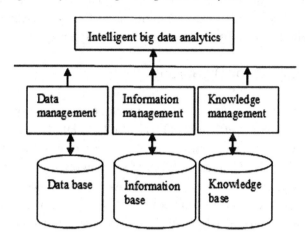

Intelligent Big Data Analytics for Management

Intelligent big data analytics should be applied to each of the main management functions in order to sustain business competitiveness, operate organizations more intelligently at all levels, and enhance management decision making (Davis, 2014), that is, it is important to look at intelligent big data analytics for planning, organizing, leading, and controlling respectively. In what follows, we will look at each of these in some detail.

Intelligent Big Data Analytics for Planning

Planning involves defining the organizations' goals, establishing an overall strategy for achieving those goals, and developing a comprehensive set of plans to integrate and coordinate organizational work (Robbins, Bergman, Stagg, & Coulter, 2012, p. 294). In the process of planning, managers define goals, establish strategies for achieving these goals, and develop plans to integrate and coordinate activities (Robbins, Bergman, Stagg, & Coulter, 2012, p. 14). To this end, the managers should define the nature and purpose of planning, classify the type of goals that organizations use, and describe related types of plans that organizations use, describe project management and discuss issues in planning. A comprehensive set of plans is the outcome of the planning process (Sun & Firmin, 2012).

Intelligent big data analytics for planning aims to imitate and automate some or all planning behaviors of managers of organizations, e.g., in corporate planning (Thierauf, 1982) and supply chain planning (Laudon & Laudon, 2014, p. 303). More specifically, they should imitate and automate definition of goals, establishment of strategies for achieving these goals, and development of plans to integrate and coordinate activities (Sun & Firmin, 2012). To this end, data management, information management and knowledge management should be the basis for any intelligent big data analytics for planning. Data mining, business analytics, knowledge base systems (KBS), expert systems and intelligent agents have been developed to aid the process of planning. All these intelligent techniques are used as a decision support tool for intelligent planning system (Smith, 1992). Case based systems as intelligent systems can also facilitate the intelligent big data analytics for planning, because "similar goals have similar strategies" for achieving these goals (Sun & Finnie, 2004) (Finnie & Sun, 2003).

Intelligent big data analytics for planning can be also called intelligent planning analytics. Intelligent planning analytics has been used to automate planning, budgeting, forecasting and analysis processes for an organization working together with IBM® Planning Analytics (Cortell, 2017).

Intelligent Big Data Analytics for Organizing

Organizing is to establish effective behavioral relationships among selected work, persons, and workplaces in order for the group to work together efficiently (Terry, 1968, p. 289). In other words, organizing means arranging and structuring work, persons, and workplaces to accomplish the organization's plans and goals (Robbins, Bergman, Stagg, & Coulter, 2012, p. 14). When organizing, managers determine what tasks need to get done, who is to do them, and how the tasks are to be decomposed and grouped, who reports to whom and at what level decisions to be made. They also allocate and deploy organizational resources during the organizing process (Robbins, Bergman, Stagg, & Coulter, 2012, p. 368).

Intelligent big data analytics for organizing aims to imitate and automate all or some organizing behaviors of managers of organizations. More specifically, it should imitate and automate decomposition of tasks, grouping of persons who complete the decomposed task, allocation and deployment of organizational resources. Intelligent big data analytics for organizing also includes intelligent customer relationship analytics (CRA) software and intelligent supply chain analytics (SCA) software. CRA software uses intelligent technologies and big data analytics to organize business processes and marketing activities including customer service and technical support. The main CRA vendors are SAP (www.sap.com), oracle (www.oracle.com) and salesforce.com (CRM, 2012). SCA software as an intelligent system involves using intelligent technology to optimally organize supply activities and associated material flows and information flows to organizations and marketing (Sun Z., 2016). SAP and Oracle are among the leading providers of SCA applications (Chaffey, 2009, p. 379).

The intelligent big data analytics tools for organizing include spreadsheets and project management specific applications. Spreadsheets are regularly used to assist managers to organize information and data. Project management applications e.g. Microsoft Project, are also used to assist managers to organize activities, in particular the planning and scheduling of activities. Tools such as Microsoft Project have intelligent capabilities evidenced through the automation and generation of management reports such as Gantt charts (Larson & Gray, 2011). Their functionality supports the organizational process to improve efficiencies and information quality (Caniels & Bakens, 2011).

Intelligent Big Data Analytics for Leading

Leading is to oversee and coordinate people to work so that organizational goals can be pursued and accomplished (Robbins, Bergman, Stagg, & Coulter, 2012, p. 467). When managers are leading, they motivate their subordinates, help to resolve work group conflicts, influence individuals or work teams, select appropriate communication channels, or deal with individual or group behavior issues (Robbins, Bergman, Stagg, & Coulter, 2012, p. 14). Leading people involves understanding their attitudes, behaviors, personalities and motivations as an individual, or a group, or a community (Robbins, Bergman, Stagg, & Coulter, 2012, p. 469) and helping them to "achieve their respective essential goals as well as their maximum potentialities" (Terry, 1968, p. 451).

Intelligent big data analytics for leading aims to imitate and automate all or some leading behaviors of managers. More specifically, it should imitate and automate how to motivate subordinates, help to resolve work group conflicts, influence individuals or work teams, select appropriate communication channels or deal with individual or group behavior issues, and understanding attitudes, behaviors, personalities and motivations of the individuals and teams (Sun & Firmin, 2012). However, understanding attitudes, behaviors, personalities and motivations of individuals and teams is still a big challenge for research and development of intelligent systems for leading (Sun Z., 2016). Although there are not special intelligent big data analytics for leading, there are intelligent analytics apps that are used to assist leading of managers. For example, enterprise networking sites as limited online social networking services have been available in many large organizations for facilitating leading of managers. Updated communication tools including emails have also facilitated the communications among the manager and his/her subordinates.

Intelligent Big Data Analytics for Controlling

Controlling is to determine what is being accomplished, that is, evaluate the performance and, if necessary, apply corrective measures to that the performance takes place according to plans (Terry, 1968, p. 544). In other words, a control mechanism has five basic elements: establish standards, supervise, monitor, compare and correct work performance (Thierauf, 1982, p. 278). Controlling of operations, processes, quantity, quality, time use, budget and cost are main job of a manager (Terry, 1968, p. 543) (Sun Z., 2016). When managers are in the process of controlling, they must monitor and evaluate the activities to make sure they are being done as planned and correct any significant deviations (Robbins, Bergman, Stagg, & Coulter, 2012, p. 645). Therefore, a control process consists of measuring actual performance, comparing actual performance against the established standards and taking managerial action, taking into account the goals and objectives of the organization (Sun & Firmin, 2012).

Intelligent big data analytics for controlling aims to imitate and automate all or some controlling behaviors of managers of organizations. More specifically, it should imitate and automate monitoring and evaluation of activities, measurement of actual performance, comparison of actual performance against the established standards and recommendations of managerial decisions (Sun & Firmin, 2012).

Intelligent big data analytics for controlling can be also called intelligent control analytics which has "the ability of comprehend, reason and learn from processes, disturbances and operating conditions" (Astriim & McAvoy, 1992). Intelligent control analytics has used intelligent techniques including knowledge base systems, expert systems, neural networks, machine learning, multiagent systems, and fuzzy logic (Astriim & McAvoy, 1992) and big data analytics to process control and process automation.

Currently, digital surveillance and CCTV (closed circuit TV) camera, and intelligent agents have been used to monitor and evaluate activities and recommendations of managerial decisions. The following proposed intelligent control analytics for controlling (ICA), shown in Fig. 5, is based on the intelligent system for process control (Astriim & McAvoy, 1992) (Sun Z., 2016), taking into account big data analytics as an intelligent system.

This ICA is a knowledge-based analytics for controlling. The knowledge base includes the performance knowledge of entity that requires control, called controllee, and knowledge for supervision, monitoring, evaluation and recommendation. The multiagent system includes multiple intelligent agents such as supervisor, monitor, evaluator and recommender. The recommender will propose alternative strategies for adjusting work of the controllee to the manager, the manager will finally select one of the alternative strategies to ask the controllee to carry out (Sun Z., 2016).

We have examined intelligent big data analytics for planning, organizing, leading and controlling respectively. In fact, many intelligent systems include not one but more than one functions of the management functions. The most comprehensive intelligent big data analytics as intelligent systems for enterprise management might be ERP (enterprise resource planning) systems which integrate all management facets of an enterprise, including accounting management, logistics management, manufacturing management, marketing management, planning management, project management, human resources management, SCM, CRM, and finance management (Schneider, 2011) (Laudon & Laudon, 2014). The two major ERP vendors are Oracle.com and SAP.com, as mentioned earlier.

There are still few attempts toward unifying main management functions into intelligent big data analytics to automate planning, organizing, leading and controlling at an organizational level. Any attempt in this direction is significant for research and development of intelligent big data analytics.

DISCUSSION AND IMPLICATIONS

This section will discuss the related work, examine theoretical, technical and social implications of this research.

Discussion

Intelligent big data analytics has drawn some attention in academia and industries. For example, two researches are related to this chapter. The first research (Chen, Li, & Wang, 2015) considers intelligent big data analytics as a big data system and uses collective intelligence model and multiagent paradigm to propose a collective intelligence framework to solve the system integration problem in big data environment. The second research (Kumara, Paik, & Zhang, 2015) uses automatic service composition to present an approach to automate the process in order to infer workflow for data analytics process. Both have not discussed the fundamental problems of intelligent big data analytics nor provided any managerial perspective on intelligent big data analytics.

Figure 5. A system architecture of an intelligent control analytics

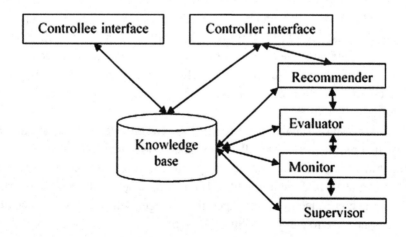

From an evolutionary viewpoint, data mining is an extended form of data analysis (Kantardzic, 2011). Data analytics is an extended form of data mining (Gandomi & Haider, 2015). For example, data analytics is considered as the whole data mining process or process of knowledge discovery in databases (KDD) (Tsai, Lai, Chao, & Vasilakos, 2015). Therefore, the relationships among data mining, data analytics, big data analytics and intelligent big data analytics can be represented as

intelligent big data analytics $\subset$ big data analytics $\subset$ data analytics $\subset$ data mining.

This means that data mining is a foundation of intelligent big data analytics. However, the difference between intelligent big data analytics and data mining is that the former discovers knowledge not only from database but also from the Web, and the big data are not only big, but also composed of various data types including streaming data, comparing with the traditional data (Tsai, Lai, Chao, & Vasilakos, 2015).

The interrelationship among big data, analytics and AI have drawn increasing attention. Sun and Wang provide a logical approach to it (Sun & Wang, 2017). Intelligent big data analytics is similar to analytics intelligence mentioned in (Wang, 2012). The difference between them is that the latter is limited to the data in cyberspace or the Web. The similarity between them is that incorporating AI into analytics is a huge global and social need in the near future (Wang, 2012). The intelligent big data analytics discussed in this chapter is an answer to address such global and social needs.

Theoretical, Technical, and Managerial Implications

The theoretical implication of this research is that the proposition that big data analytics is at the center of the age of trinity provides a new way for understanding the interrelationship among intelligent big data, analytics, and AI and their integration.

The technical implication of this research is that the proposed intelligent big data analytics for management can attract more researchers and practitioners to undertake the research and application of intelligent big data analytics for planning, organising, leading and controlling to support optimal business process and effective management decision making.

The managerial implication of this research is that the proposed managerial framework of intelligent big data analytics can help managers to better understand intelligent big data analytics as a science and technology, service, system and management and facilitate the use of intelligent big data analytics for supporting their decision making and intelligent management of organizations and businesses.

FUTURE RESEARCH DIRECTIONS

Intelligent big data analytics is an integrated paradigm of big data, analytics and AI. It is also an integrated computing, management and service paradigm and provides smart solutions to business, marketing and services through intelligent technologies, methodologies and applications. Intelligent big data analytics is a term that embodies the realization of a historic vison of how big data, analytics and AI as well as intelligent computing will revolutionize the world of business, organizations, society and our lives, forever and irrevocably (Davis, 2014). It is also a vision that create a society of intelligence through integrating big data, analytics and AI.

A limitation of this chapter is that it should consider intelligent big data descriptive, predictive and prescriptive analytics as one dimension, and the technological components of big data analytics as another dimension. Therefore, one of future research directions is to provide the matrix analysis for intelligent big data analytics.

Another of future research directions is to explore implementation issues for a managerial framework of intelligent big data analytics. The third future research direction is to present an extended framework of intelligent big data analytics for improving business decision making through reviewing the detailed technologies of AI and incorporating each of them into intelligent big data analytics.

CONCLUSION

The objective of this chapter is to provide a managerial perspective to intelligent big data analytics. The paper first looked at the age of trinity as the background of the research, and argued that intelligent big data analytics is at the center of the age of trinity. It then addressed what is a managerial perspective to intelligent big data analytics through proposing a managerial framework of intelligent big data analytics, which consists of intelligent big data analytics as a science and technology, system, service and management for improving business decision making. Then it explored intelligent big data analytics for planning, organizing, leading and controlling to some detail as an in-depth analysis of intelligent big data analytics for management. The proposed approach in this chapter might facilitate the research and development of intelligent analytics, intelligent management analytics, big data analytics, and AI.

REFERENCES

Al-Jarrah, O., Yoo, P. D., Muhaidat, S., & Karagiannidis, G. K. (2015). Efficient machine learning for big data: A review. *Big Data Research*, 2(3), 87–93. doi:10.1016/j.bdr.2015.04.001

Astriim, K. J., & McAvoy, T. J. (1992). Intelligent control. *J. Proc. Cont.*, 2(3), 115–126. doi:10.1016/0959-1524(92)85001-D

Caniels, M., & Bakens, R. (2011). The effects of project management information systems on decision making in a multi project environment. *International Journal of Project Management*, 30(2), 162–175.

Chaffey, D. (2009). *E-Business and E-Commerce Management: Strategy, Implementation and Practice*. Harlow, UK: Prentice Hall.

Chaffey, D., & White, G. (2011). *Business Information Management* (2nd ed.). Harlow, UK: Prentice Hall.

Chen, H., Chiang, R., & Storey, V. (2012). Business intelligence and analytics: From big data to big impact. *Management Information Systems Quarterly*, 36(4), 1165–1188. doi:10.2307/41703503

Chen, K., Li, X., & Wang, H. (2015). On the model design of integrated intelligent big data analytics systems. *Industrial Management & Data Systems*, 115(9), 1666–1682. doi:10.1108/IMDS-03-2015-0086

Coronel, C., & Morris, S. (2015). *Database Systems: Design, Implementation, and Management* (11th ed.). Boston: Cengage Learning.

Cortell. (2017). *IBM Planning Analytics.* Retrieved July 29, 2018, from http://www.cortell.co.za/our-partners/ibm-planning-analytics/

CRM. (2012). Retrieved 1 8, 2013, from Wikipedia: http://en.wikipedia.org/wiki/Customer_relationship_management

Davis, C. K. (2014). Viewpoint Beyond Data and Analytics- Why business analytics and big data really matter for modern business organizations. *Communications of the ACM, 57*(8), 39–41. doi:10.1145/2602326

Delena, D., & Demirkanb, H. (2013). Data, information and analytics as services. *Decision Support Systems, 55*(1), 359–363. doi:10.1016/j.dss.2012.05.044

Finnie, G. R., & Sun, Z. (2003). R5 model for case-based reasoning. *Knowledge-Based Systems, 16*(1), 59–65. doi:10.1016/S0950-7051(02)00053-9

Gandomi, A., & Haider, M. (2015). Beyond the hype: Big data concepts, methods, and analytics. *International Journal of Information Management, 35*, 137–144.

Henke, N., & Bughin, J. (2016, December). *The Age of Analytics: Competing in a Data Driven World.* McKinsey Global Institute.

Holsapplea, C., Lee-Postb, A., & Pakath, R. (2014). A unified foundation for business analytics. *Decision Support Systems, 64*, 130–141. doi:10.1016/j.dss.2014.05.013

Howson, C., Sallam, R. L., & Richa, J. L. (2018, Feb 26). *Magic Quadrant for Analytics and Business Intelligence Platforms.* Retrieved Aug 16, 2018, from Gartner: www.gartner.com

John, G. (2013). *The Age of Artificial Intelligence.* Retrieved from TEDxLondonBusinessSchool: https://www.youtube.com/watch?v=0qOf7SX2CS4

Kantardzic, M. (2011). *Data Mining: Concepts, Models, Methods, and Algorithms.* Hoboken, NJ: Wiley & IEEE Press. doi:10.1002/9781118029145

Kauffman, R. J., Srivastava, J., & Vayghan, J. (2012). Business and data analytics: New innovations for the management of e-commerce. *Electronic Commerce Research and Applications, 11*(2), 85–88. doi:10.1016/j.elerap.2012.01.001

Kumara, B. T., Paik, I., & Zhang, J. (2015). Ontology-Based Workflow Generation for Intelligent Big Data Analytics. In *IEEE International Conference on Web Services.* New York, NY: IEEE. 10.1109/ICWS.2015.72

Laney, D. (2001). *3D data management: controlling data volume, velocity, and variety, META Group, Tech. Rep.* Retrieved 10 27, 2015, from http://blogs.gartner.com/doug-laney/files/2012/01/ad949-3D-Data-Management-Controlling-Data-Volume-Velocity-and-Variety.pdf

Laney, D., & Jain, A. (2017, June 20). *100 Data and Analytics Predictions Through.* Retrieved August 04, 2018, from Gartner: https://www.gartner.com/events-na/data-analytics/wp-content/uploads/sites/5/2017/10/Data-and-Analytics-Predictions.pdf

Larson, E. K., & Gray, C. F. (2011). *Project Management: The Managerial Process* (5th ed.). New York: McGraw-Hill.

Laudon, K., & Laudon, J. (2014). *Essentials of Management Information Systems.* Boston: Prentice hall.

Lohr, S. (2012, February 11). The Age of Big Data. *The New York Times,* pp. 1-5.

McAfee, A., & Brynjolfsson, E. (2012). Big data: The management revolution. *Harvard Business Review,* (October): 61–68. PMID:23074865

McKinsey. (2011, May). *Big data: The next frontier for innovation, competition, and productivity.* Retrieved from McKinsey Global Institute: http://www.mckinsey.com/business-functions/business-technology/our-insights/big-data-the-next-frontier-for-innovation

Moutinho, L., Rita, P., & Li, S. (2006). Strategic diagnostics and management decision making: A hybrid knowledge-based approach. *Intell. Sys. Acc. Fin. Mgmt, 14*(3), 129–155. doi:10.1002/isaf.281

Pettey, C., & van der Meulen, R. (2018, April 25). *Gartner Says Global Artificial Intelligence Business Value to Reach $1.2 Trillion in 2018.* Retrieved August 04, 2018, from Gartner: https://www.gartner.com/newsroom/id/3872933

Robbins, S., Bergman, R., Stagg, I., & Coulter, M. (2012). *Management 6.* Frenchs Forest: Pearson Australia.

Russell, S., & Norvig, P. (2010). *Artificial Intelligence: A Modern Approach* (3rd ed.). Prentice Hall.

Schalkoff, R. J. (2011). *Intelligent Systems: Principles, Paradigms, and Pragmatics.* Boston: Jones and Bartlett Publishers.

Schneider, G. (2011). *Electronic Commerce* (9th ed.). Course Technology.

Smith, S. (1992). Towards an intelligent planning system. *International Journal of Project Management, 10*(4), 213–218. doi:10.1016/0263-7863(92)90080-S

Sun, Z. (2016). A Framework for Developing Management Intelligent Systems. *International Journal of Systems and Service-Oriented Engineering, 6*(1), 37–53. doi:10.4018/IJSSOE.2016010103

Sun, Z. (2018). 10 Bigs: Big Data and Its Ten Big Characteristics. *PNG UoT BAIS, 3*(1), 1–10. doi:10.13140/RG.2.2.31449.62566

Sun, Z., & Finnie, G. (2004). *Intelligent Techniques in E-Commerce: A Case-based Reasoning Perspective.* Berlin: Springer-Verlag. doi:10.1007/978-3-540-40003-5

Sun, Z., & Finnie, G. (2005). *Experience management in knowledge management. LNAI 3681* (pp. 979–986). Berlin: Springer-Verlag.

Sun, Z., & Firmin, S. (2012). A strategic perspective on management intelligent systems. In Management Intelligent Systems, AISC 171 (pp. 3-14). Springer. doi:10.1007/978-3-642-30864-2_1

Sun, Z., Strang, K., & Yearwood, J. (2014). *Analytics service oriented architecture for enterprise information systems. In Proceedings of iiWAS2014* (pp. 506–518). Hanoi: ACM. doi:10.1145/2684200.2684358

Sun, Z., Sun, L., & Strang, K. (2018). Big Data Analytics Services for Enhancing Business Intelligence. *Journal of Computer Information Systems*, *58*(2), 162–169. doi:10.1080/08874417.2016.1220239

Sun, Z., & Wang, P. (2017). Big Data, Analytics and Intelligence: An Editorial Perspective. *Journal of New Mathematics and Natural Computation*, *13*(2), 75–81. doi:10.1142/S179300571702001X

Sun, Z., & Yearwood, J. (2014). A theoretical foundation of demand-driven web services. In Z. Sun, & J. Yearwood (Eds.), Demand-Driven Web Services: Theory, Technologies, and Applications (pp. 1-25). IGI-Global. doi:10.4018/978-1-4666-5884-4.ch001

Sun, Z., Zou, H., & Strang, K. (2015). *Big Data Analytics as a Service for Business Intelligence. In LNCS 9373* (pp. 200–211). Berlin: Springer.

Tableau. (2015). *Top 8 Trends for 2016: Big Data.* Retrieved from www.tableau.com/Big-Data

Terry, G. R. (1968). *Principles of Management* (5th ed.). Homewood, IL: Richard D. Irwin, Inc.

Thierauf, R. J. (1982). *Decision Support Systems for Effective Planning and Control: A Case Study Approach.* Englewood Cliffs, NJ: Prentice Hall.

Tsai, C., Lai, C., Chao, H., & Vasilakos, A. (2015). Big data analytics: A survey. *Journal of Big Data*, *2*(1), 31–62. doi:10.118640537-015-0030-3 PMID:26191487

Turban, E., & Volonino, L. (2011). *Information Technology for Management: Improving Performance in the Digital Economy* (8th ed.). Hoboken, NJ: John Wiley & Sons.

Turing, A. (1950). Computing Machinery and Intelligence. *Mind*, *49*(236), 433–460. doi:10.1093/mind/LIX.236.433

Vardi, M. Y. (2016). The Moral Imperative of Artificial Intelligence. *Communications of the ACM*, *59*(5), 5. doi:10.1145/2903530

Wang, F.-Y. (2012). A big-data perspective on AI: Newton, Merton, and Analytics Intelligence. *IEEE Intelligent Systems, 27*(5), 2-4.

Weiss, R., & Zgorski, L.-J. (2012, March 29). *Obama Administration Unveils "Big Data" Initiative: Announces $200 Million in New R&D Investments.* Retrieved from http://www.cccblog.org/2012/03/29/obama-administration-unveils-200m-big-data-rd-initiative

Wikipedia. (2018, July 26). *List of virtual communities with more than 100 million active users.* Retrieved July 27, 2017, from https://en.wikipedia.org/wiki/List_of_virtual_communities_with_more_than_100_million_active_users

ADDITIONAL READING

Core, F. (2015). *Big data analytics: a managerial perspective*. Springer.

Finnie, G., & Sun, Z. (2002). Similarity and metrics in case-based reasoning. *International Journal of Intelligent Systems*, *17*(3), 273–287. doi:10.1002/int.10021

Information Resources Management Association. (2015). Big Data: Concepts, Methodologies, Tools, and Applications. Hershey, PA: IGI Global.

Lv, Z., Song, H., Basanta-Val, P., Steed, A., Jo, M. (2017) Next-Generation Big Data Analytics: State of the Art, Challenges, and Future Research Topics. IEEE Transactions on Industrial Informatics 13(4),7866003, pp. 1891-1899.

Manyika, J., Chui, M., & Bughin, J. e. (2011, May). Big data: The next frontier for innovation, competition, and productivity. Retrieved from McKinsey Global Institute: http://www.mckinsey.com/business-functions/business-technology/our-insights/big-data-the-next-frontier-for-innovation

Mashingaidze, K., & Backhouse, J. (2017). The relationships between definitions of big data, business intelligence and business analytics: A literature review. *International Journal of Business Information Systems*, *26*(4), 488–505. doi:10.1504/IJBIS.2017.087749

Sun, Z., & Finnie, G. (2005). *Experience management in knowledge management. LNAI 3681* (pp. 979–986). Berlin, Heidelberg: Springer-Verlag.

Sun, Z., Strang, K., & Firmin, S. (2016). Business analytics-based enterprise information systems. *Journal of Computer Information Systems*, *56*(4), 74–84. doi:10.1080/08874417.2016.1183977

Sun, Z., Zou, H., & Strang, K. (2015). *Big data analytics as a service for business intelligence. I3E2015, LNCS 9373* (pp. 200–211). Berlin: Springer.

Verma, S. (2017). Big data and advance analytics: Architecture, techniques, applications, and challenges. *International Journal of Business Analytics*, *4*(4), 21–47. doi:10.4018/IJBAN.2017100102

KEY TERMS AND DEFINITIONS

Artificial Intelligence (AI): Science and technology concerned with imitating, extending, augmenting, and automating the intelligent behaviors of human beings.

Big Data: Data with at least one of the ten big characteristics consisting of big volume, big velocity, big variety, big veracity, big intelligence, big analytics, big infrastructure, big service, big value, and big market.

Data Mining: A process of discovering various models, summaries, and derived values, knowledge from a given collection of data.

Data Science: A field that builds on and synthesizes a number of relevant disciplines and bodies of knowledge, including statistics, informatics, computing, communication, management, and sociology to translate data into information, knowledge, insight, and intelligence for improving innovation, productivity, and decision making.

Intelligent Big Data Analytics: Science and technology about collecting, organizing, and analyzing big data to discover patterns, knowledge, and intelligence as well as other information within the big data based on artificial intelligence and intelligent systems.

Intelligent System: A system that can imitate, automate some intelligent behaviors of human beings. Expert systems and knowledge-based systems are examples of intelligent systems.

Machine Learning: Is concerned with how computer can adapt to new circumstances and to detect and extrapolate patterns.

Management: The process of manager's coordinating and overseeing the work activities of others so that their activities are completed.

Chapter 2
Is Artificial Intelligence a New Dawn or Challenge for Corporate Decision Making?

Maria I. Nikishova

https://orcid.org/0000-0002-8089-1899

TopCompetence, Russia

Mikhail E. Kuznetsov
Moscow State University, Russia

ABSTRACT

The Fourth Industrial Revolution provides companies with new opportunities, and business picks up allies represented by technologies that can change mechanisms of corporate decision making in corporations. Rapid development of technologies, which allows working more efficiently with information, can lead to the creation of a new system of stakeholder interaction, thanks to better analytics, transparency, and speed of decisions. In this regard, the analyst based on big data with the use of artificial intelligence (AI) is able to significantly affect the quality of decisions. How can the application of AI for analysis of big data be able to influence the decision-making process and to what extent can it influence the system of corporate relationships? To answer this question, the authors will try to describe how transformation of decision-making methodology at the Board of Directors level under the influence of the Fourth Industrial Revolution and the development of AI technologies and big data, and what are the opportunities, limitations, and risks of the decision-making process with AI.

INTRODUCTION

In today's corporate world, the speed of change is increasing rapidly and the length of a business cycle, from initial idea to profit gain, has shrunk from several years to a couple of months. Taking all this into account, businesses have to incorporate principles of quick, flexible and intellectual enterprise. This type of development should be founded in intellectual approaches to managing the most vital resource

DOI: 10.4018/978-1-5225-7277-0.ch002

of the 21st century – information. The size and complexity of information, however, becomes both an opportunity and a big challenge. That's why classic algorithms aren't coping with Big Data, and that's why machine learning and artificial intelligence (AI) technologies are rising to the top of the agenda.

The digital economy and corporate transformation put pressure on existing mechanisms and management systems. Pressure from stakeholders, along with increasing competition, are accelerating challenges at the level of the Board of Directors – a corporate governance body instituted mainly to represent the interests of financial investors and formed for the most part by the principle of representation. In this new environment, the Board of Directors will have to transform as well; reorganizing the principles and approach to how it functions. If it doesn't do this, top management could become the weak link in the chain of business relations, due to an inability to bear the increased load of information.

As a result, companies have started to pay more attention to new technologies that allow them to process more and more information in an efficient and independent way, to avoid the phenomena of "group thinking" and "following the leader". Among these technologies, the one that stands out the most is AI-based big data analysis, which could become an effective tool for Boards of Directors in the corporate decision-making process.

Alongside this, it is necessary to manage significant unpredictable risks that arise in the application of such technology. For corporate governance, this can mean the loss of human control over algorithms during the corporate decision-making process, excess confidence in recommendations developed by AI, and dilution of the decision-making responsibility.

This begs the question: what are the conditions for the efficient implementation of AI-based big data analysis in making effective corporate governance decisions? The main goal of this research is to find the best approach to the big dilemma of the nearing future: what is the optimal structure and process for making decisions in the "new digital era" of AI-based big data analysis being used by Boards of Directors?

The need and high demand for such research has been proven by the rising interest of regulators and large corporations in IT governance issues and the use of new informational technologies and cybersecurity at the level of the Board of Directors. We can see more and more Corporate Governance Codes, regarding IT governance, cybersecurity issues and requirements for more IT expertise at the Board of Directors level (Singapore (2012), South Africa (2016), Netherlands (2016), Hong Kong (2016). One of the key issues in the discussion of IT governance is the role of the Board of Directors in controlling key technologies used by a company.

· What is the role of the Board of Directors and what are the specifics of decisions made by the Board of Directors in the "new digital era"?

· How different are the human-based and AI-based decision-making processes, what are the conditions for effective decision-making models?

· What are the applicable risks associated with AI technologies for new corporate governance technologies based on AI and big data are there? How will the fundamental "prisoner's dilemma" applied to competition based on AI be solved?

In this chapter, we are not trying to give the "final answers" to these complicated issues, but rather to set the right questions, which could become a guide to further research and practical experiments.

This topic is targeted at top managers, Board Members, company shareholders, as well as regulators and a range of professionals interested in deepening their expertise in the practical applications of AI-based big data analysis.

In this context, this chapter will consider the topic of transformation of decision-making methodology at the level of the Board of Directors under the influence of the Fourth Industrial Revolution and the development of AI technologies and big data.

BACKGROUND

Transformation of Management Systems and Corporate Governance in the Fourth Industrial Revolution

As mentioned by the researchers K. Schwab (2016), E. Toffler (2004), J. Haskel & S. Westlake (2017), J. Ito & J. Hui (2017), all of whom are engaged in the study of management transformation in the era of the Fourth Industrial Revolution, many researchers agree that the knowledge and technologies mastered over the last decades have brought humanity closer to the point at which traditional modes of production, economy, and society will undergo breakthrough changes. The hallmark of the new era — the era of the Fourth Industrial Revolution — is the high speed of such changes.

Experts such as T. Kerikmäe (2016), B. Libert (2013), E.P.M. Vermeulen (2015), W. Visser (2008), F. Möslein (2017), V.D. Milovidov (2017) and A.E. Molotnikov (2017), who deal with issues related to changes in the system of corporate relations and the role of the Board of Directors at various stages of the Industrial Revolution, are optimistic about the possibility of advanced technologies being used in corporate governance and emphasize their enormous potential and prospects, mentioning that companies are now faced with a choice: quickly adapt to the changes of the era, or die. However, many futurologists, including J. Lesli, F. Fukuyama (1992), V. Vindge (1993), N. Bostrom (2016) and E. Kuznetsov (2017), analyze opposing views, often not so optimistic about the possibilities and consequences of technological shifts in the Fourth Industrial Revolution, and pay special attention to the risks and threats posed by disruptive technologies, particularly regarding AI, which is being used by more and more companies.

For example, in 2014, the Hong Kong Venture Foundation – Deep Knowledge Ventures – was the first company to include AI in its Board of Directors, the task of which was to evaluate and rate projects being considered by the Investment Committee. The evaluation of projects is carried out simultaneously by both Members of the Board of Directors and AI, which analyzes large data sets. If votes coincide, the project is adopted, but if opinions differ between the directors and AI, an analysis is carried out, taking into account new information provided by AI, and voting is conducted until the differences are exhausted. The fact that AI is used to analyze big data at the level of the Board of Directors is testament to, as a minimum, the vast potential and prospects for the use of advanced technologies in the XXI century, and is a sign of future changes in decision-making processes at the top-management level in companies that have to adapt to the Fourth Industrial Revolution and to increasing competition. These issues are partly covered in the article *"Corporate Governance 2.0: evolution of the corporate relations system in the information society"* by V. Milovidov (2017), focusing on the future of corporate governance under the influence of various advanced technologies. But F. Möslein was the closest in studying the possibilities, prospects and risks of using AI in corporate governance. F. Möslein (2017), in his article *"Robots in the Boardroom: Artificial Intelligence and Corporate Law"*, considers the problems of introducing robots and AI into corporate governance through a "legal prism". We will try to look at the problems of using AI-based intelligent big data analytics from the point of view of managerial perspectives and risks.

And nevertheless, throughout history, with each industrial revolution, companies have had to adapt to changing conditions, but now the rate of change in accordance with The Law of Accelerating Returns has increased exponentially. As T. Urban (2015) describes, according to R. Kurzweil's (2005) calculations, the speed of progress in 2000 is 5 times faster than the average speed of progress throughout the 20th century. Furthermore, the degree of progress achieved over the course of the entire 20th century had already been reached from 2000 to 2014, and the next iteration of 20th-century-scale progress will be passed as early as 2021. As a result of the implementation of The Law of Accelerating Returns, over the course of the 21st century, the degree of mankind development will exceed the degree of mankind development in the 20th century 1000-fold.

In order to imagine the scale of the current changes, let us turn to history and recall what happened with the development of corporate relations during the industrial revolutions. A. E. Molotnikov (2017) describes how the development of management systems during each of the industrial revolutions was related to the existing technological order and the needs that it brought, and the development of production forces influenced the emergence of various forms and ways of doing business.

As several researchers note, among them the founder of the World Economic Forum, K. Schwab (2016), the 21st century is bringing the world to the stage of the Fourth Industrial Revolution, also called Industry 4.0. What changes can be expected in corporate relations?

As noted in research conducted by the World Economic Forum & Accenture (2017), breakthrough technologies that could have a significant impact on society and business in the Fourth Industrial Revolution are AI, big data analytics and cloud technologies, robots and drones, self-driving vehicles, the Internet of Things (IoT) and connected devices, social media and associated platforms, custom manufacturing and 3D printing.

The reduction in the cost of digital technologies and their availability is the most important feature of the Digital Revolution, and the combinatorial effects of technological incorporation, such as AI and big data analytics, accelerate progress exponentially. In this regard, the use of advanced technology is capable of reshaping industries by disrupting existing business and operational models. But it is also having a profound impact on society, thereby presenting a series of opportunities and challenges for businesses. What changes are expected in corporate relations?

According to McKinsey's research Digital Russia: The New Reality (2017), the top 10% of the most effectively digitized companies already bring in 2-3 times more income for shareholders and provide higher rates of growth in revenue. Thus, the results of a questionnaire survey and interviews with 51 directors and top-managers conducted by the authors showed that 64% of these expect investments in digital technologies to allow them to increase the efficiency of business processes, 60% expect to be able to improve the quality of existing products and services thanks to AI, and 48% invest in order to stay competitive (Figure 1).

Moreover, according to the authors' study, directors and top managers, in the next 2-3 years, companies' strategy will be affected to a greater extent by technologies such as the Internet of Things, AI and big data robotics

The key benefit in applying these three most promising technologies is that they involve unique opportunities to work with information – its collection, processing and more efficient application – which, thanks to better analytics, ultimately entails a new system of interaction between participants, greater transparency and increased speed in making decisions. However, analytics based on digital technologies will inevitably lead to an increase in data volume and the need to increase the speed of decision-making.

Figure 1. The benefits that managers expect from digital technology investments, according to the authors' research "Is your company ready for digital transformation in the era of the Fourth Industrial Revolution?" (compiled by the authors)

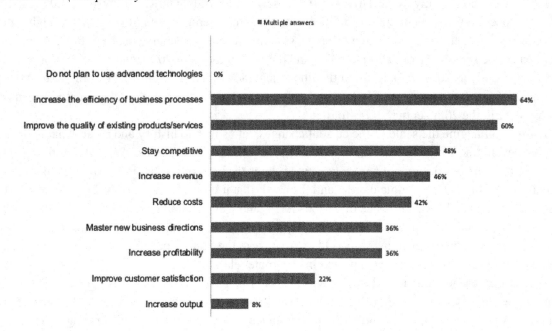

Figure 2. Technologies that will affect companies' strategy in the next 2-3 years, according to the study (compiled by the authors)

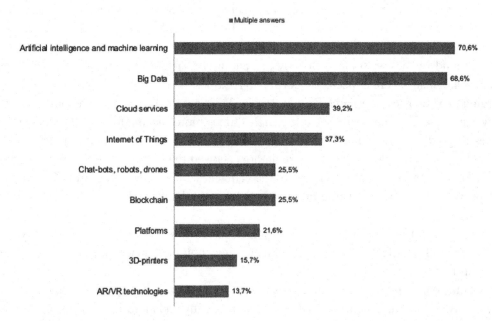

The branches of the economy and companies with access to big data that can adapt to its effective processing will have the opportunity to radically improve the quality of decisions made on the basis of big data and AI. It is expected that by 2035, AI technologies will boost corporate productivity in 16 industries in 12 countries by an average of 38%. This was shown by the Allianz Global Corporate & Specialty survey conducted in different countries in 2018. According to the survey, 66% of companies are already implementing AI in one way or another.

The introduction of the term "big data" is associated with Clifford Lynch, editor of the Nature journal, which, by September 3, 2008, had prepared a special issue on the topic "How can technologies that open up the possibilities for working with large volumes of data affect the future of science?" (2008). In this issue, materials were collected on the phenomenon of explosive growth in the volume and variety of processed data and the technological prospects in a paradigm rocketing "from quantity to quality". The term was suggested by analogy with the metaphors "big oil" and "big ore" in the English-speaking business environment.

The emergence of the term "artificial intelligence" after the Turing test and the beginning of the scientific field development is associated with Joey McCarthy, who first gave a definition of AI in 1956 at the Dortmund Summer Conference, according to which AI is the science and technology of creating intelligent computer programs. And despite the fact that research directions in the field of big data and AI appeared in the middle of the 20th century, technical opportunities for the wide application of these technologies only appeared in the 21st century.

It is expected that by 2035, AI technologies will boost corporate productivity in 16 industries in 12 countries by an average of 38%. This was shown in the Allianz Global Corporate & Specialty survey *"The rise of AI: Future Outlook and Emerging Risks"* (2018) conducted in different countries in 2018. According to a survey by MIT Sloan & BCG (2017), 66% of companies are already implementing AI in one way or another.

Nevertheless, there are different expectations and points of view on the use of AI technologies. Some authors pay more attention to the risks associated with its use.

For example, according to N. Bostrom (2016), the application of AI in management in general entails two major risks: loss of control over the technology and the risk of such technology being used with negative consequences for humanity.

As stated in the research conducted by Allianz Global Corporate & Specialty, the use of high-powered AI leads to risks in five problem areas. In the author's opinion, such risks should be fully taken into consideration when developing instruments and technologies based on AI for the support of the Board of Directors.

The authors found that the most significant risks, in the opinion of top-managers, are that of excessive confidence in AI systems, a lack of transparency in business processes, decrease in stakeholder confidence and deterioration in the level of safety (Figure 3).

Despite the risks, the authors note that world investment in the development of AI is still growing. According to the analysis conducted by *PWC's Strategy and Part* (2018), in the first three months of 2018, a record was set for financing in the field of AI – the total investment volume exceeded US$1.9 bil. Compared to the same period in 2017, this amounts to growth of 69%. And at the same time, according to the *NVP Big Data Executive Survey* (2017), 37.2% of executives say their companies have invested more than US$100 mil on big data initiatives over the past 5 years, with 6.5% investing over US$1 bil.

Figure 3. The most significant risks for companies associated with the use of AI (compiled by the authors)

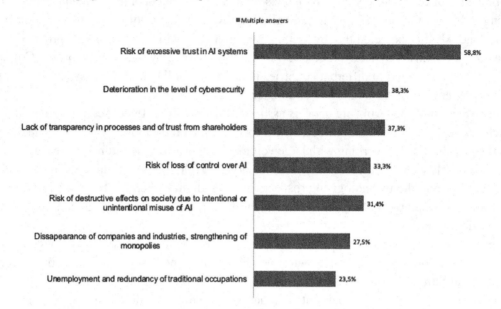

Given such high rates and development prospects, AI technology combined with big data analytics can significantly influence the mechanisms for corporate decision-making, since these are associated with the processing of big data which AI can handle most effectively. This can serve as a good foundation for managers, who can shift some of the analytical functions that machines are better able to cope with over to AI, leaving them to concentrate on less routine tasks. The results of the McKinsey Global Institute study *A future that works: automation, employment, and productivity, US* (2017) confirm that professions and activities related to data processing could soon be automated. At the same time, according to this research, management and director activity is less likely to be automated in the near future.

However, there are also opposing points of view. According to a study by the International Expert Council of the World Economic Forum (2015), 45.2% of the directors surveyed believe that AI (a robot) will be able to become a member of the corporate Board of Directors by 2025.

But regardless of contrasting views on the possibility of automating the activities of company managers and directors, Boards of Directors and top management will have to change the principles of decision making in order to remain competitive. The authors came to the conclusion that this is the greatest benefit AI-based innovation can bring.

Analyzing procedures for making corporate decisions, the authors identified several levels: the level of the shareholders, of the Board of Directors, and of top management. In this regard, it is necessary to recall the classic problem of corporate governance – "information asymmetry".

So, if top management, as a classic "insider", sees the company and all its processes from within, then the Board of Directors and shareholders are often limited in their access to information about the company, which lays the ground for corporate conflict and increases the costs of miscommunication between participants in corporate relations.

At the same time, decisions made at the shareholder level are clearly structured, (the competence of shareholders is limited by law), and less complicated in the sense that they consist of previously worked out and proposed (usually by the Board of Directors) options, for example, approving amounts of dividends (yes/no), approving a transaction (yes/no), etc.

Meanwhile, decisions made by the Board of Directors are usually based on a large amount of conflicting information coming from top management, often involving a conflict of interest. At the same time, the decisions of the Board (for example, approval of a development strategy, the budget, hiring/firing of managers) are complex and structured, and involve risk taking and a higher level of responsibility compared to shareholders.

The decisions made by top management are similar to the decisions made by the Board in terms of complexity, but top managers have incomparably greater information support, time and personnel resources for making decisions in comparison with decisions of the Board and shareholders. In addition to this, the "error cost" of operating decisions made by management is usually much lower than the cost of strategic errors made by the Board of Directors.

In this regard, it is most likely that AI at the level of the Board of Directors can be used primarily as a tool to overcome the asymmetry of information and as predictive analyst.

Therefore, at the level of corporate directors, the need has arisen to adapt processes to new technological developments. In this regard, at all levels of management there will be need to rebuild decision-making mechanisms, using advanced technologies that allow faster and more efficient analysis of information, ensuring the independence and objectivity of decisions. So, what could be the optimal structure and process of decision making in the era of AI and big data supporting management and directors in decision making?

The question remains open: in which decisions undertaken by Boards of Directors and under what conditions will AI and big data analysis be most effective?

APPLICATION OF AI BASED ON BIG DATA ANALYSIS IN CORPORATE GOVERNANCE

The Role of the Board of Directors and Specifics of Decisions in the "New Digital Era"

Considering the increasing attention of regulators to the topic of IT governance, reflected in the national Corporate Governance Codes of countries such as Singapore (2012), South Africa (2016), Netherlands (2016) and Hong Kong (2016), the role of the Board of Directors on issues of disruptive technologies and digital trends in the "new digital era" is evidently strengthening. Taking into consideration the development of big data technology, which is most effectively handled by AI, the Board of Directors needs to look to the future, basing their decisions on predictive analytics, and not on analyzing disparate data from the past. Advanced technologies therefore change the role of the Board of Directors to a proactive one in the development, application and search for opportunities to use advanced technologies. Thus, as respondents to the authors' study note, technologies, such as AI and big data, will soon be able to be used as a tool to support the Board of Directors in making decisions.

Table 1. Areas of decisions made by the Boards of Directors at present and possibilities for their algorithmization (compiled by the authors)

Main Areas of Decisions Made at the Level of the Board of Directors	Possibilities for Algorithmization of Decision Areas
Strategy	· Conducting competitive analysis · Conducting consumer analysis
Investment policy	· Evaluation of investment projects · Analysis of investments
Internal control and audit	· Internal control · Audit
Risk management	· Compliance · Risk analysis
Personnel actions regarding top management	· Evaluation of activities, taking into account KPIs · Recommendations on amounts of remunerations for top management based on remuneration policy
Material deals control	· Analysis of stakeholder affiliation · Analysis of counterparties · Analysis of the connectivity of transactions
Issues of sustainability and CSR	· Issues of sustainability and CSR

Summarizing the best practice of corporate governance presented in the OECD Principles of Corporate Governance and National Corporate Governance Codes, the authors identified the main areas of decisions made at the level of the Board of Directors. In a survey of 51 Board Members and top managers of large and medium-sized companies, the leaders were given recommendations with possible areas of algorithmization of decision making. Table 1 shows the areas that can be automated, according to the leaders.

From Table 1 we see that some of the decisions of the Board can potentially be entrusted to AI. In addition to this, AI is able to react quickly to various kinds of events. Therefore, in order to make decisions in difficult structured situations, it might be useful for company Board Members to be able to receive effective independent grounded answers to questions posed about the company's activity and the real situation on the market. The last thing is to determine the conditions for effective decision making by a human and by AI.

If we turn to history and recall the cases of the largest corporations collapsing after incorrect decisions were made by Board Members of the well-known companies Enron, WorldCom, Vivendi, and Parmalat, described in detail by M. Beare, we find that the causes of wrong decisions were associated with various factors that influenced decision making:

- The Board of Directors made decisions under the strong influence of the owner, that is, it was not independent in making decisions.
- Members of the Board did not have sufficient information; some data were hidden from them.
- Directors did not have enough time to analyze all the necessary information.
- Directors relied on the opinion of top management, not making their own assessment of the state of affairs in the company on strategically important issues.
- Stakeholders who influenced the adoption of corporate decisions differed in their values and interests; they had a desire to own a certain resource.

All these factors indicate the impact of characteristically human elements on the decision-making process: a high degree of suggestibility; significant influence of emotions, habits and customs on decision making; loss of independence due to resource constraints; and limited ability to process a large body of information over a small period of time.

Furthermore, group and personal values and corporate culture have a significant influence on decision making. The "tunnel effect", described by D. Kahneman & A. Tversky (1987), intertwined interests of shareholders, and the "pressure of intuition" also have a big impact.

Is the "human" method of making decisions, taking into account the above factors, the most effective in the current and potential conditions of the unfolding Fourth Industrial Revolution, the resulting global uncertainty, the "information storm" and the unpredictable development of technology?

It is obvious that, under modern conditions, at the level of the Board of Directors, the processing of more and more data is required in decision making, while independent interpretation and a high level of reliability of both data and of the analysis based on them are important. Moreover, the more complex the decision is, the more data is needed to adopt it on a rational, independent basis. The amount of new factors, ideas and other information that a person can assimilate and analyze in a certain period of time is limited.

And since AI is especially suited to processing large volumes of data, it would be able to help improve the efficiency of decision making, reducing all kinds of uncertainties through forecasting. Thus, issues related to the automation of information flows and intensification of intellectual activity at the level of the Board of Directors require special attention.

To make sure that AI is able to increase the efficiency of the decision-making process, let us examine in more detail some of the limitations in decision making that are typical of Boards of Directors in Table 2.

The limitations in making decisions listed in Table 2 are "human" limitations only. In this regard, the question is can AI completely replace a person as a Member of the Board of Directors. To answer this question, we should consider the field of decisions made by Boards of Directors today and compare them with the possibilities of their algorithmization.

Table 2. Restrictions in decision making typical of Boards of Directors (compiled by the authors)

Cognitive and Behavioral Characteristics of a Person	Limitations Related to the Professional Activities of Director and the Activities of the Company
· The slow reaction to various kinds of events as a consequence of slow information flows. · Decision making is influenced by emotions, human values, and expectations of personal gain. · Decision making is influenced by the "group thinking phenomenon" (*I. Janis, 1972*). · Decision making is influenced by the "tunnel effect". · A person's confidence in their intuition and competence, failure to understand the limits of their professional skills (*D. Kahneman, 2014*).	· Board Members have a small amount of time available for solving problems. · A large amount of "white noise" prevents them from seeing and understanding the risks in time. · There is the need to regulate the interests of stakeholders and make decisions taking into account their expectations. · The values and corporate culture of a particular company can influence decision making. · Over-reliance on management. · There is a high level of both cost and redundancy in internal control and reporting systems for providing high-quality analytics to the Board of Directors · There is an inability to obtain additional expertise and involve consultants and experts to make better decisions on specific issues at the company's expense.

Specifics of Decisions Made by the Board of Directors in the "New Digital Era"

In the opinion of the futurologist Ian Pearson, the ability of people to think creatively could protect their profession from being replaced by AI. Company management is among those professions requiring creative thinking.

In the opinion of the managers surveyed by the authors of the survey (Figure 4), by 2025, AI will most likely only perform the functions of an analytical assistant to top management (66.7% of the surveyed managers) and look for bottlenecks in business processes (64.7%).

However, the fact that AI AlphaGo was able to win a game of weiqi, which requires non-standard creative and improvisational solutions (the withdrawal of some symbolic logic from the statistical system), suggests that "machines" may be able to learn creativity in the near future, and thereby replace managers.

In this case, in order to prevent the risks associated with the use of AI in management, we examine the dilemma: which model of decision making will be more effective – one with a person at its center, or one which at its center, instead of a person, has AI analyzing big data and actually making the basic decisions?

In systems using AI to analyze big data, the authors distinguish two main applications for this technology in the process of corporate decision making: it could potentially be used as a decision support system for the Board of Directors, or it could become a full member of the Board of Directors, alongside the human Directors. However, before implementing AI in the process of making corporate decisions, let us compare the main characteristics and the degree of effectiveness of decisions made by a human, made by AI, and made by a human using a system based on AI and big data for making decisions.

We will compare these using existing research (*Management Sciences in the Modern World* (2018), which outlines the following unique features in making decisions characteristic of humans and AI respectively:

Human:

Figure 4. Functions that managers believe are most likely to be performed by AI by 2025, according to the authors' study (compiled by the authors)

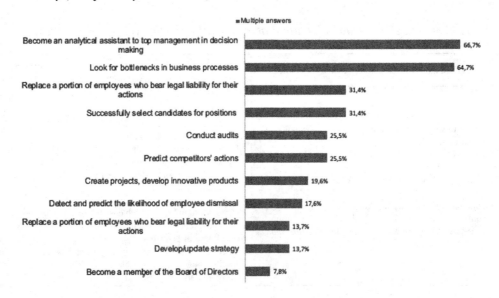

- Able to solve unformalized tasks.
- Able to think critically, make nontrivial conclusions.
- Able to communicate interpersonally – negotiate, develop common views and values.
- Able to understand shareholders' interests intuitively.

AI:

- In a number of cases, instant decision-making.
- Great manageability with big data – the ability to produce more accurate results, operating in millions of variables and searching for the most optimal solutions.
- Absence of fatigue.
- Independence in decision-making.
- Can produce a more creative result by using patterns uncharacteristic of a person.
- Low costs – there are no costs for employee leave, days off, medical insurance, bonuses, etc.

Based on these characteristics, we can assume that the decisions made by human and those made by AI will each have their pros and cons.

Next, in Table 3, let us consider the degree of effectiveness of a human, a human using a decision support system based on AI, and AI as a Member of the Board of Directors. The analysis of the effectiveness of decision-making processes was conducted on the basis of a survey of 34 leaders of medium-sized and large Russian companies on a 3-point scale. 0 – inefficient, 1 – minimally efficient, 2 – averagely efficient, 3 – highly efficient.

From Table 3 and the comments of leaders we can conclude that a person using a support system for decision making based on AI is able to improve the process of making decisions and demonstrates better results in comparison with decisions made by a person not using such support systems, as AI demonstrates considerably better performance in collecting and processing information, finding uncon-

Table 3. The degree of effectiveness at each stage of the decision-making process (compiled by the authors)

The Degree of Effectiveness at Each Stage of the Decision-Making Process	Human	Human With Decision Support System Based on Big Data and AI	AI–Director
Ability to identify a problem	2	2	2
Ability to collect information	2	3	3
Ability to handle large amounts of data	1	2	3
Development of new solution	2	2	2
Ability to find ready-made solutions	2	3	3
Ability to find unconventional correlations and solutions	1	3	3
Ability to compare various alternatives, evaluate and select	2	3	3
Ability to negotiate	3	3	1
Ability to approve and be accountable for decisions	3	3	0

ventional correlations, comparing with decisions that have already been made, and selecting alternatives, and performs these tasks with a higher operating speed than a person who is not using any additional systems based on AI and big data.

However, AI faces some problems in negotiating, regarding taking into consideration and correlating shareholders' interests, and in being accountable for decisions made. A person will do a better job in dealing with these issues, therefore, at this stage, AI operating without a human is less effective. Quite often, when assessing the needs of the shareholders, a person acts on intuition, whereas AI is likely to make a decision, for example, about reorganization based on the notion that it would be more economically effective, ignoring the interests and wishes of the owners.

Thus, in the process of decision making by a Board of Directors, AI will be most effective as an assistant-analyst.

In this case, the process of making decisions will differ from the "classic" model. In Figure 5, the authors present the stages of a Board of Directors in making decision by adding stages involving learning AI (a neural network) to G. Mintzberg's algorithm of decision making (1976). It should be taken into consideration that before using AI, an intelligent system needs to be made and "set". This should include a preliminary stage, which consists of three substages:

1. Collection of all possible specifications and their interrelations, which will then be analysed by the AI: base materials, which the AI will use to learn, are uploaded to the system - these materials could be the minutes of all previous Board meetings together with all the approved and dismissed decisions, examples of logic behind the decisions, budgetary and other limitations, performance results of competitors and any other information which has an effect on the process of decision making.
2. Then all the methods of machine learning should be sorted and, after selecting the optimal approach, machine learning can begin.
3. After the results have been interpreted and by testing on the actual objectives of the Board, the system is applied to the process of making decisions.

After going through the preliminary stage, the "classic" decision-making process can be supported by parallel analytics and recommendations given by AI, however it is still the Board of Directors who should make all the final decisions (Figure 5).

Based on current practice of the application of AI technologies, the crucial role in its introduction and development is played by the work of analysts and data scientists. Essentially, the effectiveness of the whole system of decision making, as well as the risks and respective limitations related to the application of AI, all depend on their actions and interpretations.

Thus, one of the promising applications of AI technologies by Boards of Directors is its application in an intellectual decision support system that works in parallel with the Board of Directors.

Thus, some questions arise: how reasonable is it to introduce AI into the management corporate governance system? What are the risks of its application in corporate governance?

Figure 5. The process of making decisions by the Board of Directors using AI according to the authors'
research"Is your company ready for digital transformation in the era of the Fourth Industrial Revolu-
tion?" (compiled by the authors)
Source: M. Nikishova. AI application in the system of corporate governance (Unpublished PhD dissertation thesis). Financial
University under the Government of the Russian Federation. Russia, 2018.

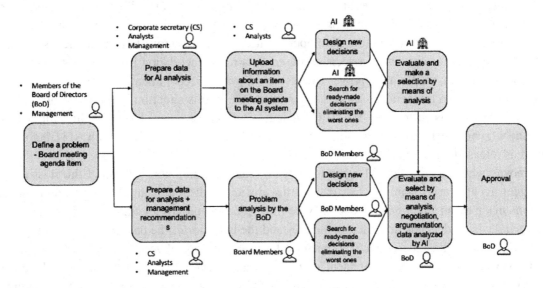

Risks Associated With AI Technologies Based Big Data in Corporate Governance

Looking at AI implementation, we could state that the biggest corporations, such as Google, Microsoft, IBM, Apple etc. are competing to develop AI platforms, and thereby moving the technology forward.

And if we multiply this situation by rising competition between nations, we find ourselves in the classic "prisoners' dilemma". But what will happen in the future if the key players in the field (big nations and large international corporations), according to the "prisoner's dilemma", always prefer competition to cooperation?

Oxford philosopher N. Bostrom (2016), in his famous book on AI, has already raised this discussion.

He analyses a hypothetical arms race in the use of AI, where several teams compete to be the first to create super-intelligence. What risks does this situation lead to?

In this case, suggests N. Bostrom (2016), If the competitors cannot reach a consensus (due to the differences in their positions and failure to control compliance with their agreement) the race can become fatal, with each team spending only minimal resources on safety.

Moreover, the level of danger of such a race increases with the number of competing teams, as vicious competition increases participants' exposure to risk. In this case, according to Bostrom, teams may accelerate the development of "super intelligence", decreasing their investments in safety. Under these circumstances, when "the winner takes all" and the cost of falling behind is the existence of a player, the safety of such new technology can in fact become less of a priority.

And so, according to classic "prisoner's dilemma" theory, in competitive markets all the companies will inevitably turn to the use of AI, because constant improvement of AI will become the only logical strategy for survival in a competitive environment. And the decision making by the board of directors will be carried out taking into account the competition based on the more prepared predictive analytics based on big data.

The use of AI in management and corporate governance also raises another a critical issue - that of accountability. Although in practice "intelligent agents" can take responsibility for a large number of decisions that used to be made by humans, according to law the final responsibility for such decisions still lies with people - usually with the developers or users of the systems. Let's imagine a situation in which a Board of Directors makes a decision based on a recommendation from an AI system. In this hypothetical situation, the Board approves a decision following a recommendation from AI, but, in the end, this deal leads to financial losses. Who is responsible in this situation? The Board of Directors, the system creators, its customizer, the CEO? A legal conflict can arise. The most difficult task is to determine who exactly holds responsibility and what the legal basis for working with AI is, before such software is released on the market.

Moreover, when dealing with AI, ethical issues become more and more relevant. Ethical issues with "intelligent agents" arise from the fact that AI has difficulty distinguishing between good and bad. Decisions made by an "intelligent agent" may be more precise and proficient, however, in many cases an optimal decision depends on ethical principles and the behavior of the parties involved. The human brain has "social intelligence", which has been evolving for millions of years, and is capable of making such decisions, while an "intelligent agent" is not - it cannot take into consideration such abstract notions as conscience, honor, happiness, values, and therefore it may sometimes act in contradiction with the interests of people or a company.

Any Board of Directors will deal with complex decisions on a regular basis. For example, an "intelligent agent" can rationally make a decision about the dismissal of a significant number of employees, about the reduction of expenses on the development of a product or about its "appropriate" decrease in consumer performance, solely from the perspective of the value maximization function. "Human" Boards of Directors, when making a decision, are more likely to take into account ethical and behavioral nuances.

A whole range of risks in applying AI have a direct influence on business.

According to research conducted by the authors (Figure 6), constraining factors for the introduction of AI in business are the lack of competent staff, budget constraints, limitations of technological capabilities, inflexible processes in organization, and lack of a clear understanding of the processes.

The PWC study (2017) adds a number of barriers to this list: increase in volatility caused by "groundbreaking technologies"; increase in the risk of potential mistakes and the lack of transparency and certainty in the ability to control AI; as well as moral dilemmas such as the trust of shareholders, potential destructive effects on society and a lack of adequate regulations.

Another set of risks is related to the specifics of applying AI in management practices. Let's define some of these.

When we talk about "making AI (a neural network) behave in sensible way, like a human being" we usually mean the left brain hemisphere working independently of the right one. The left side of the brain, as noted by S. Springer & G. Deutsch (1983), is responsible for abstract logic, analysis and verbal thinking. The application of AI as a wide-spread support system may cause a decline in "management diversity". Nowadays, it is commonly accepted that "diversity" at the level of Directors improves the quality of their decisions and the effectiveness of management. Generic decisions suggested by AI could contribute to "tunnel" thinking at the level of the Board and management.

Figure 6. Constraining factors for the introduction of AI in business (compiled by the authors)

Moreover, solutions and decisions suggested by AI could lead to "a self-fulfilling prophecy", as described in 1949 by R.K. Merton (1949) and further studied by G. Soros (2013), who suggest that a prophecy directly or indirectly influences reality in such way that the prophecy eventually turns out to be true. This can happen if an inaccurate understanding of a situation causes new forms of behavior, which transform the initial false assumption into reality. Imagine a situation in which a glitch in a "self-confident" system based on AI causes mass sales on the stock market, which in its turn, acts as a "trigger" to an "automatic" financial crisis.

One more, strictly psychological, risk is caused by the possibility of suffering from the "syndrome of superfluous trust" toward AI systems.

Other risks specific to the use of big data, such as lack of infrastructure, culture of data storage, duplication and mismatch of data sources, unstructured information, statistical mistakes etc., from our point of view are less significant relative to the use of AI, and could be minimized with the further development of the technologies.

Consequently, all risks related to the use of AI based on big data should be governed, and the management of such risk can not be designated to AI itself. In each system using AI, there should be an analogue of the "red button overriding autopilot", which is able to switch the system to "human" mode.

It is worth mentioning that, on the state level, several countries have already made some attempts to regulate the spheres of robotics and AI.

The first approaches to dealing with such issues were developed in South Korea. In 2007, the development of the Robot Ethics Charter was announced, and later the "Intelligent Robots Development And Distribution Promotion Act" (2008) was implemented.

China has also already developed a detailed "New Generation of Artificial Intelligence Development Plan" (2017) on promoting the development of a new-generation of AI technologies, which includes some ambitious plans to be fulfilled by 2030. It's also been indicated that the country intends to create the first laws dedicated to the regulation of this sphere by 2020.

In 2016, the European Parliament accepted for consideration a resolution on the "Civil Law Rules on Robotics" (2016). It consists of several sections: general understanding of robots; their classification; responsibility issues; and establishment of a code of ethics for developers of robots.

At this point, all the listed documents are nothing more than general principles on robotics and AI. However, with the development of practical application in business, more elaborate regulation will be required.

Corporate law allows the Board to delegate their decision making rights to algorithms, however with certain limitations. Moreover, the law can even force the application of algorithms as a mean of control of the decisions made by the Board. But the other side of the question should also be discussed: can Directors demand the right to delegate their decision-making authority to algorithms, at least under certain circumstances?

In terms of legislation it is also important to consider the questions of guilt and accountability of the people who regulate the configurations of algorithms in companies, developers of software, and Directors, when making decisions using AI or refusing to do so. This question is especially important in complex situations, often involving ethical issues or issues related to corporate social responsibility.

SOLUTIONS AND RECOMMENDATIONS

In the 21st century, the corporate world is experiencing changes at a drastically increasing pace. Digital technologies are rapidly developing and the length of business cycles is decreasing from several years to several months. Companies therefore need to react quickly and adapt to such changes by becoming agile and increasing the effectiveness of their work with information.

The growth rate of innovations and the scale and the diversity of existing information create the need to change approaches in management and in decision-making processes. Under such conditions, AI technology is capable of assisting management in processing the large amounts of information required for making corporate decisions, taking into account the increasing competition and pressure from shareholders.

Decisions made by a person and by AI each have their limitations, advantages and disadvantages, which leads to the fact that the most ideal option for improving the effectiveness of such decisions is the use of AI for analysing Big Data as a support system in making such decisions.

Based on the authors' research, Board Members and top managers could be advised to pay attention to the following issues:

- Every company is becoming more and more dependent on new digital technologies; big data technologies provide opportunities only to those who have the appropriate technologies, including AI.
- The role of the Board of Directors is shifting from a "compliance only" approach to a more comprehensive and proactive approach based on setting visions and managing risks.
- Decisions made by Boards of Directors are characteristically based on big data and at the same time include a lot of "subjective noise", which could be decreased by the professional implementation of AI based on big data.
- At the same time, Boards of Directors should pay attention to the risks associated with AI based on big data, including rising volatility, complexity and unpredictability of the consequences of a decision.

- Every board should raise the personal and collective competence in AI and big data technologies and their applications, including "digital experience" in the perspective competence model of the Board of Directors.
- Regulators should pay attention to the amendment of the law about the application of AI based on big data. Corporate Governance Codes should include basic principles for application and ways to manage the risks associated with processing big data and applying AI.

The application of AI based on big data will allow companies to change the process of making decisions by introducing parallel analysis of issues to the agenda of Board meetings and developing alternative independent solutions. However, the decision itself and the responsibility for it should remain with the Board of Directors.

At the same time, when introducing the most effective analysis technology of big data– AI - all risks and possibilities should be thoroughly evaluated, and questions of responsibility and regulations should be thought through both on a state and corporate level.

FUTURE RESEARCH DIRECTIONS

In the 21st century we could witness the Fourth Industrial Revolution, which has been felt since the end of the 20th century, and now the digitalization of the society, technological development, and the transformation of corporations both challenge us and at the same time lead us to new changes in business models and in the processes of how decisions are made, which brings us to intellectualization and higher transparency of management, as well as to the modification of potential conflicts of interest, which lay at the base of corporate governance.

Consequently, the authors will continue their research on the following subject: analysis of the tendencies and perspectives of the corporate governance system in the "digital era"; its transformation to Corporate governance 2.0; and technical aspects of the use of big data technologies and AI in corporate governance.

CONCLUSION

In this study, the authors aim to find an approach to the question 'What is the optimal structure and process for decision making using AI based on big data to support Boards of Directors in decision making in the "new digital era"?', while not focusing on the methods of processing information and other technical aspects of the issue, which have been left for the continuation of this study. Due to higher quality analytical abilities, the increase of transparency and the ability to speed up the decision-making process using AI technologies and big data, corporate governance models will transform, and, in doing so, will create new systems of interaction between shareholders, and will change the methods and business models used in making corporate decisions. In the face of constantly increasing amounts of information and technology development, Boards of Directors need to look to the future, basing their decisions on predictive analytics, rather than analyzing past unstructured data.

Analyzing the system of decision making used by the Board of Directors, it can be concluded that there is a certain set of limitations arising from qualities associated only with human behavior. In order to avoid such limitations, a part of Board's decisions and processes can potentially be automatized and complemented/replaced by analytic systems using AI based on big data. However, full replacement, contrary to the opinions of some authors, and fortunately for humanity, is very unlikely, as the nature of some decisions requires not only analytical abilities (in which AI based on big data can be superior to the human brain), but also emotional and "social" competencies, which AI does not and will not possess in any foreseeable future.

At the present moment, comparative assessment of the effectiveness of AI and people in different types of managerial activities leads to the conclusion that partial automatization is possible when the decision-making process is related to analytic thinking, and that AI is incapable of balancing the interests of shareholders, holding negotiations, approving decisions and taking responsibility for them. Thus, the most effective approach at this point is the introduction of AI in management and corporate governance systems as a support system for making decisions.

However, it should not be forgotten that competition, as one of the most important triggers for the further involvement of AI in management, could lead to major development of AI up to an unpredictable point of singularity. So before such new technology is applied, it is crucial to assess all possible risks and create a control system for these.

Moreover, the risks of using AI should be taken into consideration on governmental, legislative and corporate levels. On the governmental level, it is important to regulate questions of responsibility for decisions made using AI. On the corporate level, internal acts should regulate algorithms of new processes, means of verification, accountability of those responsible for setting up the support system and for the decisions made, and potential consequences and risks.

Consequently, taking into account the possibilities and risks of using AI in corporate governance, AI, which is capable of analyzing big data, could become an effective ally to the Board of Directors in the process of making decisions, by providing them with high-quality, objective information in a short period of time.

REFERENCES

Allianz Global Corporate & Specialty. (2018). *The rise of AI: future perspectives and potential risks.* Retrieved from https://allianz.ru/ru/stuff/Взлет%20искусственного%20интеллекта.pdf

Beare, M. E. (2012). Encyclopedia of Transnational Crime and Justice. Toronto: Academic Press. doi:10.4135/9781452218588

Bostrom, N. (2016). *Artificial Intelligence. Stages. Threats Strategies.* Moscow: MIF.

Centre for Effective Altruism. (2017). *Changes in funding in the AI.* Retrieved from: https://www.centreforeffectivealtruism.org/blog/changes-in-funding-in-the-ai-safety-field/

Chernyak, L. (2011*). Big Data - a new theory and practice. Open systems.* Retrieved from https://www.osp.ru/os/2011/10/13010990/

Corporate Governance Codes and Principles. (2012). *Singapore*. Retrieved from http://www.ecgi.org/codes/code.php?code_id=354

Deep Knowledge Venture's Appoints Intelligent Investment Analysis Software VITAL as Board Member. (2014). Retrieved from: http://www.prweb.com/releases/2014/05/prweb11847458.htm

Eggertsson, T. (2001). Economic behavior and institution. Moscow: Academic Press.

Financial Reporting Council. (2016). *The UK Corporate Governance Code*. Retrieved from https://www.frc.org.uk/directors/corporate-governance-and-stewardship/uk-corporate-governance-code

Fukuyama, F. (1992). *The End of History and the Last Man*. Toronto: Maxwell Macmillan.

Hacker's guide to Neural Networks. (n.d.). Retrieved from: https://karpathy.github.io/neuralnets/

Haskel, J., & Westlake, S. (2017). *Capitalism without capital*. Moscow: Princeton University Press.

Hong Kong Corporate Governance: a practical guide a practical guide. (2016). Retrieved from http://www.hkcg2014.com/pdf/hong-kong-corporate-governance-a-practical-guide.pdf

Intelligent Robots Development and Distribution Promotion Act. (2008). Retrieved from http://elaw.klri.re.kr/eng_mobile/viewer.do?hseq=17399&type=part&key=18

Ito, J., & Hui, J. (2017). *Shift*. Moscow: MIF.

Janis, I. (1972). *Victims of group-think*. Boston: Houghton Mifflin.

Jensen, M., & Meckling, W. (1976). Theory of the firm: Managerial Behavior, Agency costs and Ownership Structure. *Journal of Financial Economics*, *3*(4), 305–360. doi:10.1016/0304-405X(76)90026-X

Kahneman, D. (2014). *Thinking, Fast and Slow*. Moscow: AST.

Kahneman, D., & Tversky, A. (1987). Rational choice and the framing of decisions. *The Journal of Business*, (4), 251–278.

Kerikmäe, D., & Rull, A. (2016). *The Future of Law and eTechnologies*. Springer. doi:10.1007/978-3-319-26896-5

KING IV Report on corporate governance for South Africa. (2016). Retrieved from https://c.ymcdn.com/sites/www.iodsa.co.za/resource/resmgr/king_iv/King_IV_Report/IoDSA_King_IV_Report_-_WebVe.pdf

Kurzweil, R. (2005). *The Singularity Is Near*. New York: Viking.

Kuznetsov, E. (2017). The last line of defense of a person is surrendered. *The Platform, 2*, 6-12.

Libert, B. (2013). *Governance 2.0: the future for boards in the age of big data*. Retrieved from https://www.kornferry.com/institute/579-corporate-governance-2-0-the-boardroom-collides-with-the-digital-age

Management Sciences in the Modern World. (2018). Book of reports of Scientific-Practical conference: Financial University under the Government of the Russian Federation. Saint-Petersburg: Publishing house "Real Economy".

McKinsey Global Institute. (2017). *A future that works: automation, employment, and productivity, US*. Retrieved from https://www.mckinsey.com/~/media/mckinsey/featured%20insights/Digital%20 Disruption/Harnessing%20automation%20for%20a%20future%20that%20works/MGI-A-future-that-works-Executive-summary.ashx

Merton, R. K. (1949). *Social theory and social structure*. New York: Free Press.

Milovidov, V.D. (2017). Corporate governance 2.0: Evolution of the system of corporate relations in digital society. *Problems of the National Strategy, 4*(43), 171-189.

Mintzberg, G., Raisinghani, D., & Théoret, A. (1976). The Structure of "Unstructured" Decision Processes. *Administrative Science Quarterly, 21*(2), 246–275. doi:10.2307/2392045

MITSloan & BCG. (2017). *Global executive study. Reshaping Business With AI*. Retrieved from https://sloanreview.mit.edu/projects/reshaping-business-with-artificial-intelligence/

Molotnikov, A. E. (2017). *The forth industrial revolution and modern understanding of corporate business forms. Business law. N 2* (pp. 3–16). Moscow: Lawyer.

Möslein, F. (2017). Robots in the Boardroom: AI and Corporate Law. *Research Handbook on the Law of Artificial Intelligence*, 10-15.

New Generation of Artificial Intelligence Development Plan. (2017). Retrieved from https://chinacopyrightandmedia.wordpress.com/2017/07/20/a-next-generation-artificial-intelligence-development-plan/

New Scientist. (2007). *South Korea creates ethical code for righteous robots*. Retrieved from https://www.newscientist.com/article/dn11334-south-korea-creates-ethical-code-for-righteous-robots/

Nikishova, M. I. (2018). *Application of AI technologies in the system of corporate governance* (Unpublished PhD thesis). Financial University under the Government of the Russian Federation, Russia, Moscow.

NVP. (2017). *Big Data Executive Survey*. Retrieved from http://newvantage.com/wp-content/uploads/2017/01/Big-Data-Executive-Survey-2017-Executive-Summary.pdf

OECD. (2015). *G20/OECD Principles of Corporate Governance*. Retrieved from http://www.oecd.org/daf/ca/principles-corporate-governance.htm

Pearson, Y. (2017). *The interview for the Mail.ru company*. Retrieved from https://hi-tech.mail.ru/review/ian-pearson/

Policy Department Citizens' Rights and Constitutional Affairs. (2016). *European Civil Law Rules in Robotics*. Retrieved from http://www.europarl.europa.eu/RegData/etudes/STUD/2016/571379/IPOL_STU(2016)571379_EN.pdf

Principles of Corporate Governance. (2016). Retrieved from https://businessroundtable.org/sites/default/files/Principles-of-Corporate-Governance-2016.pdf

PWC. (2017a). *Annual corporate directors survey*. Retrieved from https://www.pwc.com/us/en/governance-insights-center/annual-corporate-directors-survey.html

PWC. (2017b). *CEO Pulse*. Retrieved from https://www.pwc.com/gx/en/ceo-agenda/pulse.html

PWC. (2017c). *The acceleration of innovative development.* Retrieved from https://www.pwc.ru/ru/assets/pdf/artificial-intelligence-realizations-rus.pdf

Russian dialogue of cultures and civilizations - mutual enrichment. (n.d.). Retrieved from http://svop.ru/проекты/lectorium/17025/.

Schwab, K. (2016). *The Fourth industrial Revolution.* Moscow: Publishing house.

Soros, G. (2013). Fallibility, reflexivity, and the human uncertainty principle. *Journal of Economic Methodology, 20*(4), 309–329. doi:10.1080/1350178X.2013.859415

Springer, S., & Deutsch, G. (1983). Left brain, Right brain. Moscow: Mir.

StrategyandPart of the PWC. (2018). *Review of the global venture market and the most advanced technologies, new business models.* Retrieved from https://www.strategyand.pwc.com/media/file/Next-Big-Thing_RU.pdf

The Civil Law Rules on Robotics. (2016). Retrieved from http://www.europarl.europa.eu/RegData/etudes/STUD/2016/571379/IPOL_STU(2016)571379_EN.pdf

The Dutch Corporate Governance Code. (2016). Retrieved from https://www.mccg.nl/?page=3779

The State University of Management. (2017). *Proceedings from the 1st scientific-practical Conference Step into the future: AI and digital economy.* Moscow: Author.

Toffler, E. (2004). *The third wave.* Moscow: AST.

Urban, T. (2015). *The AI Revolution: The Road to Superintelligence.* Retrieved from https://waitbutwhy.com/2015/01/artificial-intelligence-revolution-1.html

Vermeulen, E. P. (2015). *Corporate Governance in a Networked Age.* Tilburg Law School Legal Studies Research Paper Series No. 16/2015.

Vinge, V. (1993). *The Coming Technological Singularity.* Retrieved from http://www.accelerating.org/articles/comingtechsingularity.html

Visser W. (2008). CSR 2.0: The new era of corporate sustainability and responsibility. *CSR International Inspiration Series, 1,* 1-2.

World Economic Forum & Accenture. (2017). *Digital Transformation Initiative.* Retrieved from https://www.accenture.com/t20170411T120304Z__w__/us-en/_acnmedia/Accenture/Conversion-Assets/WEF/PDF/Accenture-DTI-executive-summary.pdf

KEY TERMS AND DEFINITIONS

Artificial Intelligence: Systems able to independently react to signals from the outside world (i.e., signals not directly controlled by programming specialists or anyone else), which therefore cannot be foreseen, in comparison with systems based on algorithms.

Big Data: A means of identifying structured and unstructured data of large volumes and considerable diversity which is hard to process using traditional methods, including structured data, media, and random objects.

Chapter 3
The Strategic Adoption of Big Data in Organizations

Nabeel Al-Qirim
United Arab Emirates University, UAE

Kamel Rouibah
Kuwait University, Kuwait

Mohamad Adel Serhani
United Arab Emirates University, UAE

Ali Tarhini
Sultan Qaboos University, Oman

Ashraf Khalil
United Arab Emirates University, UAE

Mahmoud Maqableh
The University of Jordan, Jordan

Marton Gergely
United Arab Emirates University, UAE

ABSTRACT

This chapter investigates the strategic adoption of big data (BD) and analytics (BDA) in organizations. BD represents a large and complex phenomenon which spans different disciplines. BD research is fraught with many challenges. This research develops BD adoption model that could aid organizations in assessing the strategic importance of BD to gain different advantages including gaining a competitive advantage. BD is considered a radical technology and realizing its advantages in organizations is challenged with many factors. The research attempts to outline the different aspects of BD highlighting different contributions, implications and recommendations.

DOI: 10.4018/978-1-5225-7277-0.ch003

INTRODUCTION

With the current pace of technological development and increased interconnectedness, global competition is soaring and is witnessing ferocious acquisitions, alliances, mergers, and this sometimes lead to the complete abolishment of well established businesses (i.e., Nokia). Technologies such as Internet and social media, electronic commerce, Internet of Things (IoT), sensory data, genomics, and Cloud computing (CC) have led to the exponential growth of data far beyond the comprehension of both technology and people.

There is a big hype around big data (BD) and indeed, it is becoming a very attractive topic for researchers, professional and policymakers around the world. Columbus (2016) indicated that the global BD market will grow from 18.3 Billion US Dollars (BUSD) in 2014 to 92.2 BUSD by 2026, representing a compound annual growth rate of 14.4 percent (Wheatley, 2016); BD and corresponding business analytics software worldwide revenues will grow from nearly 122 BUSD in 2015 to more than 187 BUSD in 2019, an increase of more than 50% over the five-year forecast period; The market for prescriptive analytics software is estimated to grow from approximately 415 Million in 2014 to 1.1 BUSD in 2019; by 2020, predictive and prescriptive analytics will attract 40% of enterprises' net new investment in business intelligence and analytics; and according to Gartner the prediction that BI and analytics market is in the final stages of a multiyear shift from IT-led, system-of-record reporting to business-led, self-service analytics. This is a crucial shift.

The share of global BD market revenues is split amongst professional services (40 percent of all revenues in 2015), hardware (31 percent) and software (29 percent) where it is predicted that a significant growth in all four sub-segments of BD software through 2026: Data management (14% The compound annual growth rate (CAGR)), core technologies such as Hadoop, Spark and streaming analytics (24% CAGR), databases (18% CAGR) and BD applications, analytics and tools (23% CAGR) (Wheatley, 2016)

THE STRATEGIC ADVANTAGE OF BDA

IDC (2012) projects that by 2020 the digital universe will reach 40 zettabytes (ZB), which is 40 trillion GB of data and that the amount of B2C and B2B transactions will be 450 billion per day. The challenge here is that will we be able to deal with such amount of data as existing technologies in place are still handles terabyte to PB data only. This development in data has led to the growth of BD repositories, BD analytics/mining (BDA), and business intelligence (BI) which is driven mostly by the need of enterprises to be more competitive in: becoming more customer-centric, entering new markets and creating new business models and improving operational performance (Columbus, 2016) including improving decision making (Janssen et al., 2017). BDA is the process of uncovering actionable knowledge patterns from BD (in Habib ur Rehman et al., 2016). From now onwards BD and BDA are used interchangeably here to refer to big data.

Côrte-Real et al. (2017) found that BD can provide value at several stages: knowledge, dynamic capability (organizational agility), business process, and competitive performance. Habib ur Rehman et al. (2016) found the literature praising BD in that it could help enterprises maximize their profits by optimizing business process models and improving internal business processes. They also found that the convergence of IoT with BD and CC has taken enterprises to the next level for value creation. BD is seen as a way to enhance organizational agility and to survive in competitive markets in areas of production and operations or product and service enhancement (Côrte-Real et al., 2017). Frizzo-Barker et al. (2016) contributed the hype surrounding BD to the fact that data has become cheaper to store and analyze and easier to collect through web clicks, RFID tags, sensors, loyalty cards and barcodes. They highlighted the following benefits of BD: availability, visibility, and transparency of information and in helping businesses market products and services in a new way, optimizing operations and processes, measure and manage predictive-ity by finding new patterns and connections. However, they found most of the BD research is concentrated in large in the USA followed by Europe and Asia respectively and in large organizations only.

Frizzo-Barker et al. (2016) found that many researchers continue to define BD in different ways, throughout time, which further confirms the lack of agreement on defining BD. It is obvious that BD resembles massive and complex datasets that are hard to capture, collect, analyze, control and manipulate by traditional IT and software/hardware tools in an acceptable time. This includes structured data and unstructured data as well including text, audio, video, posts, log files etc. However, it seems there is an inclination to define BD in terms of its three features volume, variety and velocity (3Vs) (Frizzo-Barker et al., 2016) as explained later in this research. Habib ur Rehman et al. (2016) confirmed the same and pointed to inbound and outbound data sources where inbound handle data generated from internal business operations, such as manufacturing, supply chain management, marketing, and human resource management, etc. Outbound data sources handle customer-generated data which are acquired directly or indirectly from customers, market analysis, surveys, product reviews, and transactional histories.

BDA tools, technologies and infrastructure including social media, mobile devices, automatic identification technologies enabling IoT, and CC platforms enabled firms' operations to achieve and sustain competitive advantage, innovation, and productivity (Fosso et al., 2016). The same researchers emphasized the operational and strategic importance of BD in justifying information systems investment decisions and the improvement of business efficiency and effectiveness (Fosso et al., 2016).

Wheatley (2016) indicated that the demand-side will drive the rapid adoption of BD in addition to other drivers like maturing data lakes, evolving intelligent systems of engagement and emerging intelligent self-tuning systems. He further highlighted that the supply-side such as CC and increasing administrator and developer productivity as well as adjacent technology such as the IoT and rich media represent a significant opportunity in healthcare, entertainment and surveillance industries. To initiate the value creation process enterprises must invest in an effective BDA program and use BDA knowledge to develop capabilities that will help to maintain competitive advantages (Côrte-Real et al., 2017).

BDA RESEARCH IMPLICATIONS

However, realizing such BD advantages is not a straightforward process. A comprehensive review of the BD literature pointed to its fragmentation and to its weak theoretical grounding, methodological diversity and empirically oriented work (Frizzo-Barker et al., 2016). In their review of the literature, Côrte-Real et al. (2017) found that existing BDA research is focused on the adoption and use of BDA; in terms of BD value, most research is focusing on analyzing business value from a data or system perspective; from a strategic management perspective only one conceptual research explored how BDA affects several marketing activities; and the remaining research addresses industry primarily. Frizzo-Barker et al. (2016)

noted that despite the newest of the BD field there was a clear evidence of the increasing interest on BD; BD research remains in the preliminary stages of investigating as it is dominated by conceptually-based research; BD orientation focused more toward BD tools than any other BD issues; much of the literature is more focused on the what or how type questions around integrating BD into business, but far less on whether or even if all organizations or their stakeholders will benefit from using BD; limited coverage on critical, ethical or socio-economic aspects of BD or even the politics of BD algorithms; limitations in the literature relating to small and medium enterprises; lack of global diversity where conducting future empirical work is necessary to determine what types of data-driven best practices are most useful for diverse users; based on the growing trend of empirical studies, it is expected to see more studies in the near future with an eye toward which BD techniques work and which do not, in the context of practical application.

At the outset, Côrte-Real et al. (2017) highlighted that although BDA technologies have been recognized as the "next big thing for innovation", BDA value chain remains relatively unexplored and needs further investigation. They highlighted that the literature found BDA adopters to gain an advantage over their competitors by 5% in productivity and 6% in profitability which encouraged enterprises to invest heavily in BDA technologies. On the other hand, this success is faced with scant empirical research, that needs to extend beyond post-adoption stages toward competitiveness, assessing how BD can bring business value, establishing linkages between knowledge assets, organizational agility, performance (process-level and competitive advantage) and how to use the appropriate technology and organizational resources to gain a competitive edge.

Using Gartner's hype cycle methodology, Frizzo-Barker et al. (2016) concluded that BD has moved through the initial hype and now is still in the preliminary stages of the disillusionment stage. Therefore, they blamed the complexity of the BD field to its infancy as a field and to the limited understanding of what BD is and what it means for organizations. This complexity also stems from difficulties in dealing with large data repositories (infrastructure), data itself (integrity, authenticity, validity, reliability, etc.) and data processing (analytics) to generate insights and strategic decisions concerning BD assimilation in business. In addition BD is often related to predictive analytics and hence, using different techniques to predict future insights by looking for patterns and relationships in data is not that easy process (Gandomi & Haider, 2015). Further, BD processes and data collection strategy increases operational costs and privacy threats, resulting in customer dissatisfaction (Habib ur Rehman et al., 2016).

Similarly, Shin (2016) reported that BD is one dominant strategy in a smart society and found the literature pointing to the wide enthusiasm, hype and potential importance of BD to the economy of the different countries in the world. But this literature was pointing to different implications: both public and privates sectors are still not actively applying BDA; current initiatives are technologically biased and industry-specific; and most development efforts have been focused on the industrialization and commercialization of data technologies and infrastructure and ignored the social dynamics and organizational, political, and managerial decisions on BD success (i.e., privacy, security, interoperability).

Given these challenges and considering the strategic importance of BD to enterprises and their stakeholders, it is very important to understand the innate of BD and how it could be exploited to the benefit of organizations. For example, there is a considerable pre-adoption stage where enterprises should invest money and time to explore how BD can be applied in their business processes in order to develop skills and gain experience. Therefore this research depicts the following research question: *how can enterprises adopt BD successfully*. This question entails answering several sub-questions including what BD means to organizations and how such organizations adopt and implement BD by avoiding hindrances and capitalizing on accelerating factors. In the following sections, the research progresses BD features and tools followed by BD drivers and challenges. Finally the research discuss the results and ends with a conclusion.

BD FEATURES AND TOOLS

In their review of the literature, Janssen et al. (2017) found researchers employing different analytical steps involved in the BD process without specifying who executes these steps and the effects of one step on the other steps: six-model steps (data capturing, data storage, data searching, data sharing, data analysis, and data visualization); three steps (data handling, data processing, and data moving); five steps (problem definition, data searching, data transformation, data entity resolution, answer the query/solve the problem); and data collection, data storage, data management, data manipulation, data cleansing, and data transformation.

CC, new programming models, and scalable high-performance databases, are emerging as BD's core technologies. BD tools are categorized into (Frizzo-Barker et al., 2016):

1. programming models, e.g., MapReduce and Matlab (Matrix lab)
2. data collection, processing and storage, e.g., AaaS, Amazon Web Services
3. data extraction and monitoring, e.g., Amazon Mechanical Turk, Techn orati
4. data management, modelling, and analytics, e.g, Hadoop (based on MapReduce), Apache,

Habib ur Rehman et al. (2016) found the literature splitting the BDA processes into descriptive (e.g., mean, median, mode, standard deviation, variance, and frequency) or prescriptive (cause-effect, optimize business process models based on feedback from predictive analytic) or predictive (supervised, unsupervised, and semi-supervised learning models) analytic models. They also listed the following BDA software tools including Accenture, Alpine Data, Alteryx, Angoss, BigML, BIME, Clario, CoolaData, CoreMetrics, Data Applied, Dell, FICO, IBM, KNIME, Kognitio, Lexalytics, Microsoft, MicroStrategy, Predixion Software Prognoz, RapidMiner, SAP, SAS, SqlStream, etc. Again, the same researchers highlighted different BDA methods. Initially, there is Machine Learning type which include different methods such as Supervised Learning, Unsupervised Learning, Semi-Supervised Learning and Deep Learning. Secondly, Data Mining which include the following different methods: Classification, Association Rules Mining, and Regression Analysis. Finally, the Statistical Methods including Descriptive Statistics and Inferential Statistics.

In looking at BD, volume seemed to be the most obvious attribute here. Variety describes the diversity of structured and unstructured data that can be collected. Velocity refers to how quickly data can be made available for analysis (Frizzo-Barker et al., 2016). However, such a 3Vs model is not enough to warrant companies a competitive position as such. Adding more features such as Variability, Veracity and Visualization (Gandomi and Haider, 2015) provide surrogates to the previous 3Vs in the form of enhanced decision making, further insight discovery, and process optimization. Veracity means how much of the collected data was precise and accurate. This is especially so with data collected from social media avenues and how to trust decisions that were based on such data. Variability considers if the data collected from variety source are consistent and semantics. The variability property determines the internal variability in BD with multiple information-shifts as time passes. The information shift is defined as the difference between states of knowledge in BD systems (Habib ur Rehman et al., 2016). Visualization refers to data presentation as i.e., images, statistical graphs or chemical structure to easily understand the meaning of the data. Others added value to the above six Vs to measure the usefulness of data for an intended purpose (Frizzo-Barker et al., 2016). BD's volume, velocity and variety poses new challenges for aggregating, classifying, storing, and deciphering value out of data (Frizzo-Barker et al., 2016). The challenge here is that the veracity (manipulation, noise), variety (heterogeneity of data) and velocity (constantly changing data sources) amplified by the size of BD calls for relational and contractual governance mechanisms to ensure BD quality and being able to contextualize data (Janssen et al., 2017).

BD DRIVERS AND CHALLENGES

Frizzo-Barker et al. (2016) attributed the success of BD to the: ease of obtaining data through e.g., web clicks, RFID tags, sensors, loyalty cards and barcodes; data has become cheaper to store and analyze; the volume capacity and performance quality of BD tools; the greater availability, visibility, and transparency of information; data analysts and data-mining techniques can find new insights; and help businesses measure and manage predictiv-ity.

BD is considered a disruptive technology and hence, the majority of these challenges (Frizzo-Barker et al., 2016) range from organizational BD design issues and management, BD in relation to innovation, computing technologies, analytics, social media, marketing, inventory management, talent management, and customer experience. Wheatley (2016) highlighted that the skill-gap remains the number one barrier to BD followed by the lack of standards and conventions for BD programming models, administration processes and insight-delivery methods. In the same vein, Janssen et al. (2017) pointed to the BD capac-ity and capabilities of people involved in collecting and processing BD. Secondly, the relative imma-turity of technologies which hinders BD growth, even e.g. Hadoop and data lakes are still need a lot of transformation to be simpler. Finally, BD governance, or rules for use is more complex as it transcends technology boundaries. Similarly, Frizzo-Barker et al. (2016) confirmed the same and highlighted other challenges: lack of skillsets; lack of tools required to carry out BD strategies; concerns about privacy and surveillance; various disruptions of conventional methods, labor, and legality; incorporate BD into business, challenges organizational structures themselves, as new workflows and incentives must be designed to prioritize data-driven decision-making; risk of data privacy and ethical infringements, lack of BD policy; cost versus benefit of using BD for decision-making; the validation and integrity of collected data, and the complexities of dealing with highly distributed data sources; and how to take advantage of the unprecedented scale of available data:

1. Need for BD scientists and programmers
2. Integration of new technical tools required to collect, store, analyze and use BD

Côrte-Real et al. (2017) research indicate that although BDA technologies call for substantial investment in implementation and maintenance, European firms are aware of BDA's potential value and benefits. Let's not forget BD may incur indirect costs. For example, CC utilization costs increase because of BD analytics and value creation activities for enterprises and customers (Habib ur Rehman et al., 2016). Despite its significance, the effect of BD on decision-making quality has been given scant attention in the literature (Janssen et al., 2017). This is attributed to the complexity of creating value from BD sets that are collected from different and heterogeneous sources that have various data qualities and are processed by various organizational entities resulting in the creation of a BD chain (collecting the data from the sources and ends when data-based decisions are taken) involving a myriad of multidisciplinary players.

Therefore, it is not surprising that the majority of adopters are concentrated within real-time, large and multinational organizations but even though, such corporations are still struggling to integrate BD into their organizational cultures where questions like what BD is, who is using it, and what benefits, opportunities, and risks does it present to organizations and firms are not yet answered in large (Frizzo-Barker et al., 2016). Those organizations spanned different industries including finance and management sectors (banking and accounting), law and governance (military, policy-making, and national security), Information technology (IT) (data analysis, technical platforms, crowdsourcing, and information systems strategy), healthcare represented (genomics, medicine, hospitals and drug administration), education (BD in higher education, research and libraries), and finally, limited participation from other industries including trade and manufacturing, agriculture, music and entertainment, insurance, media, non-governmental organizations, and the environment.

While some challenges are related to data such as acquisition and storage and the risk of the confidentiality aspect others related to management and analysis (Janssen et al., 2017). Further, they highlighted that BD is noisy, messy, constantly-changing, and comes in different formats. They found the literature highlighting that an effective BD chain requires building capabilities and capacity for data management and BD analytics (descriptive, exploratory, inferential, predictive, causal and mechanistic techniques). For that reason, various methods are employed such as natural language processing, text mining, linguistic computation, machine learning, search and sort algorithms, syntax and lexical analysis, etc. They found the following conditions important for BD and BD analytics success: contractual governance concerning making agreements and contracts (SLAs) with BD providers to ensure mutual understanding of BD; relational governance is important to establish trust among involved organizations; the ability to collaborate among BD providers, BDA analysts and decision-makers; BDA domain-based capabilities in identifying the right tools for analyzing, which techniques to use and how to visualize B; data and knowledge exchange about the data in order to facilitate BDA analysis; process integration and standardization; routinizing and standardization BD chain improves BD velocity and decision making; flexible infrastructure determines the ability and the amount of effort necessary to handle and process the data; systems integration improves the handling of BD in order to avoid tedious manual work; scarce BD and BDA expertise who could communicate and interpret results; data quality of the BD sources; and the quality of decision-maker decisions

Côrte-Real et al. (2017) stressed on the following antecedents to realizing BDA value: initially, making sense of the way firms use the technologies available to manage internal and external knowledge (helped through training); second, by effectively using BDA, firms can acquire capabilities to innovate and rapidly adjust to external demands (building organizational agility); thirdly, these capabilities will encourage specific business areas to involve the whole organization, when an effective bottom-up strategy is followed, supported by good communication practices; and finally, a performance metric to gauge the impact of BDA.

Habib ur Rehman et al. (2016) noted from the literature that data scientists spend 57.5% of their time on data preparation and hence, following a data reductionist strategy could further facilitate workload optimization, uncover the semantic relationship between data points and reduced BD streams before entering CC systems through compression and decompression techniques to reduce in-network bandwidth, sizing datasets, reduce dimensionality, remove duplicated data, minimize the financial cost of data storage services (by CC providers) and finally using datamining and machine learning methods could be used to uncover the knowledge patterns for lateral utilization instead of iterative raw data processing. They further noted that the prior knowledge of customers' behaviors could help in reducing processing the same raw data. In addition, security breaches are on the rise which should be addressed.

It is worth noting that BD capabilities is a function of management (planning, investment, coordination, control), infrastructure flexibility (connectivity, compatibility, modularity), and personnel expertise (technical knowledge, technology management knowledge, business knowledge and relational knowledge) capabilities (Fosso et al., 2016)

BD ADOPTION MODELS

9S Framework

To be able to understand the impact of BD in business; firms and managers can view BD from the perspective of the 9S framework (or BD Wheel) (Lake and Drake, 2014). The 9S framework allows managers to see broadly the interplay between data and analytics from different technical and managerial strategic directions e.g., hard technologies, security and system, style, staff (Figure 1). As shown in Figure 1 statistical thinking sets at the center of the BD Wheel since it is the common perspective across all others aspect of BD. Strategy and structure are tightly coupled in a way to show how organizations are structured and where the power lies which influences the way strategy is developed. Also, such strategies and their results may change the organization structure. Moreover, the type of staff employed as well as the structure and strategy of the organization are tightly coupled with the management styles.

Figure 1. 9S Framework

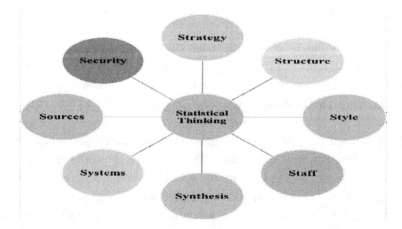

PRACTICE FRAMEWORK

There are other frameworks which could help business to ensure a successfully BD analytics. The following framework consists of two perspectives: business perspective, technological perspective (Singh H. 2015).

Business Perspective:

1. Selecting the right strategy: Business must be able to provide clear business case on the problem they want solve analytically.
2. Connect the Stakeholders: such as active senior management support and involvement.
3. Establish Critical Success Factors CSFs: that focuses on employee usage of the resulting intelligence and key performance indicators for the processes where analytics will be used e.g., customer satisfaction, supply chain efficiency, etc.
4. Run a Pilot Project.

Technological Perspective:

1. Evaluate data requirements
    a. What is the structure of data sources: For example, external structured data, external unstructured data such as social media posts, internal unstructured data such as sensor data and internal structured data such as Customer Relationship Management (CRM) (Ebner et al., 2014).
    b. Data frequency of the data being processed.
    c. Is it on-demand, continuous feed or real-time.
    d. What is the analysis type which should be used?
    e. Is this batch or streaming/real-time?
    f. What is the volume of data received.
    g. Are these massive chunks or small and fast chunks?
    h. How to store data or how to process it.
    i. How to visualize results.
2. Take a structured approach: such as using an agile and iterative implementation technique that delivers quick results addressing the business requirement instead of a considerable SDLC application development. It is recommended to start small by meeting the requirement identified in the business case and gradually expand the project while not losing sight of the bigger business strategy.
3. Pick the right tools and technology for the requirement: it is recommended to technically and financially evaluate the different tools provided by different BD commercial vendors.
4. Define data governance early: as businesses adopt BD for competitive purposes, it is as important to address security threats and issues relating to realigning organizations security, privacy and governance policies especially if data transcends countries and continents privacy laws.

There are other competing frameworks that help organizations adopt BD strategically. Most importantly is that organizations could use combined approaches, for example, combining best aspects from both the 9S and the 8 practices frameworks, to reach to a set of variables that best fit their needs.

BD Strategies

Selecting the right BD strategy can be categorized into three dimensions: strategic elements, resource, and operating environment. The first dimension refers to the strategic factors, which include the relevance of BD, sponsorship level, and urgency. The second dimension refers to the resource factors, which include the IT personnel abilities, resource availability and absorptive capacity. The last dimension is operating environment, which involves the task routineness and data privacy (Ebner et al., 2014).

DISCUSSION

At the outset, the hype surrounding BD spurred global competition in that companies are pushed to adopt BD out of fear of being left behind. With such dependency on technology, organizations are becoming increasingly more data-dependent. At this stage organizations are still driven by technology and what it can do for them. On the other hand, being a disruptive technology, it possesses a variety of challenges which challenges organizations in using BD more effectively and ethically (Frizzo-Barker et al., 2016). This will further strain top executives in considering the following options: whether to proceed with a considerable initial investment in e.g., "risky" BD endeavors or trialing with BD across their learning curves using incremental and small investments or take a wait-and-see posture until BD stabilizes and matures. All these options are difficult ones because once the BD adoption and implementation process starts it will be very difficult to reverse the process if not impossible. Preparing the organization and Building the well-integrated infrastructure and unifying all sources of data across the BD chain will already consume large amounts of resources. At this stage, such processes are still technically feasible but the following processes in dealing with the raw data, cleansing it, standardizing it and then analyzing it using the right strategic model and interpreting results are still lurking challenges both technically and cognitively in addition to the needed considerable investments on consultants, hardware and software and training. The most important part here is the needed intelligence to make sure that what the organization is looking for is in line with its strategy and how to make sense of these exorbitant data. In addition, these processes should proceed in a smooth intra- and inter-organizational manner. This will require painstakingly close cooperation and collaboration between diverse range (sometimes with conflicting views and agendas) of stakeholders and organizational silos. This is an exhausting process financially, mentally, socially, etc.

There are already large players in the game and those are learning the hard way if not the hardest, but they have no option especially companies that deal with real-time data like Facebook and Twitter. Lessons from the history of technology adoption and diffusion have always taught us that leaders will always reap most of the benefits and laggards will always be left with leftovers or nothing. Technology is evolving so rapidly that what comes soon could be something totally unprecedented. For example, blackberry have lured large numbers of Nokia's mobile users for some time with its push-email-services feature but when iPhone emerged it overtook almost all mobile phone users and set the standard for the mobile industry once and for all.

The last option of wait-and-see is no longer an option. The huge hype and drive behind BD meant that everybody large and small enterprises should jump into the speedy BD wagon. Now, the difference is that there are enterprises that are already thrusting on the different phases of the BD's lifecycle driven mostly by its strategic necessity to their existence like Facebook. They could afford integrating phases or paralleling them in order to get the job done. But other enterprises are not faced with such urgency to adopt BD. The whole issue really dictates having critical and clear vision and leadership to push BD forward.

Accordingly, BD adoption and implementation decisions should be both rationalized but at the same time should be pushed forward. This hybrid approach in "incrementally pushing" BD is highly envisaged here for organizations alongside BD's metamorphological stages. Even if BD takes a sudden change in direction, such enterprises could still be present and active in the BD game. For example, investing in building BD intelligence (internally and externally) and integrating the BD infrastructure are steps in the right direction in general. The rest of the phases could be picked up and prioritized alongside the learning curve of such enterprises. The speed on this learning curve could be steep or gentle depending on the BD's strategic understanding and priorities of such enterprises.

Indeed, the whole BD issue is overwhelming in that the road to the full realization of the "emergent" BD field is fraught with many challenges and CEOs and CIOs will face tough decisions to make. Therefore, it is not surprising that BD became everyone's most hated buzzword in 2013 (Datoo, 2014). What is encouraging here is that there is a general optimism around BD and its importance which will create the needed momentum to push it forward.

CONCLUSION

This research attempted to shed light into the BD field by highlighting and explaining its different components, theoretical implications, and drivers and challenges. What this research attempts to stress on here is that although BD represents a crucial strategic information systems tool for organizations, its adoption and implementation should be carefully considered and assimilated alongside different contextual levels. The earlier failure stories of enterprise information systems adoption and implementation in the past stands as painful reminders.

REFERENCES

Columbus, L. (2016). *Roundup of Analytics, Big Data & BI Forecasts and Market Estimates, 2016, AUG 20*. Retrieved January 16, 2017 from: http://www.forbes.com/sites/louiscolumbus/2016/08/20/roundup-of-analytics-big-data-bi-forecasts-and-market-estimates-2016/#4ea4c90849c5

Côrte-Real, N., Oliveira, T., & Ruivo, P. (2017). Assessing business value of Big Data Analytics in European firms. *Journal of Business Research*, *70*, 379–390. doi:10.1016/j.jbusres.2016.08.011

Datoo, S. (2014). Big data: 4 predictions for 2014. *The Guardian*. Retrieved January 20, 2017 from: https://www.theguardian.com/technology/datablog/2014/jan/14/big-data-4-predictions-for-2014

Ebner, K., Buhnen, T., & Urbach, N. (2014). Think Big with Big Data: Identifying Suitable Big Data Strategies in Corporate Environments. *2014 47th Hawaii International Conference on System Sciences*.

Fosso Wamba, S., Gunasekaran, A., & Akter, S. (2016). Big data analytics and firm performance: Effects of dynamic capabilities. *Journal of Business Research*, *70*, 356–365. doi:10.1016/j.jbusres.2016.08.009

Frizzo-Barker, J., Chow-White, P., Mozafari, M., & Ha, D. (2016). An empirical study of the rise of big data in business Scholarship. *International Journal of Information Management, 36*(3), 403–413. doi:10.1016/j.ijinfomgt.2016.01.006

Gandomi, A., & Haider, M. (2015). Beyond the hype: Big data concepts, methods, and analytics. *International Journal of Information Management, 35*(2), 137–144. doi:10.1016/j.ijinfomgt.2014.10.007

Habib ur Rehmana, M., Changb, V., Batoolc, A., & Wah, T. (2016). Big data reduction framework for value creation in sustainable enterprises. *International Journal of Information Management, 36*, 917–928.

IDC. (2012). *Digital Universe study*. Retrieved January 1, 2017, from: http://www.kdnuggets.com/2012/12/idc-digital-universe-2020.html

Janssen, M., Van der Voort, H., & Wahyudi, A. (2017). Factors influencing big data decision-making quality. *Journal of Business Research, 70*, 338–345. doi:10.1016/j.jbusres.2016.08.007

Lake, P., & Drake, R. (2014). *Information systems management in the big data era*. Springer International Publishing; doi:10.1007/978-3-319-13503-8

Shin, D. (2016). Demystifying big data: Anatomy of big data developmental process. *Telecommunications Policy, 40*(9), 837–854. doi:10.1016/j.telpol.2015.03.007

Singh, H. (2015, August 24). *8 Best Practices for Executing a Successful Big Data Analytics Strategy*. Retrieved May 1, 2016, from https://www.linkedin.com/pulse/8-best-practices-executing-successful-big-data-analytics-singh

Wheatley, M. (2016). *Wikibon forecasts Big Data market to hit $92.2B by 2026*. Retrieved January 1, 2017, from: http://siliconangle.com/blog/2016/03/30/wikibon-forecasts-big-data-market-to-hit-92-2bn-by-2026/

Chapter 4
Managerial Controversies in Artificial Intelligence and Big Data Analytics

Kenneth David Strang
iD https://orcid.org/0000-0002-4333-4399
Multinations Research, USA

Zhaohao Sun
iD https://orcid.org/0000-0003-0780-3271
Papua New Guinea University of Technology, Papua New Guinea

ABSTRACT

This chapter discusses several fundamental and managerial controversies associated with artificial intelligence and big data analytics which will be of interest to quantitative professionals and practitioners in the fields of computing, e-commerce, e-business services, and e-government. The authors utilized the systems thinking technique within an action research framework. They used this approach because their ideology was pragmatic, the problem at hand, was complex and institutional (healthcare discipline), and they needed to understand the problems from both a practitioner and a nonhuman technology process viewpoint. They used the literature review along with practitioner interviews collected at a big data conference. Although they found many problems, they considered these to be already encompassed into the big data five V's (volume, velocity, variety, value, veracity). Interestingly, they uncovered three new insights about the hidden healthcare artificial intelligence and big data analytics risks; then they proposed solutions for each of these problems.

DOI: 10.4018/978-1-5225-7277-0.ch004

INTRODUCTION

Technological entrepreneur and UK-based venture capitalist Viktor Prokopenya (2018) pointed out that artificial intelligence applications like machine learning have many limitations especially that many tasks have too much data and are simply too complicated to program. Scholars already know about the major challenges faced by big data analytics practitioners across all disciplines which are described as the five V's (Jovanovi et al., 2015, Terry, 2015) or sometimes more (Sun et al., 2016). The big data five V's are commonly phrased as high volume (Chen and Zhang, 2014), complex variety (Kessel et al., 2014), large velocity (Ekbia et al., 2015), strategic value (Gandomi and Haider, 2015), and more recently veracity (Strang and Sun, 2016). Value in big data can be viewed as a constraint because it can be challenging to derive a benefit from analytics that is worth the investment time and cost to accommodate the other factors. Big data veracity can refer to ethics, accuracy, validity, or truthfulness (Vajjhala et al., 2015) as well as social-cultural relevance (Vajjhala and Strang, 2017). In addition to the above characteristics, each discipline and industry has unique big data analytics issues.

In the healthcare discipline researchers have posited that privacy is one of the biggest problems associated with the big data paradigm (Thorpe and Gray, 2015, Hoffman and Podgurski, 2013, Kshetri, 2014, Filkins et al., 2016, Rothstein, 2015). Most countries have legislation to uphold the privacy of individuals, such as the *Health Insurance Portability and Accountability Act* in USA (Brown, 2008). However, we propose there are important hidden big data analytics issues in the healthcare industry that are not documented in the literature. In this study we review the literature and collect information from practitioners about tacit problems associated with healthcare big data analytics and then summarize the results in a visual model.

The big data paradigm is relatively new since it formally commenced in 2011 (Salleh and Janczewski, 2016, Burrows and Savage, 2014, Strang and Sun, 2017) so there is roughly half a decade of research at the time of writing. Most of the published big data research has been focused on technology-related keywords like data mining, cloud computing, machine learning, electronic data processing, algorithms and others (Strang and Sun, 2017). According to a recent meta-analysis of the big data literature only 2% of peer-reviewed publications examined privacy and security topics including healthcare during 2011-2016 that that decreased to 1% for the first three months of 2017 (Strang and Sun, 2017). Many researchers have called for more studies about big data privacy (van Loenen et al., 2016, Eastin et al., 2016, de Montjoye and Pentland, 2016, Salleh and Janczewski, 2016, Chen and Zhang, 2014), and particularly in healthcare (Jungwirth and Haluza, 2017, Filkins et al., 2016). This is strong evidence that more research about healthcare big data analytics is needed. This also implies there may be unseen risks that practitioners know exist in healthcare big data analytics. We attempt to articulate these obscure issues in healthcare big data analytics through a literature review and from discussions with other practitioners.

LITERATURE REVIEW

Overview of Big Data Literature

Chen and Zhang (2014) reviewed the literature several years ago and came to the conclusion that privacy was not adequately investigated within the big data body of knowledge. However, in addition to being dated, they did not perform a longitudinal structured review of the literature. Therefore we conducted a thorough review of the big data literature published during the last decade.

We start with a summary of the literature before we review the relevant healthcare data analytics papers. Using "big data" as the search term, we closely examined 13,029 manuscript titles, abstracts and keywords published in journals during 2011-2017 (only the first three months of 2017 were included). We used the title, abstract and keywords to a dominant theme for every article. We counted the frequencies of the themes which resulted in 49 topics consisting of 1-3 words like 'data mining', 'artificial intelligence' and 'online social networks'. We then factored the journal big data from 2011-2017 into a displayable short-list of 10-15 dominant themes using the frequency, and grouped all remaining low-count topics into a new category called '<1%'.

The results revealed that the most frequent big data topic published in journals was data mining (N=1186) at 9.1%. The next three topics were similar in frequency, namely data analytics (N=979, 7.5%), cloud computing (N=808, 6.2%), and literature reviews (N=784, 6.0%). For reference purposes we could classify the current study as either a big data literature review (or under the others topic). Machine learning (N=493, 3.8%) and social media (N=466, 3.6%) came next but were a third less frequent than data mining. The following seven big data topics were somewhat equivalent in frequency: electronic data processing (N=455, 3.5%), algorithms (N=388, 3.0%), databases (N=360, 2.8%), map reduce (N=358, 2.7%), research methods (N=302, 2.3%), human behavior (N=282, 2.2%) and privacy & security (N=280, 2.1%). As shown in figure 1, the remaining articles generated frequencies at or less than 1% so all were grouped into the '<1%' category which amounted to 6752 or 51% of the manuscripts in the meta-analysis. This other category included 36 topics like information technology, concepts or frameworks, hadoop, acquisition of data, computer algorithms, as well as healthcare.

These 13 dominant topics represented 49% of the big data body of knowledge production in scholarly journals during the literature review sample time frame. Only a very small proportion of the privacy & security articles were grounded in the healthcare discipline. Thus, it was clear that published research about privacy in big data was scarce (at 2.1%) and this included all disciplines not just healthcare. This shows that there was a shortage of big data analytics research about privacy.

In our literature meta-analysis of big data we grouped privacy and security together because researchers often did that despite that they meant one or the other term. To clarify, privacy in big data is the claim of individuals to have their data left alone, free from surveillance or interference from other individuals, systems or organizations (Kessel et al., 2014, Kshetri, 2014). In the healthcare discipline privacy can be further defined as an individual's right to control the acquisition, use, or disclosure of his or her identifiable health-related data even if it does not contain personal identifiers. In contrast, big data security refers to the technology, software, policies, procedures, and technical measures used to prevent unauthorized access, alternation, theft of data or physical damage to devices and systems (Gandomi and Haider, 2015, Jovanovi et al., 2015). In the healthcare discipline, security is further refined as the physical, technological, or administrative safeguards or tools used to protect identifiable health data from unwarranted access or disclosure. In this study we focus on healthcare big data privacy and not security – not that the latter is any less critical but it is beyond the scope.

Positive Impact of Big Data in Healthcare

Notwithstanding the five or more challenges with big data (volume, velocity, variety, value, veracity), there are many positive benefits for healthcare practitioners and researchers. Detailed big data on people can be used by policymakers to reduce crime or terrorism, improve health delivery, and better manage cities (Strang and Alamieyeseigha, 2015, Terry, 2015). Organizations and nations can benefit from big data because research indicates that data-driven businesses were 5% percent more productive and 6% more profitable than their competitors (Chen and Zhang, 2014, Burrows and Savage, 2014). The macro-economic impact is that the gross domestic product of a country could increase due to big data analytics (Gandomi and Haider, 2015).

We have seen big data analytics used to help combat global and domestic terrorism (De Zwart et al., 2014, Strang and Sun, 2016). The American military has tapped into big data to uncover and mitigate terrorist plots (Strang, 2015a). For example geo-location smart phone big data was helpful for investigating the Boston bomber and his accomplices (Strang and Alamieyeseigha, 2017) and many other terrorist plots have been foiled (Lichtblau and Weilandaug, 2016).

Big data analytics can assist with decision making in all disciplines and industries, from commercial entities to government policy makers (Eastin et al., 2016, Kessel et al., 2014). Big data is valuable to commercial businesses to improve target marketing and thereby increase effectiveness on a microeconomics level but the benefits go further to the macroeconomic environment as a cost reduction and increased goods production using the same scarce resources (de Montjoye and Pentland, 2016).

The benefits of big data analysis for improving healthcare medical research are well-known (Lusher et al., 2014, Thorpe and Gray, 2015). These benefits include facilitating evidence-based medical research to detect diseases at the earlier stages (ADA, 2015, Rothstein, 2015), minimizing drug surpluses and inventory shortfalls in pharmaceutical (Zhong et al., 2015), and better tracking of viruses through location-enriched social media big data (Vaidhyanathan and Bulock, 2014). As with the other disciplinary benefits, this has a positive domino effect by improving microeconomics and macroeconomics (Chen and Zhang, 2014).

Environmental monitoring has generated useful big data that can help to identify virus and disease spreading patterns through global position system (GPS) location-coding (Leszczynski, 2015, Zhong et al., 2015) and from patient symptom-related messages in social media posts (Jungwirth and Haluza, 2017, Hogarth and Soyer, 2015). Hospital executives and management have used administrative big data to monitor patient quality and staff feedback, which affords information that may not otherwise be forthcoming (Hoffman and Podgurski, 2013). Interestingly, when individual patient data is aggregated together for an entire hospital or facility, fluctuations in vitals could indicate a major problem such as poor air quality or a pandemic like pneumonia (Jungwirth and Haluza, 2017, Kshetri, 2014).

Healthcare researchers have gained the most from big data because this has become another rich data collection avenue providing more volume, velocity, variety, and potential value, as compared with surveys, observation, and physical vitals capture (Kshetri, 2014, Lusher et al., 2014). Healthcare big data tends to be categorized into two streams: Vitals and social. The vitals are the obvious value-laden form of big data in healthcare. However, social big data can also be useful to the healthcare industry by allowing practitioners to detect attitudes through sentiment analysis (Zikopoulos et al., 2011, Gandomi and Haider, 2015).

Unintended Healthcare Big Data Access

The literature is ripe with the benefits of big data but there are also some unadvertised pitfalls. In these next three sections we will examine the three hidden problems of healthcare bug data analytics. Wireless micro-technology advances have given healthcare professionals insights into diseases and medical conditions. What puts wireless healthcare technology into the big data analytics domain is that micro-technology implants and devices can generate huge volumes of high velocity and a wide variety of valuable 'personal data'. Personal data generated by healthcare devices and implants may contain date of birth, social security number or other healthcare patient identification, gender, address with geo-location coordinates, along with the high volume high velocity probe readings such as blood pressure, counts, etc. (Lusher et al., 2014, Ward, 2014).

Wireless healthcare devices and implants are similar to SCADA systems used for environmental monitoring in that a huge amount of readings are generated – more big data than could possibly be stored or analyzed (Strang and Sun, 2016). Likewise in healthcare wireless devices or implants, there are so many probe readings that only a small number are processed by the receiving station (Filkins et al., 2016). The personal identification data is more extensive during the initiation sequence with a receiving station (to authenticate the connection), and while this may be encrypted, it is transmitted either randomly or at specific intervals to maintain a connection with a receiving station (Lusher et al., 2014).

Healthcare wearable devices or internal implants are generally connected to servers through a pervasive computing application, with the purpose to monitor a patient from sensor readings so as to warn physicians if a pattern changes for the worst or for the better (Lusher et al., 2014). Sensors are not new technology because they have been used with pervasive computing applications to gather data from the physical environment such as binary (1=on or 0=off) sensors attached to household objects or infrastructure like movement detectors, door sensors, contact switch sensors and pressure pads (Shen and Zhang, 2014). Healthcare specific devices or implants tend to collect readings on body temperature, blood pressure, pulse, blood–oxygen ratios, heart ECG or glucometers, movement (e.g., a fall), and chemical presence (Vaidhyanathan and Bulock, 2014). Radio frequency identification data (RFID) chip tags or Quick Response (QR) codes can be used to uniquely identify and locate tagged objects (e.g., a medical device presence), or to store (a link to) relevant information such as medication instructions (van Otterlo, 2014). Similarly, Bluetooth or modulated illumination-based beacons deployed throughout the user's environment can be used to transmit unique location identification codes, which a hand-held device or wearable badge can detect in order to locate the user through GPS coordinate (van Otterlo, 2014).

Some type of personal identification is included in every healthcare wireless broadcast to ensure that a receiving station does not confuse the patient's device device/implant with another close by patient. Although the identification in pure data reading transmissions may be a unique number generated for the patient, it is nevertheless linked to the patient as well as to the location of the patient. This is what makes wireless healthcare personal big data subject to the veracity or viability characteristic – many people do not want their wireless-transmitted personal data to be captured by anyone other than the intended receiving station. Unfortunately, the nature of wireless transmissions is that even encrypted data could be easily intercepted and decoded with currently available software (Al-Ameen et al., 2012).

The capability of identifying individuals in big data even when personal attributes have been removed is a risk. There are several well-known cases in the literature. Likelihood algorithms have been used to link big data streams without personal identifiers to a master file based on information that could estimate age, gender, location, and employment characteristics (Angiuli et al., 2015, Wang et al., 2015. Winkler, 2005). If the social media big data include even a few direct identifiers, like names, address, cell phone numbers, social security numbers, or company numbers, the risk is high that a match could be made with organizational or government data (Wang et al., 2015, Zikopoulos et al., 2011).

Most healthcare devices or implants have physical machine addresses (MAC's) and Internet Protocol (IP) addresses if they are online. The MAC address is hard-coded at the factory and is detectable in cellular data networks or on the Internet, while IP addresses are usually active only when on the Internet but they can still be read with the appropriate software (Wang et al., 2015). These addresses are necessary for the device/implant to connect to a peer or network receiver in order to transmit their data (Wang et al., 2015). The problems is that since these network addresses can be accessed, they can be linked to location and device owner so that when combined with the transmitted data it could identify an individual including financial and other confidential information. There are free open software applications that can track cell phone locations and social media user names through the MAC and GPS big data which are being used for malicious reasons (Shen and Zhang, 2014, Shull, 2014).

At the other end of the situation is the informed consent presented to the healthcare patient and/or physicians. Usually a healthcare device/implant will contain a privacy policy declaration that must be signed before surgery or application. Secondly, any mobile software being used in conjunction with the device/implant, such as a smartphone application would contain a privacy policy that would require patient consent. However, the Internet generation of people are accustomed to seeing software agreements due to downloading applications on smartphones, laptops, and other products so there is a tendency to hastily recklessly agree out of frustration or habit. Therefore, more attention must be given to informed consent when wireless healthcare big data collection is being authorized.

Most developed countries have legislation to protect individual privacy in healthcare big data, such as the Health Insurance Portability and Accountability Act (HIPAA) regulations under the Privacy Rule of 2003 in USA (Brown, 2008). HIPAA requires healthcare providers to remove 18 types of identifiers in patient data, including birthdate, vehicle serial numbers, image URLs, and voice prints (Brown, 2008). However, even seemingly innocuous information makes it relatively easy to re-identify individuals through wireless healthcare big data, such as finding sufficient information that there is only one person in the relevant population with a matching set of unique conditions (van Loenen et al., 2016).

Data generated by interacting with recognized professionals, such as lawyers, doctors, professors, researchers, accountants, investment managers, project managers or by online consumer transactions, are governed by laws requiring informed consent and draw on the Fair Information Practice Principles (FIPP) legislation (Brown, 2008, Terry, 2015). Despite the FIPP's explicit application to protect individual data, the rules are typically confined to personal information such as social security number and do not encompass the large-scale data-collection issues that arise through location tracking and online social media postings or Internet site visits (Terry, 2015).

Ultimately, the major drawback of wireless healthcare big data is that it takes place in the open public domain outside of a healthcare provider jurisdiction, and therefore it is not covered by privacy legislation (Brown, 2008). Two practitioner examples from colleagues of the first author illustrate the extreme risk of what can happen. In one case a licensed medical physician from Sydney Australia specializing in pediatric immunology (children allergies, asthma, rhinitis, sinusitis, atopic dermatitis, urticarial, anaphylaxis and immune disorders) missed two days of the IEEE Big Data conference. When he was pulled aside for a detailed interview at the Dulles Washington International airport immigration he did not realize that his foreign passport contained a readable electronic passive chip that contained his place of birth, which happened to be Tehran but his parents had emigrated from Iran to Australia when he was one year old. It is easy to sympathize with anyone held up in immigration-customs especially in his predicament where he was asked "so prove to me that you are a doctor in Australia." After several hours of interrogations he was able to produce several of his journal papers stored on his laptop and by later in the evening EST the Sydney clinic had opened for their early morning so they were able to confirm his identity through a Skype call. During immigration apparently humans are guilty until proven innocent.

A piping engineer in the oil-gas industry was living in Houston, TX while completing his doctorate at an American university under the guidance of the first author. Since he travelled frequently for work and university the engineer used a wireless pass card for toll roads and he had an enhanced driver license that facilitated his passing through land and water borders between USA and Mexico. When he was finishing his dissertation he took several months off and became annoyed at receiving what he thought were scam collection letters in the mail. After a visit with his bank and discussions with a credit counselor, he found that his identity had been stolen and over $20,000 in debt had been incurred in his name in addition to his student loan. Investigators believed that the wireless passive chip in his driver license had been read to furnish his birth date, citizenship information and address, and some credit card data along with other vehicle identifiers were somehow captured from the toll-pass-card and their billing system. The culprits were professionals because there was no evidence to charge them so he was forced to declare bankruptcy.

The prevalence of multiple digital devices of the sample person being connected to the Internet has resulted in personal information being inadvertently collected by legitimate providers, which when combined across sources can become powerful big data. For example, as Ohm (2010) proved, a marketing specialist or a hacker could re-identify more than 80% of Netflix clients using an individual's zip code, birthdate, and gender along with viewing history. Netflix is a popular entertainment site but it is unlikely that high ranked officials would necessarily want their viewing information or other online behaviors revealed to the world. Another example of big data caveats occurred when Target was able to predict a teenage girl was pregnant due to her online browsing activity and sent baby coupons to her house which were not well-received by her father (Duhigg, 2014). The same problems can occur in the healthcare discipline because professionals may have their online Internet behavior linked to their personal identity, or patients may have their Internet activity, location, and other personal details connected together using big data analytics (Lusher et al., 2014, Leszczynski, 2015).

METHODS

We utilized the systems thinking technique popularized by Checkland (1999) which Strang (2015b) classifies as an action research method where practitioners apply a pragmatic ideology towards a study. "The action research method starts by the researcher reviewing the literature either before or after the analysis, so as to validate or improve upon existing theories" (Strang, 2015b, p. 59). This systems thinking technique differs from the critical analysis method in that the latter attempts to find gaps or inaccuracies in the literature using only the literature with deductive reasoning, but the former also collects practitioner or process data and attempts to find a solution to an institutional problem (Strang, 2015b). An advantage of the systems thinking approach over other traditional research methods is that it helps to "understand group and nonhuman processes" (Strang, 2015b, p. 403) such as in healthcare informatics. This approach is ideal for examining the complicated hidden big data analytics problems in the healthcare discipline which is dominated by subject matter specialists and leading edge technology.

A pragmatic ideology is pluralistic in that a study "begins with research questions focused on a problem, with a process improvement unit of analysis and a community of practice level of analysis", using mixed data types interpreted by the researcher and participants (Strang, 2015b, p. 23). This may be contrasted to a positivistic worldview where the data is fact-driven and hypothesis testing is often employed, or at the other philosophical extreme point is a constructivist ideology where participants provide rich data and communicate their own socio-cultural meaning reported verbatim by the researcher (Strang, 2015b).

In this study we do not make any cause-effect, correlation, deductive or inductive propositions, nor do we merely report practitioner opinions – we interpret what we discover in an open-minded practical manner. We first review scholar perspectives from the literature, we collect big data analyst practitioner opinions, and then we integrate results produced by statistical techniques. The practitioner opinions were collected through two channels. The first was direct interviews and discussions during the IEEE Big Data Conference held at Washington DC December 3-5, 2016. The second was also from direct discussions with practitioners through emails and using discussions on the Research Gate scholar social network system during the first six months of 2017.

According to Checkland (1999), after the literature review and subsequent knowledge assessment are completed, the key output of the systems thinking method is a visual model of the proposed critical real-world and tacit processes needed to solve the problem(s). The systems thinking model has two areas separating the known practices from the uncertain issues or processes with strategic links intended to bridge the gap or reduce risks. The model does not replace a discussion, but rather it summarizes the findings in a systematic diagram. A visual model will assist in communicating the findings to the healthcare discipline stakeholders as well as to researchers in this or any related discipline.

A pragmatic action research systems-thinking type of project does not necessarily follow the introduction-literature-method-results-discussion paper sequence. The rationale for choosing a pragmatic ideology is that proven techniques must often be adapted to accomplish the research goal(s) because formal methods do not necessarily accommodate messy problems or the complex mixed data collected (Strang, 2015b). Our research design is pragmatic, with a manuscript containing an introduction to the problem(s), methodology explanation, literature review, subject matter expert discussions, synthesis and assessment of data, recommendations to solve problem(s), conclusions and reference listing. Here we integrate our discussion into the literature review and close with a combined recommendations-conclusions section.

DISCUSSION

Earlier we stated that there are many benefits to having wireless healthcare big data but if it used unethically or outside of a personal privacy stipulation, the result can be harmful to individuals. For example, high blood pressure and other poor health indicators could trigger higher insurance premiums or prevent being hired. Inadvertent release of personal healthcare information such as a patient's mental illness, dementia, or other cognitive impairments could result in losing a job, losing their driver license, failing to obtain a mortgage/loan, losing friends, and at the extreme it could lead to depression, premature forfeiture of independence to caretakers or even suicide.

We will overlook the pure technology related issues with healthcare big data problems. For example, electromagnetic interference could scramble some or all of the data, a natural or anthropogenic disaster could compromise the device/implant or server, and device or server could simply overheat and fail. These problems are beyond the scope of our healthcare big data privacy study – but these risks do exist and they ought to be examined by other researchers.

We will categorize the above risks associated with wireless/remote healthcare device/implant big data being available and usable outside of its intended purpose as the hidden problem of unintended healthcare big data access. Although we found most unintended access was through wireless technology, this definition should also encompass other media, such as inadvertent use or covert theft of a clinic's data files along with other big data in ways that were not originally authorized.

The first proposed solution to this 'unintended healthcare big data access' problem seems intuitive. Strong public or private key encryption could be added as a security layer, and actually this is already being done. As software becomes more powerful encryption algorithms will run fast enough to permit more real-time use. Additionally, a government managed security clearing network could be built to serve as an intermediary between healthcare devices/implants and the outside connection to another other system. That is obviously a monolithic costly suggestion if implemented at the national or global level. The other potential solution is simple: Eliminate factory-coded MAC addresses and instead use temporary ones. Actually that is more difficult to achieve in practice due to the dependencies of the MAC address. Another constraint associated with MAC addresses is that they are useful to investigate criminal activity as well as domestic and global terrorism (Strang and Alamieyeseigha, 2015, Strang, 2015a). More research into this problem and these proposed solutions will be needed.

Healthcare Big Data Statistical Sampling Violations

Healthcare big data and big data in general tends to measure patterns in behavior (physical or mental), not internalized states like attitudes or beliefs that would be captured through other collection methods such as interviews, surveys, observations, or literary records. Healthcare big data is near-real-time and has a high granularity of details, owing to the high volume, velocity and variety.

Healthcare big data are usually high in volume and velocity but at any given point there are very few variables or fields transmitted. Social media big data often contains only a GPS location code and a text message (Strang and Sun, 2016). In healthcare big data it is typical to see four fields, an identifier, a timestamp, a GPS coordinate and some sensor reading (Strang and Sun, 2016). Some sensor readings contain several numbers but others are simplistic, such as a decimal 1 or 0 meaning yes or no, on or off, ok or not ok, etc. In a technical sense, a single byte has 8 bits which could each be a code. In a simple example, let's say a medical device transmitted a patient number, the time, their location, and their body temperature, every second, which would result in 3600 records per hour 86,400 per day and 31,536,000 per year, for every device per patient. This is why healthcare devices/implants generate big data. Let's say that researchers want to determine if there is a correlation or a cause-effect between the drugs administered to their 100 patients and their body temperatures during the year, and that an equally sized data was generated per patient for the drug administration processes. This would conceptually require 6,307,200,000 records which we can round up to 6.4 billion.

The problem is that it is difficult for healthcare researchers to perform statistical analysis on healthcare big data because even without the addition of the drug information for this anecdote, the desktop version of one of the most powerful statistical software programs SPSS can hold only 2 billion cases in a dataset since the file format includes a count of the cases in a 32-bit signed integer with the high order bit devoted to the sign (IBM, 2013); thus, the largest record number that can be stored is 2(31)-1 = 2,147,493,647. Thus, we could not store all the healthcare big data even for a simple drug-temperature analysis! No problem though, IBM have a mainframe version of SPSS without these big data file size constraints that can be purchased with hardware facilities for a few million USD.

Actually, several researchers had already pointed out that a barrier to performing big data analytics was that most statistical software could not handle the large file sizes (Vajjhala et al., 2015). However, researchers have found ways around the big data five V's – at least the volume, velocity and variety attributes – by using could-based and distributed software such as Hadoop along with sampling techniques to reduce the five V's (Couper, 2013, Varian, 2014, Strang and Sun, 2016). Nonetheless, this is where another hidden healthcare big data problem lurks. There are several tacit issues that revolve around research design assumptions and statistical sampling assumptions.

Social media big data was once criticized for being focused on the young generation but paradoxically the modern products like Facebook and Twitter are now used older baby-boom adults whereas Instagram and Snapchat tend to be preferred by the younger generation (Ekbia et al., 2015). In the healthcare industry medical devices/implants that generate wireless big data are used by people with injuries, viruses, diseases or illnesses (Rothstein, 2015). Additionally the popular social media products with big data available are predominately in English (Filkins et al., 2016). In laymen terms, researchers of social media big data do not know who in the population is excluded, who is not texting or responding, or even the true extent of the underlying population. Thus it is clear there is a sampling bias beyond nonresponse in the entire big data paradigm (Couper, 2013, Varian, 2014). Almost an entire global generation and many world-wide non-English speaking cultures could be missing in popular social media big data files, depending on the situation.

Obviously if only sick people are included in most healthcare big data analytics this would be a biased very small sample of humans. More so, it could be difficult to convince a significant sample of healthy people to have medical devices implanted to participant without offering a huge monetary incentive and even if they agreed it could present a new obstacle of statistical self-selection bias. Additionally, healthcare big data usually represents a large volume of readings collected from a very small number of patients in close proximity at a medical facility (Al-Janabi et al., 2016). For example, in the anecdote above the healthcare big data collection of body temperature reading records at 86,400 is well beyond the minimum statistical sample size of 30 but it is useless for estimating correlations or cause-effect predictions to the underlying population. Likewise, when social media big data is applied for healthcare research, generational, language and socio-cultural barriers would likely confound the statistical sampling principles. Therefore it is likely that all healthcare big data collected violates the statistical sampling principles of randomness and population representation (Strang, 2015b). There are exceptions to this problem in healthcare big data analytics because some medical devices are used for single patient emergency monitoring and decision making such as spatiotemporal sensing to alert staff when a patient falls or if vitals abruptly change – there is no logical reason to improve sampling of this type of healthcare big data.

The difference between primary and second research collection is that primary research data collection involves conducting research oneself, or using the data for the purpose it was intended for. Secondary research data, on the other hand, was collected by a third party or for some other purpose (Couper, 2013). An advantage of using primary data is that researchers are collecting information for the specific purposes of their study. In essence, the questions the researchers ask are tailored to elicit the data that will help them with their study (Couper, 2013, Varian, 2014) such as to test hypotheses or answer complex research questions. Researchers collect the data themselves, using surveys, interviews, direct observations or from records (namely reports or transaction files designed to capture information specific to the study). This is called the research design, that is, the articulation of the study goals, unit of analysis, generalization targets (Strang, 2015b). In the healthcare discipline, most scholarly research takes place in the field – the hospital or clinic – using primary data collection techniques like observations (of physical vitals included), visual observations, interviews, and sometimes surveys if controlled experiments are conducted. The hidden problem is that healthcare big data is being used as a replacement for accessing secondary data but the issue is the secondary data was not collected as a proper research design.

There are substantial risks associated with replacing traditional data collection methods, such as a misallocation of resources. For example, there have been many social media big data studies to improve emergency management practices during natural disasters like hurricanes (Strang, 2013) and tornados (Strang, 2012). On the other hand there has been an overreliance on Twitter data in deploying resources in the aftermath of hurricanes which has led to the misallocation of resources toward young, Internet-savvy people with cell phones and away from elderly or impoverished neighborhoods lacking in social medial access and literacy (Ohm, 2010). A famous example of poor survey methodology led the Literary Digest to incorrectly predict the 1936 presidential election results (Ohm, 2010). Inadequate understanding of sample coverage, incentive, and the lack of a comparison control group when analyzing administrative criminal big data records unfortunately led to incorrect inferences being made that a death penalty policy reduces state crime (Ohm, 2010).

One of the main reasons for applying statistical techniques and the *Central Limit Theorem* is for inferential thinking, that is, to show there is a link between variables or a predictive cause-effect trend in the entire underlying population by using an efficient cost-effective sample (Couper, 2013, Varian, 2014). Therefore, much work must be done to adapt statistical techniques that can exploit the richness of healthcare big data but preserve inference principles (Varian, 2014). We will categorize the above risks associated with wireless/remote healthcare device/implant big data collection as 'statistical sampling violations'. A straightforward solution to this 'statistical sampling violations' is to correct the research design using stratification, systematic or other generally-accepted sampling technique to collect a more representative sample. Due to the big data five V's, this will likely require sampling from multiple sources and combining the results as a single input to parametric or nonparametric statistical techniques. Strang and Sun (2016) discussed how this could be done with global terrorism big data so this could be applied to healthcare big data analytics.

There may be other solutions to the 'statistical sampling violations' healthcare big data analytics problem. Much of our discussion in this section has been positivist but a pragmatic approach could also be taken. Healthcare big data could be collected about each patient from multiple sources so as to achieve data triangulation. Healthcare big data could be collected to sample the entire context of the patient including the room conditions, nearby patient readings, atmospheric radiation, and so on. A constructivist approach could also supplement healthcare big data by adding qualitative patient feelings and physician opinions into the file to be analyzed.

Healthcare Big Data Statistical False Positives

We found more hidden problems with healthcare big data. Other researchers have articulated the data quality issues with big data, such as missing or incomplete data, errors due to technical interference like delays or magnetic fields, and duplicated values (Ekbia et al., 2015, Hoffman and Podgurski, 2013).

A common error with healthcare big data is inaccurate or erroneous labeling of the column data (Couper, 2013, Chen et al., 2014). As an example of this error consider a hospital register may include a column labeled 'number of employees' defined in the data dictionary as the number of persons in the company that received a payroll check in the preceding month but instead the column contains the number of persons on the payroll whether they received a check last month or not, including persons on leave without pay. Other types of big data healthcare errors could rest with the analysts if they perform manipulation or transformation of the values. For example, perhaps changing a timestamp signed integer into a character field representing a calendar day, or transforming ordinal data into a low-medium-high scale. Transformation of data is acceptable for some types of regression and categorization analysis, but since it is literally impossible to see the big data, care must be taken when researchers are transforming values. Additionally, traditional content errors use for master files in a healthcare big data analysis could cause errors, such as keying, coding, or editing of drug or patient characteristics in a master file which is linked to the healthcare big data sensor stream. However, these errors are not unique to healthcare big data – the problem of data entry errors and incomplete inaccurate data is widespread with all manual or machine coded data.

On the other hand there is potentially a new hidden problem associated with healthcare big data. A well-known example of this healthcare big data risk was the error produced by the Google Flu Trends series, which used Google searches on flu symptoms, remedies, and other related keywords to provide near-real-time estimates of flu activity in the United States and 24 other countries worldwide (Lazer et al., 2014). The USA Center for Disease Control (CDC) regularly predicts the flu trends in order to ensure there will be enough vaccinations and healthcare facilities to accommodate the need. According to Lazer, Kennedy, King and Vespignani (2014), Google Flu Trends provided a remarkably accurate indicator of the flu cases in the United States between 2009 and 2011, which was significantly more accurate than the CDC predictions. However, Google Flu Trends was inaccurate thereafter for 2012–2013, more than twice as high as the CDC predictions of which the latter were accurate (Lazer et al., 2014). Thus, Google Flu Trends used healthcare big data analytics to incorrectly forecast future flu trends resulting in more than double the proportion of vaccinations and doctor visits scheduled.

The Google Flu Trends healthcare big data incident may have been caused by social media herd-behavior and commercial search engine manipulation. Apparently the healthcare big data-generating engine at Google was modified in such a way that the formerly highly predictive search terms eventually failed to work, for example, when a user searched on fever or cough, Google's other programs started recommending searches for flu symptoms and treatments, which had a domino impact on other user searches because they would be redirected to flu sites which was counted in the predictor variable (Lazer et al., 2014). These types of problems are programming errors made by Google. There have been similar problems reported by other social media platforms like Twitter, Facebook, and Microsoft Bing in their attempt to improve the user experience (Lazer et al., 2014).

Fan, Han, and Liu (2014) stood out in the literature as researchers that identified several legitimate hidden healthcare big data problems, which they referred to as (1) noise accumulation; (2) spurious correlations; and (3) incidental endogeneity. To illustrate noise accumulation suppose a practitioner is comparing patients in two hospital wards A and B based upon the values of 1,000 features (or variables) in a healthcare big data file but unknown to that researcher the mean value for participants in A is 0 on all 1,000 features while participants in B have a mean of 3 on the first 10 features and a value of 0 on the other 990 features. A big data machine learning classification rule based upon the first $m \leq 10$ features performs quite well, with little classification error, but as more and more features are included in the rule, classification error increases because the uninformative features (i.e., the 990 features having no discriminating power) eventually overwhelm the informative signals (i.e., the first 10 features). We agree with this if you are using contemporary big data machine learning algorithms. We suggest that big data algorithms be used in parallel with other recognized statistical techniques as methodical triangulation (Strang, 2015b).

Fan, Han, and Liu (2014) describe spurious correlations as healthcare big data files that have many unrelated features but which may be highly correlated simply by chance, resulting in false discoveries and erroneous inferences. For example, using simulated populations and relatively small sample sizes, Fan, Han, and Liu (2014) proved that with 800 independent features, there was 50% chance of observing an absolute correlation that exceeded R=0.4 which would be statistically significant (p<.05) and amount to a small effect size of 16% (r^2=0.16). Their results suggest that there are considerable risks of false inference associated with a purely empirical approach to predictive analytics using high-dimensional data. We agree and we will explore this in more detail later.

Thirdly, Fan, Han, and Liu (2014) assert that endogeneity is a problem when performing regression analysis on big data that results in a model with covariates correlated with the residual error. For high-dimensional models, with many factors, this can occur purely by chance. We agree this is possible but statistically it is an extension of the same spurious correlation phenomenon identified above. Regarding all he above potential hidden problems, we suggest that all but the spurious correlations could be avoided by following the 'statistical sampling violations' solution of improving the research design through rigorous sampling collection plans. Additionally the recommendations of Hair, Black, Babin, Anderson and Tatham (Hair et al., 2006) should be reviewed when designing complex multiple or multivariate regression models in any discipline regardless of whether they are healthcare big data sourced.

The third category of hidden healthcare big data analytics problems is also statistical in nature. When Dr. Gauss invented the student t-test using the normal distribution he probably did not envision the large sample sizes characteristic of the big data five V's. The root of this problem stems from the sample size which is used in many nonparametric as well as parametric formulas (Strang, 2015b). For example, the well-known formula for standard deviation is shown in equation 1 where X is the big data value, μ is the mean, and N is the total sample size.

Table 1. Descriptive statistics of anecdotal healthcare small and big data samples

	Small Sample	Big Data Sample
N	30	3600
Mean	73.5	96.804
SD	23.902	3.027
Median	73.5	97
Correlation	-0.867	-0.112

$$\sqrt{\sum \frac{\left(X - \mu\right)^2}{N}} \tag{1}$$

Going back to the patient temperature anecdote, let's say that we received 30 readings in a small sample and 3600 readings in a small big data sample over the span of one hour (60 seconds * 60 minutes). All the temperature readings were 97F except that last 15 readings were 50F to simulate patient going into a serious medial trauma. In the big data file all the values were 97F except for the last 15. Any practitioner or researcher could easily reproduce the data in this anecdote. Table 1 lists the descriptive statistics of these two samples (all estimates rounded for display).

The anecdotal descriptive statistics in table 1 illustrates the fallacy of healthcare big data. By the way each has the same minimum and maximum readings. In the small sample, the mean (M) is 73.5F with a huge standard deviation (SD) of 23.902, which is a coefficient of variation of 33% (SD/M*100). The median is also 73.5F. This clearly indicates the patient is in medical trauma distress. Unfortunately, the healthcare big data descriptive statistics shows that despite recording data for an hour, that the mean temperature is 96.8F with a minor SD of 3.027 which is a small effect size of about 3% (SD/M*100). The healthcare big data makes us believe the patient is doing well, maybe feeling a bit chilly so they could use a sweater. The median is 97F which is further misleading. Actually, having more data would only further obscure the medical emergency for this healthcare patient.

Additionally, going back to the table 1 anecdote, how could we be sure that the temperature of 50F was not created through imputation, with the remaining 50 values being created by copying the change from 97 to 50, or maybe simple duplication, or perhaps a spurious value of 50 created by wireless network electromagnetic interference. Of course the same arguments could be made against the small sample too.

Another problem with healthcare big data is that parametric statistics will be unknowingly impacted by the sheer sample volume, velocity and variety. In the anecdote, assume we have the time sequence number for each reading and we performed a correlation of the temperature against the time sequence. In the small sample of table 1, the correlation was significant between time and temperature with R=-0.867, p<.05 (two-sided). The effect size of the small sample correlation of temperature with time was 75% (r^2 =0.751, N=30) which shows a significant negative correlation between temperature and time, meaning that temperature is quickly falling as time progresses. This is valuable to know because the healthcare staff could be alerted and the patient could be treated in order to save their life.

Unfortunately, based on the table 1 anecdote with the healthcare big data sample, the correlation between temperature and time sequence was -0.112 (p>.05) which was insignificant. This could be interpreted that there is no statistically significant relationship between patient temperature falling and time. Perhaps the big data value in this would be that the hospital will soon have an extra bed available in their facility. The same phenomenon occurs when using more advanced parametric statistical techniques such as regression to estimate cause-effect predictions on healthcare big data.

As further test we used random sampling on the 3600 healthcare big data records in the table 1 anecdote, and after 360 iterations (10% of the data) all values were 97F. Thus, even random sampling of healthcare big data is not reliable for parametric statistics. The fallacy of healthcare big data should now be obvious. Therefore, even if the earlier 'statistical sampling violations' hidden problem was not present, the large sample size of healthcare big data could present a type I error or rejecting the null hypothesis when in fact it was true there was no statistically significant result, which is known as a false positive (Strang, 2015b). We will classify this hidden healthcare big data problem as 'statistical false positives'.

The solution we propose to the hidden healthcare big data problem of 'statistical false positives' is to use nonparametric techniques. This advice has been applied to analyze terrorism big data (Strang & Alamieyeseigha, 2017) as well as financial market collapse portfolio manager behavior big data (Strang, 2015b). To prove our point we applied nonparametric techniques in SPSS and Minitab software to test a medical-related hypothesis that the anecdotal patient temperature is no different than an expected average of 97F. The distribution free one-sample Wilcoxon signed rank test on the small sample from table 1 verified as anticipated that the patient temperature was significantly different than the benchmark median of 97F, based on the results of $W(30)=15$, $p=.001$ (two-sided). The interesting result was the same finding from the healthcare big data sample in table 1, with a $W(3600)=15$, $p=.001$ (two-sided). Thus, the nonparametric test on the healthcare big data sample was able to correctly identify that the patient temperature was significantly different than the expected median. We ought to disclose though that parametric one-sample t-tests on the same data produced the same results. Nonetheless, we highly recommend nonparametric statistical techniques become the norm when analyzing healthcare big data.

CONCLUSION

Our literature review of 79,012 journal articles from 2011-2016 confirmed the astonishing situation that healthcare privacy and security related topics accounted for only 2% of the total research production, and this rate had fallen to 1% during the first three months of 2017. Healthcare big data analyst practitioner interviews were therefore used to supplement our research.

The results of our literature review and practitioner interviews verified that the healthcare discipline suffers from the same problems endemic to any type of statistical analysis, namely data entry, coding, mislabeling, missing/inaccurate values, and poor research design. Additionally, healthcare big data suffers from electromagnetic interference, network delays or outages, and the same factors which impact any technology. The same cautions would thus apply to mitigate against those risks. Additionally, the healthcare big data faces the big data five V's: high volume, complex variety, large velocity, strategic value tradeoffs, and more recently veracity (accuracy, ethics, privacy, socio-cultural meaning).

Healthcare big data analytics in particular is prone to veracity privacy violations, perhaps more so than other disciplines. Although most countries have legislation to protect patients against inappropriate use of their data, this only forces providers within the healthcare domain to avoid recording certain identifying attributes. Even the HIPAA in USA allows a hospital to override the rules if they have a justifiable reason – which seems hard to fathom for a healthcare big data collection context. Additionally, informed consent may not be getting the scrutiny it deserves from patients or physicians. Healthcare medical devices/implants transmit wireless readings which could be intercepted. For example a patient driving through a weight station, toll bridge, parking lot, border entry could have their personal data read without their knowledge or consent. Encryption may be a solution to this common big data privacy problem when software and hardware improve to make it faster and affordable in the healthcare industry.

Although there were many issues found, we considered these to be already encompassed into the big data five V's. We uncovered several insights about the hidden healthcare big data analytics risks. We grouped these new hidden problems into three logical categories, and we also provided recommended solutions for each. Furthermore, we applied the action research systems thinking technique to organize the insights into a diagram, as summarized in figure 1. This diagram will facilitate communicating the information to other stakeholders such as healthcare practitioners, researchers, decision makers and policy administrators. The three hidden healthcare big data analytic problem categories are briefly enumerated below.

1. Unintended healthcare big data access – inadvertent or intentional wireless eavesdropping – this could be mitigated by using strong public or private key encryption once software becomes more powerful and affordable for the healthcare industry/patients;
2. Statistical sampling violations – non-coverage, lack of random selection, nonresponse, self-selection bias caused by lack of a research design – this could be fixed by a research design using stratification, systematic or other generally-accepted sampling technique to collect a more representative multiple-sourced sample (pragmatic and constructivist approaches were also mentioned);
3. Statistical false positives – caused by mathematical formulas that use sample size in calculations resulting in spurious relationships, correlations, and other inaccurate estimates (a healthcare big data simulation was used to prove this) – this risk could be reduced by applying nonparametric statistical techniques and methodological triangulation (use of multiple parametric, distribution free and qualitative methods).

We feel we uncovered several insights about the fundamental and managerial controversies associated with big data analytics and artificial intelligence that will be of interest to quantitative professionals and practitioners in the fields of computing, e-commerce, e-business services, and e-government. The goal of this chapter was to explain contemporary managerial and conceptual problems concerning big data analytics. We utilized the systems thinking technique within an action research framework. The methodology that we applied was unique and worth considering by other researchers. We utilized the systems thinking technique popularized within an action research framework. We used this approach because our ideology was pragmatic, the problem at hand was complex and institutional (healthcare discipline), and we needed to understand the problems from both a practitioner group and nonhuman process (technology). We used the literature review summarized above along with practitioner interviews collected at a big data conference. According the systems thinking methodology, after the literature review and

Figure 1. Hidden healthcare big data analytics problems

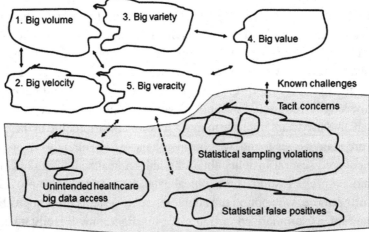

subsequent knowledge assessment were completed, we organized the key results into a visual model of the proposed critical real-world and tacit processes that could identify and solve the problems.

In conclusion, big data and artificial intelligence privacy is an important topic that was not adequately covered in the existing literature, so more research is needed. Additionally, while our findings that the traditional five big data challenges also impact the healthcare discipline, we identified three new tacit issues that are essential to address in future studies. We could not locate any other publication that identified and explained these three new hidden problems in healthcare data analytics so we feel this is a worthy contribution to the community of practice literature. In closing we will make our data available to anyone by request to the corresponding author.

REFERENCES

ADA. (2015). Harnessing Big Data to Help Stop Diabetes. *The American Journal of Managed Care*, *9*(1), 1–4.

Al-Ameen, M., Liu, J., & Kwak, K. (2012). Security and privacy issues in wireless sensor networks for healthcare applications. *Journal of Medical Systems*, *36*(1), 93–101. doi:10.100710916-010-9449-4 PMID:20703745

Al-Janabi, S., Al-Shourbaji, I., Shojafar, M., & Shamshirband, S. (2016). *Survey of main challenges (security and privacy) in wireless body area networks for healthcare applications.* Egyptian Informatics Journal.

Angiuli, O., Blitzstein, J., & Waldo, J. (2015). How to De-Identify Your Data. *Communications of the ACM*, *58*(12), 48–55. doi:10.1145/2814340

Brown, B. (2008). HIPAA Beyond HIPAA: ONCHIT, ONC, AHIC, HITSP, and CCHIT. *Journal of Health Care Compliance*, *10*(41), 1–21.

Burrows, R., & Savage, M. (2014). After the crisis? Big data and the methodological challenges of empirical sociology. *Big Data & Society Journal*, *12*(2), 1–6.

Checkland, P. (1999). *Systems Thinking, Systems Practice*. Chichester, UK: John Wiley & Sons Ltd.

Chen, C. L. P., & Zhang, C. Y. (2014). Data-intensive applications, challenges, techniques and technologies: A survey on big data. *Information Sciences Journal*, *275*(1), 314–317. doi:10.1016/j.ins.2014.01.015

Chen, M., Mao, S., Zhang, Y., & Leung, V. C. (2014). Open issues and outlook in big data. In Big Data: Related Technologies, Challenges and Future Prospects (Vol. 1, pp. 81-89). Springer.

Couper, M. P. (2013). Is the sky falling? New technology, changing media, and the future of surveys. *Survey Research Methods Journal*, *7*(1), 145–156.

de Montjoye, Y.-A., & Pentland, A. S. (2016). Response to Comment on "Unique in the shopping mall: On the reidentifiability of credit card metadata". *Science Journal*, *351*(6279), 1274.

De Zwart, M., Humphreys, S., & Van Dissel, B. (2014). Surveillance, big data and democracy: Lessons for Australia from the US and UK. *The University of New South Wales Law Journal*, *37*(2), 713–747.

Duhigg, C. (2014). *The power of habit: Why we do what we do in life and business*. New York: Penguin Random House.

Eastin, M. S., Brinson, N. H., Doorey, A., & Wilcox, G. (2016). Living in a big data world: Predicting mobile commerce activity through privacy concerns. *Computers in Human Behavior*, *58*(1), 214–220. doi:10.1016/j.chb.2015.12.050

Ekbia, H., Mattioli, M., Kouper, I., Arave, G., Ghazinejad, A., Bowman, T., ... Sugimoto, C. R. (2015). Big data, bigger dilemmas: A critical review. *Journal of the Association for Information Science and Technology*, *66*(8), 1523–1545. doi:10.1002/asi.23294

Fan, J., Han, F., & Liu, H. (2014). Challenges of Big Data Analysis. *National Science Review Journal*, *1*(1), 293–314. doi:10.1093/nsr/nwt032 PMID:25419469

Filkins, B. L., Kim, J. Y., Roberts, B., Armstrong, W., Miller, M. A., Hultner, M. L., ... Steinhubl, S. R. (2016). Privacy and security in the era of digital health: What should translational researchers know and do about it? *American Journal of Translational Research*, *8*(3), 1560–1580. PMID:27186282

Gandomi, A., & Haider, M. (2015). Beyond the hype: Big data concepts, methods, and analytics. *International Journal of Information Management*, *35*(2), 137–144. doi:10.1016/j.ijinfomgt.2014.10.007

Hair, J. F., Black, W. C., Babin, B. J., Anderson, R. E., & Tatham, R. L. (2006). *Multivariate data analysis* (6th ed.). Upper Saddle River, NJ: Prentice-Hall.

Hoffman, S., & Podgurski, A. (2013). Big Bad Data: Law, Public Health, and Biomedical Databases. *The Journal of Law, Medicine & Ethics*, *41*(1), 56–60. doi:10.1111/jlme.12040 PMID:23590742

Hogarth, R. M., & Soyer, E. (2015). Using Simulated Experience to Make Sense of Big Data. *MIT Sloan Management Review*, *56*(2), 49–54.

IBM. (2013). IBM SPSS Statistics for Windows (21st ed.). International Business Machines Corporation (IBM).

Jovanovi, U., Stimec, A., & Vladusi, D. (2015). Big-data analytics: A critical review and some future directions. *International Journal of Business Intelligence and Data Mining*, *10*(4), 337–355. doi:10.1504/IJBIDM.2015.072211

Jungwirth, D., & Haluza, D. (2017). Information and communication technology and the future of healthcare: Results of a multi-scenario Delphi survey. *Health Informatics Journal*. doi:10.1177/1460458217704256 PMID:28438103

Kessel, P. v., Layman, J., Blackmore, J., Burnet, I., & Azuma, Y. (2014). *Insights on governance, risk and compliance: Big data, changing the way businesses compete and operate*. Ernest and Young.

Kshetri, N. (2014). Big datas impact on privacy, security and consumer welfare. *Telecommunications Policy*, *38*(11), 1134–1145. doi:10.1016/j.telpol.2014.10.002

Lazer, D. M., Kennedy, R., King, G., & Vespignani, A. (2014). The parable of Google Flu: Traps in big data analysis. *Science Journal*, *343*(1), 1203–1205. doi:10.1126cience.1248506 PMID:24626916

Leszczynski, A. (2015). Spatial big data and anxieties of control. *Environment and Planning. D, Society & Space, 33*(6), 965–984. doi:10.1177/0263775815595814

Lichtblau, E., & Weilandaug, N. (2016). Hacker Releases More Democratic Party Files, Renewing Fears of Russian Meddling. *New York Times*, pp. A12-A14.

Lusher, S. J., McGuire, R., van Schaik, R. C., Nicholson, C. D., & de Vlieg, J. (2014). Data-driven medicinal chemistry in the era of big data. *Drug Discovery Today, 19*(7), 859–868. doi:10.1016/j.drudis.2013.12.004 PMID:24361338

Ohm, P. (2010). Broken promises of privacy: Responding to the surprising failure of anonymization. *UCLA Law Review Journal, 57*(1), 1701–1818.

Prokopenya, V. (2018). *Truths, half-truths and lies about artificial intelligence.* The European Financial Review. Available http://www.europeanfinancialreview.com/?p=25629

Rothstein, M. A. (2015). Ethical Issues in Big Data Health Research: Currents in Contemporary Bioethics. *The Journal of Law, Medicine & Ethics, 43*(2), 425–429. doi:10.1111/jlme.12258 PMID:26242964

Salleh, K. A., & Janczewski, L. (2016). Technical, organizational and environmental security and privacy issues of big data: A literature review. *Procedia Computer Science Journal, 100*(1), 19–28. doi:10.1016/j.procs.2016.09.119

Shen, Y., & Zhang, Y. (2014). Transmission protocol for secure big data in two-hop wireless networks with cooperative jamming. *Information Sciences, 281*(1), 201–210. doi:10.1016/j.ins.2014.05.037

Shull, F. (2014). The True Cost of Mobility? *IEEE Software, 31*(2), 5–9. doi:10.1109/MS.2014.47

Strang, K. D. (2012). Logistic planning with nonlinear goal programming models in spreadsheets. *International Journal of Applied Logistics, 2*(4), 1–14. doi:10.4018/jal.2012100101

Strang, K. D. (2013). Homeowner behavioral intent to evacuate after flood warnings. *International Journal of Risk and Contingency Management, 2*(3), 1–28. doi:10.4018/ijrcm.2013070101

Strang, K. D. (2015a). Exploring the relationship between global terrorist ideology and attack methodology. *Risk Management Journal, 17*(2), 65–90. doi:10.1057/rm.2015.8

Strang, K. D. (2015b). *Palgrave Handbook of Research Design in Business and Management.* New York: Palgrave Macmillan. doi:10.1057/9781137484956

Strang, K. D., & Alamieyeseigha, S. (2015). What and where are the risks of international terrorist attacks: A descriptive study of the evidence. *International Journal of Risk and Contingency Management, 4*(1), 1–18. doi:10.4018/ijrcm.2015010101

Strang, K. D., & Alamieyeseigha, S. (2017). What and Where Are the Risks of International Terrorist Attacks. In Violence and Society: Breakthroughs in Research and Practice. IGI Global. doi:10.4018/978-1-5225-0988-2.ch026

Strang, K. D., & Sun, Z. (2016). Analyzing relationships in terrorism big data using Hadoop and statistics. *Journal of Computer Information Systems, 56*(5), 55–65.

Strang, K. D., & Sun, Z. (2017). Scholarly big data body of knowledge: What is the status of privacy and security? *Annals of Data Science, 4*(1), 1–17. doi:10.100740745-016-0096-6

Sun, Z., Strang, K. D., & Li, R. (2016). Ten bigs of big data: A multidisciplinary framework. *Proceedings of 10th ACM International Conference on Research and Practical Issues of Enterprise Information Systems (CONFENIS 2016), 1,* 550-661.

Terry, N. (2015). Navigating the Incoherence of Big Data Reform Proposals. *The Journal of Law, Medicine & Ethics, 43*(1), 44–47. doi:10.1111/jlme.12214 PMID:25846163

Thorpe, J. H., & Gray, E. A. (2015). Law and the Public's Health: Big data and public health - navigating privacy laws to maximize potential. *Public Health Reports, 130*(2), 171–175. doi:10.1177/003335491513000211 PMID:25729109

Vaidhyanathan, S., & Bulock, C. (2014). Knowledge and Dignity in the Era of Big Data. *The Serials Librarian, 66*(1-4), 49–64. doi:10.1080/0361526X.2014.879805

Vajjhala, N. R., & Strang, K. D. (2017). Measuring organizational-fit through socio-cultural big data. *Journal of New Mathematics and Natural Computation, 13*(2), 1–17.

Vajjhala, N. R., Strang, K. D., & Sun, Z. (2015). Statistical modeling and visualizing of open big data using a terrorism case study. *Open Big Data Conference,* 489-496. 10.1109/FiCloud.2015.15

van Loenen, B., Kulk, S., & Ploeger, H. (2016). Data protection legislation: A very hungry caterpillar: The case of mapping data in the European Union. *Government Information Quarterly, 33*(2), 338–345. doi:10.1016/j.giq.2016.04.002

van Otterlo, M. (2014). Automated experimentation in Walden 3.0: The next step in profiling, predicting, control and surveillance. *Surveillance & Society, 12*(2), 255–272. doi:10.24908s.v12i2.4600

Varian, H. R. (2014). Big data: New tricks for econometrics. *The Journal of Economic Perspectives, 28*(2), 3–27. doi:10.1257/jep.28.2.3

Wang, H., Jiang, X., & Kambourakis, G. (2015). Special issue on Security, Privacy and Trust in network-based Big Data. *Information Sciences, 318*(1), 48–50. doi:10.1016/j.ins.2015.05.040

Ward, J. C. (2014). Oncology Reimbursement in the Era of Personalized Medicine and Big Data. *Journal of Oncology Practice / American Society of Clinical Oncology, 10*(2), 83–86. doi:10.1200/JOP.2014.001308 PMID:24633283

Zhong, R. Y., Huang, G. Q., Lan, S., Dai, Q. Y., Chen, X., & Zhang, T. (2015). A big data approach for logistics trajectory discovery from RFID-enabled production data. *International Journal of Production Economics, 165*(1), 260–272. doi:10.1016/j.ijpe.2015.02.014

Zikopoulos, P., Eaton, C., DeRoos, D., Deutsch, T., & Lapis, G. (2011). *Understanding Big Data: Analytics for Enterprise Class Hadoop and Streaming Data.* McGraw-Hill Osborne Media.

Section 2
Technologies for Intelligent Big Data Analytics

Chapter 5
Using Intelligent Agents Paradigm in Big Data Security Risks Mitigation

Mihai Horia Zaharia
"Gheorghe Asachi" Technical University, Romania

ABSTRACT

Big data has a great potential in improving the efficiency of most of the specific information society instruments. Yet, because it uses the newly introduced cloud technology support, it may need continuous improvements especially in the security assurance area. In this chapter, a possible solution based on the intelligent agent paradigm in securing the big data infrastructure is presented. This approach will also require some changes at the general strategy level. The main accent is on using big data techniques and tools to ensure data security. Unfortunately, due to some security-related issues at the global level, the business environment must increase the amount of resources driven to this area.

INTRODUCTION

The potential of the big data approach is far from being fully exploited nowadays. This happens due to the slow adoption of cloud based architectures that are big data main support technologies. The interest in cloud adoption is high at the level of economical and research based environments (HARDY, 2016). Yet, there are a lot of problems that make this transition slow. One consists in the higher costs involved by rewriting the commonly used applications as native ones. To solve this transition the most common method is to virtualize the real machine together with its applications. This solves the cloud transition and decreases long time maintenance costs. Unfortunately this means an inefficient use of the cloud resources, so the porting of the used application or movement to newly appeared native similar cloud applications is required (Badola, 2015).

The cloud solution has not yet reached its maturity as technology. As a result there are a lot of problems concerning its security (Khana & Al-Yasirib, 2016). The same security problem appears in the majority of applications because the process of designing and implementing a secure application is at

DOI: 10.4018/978-1-5225-7277-0.ch005

least twice expensive than making an application with a reasonable security level. So, many common applications are not adapted to the asymmetric informational war that is ongoing nowadays at global level (Lasconjarias & Larsen, 2015). This must involve fundamental changes at any levels of the information society beginning with the application design level (Mumtaz, Alshayeb, Mahmood, & Niazi, 2018) and ending with paradigm changes in global security approach.

The public cloud based systems or private ones will be the computing nodes in future global cyberspace (Sharma, 2016). If we take this into account, then there is a need of fundamental changes in the used methods for security risks mitigation. A good idea will be to use some of the military grade protocols. If this approach is chosen it may involve a significant deployment cost increase. It is true that military approaches are better prepared from a security point of view (Eggen, et al., 2013) and in many cases there is a physical isolation between public communication networks and their internal ones. Yet, as normal, there are still two situations when this isolation is partially broken. One situation concerns the needed intersection points among the public domains and the military ones. Inhere there are a lot of problems generated due to disrespecting the internal security procedures by the people or targeted attacks of the third parties (private or from governmental level). The other one refers to the cases when, sometimes, the existing public communication network is used to handle high sensitive information. In these cases even if supplementary security measures are taken, no one can guaranty a full security.

To make the situation even worse, a new era in designing cryptographic algorithm begins due to the fragility of current approaches when quantum computing is used (Mood, 2016). Besides that, the information flows grow exponentially and the dedicated existing structures specialized in information security assurance begin to be overcome. As a result, major changes at the level of used cyber defense paradigms are required no matter if the military public or private domains are analyzed.

To design a new cyber defense paradigm for big data specific infrastructure some aspects must be taken into account:

- The redesign of the main big data architecture by increasing the security involvement.
- The use of the Artificial Intelligence (AI) based assisted decision support systems.
- The use of the AI dedicated entities that will emulate at low and middle level a security expert administrator.
- To make a leap from a static based structure of the cyber defense networks to a dynamic one that will have a better reaction time and collaboration in handling the current attacks.

Background

The secure design of cloud based application methodology is still at the beginning. One reason is the extreme fluidity of the related software frameworks and technologies that are in a continuous transformation. The SOA specific security design patterns (Erl, 2009) are redesigned due to the necessary refactoring, specific to transition from service based architectures to hybrid or full micro services based architectures. As a result, the experts must improve, adapt or propose new security related design patterns (Amato, Mazzocca, & Moscato, 2018). Efforts in securing code are done at any level, even at the object communication related one (Mourad, Laverdiere, & Debbabi, 2008).

One possibility is to use decision support systems in handling the cloud, both hardware and software security. In the future cyberspace the decision support systems will play a major role in driving the society. They are not new in the governmental or private sector (Arnott, Lizama, & Song, 2017; Sun, Sun,

& Meredith, 2012). This is due to the complex problems that must be simultaneously managed at higher decisional levels which are almost impossible to be handled by human mind. Unfortunately, these solutions have their own risks. Since the beginning of human society, the information validity verification was crucial in making correct (or at least as good as possible) decisions. The dimension of nowadays informational flows is beyond human comprehension. Hence, some automated processing of the primary data is required. Until now statistical method were used to detect the injection of false information in the system. These methods are now deprecated because the existing malicious software already has all the needed ability to fully intoxicate with false data (e.g. data injection) any system (Hu, Wang, Han, & Liu, 2018). Moreover, the process of validation using humans from various governmental security systems (classical approach) is so slow that, until an injection of false data in the system is detected and corrected, many real-time critical decisions may be done based on false information. This is a common aspect of the existing asymmetric informational war. This is another reason for the need in changing the main used cyber defense paradigms. The problem can be partially solved if some measures are taken on both levels: human and informational systems.

At the human level this means that the human experts involved in various security related structures must be reeducated to properly use the existing informational tools in order to increase the communication and validation speed but without renouncing to use the existing standard techniques.

At the informational system a quality of information service method must be used (Shrivastavaa, Sharmab, & Shrivastavac, 2015). The approach is not new and the security system classifies, since the beginning of time, the used human informational sources. This must be translated into a rating for various automated gathered data. Unfortunately, in the human approach any informational source cannot be seen as fully trusted even if their existing trust rates are very high. This will imply that AI techniques must be used in the analysis of all gathered data according to a set of rules that is continuously improved. Due to the already mentioned magnitude of informational flows, it is clear that most of the existing informational systems are not efficient enough. Yet, there is a solution to exponentially increase the ability of the system in properly handling these complex operations. The big data specific methods that are nowadays used in the economic related studies can be retrofitted with some effort in solving the previously mentioned problems. So, the evolution of the assisted decision systems must be directed in using these newly emerged tools, but without disbanding existing solutions. This double approach is highly costing but will provide a supplementary redundancy that is critical at these levels of decision.

The big data security problem is reduced in fact to its main support associated risks - the cloud technology. The security risks are as big as are the complexity of hardware and software of the cloud. At any layer or even tier various types of problems may occur (Singh & Chatterjee, 2017). This diversity can be handled only by the use of a variable grain architecture intelligent autonomous entity, such as an intelligent agent. In order to implement it, the big data native techniques, as information retrieval or knowledge extraction, must be used. As a result, the agent will be implemented as service composition (Zaharia, 2014).

The agent based approach can be an integrator also for insuring the cyber physical systems security (Ashibani & Mahmoud, 2017) because it has the needed granularity at the software level. Moreover, the autonomous, intelligent and, if it needed, partially supervised behavior can hide the inherent heterogeneity at the hardware level under a common view (Tao, Zuo, Liu, Castiglione, & Palmieri, 2018). This is important especially when the already deployed systems must be emerged into the big data stream.

Handling Worldwide Informational Attacks

Due to the inherent distributed architecture of the Internet, most types of attack are almost instantly replicated all around the world. This will always be a problem. The human administrators are organized in well structured networks that handle the distributed attack in the same way an elastic mesh will handle a high speed ball (NIST, 2017). In fact there are more overlapped meshes that are interlinked in order to properly handle the attack. The system works acceptable under the current conditions. Unfortunately, the future cyberspace will provide too much computing power and access to high speed communication channels so this static approach may be insufficient. In this case the security structures must be capable of increasing their reaction speed and also all available resources should be temporarily accessible as much as possible nearby the attack origin zone. One possibility is to use a scheme similar to the immune system of the mammals (Hamon & Quintin, 2016). This will involve that the dedicated agents migrate using the communication network around the initial zone. This may be difficult because, in most cases, the communication networks themselves, or access gates may be highly compromised. Another problem is that these agents will require a lot of supplementary computing power in order to do their job and this may not be possible. Finally, it is clear that all the agents can mostly do their main aims, but cannot adapt quickly enough, if the attacker manages the attack in real time. Thereupon, supplementary human resources (experts) must also be joined if they are in the area (US-CERT, 2017). It is possible that if they exist, they may have enough knowledge to offer a real help, but they are either yet unaware of the attack or do not have the required credentials to act at this level. In this situation their level of access can be highly increased in order to help, if this it is required. Inhere a problem of grant and revocation of higher access level emerges. Also, consider the problem of communication with affected areas. This can be solved using a virtual security assistant agent that may receive the needed credentials. This is possible because these agents are not fully under the control of their owners. Moreover, the agents can use different, more secured communication channels to interoperate.

This solution may also involve supplementary security access risks but there is no perfect choice in solving this problem. Overall, it is possible that the benefits given by this approach could overcome the inherent risks. This solution represents in fact the change from a static method of handling the problems to a dynamic one.

The specialists involved in this supplementary reaction force can be selected, with their consent, from the private security companies, from the white hat community experts and also, in high-risk situations, from the army and any governmental security related bodies that may be involved. The problem of paying these services can be easily handled due to the recording of all activity at the level of the virtual agent associated to each one.

This approach may be in a partial contradiction with the political main directions, yet any government must accept the fact that in a fully information based society that interacts using a common place – the cyberspace – the higher goal is for this place to remain stable. The old approach in securing most of their geographical influence zones may highly decrease the economic efficiency of the global market concept.

MAIN FOCUS OF THE CHAPTER

Cyber Defense Paradigm Changes

Most of the cyber defense related strategies are territorial oriented, as it is natural. The current solutions are based on concentric circles of protection (US Department of Defence, 2015). These circles concern various strategic infrastructures, each of them with its proper clearance levels and proper access protocols. This was enough until now. Unfortunately, in the future, some aspects concerning the current approach will appear as follows.

Credential Checking

In most cases this is the most important problem in software systems, as well as in human interaction. Most of the attacks are based on social engineering (Lord, 2017) or on altering the credential associated to an entity at any granularity level of software architecture.

The social engineering attack can be easily handled using two approaches. First, it is based on laws and internal constraints specific to each organization. As already known, the human nature is volatile enough to avoid, in various degrees, these rules (Howarth, 2014). The motivations are complex and are driven by the lack of attention due to fatigue or lack of fully understanding of the internal protocols and laws. To properly solve the problem, a simplified version of a virtual security officer can be used as a supplementary control to mitigate the possible risks, by direct interaction with its user. This cannot solve everything because the ultimate decision must remain at the user level, but at least its decision is recorded and submitted to the upper decisional levels by the virtual agent.

In case of software impersonation (object ACL modification, rights elevation, ticket or cookie tampering and login account breach) another version of virtual security agent may be used (Harris & Maymi, 2016). In this case the structure and complexity of the agent may be used depending on the level of complexity of the supervised problem. As previously stated, this supplementary cross check may involve a significant use of the system resources, but in the context of cloud computing this will mostly drive only to costs increase. This is very good because it fits perfectly with the way of computing the level of security associated with a piece of information. The golden rule in information security is that information is well protected when the cost associated in gaining it overcomes its intrinsic value. Thus, the decision of spending supplementary computing in order to protect the information will become more easy to take and with a smaller margin of error.

Required Support Mechanisms

At the level of each cloud provider a dedicated set of services that will be the basis of the virtual agents must be installed (Zaharia, 2014). As already mentioned above, in case of emergency, they may have access to the alternate, more secured communication network in order to properly help in handling any cybernetic attack. Given the fact that their main role is to help in cyber infrastructure, the costs may be split between the government, and also the private body that maintains the cloud. Still, due to their importance, the main control must remain at the governmental level.

The security provider agents will be designed using services from each level of cloud and big data architecture. The primary layer of services will be on top of the hypervisor level inside cloud architecture. These services are required for basic monitoring at the lower levels. Because cloud also offers virtualization, a possibility may be to create some minimal agents inside virtual machines. Unfortunately, this is not a feasible approach because the variety of virtualized software is too high. Instead, the agents will externally monitor all communication of each virtual machine. This will involve supplementary security risks at the virtual machine level. Because the virtualization is used to help the transition from existing applications to new ones, cloud native, this risk can be neglected. The virtualization will be used in new cloud based applications but, in this case, the basic services offered at the hypervisor level will give enough information to the agents in order to ensure a good security. Because most of the cloud solutions are open, inserting an agent layer can be easily done. Until know the agent has similar abilities with the Internet security solutions. These ones also use a swarm based approach in order to improve the rate of detection. The proposed virtual agent will use a similar approach, but a more general one. It will have a basic function as an Internet security (possibly, specific services from experienced providers can be used in agent construction) but it will also use the inference rules extraction mechanisms provided by services on upper architectural layers. This will give the agent enough computing power to be more reactive to the complex attacks, such as impersonation based ones.

All virtual agents will communicate indirectly by using collective intelligence, continuously improved by big data specific information retrieval instruments.

Big Data Architecture

A big data specific architecture is usually based on the standard multi-layer multitier approach but it also complies with the specifics of big data support (cloud and SOA). It involves the use of dedicated tiers needed for inter-tier or inter-layer translation, security or even some parts from business logic layer (Erl, 2009).

In Figure 1 a simplified architecture of big data is presented. The big data consists in fact of a worldwide big analytics system. The data can be provided from the existing databases or by interacting with live data streams (e.g. economic ones) and gives the user a global view analysis of his queries. In order to maintain functional a system of this magnitude, supplementary layers are required: the Integration, the QoS the System Management and the big data Governance. From user's point of view these layers are transparent because there are specific to the internal control of the system.

At the business logic level the use of analysis frameworks begin to increase (Inoubli, Aridhi, Mezni, Maddouri, & Nguifo, 2018). It may not be a fine tuned solution, because the granularity of application may thus significantly decrease its immediate flexibility or life time one. Yet it is a cheap and quick solution and these arguments make this approach so used. Of course this raises two major classes of problems. One concerns the inefficient use of the resource (a general approach versus a dedicated one), the other refers to the security aspects because the frameworks designers are, in most of the cases, focused mainly on giving the needed results and on leaving the security aspect at the minimum because they expect those problems to be handled only outside their framework.

A concurrency based market will provide many and sometimes different solutions to solve the same problems. So it is possible that even in the future a cyberspace similar approach will be used. This will further increase the problems associated with the framework use in rapid application development (Mar-

Figure 1. Typical big data architecture

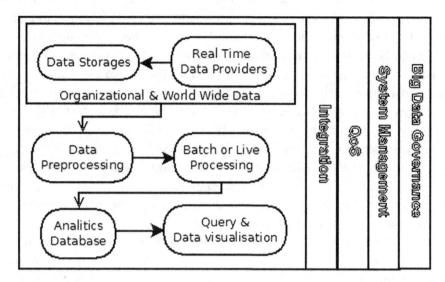

tin, Raponi, Combe, & Pietro, 2018; Pekka Pääkkönen, 2015). Therefore, new rules related to increased granularity, flexibility, interoperability must be added when designing a framework. Also, there should be more focus on security aspects such as code execution monitoring, data path analysis for virtual execution and the list may continue.

At the upper levels of the software architecture (commonly known as "front end") the security problems are increased because, in most of the situations, these applications are executed in less secured environments, no matter if the system consists either of a mobile one or an Internet enabled user workstation.

The main problem of a worldwide big data system concerns the fact that it is composed by various hardware and software pieces that are literally forced to work together by some supplementary software layers. There was no uniform view in designing this system because this is not possible. As a result, at least from security related analysis point of view, the general model must be taken into account. Because the modern technologies used in constructing various applications that stand in each layer of the model are also designed using the multi-layer multitier approach, a natural conclusion is to continue the design and analysis of this subject in the same manner. The main aim will be to find a way in increasing the security of the system as a whole. Unfortunately, due to its heterogeneous nature, this means that the security analyst must consider each component or subcomponent as a black hole and also not make false assumptions concerning the security of any component. It is enough to look at the continuous emergence of the vulnerabilities reports to justify it.

So, from big data security point of view, two different zones (that will enclose various layers from classic architectural model) with different security constraints will emerge. This may not comply with the standard approach but when the multilayer architectures were designed the security aspects were at the same level of importance as the others. Nowadays, the security analysis must be made from the attacker's point of view. As a result, the statistics regarding the most used entry points or attacked zones must be taken into account (Broeders, et al., 2017). This happens because the software architect must maintain a common view of all layers and equilibrium among them with respect to the development costs. The attacker usually uses all resources to find an entry point.

The first zone will enclose the lower layers beginning with the hardware support, communication network and persistence area and in many cases even the business layer (or at least a part of it). The risks in attacking these areas are high but so is the reward. This zone usually handles the most valuable organization data.

The other zone concerns the user levels (hardware and software) and it is easier to be penetrated, but in most situations, only user personal data is exposed. Of course, when the internal organizational rules concerning information security are now well known or respected by the user, the attacker can gain supplementary information (that is sometimes vital) needed to attack the other zones by the use of social engineering based attacks or the other standard methods.

This is possible due to the local view of security analysis because each software provider tries to mitigate only the reported security problems and there is no one to make a continuous analysis of the system as a hole. It is also clear that doing this type of analysis is impossible for a human mind. It is the same limit that appears in microprocessor design where the people only make the design and the test at the general high level and all details are handled by specific software. So the only natural way in increasing the big data security is to design a global approach that will significantly increase the control of the system for the administrators.

Secure Big Data Architecture

If we analyze the Big Data Architecture proposed by NIST (NIST, 2015), it seems that the classical multilayer - multitier architecture was redesigned according to the new existing support hardware and software architecture. As a result, the user interface zone is redefined as Data Usage, a more generic term, because there is the idea of continuously increasing the homogeneity of used interfaces, thus simplifying the design and implementation at the front end level.

The Data Transformation Layer encloses both the business and local persistence layer. This will take the advantage of centralized management and security provided by the cloud.

The third layer is similar to adaptation layer used in federative systems architecture, because it provides the interoperability with any type of existing system external data providers. This will provide backward compatibility with older infrastructures that must be also connected to the big data main stream.

This approach is tuned in with new and future big data architecture but it may confuse sometimes the new generations of system architects, due to transition from older solutions, that are more diverse, to the more homogeneous big data approach and because the life cycle for a information system may be (especially in database solutions) over thirty years.

There is also a deeply covered problem concerning the model security because the uncoupling given by service oriented architectures and the new stratification of the architecture may induce the idea that if anyone will handle its security related aspects at the needed level, the system will be secure. This is exactly the expected behavior from an attacker point of view because this thinking will significantly increase both his rate of success and the time until breach discover and risk mitigation.

Due to the high complexity of the big data systems, the classic solution of human administrators handling any security aspects is not feasible especially if we take into account the virtualization. The virtualization has a lot of advantages in auto-isolation of something that cannot be clearly classified as malicious. Unfortunately, if a lot of processes or even full servers with their applications are virtualized

Figure 2. Secure big data architecture

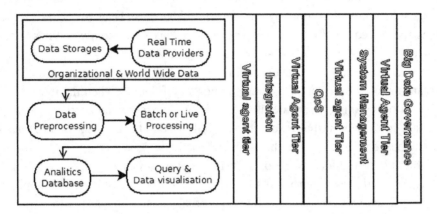

without having automatic data path checking, it can hide existing security many problems. Moreover, many virtualization technologies that seem to be attack-proof due to virtualization (e.g. Dockker & Kubernetes) are not (Martin, Raponi, Combe, & Pietro, 2018; Kozhirbayev & Sinnott, 2017).

In this context, one possible solution is to create virtual assistants for information security officers. In order to be efficient this solution must be a global one going across the architectural layers of the big data infrastructure. Hence, a new architecture for big data may be the one depicted in Figure 2, and it is based on using intelligent agents to insure security on top of already existing methods.

Inhere the bridge tiers between each layer (presentation, business logic and persistence) are not depicted. Virtually at each big data specific processing stage some security related virtual agents must reside in order to gain full control of the system. This is required because all the pieces are interrelated and the encapsulation paradigm is not enough if the system complexity is high. Securing the interaction between Big Data systems and old data repositories is also important because there are a lot of problems concerning the transition and interoperability. It is true that, in time, most of the existing infrastructure will be gradually replaced; yet, until this process is completed, the security related aspects are very important. These old infrastructures also have the problem of database migration into cloud, which is expensive and difficult.

As previously mentioned, the Security Intelligent Agents layer will provide the needed global security mechanism. This is possible because the big data architecture provides almost anything as a service, thus the dedicated agent orchestration can be automated (Elshawi, Sakr, Talia, & Trunfio, 2018).

Artificial Immune Systems in Big Data

The Artificial Immune Systems (AIS) is a research direction within the field of computational intelligence that emerged in the early 1990s and is based on the studies over the mammalian immunology. Most of the research is based on various solutions implemented using genetic algorithms. Inhere dominant classes are clone based selection algorithms, immune network algorithms and negative selection algorithms (Brownlee, 2011). Due to the inherent complexity of genetic algorithms and because of parallel architecture generalization at the processor or video processor level, new classes of parallel algorithm are being developed (Cao, et al., 2018).

Due to the inherent diversity existing nowadays in the cloud, that represents the main big data support technology, one of the most interesting solutions in assuring security may be the use of the biology inspired systems, such as the immune one. It has some unique features that make it best fitted for the job.

The latest solutions begin to reevaluate de immune system approach in order to use it as a system architecture design patterns. As a result, the original model is reanalyzed. In the case of biological immune system of a new born, he will inherit the mother's immune system. Due to its high adaptability, after a period the immune system will continue to adapt to the new host body and also to gain, on long term, specific particularities depending on the illnesses specific to his host. Consequently, an immune system can be considered unique for each human. In fact, only a part of it will be different, otherwise no vaccine would ever succeed. An immune system also has abilities such as (Diogo A.B. Fernandes, 2017):

1. **Distributed Detection:** Due to the large amount of T cells that are distributed all over the body and quickly gather around the entry point of the infection.
2. **Self-Regulation:** Because no central coordination and control are present. In fact, this is a simplistic view only at the mobile units because the human immune system is too complex to be modeled only at the mathematical level. The role of the brain is not yet clarified in the direct or indirect control of this system, but from the biological inspired systems point of view the following model is enough at this stage.
3. **Approximate Detection and Pattern Matching**: The granularity at the specific receptors is lower than the one specific to most of the attackers; as a result these receptors will only bind to portions of antigen peptides. That will avoid the need for absolute detection of every pattern. There is a price paid for this solution. There are sometimes risks of autoimmune diseases or some illnesses cannot be recognized at all but in most cases it is the best approach. From nature's point of view the death of some part of the population is a simple illness negotiation problem if the other part will adapt and survive.
4. **Diversification:** That is assured by constant clone-based selection and hyper mutation gives its unique adaptability at the mobile agents' level.
5. **Anomaly Detection:** Refers to the ability of identifying the host cells as friendly, in comparison with anything else that will be classified as unknown patterns, thus being considered enemies.
6. **Learning and Memorizing:** Is gained by its continuous adaptability to various attacks and the new constructed antigens remain forever available after creation, resulting in future immunity in front of the same type of attack.
7. **Self-Protection:** Is indirectly obtained because the protection is offered to the whole organism, therefore to itself.

When new rules are created in centralized approach, some of the old rules may be considered as obsolete and deleted. Also, the centralized solution decreases the reaction speed if the incident is located far away or if the attack already isolates the center. The immune based approach must be a hybrid one. The newly gathered rules must be submitted to the center, but each agent that fights and cooperates with others by making continuous adaptation to the attacker's strategy and exchanges rules with other peers must retain its own knowledge. This particular knowledge must be also indexed at central points in order to be used, if a local rule seems inappropriate.

In most computer systems the security systems are not shuffled at intimate level with the security system components (Stewart, Tittel, & Chapple, 2005) because, ultimately, it is a question of economic efficiency. This type of protection exists at the top level secure operating systems and applications but the costs are prohibitive in many cases.

The proposed solution is based, at a higher level, on this approach. Due to the high complexity of a big data system there will be a cooperation between various agents or even agent societies using the pattern of an immune system, but at middle or lower level there are various degrees of autonomy needed in order to handle the local problems and also to process the user or the expert input related to risk mitigation.

The distributed detection will be automatically provided by dedicated agents' custom made from scratch for some particular cases or assembled from libraries provided by the internet security solution providers.

The self regulation is implicit because, at each level the agents are destroyed if they have no jobs, in order to maintain at reasonable levels the system load, given by the security framework. This is possible because the knowledge of each agent is stored before its destruction.

The approximate detection and pattern matching is a simple question of using rule sets for inference engines.

The diversification is immediate because, with every solved problem new rules are added to knowledge database, thus the new created agents (when a new similar attack appears) will inherit all needed rules so they will be better adapted in handling the specific problem.

The anomaly detection is also a simple question of verifying the agent credential (certification authority, hash based token, access control lists or any required combination).

Learning and memorizing are also implicit abilities given by the use of artificial intelligence at the level of any required agent.

The self protection is partially based on the encapsulation and access rights maintained at the level of operating system, but also on constant and sometimes reciprocal supervising among agents.

Hence, the use of this approach in designing a global level security system may be a complex but not an unfeasible task for the big data system architects.

Big Data Persistence Layer

Due to inherent different types of data sources and various technologies that begin to be emerged in the Big Data mainstream, a possible solution for databases' integration is based on intelligent agents grouped in architectural tiers similar to the one specific to federative systems. In this tier, the agent will be used only as design pattern concept applied over service based architectures that are cloud native. This high level architectural design level approach is required due to the various service providers existing nowadays on the market (Erl, 2009). At this level the intelligent agents must be also used to supervise inter-tier or inter-layer communications in order to provide load balancing and security mechanisms. The decision to create a distinct tier for service security may or may not depend on the complexity of the required architecture. From the chosen deployment architecture the persistence level can be located on the same cloud or virtual machine, or outside the current cloud. In both situations, to ensure a good protection level, basic services from Internet security solution providers can be encapsulated at the agent level in order to ensure homogenous software architecture.

A better resource handling, in terms of system load, can be acquired if a dedicated tier will be implemented. Typically, at the persistence level access layer, this may not be required. In real life, there are many applications (especially mobile related ones) that may have a minimal business logic layer that is executed locally and then remotely access the persistence level. It is true that, in theory, the majority of database systems may provide some degree of scalability on some internal load balancing in order to provide a homogeny quality of service for each client. But some order in accessing this layer may be chosen by taking into account supplementary parameters, such as client priority, or its connection quality. Also, inhere the agent based tier may provide increased flexibility in changing the communication specific protocols.

Resource Agent Based Monitoring

Monitoring all kinds of resources could be more important than it may initially seem. For instance, monitoring energy consumption for a resource can provide early advertisements regarding an unknown activity that appears. The complexity of the actual malicious eco system makes the dedicated internet security solutions overloaded sometimes, until it totally neglects some class of attacks. One reason is that the use of the swarm intelligence (cloud knowledge based) provides a highly reactive structure, but in case of an unknown class of attack (in early stages) this approach is not efficient due to the inherent lack of information regarding the subject. Given the existing system complexity, the human experts cannot handle all new emerged attacks, consequently supplementary means of suspicious activity detection must be provided. Monitoring the energy consumption at any physical device level can be an asset, especially in the context of newly emerged IoT/IoE and fog computing directions (Zhang, Zhou, & Fortino, 2018). For instance, making profiles for normal activity and monitoring each resource spike can help the administrator to monitor the Wireless Sensor Networks – WSN (Ziwen, Yuhui, & Li, 2018). The same observation is also valid for monitoring the memory, disk and CPU. Inhere there is a special problem which is difficult to handle, yet it concerns monitoring, from the security point of view, of the hypervisor of a virtual machine, because it is an important security hole that is already used by the hacker. Hence, a data path automatic validation mechanism must be deployed; probably using an AI based system. This checking may be done differently, depending on the architectural chosen solution.

There is a problem regarding the performance counters provided by the operating system for processor load in terms of fine tuning over the process (Shao, Li, Gu, Zhang, & Luo, 2018). For instance, the processor can be reported at higher load due to overload of one core but, at the same time, the others may have lower load. Hence, new ways of measuring it must be developed. A possible solution is to use a centralized architecture. Another, more efficient, possibility would be to monitor the performance counters for each application. In the context of cloud, where there is no bottleneck problem, the last one seems more appropriate. All modern operating systems provide performance counters for any application or its processes, thus there will be no other problem in monitoring virtual machines' use of the resources. All gathered data can be stored by one agent and can be accessed and processed by another, if so. The application/process induced load is usually monitored only by load balancing reasons, but it can be used for tampering or for unauthorized application detection. This profile can also be used to have internal cloud related execution cost estimation. This may be an asset in the years to come, because it will give the owner the possibility of fine tuning its cloud related costs by updating or changing any application that proves to be economically inefficient.

In this context, dedicated hardware monitoring agents must be used. When an activity spike is detected, more specialized agents may begin to monitor the suspect device in order to see if the alert was real or not. This process can be also used in application behavior monitoring. If the problem proves to be real, the help of a human expert can be asked by an interface agent. The same way, we can use timestamp patterns dedicated agents (Ho, Kao, & Wu, 2018).

To make the automatic rule extraction, a local agent must reside on each virtual or real machine in order to collect all required information. The agent must have the ability to use the available parallelism in order to ensure a good performance of the process. The gathered information must be stored only locally. The other involved agent must extract the specific behavior pattern using data mining techniques. This agent can be implemented from scratch or will simply call an available data mining service in order to obtain the rules. In the second case, native big data instruments can be used (Elshawi, Sakr, Talia, & Trunfio, 2018). It will locally store the gathered rules and it will continuously enhance them. These rules will be also be uploaded to a central database where they will be further processed using full power of the big data. As a result, the local agent will receive updates on its rules. The method is not new and it is already used in Internet security related products that use a cloud to process all information gathered by all the worldwide installed clients. The third agent will make a continuous assessment using the rules database in order to observe if a file or a set of files begin to breach its normal timestamp pattern and then the suspicious file can be sent for further verification to an antivirus antimalware dedicated service.

An agent for traffic monitoring is also required. The content of the traffic is usually assessed by dedicated applications or services from most of the security problems. Its role in the system is to monitor the traffic overload and to detect if this is legitimate or not. Most of the Internet security solutions do not take into account this aspect in their detection schemes. This will also involve the need for communication pattern extraction for each process or application.

Due to the high load involved in the monitoring of all involved applications, a system based by training and then offset/error based monitoring triggering must be used in all monitoring schemes.

Of course, this can raise a problem regarding the costs, but the decision in using this approach may depend strictly on the importance of protected data. Also, it is possible that some of the rules created by actors with economic power to be freely distributed among the community.

Intelligent Agent as a Virtual Information Officer

There are two major sub-domains where this approach is used. One concerns the social network monitoring and control and has, as main purpose, the information control. The other is targeted on data monitoring and gathering at various levels. Both approaches are sensible of attack using the same methods. Nowadays, solutions follow the existing structures at the governmental security related departments. This stratification, that has strong reasons, must be overlapped at the information systems levels because this will further decrease the risks of false information injection or data manipulation. The other reason in doing that concerns the long time needed to adapt the informational systems to the new cryptographic solutions that will resist to quantum based attacks, and also to change the cyber defense paradigms (Mood, 2016).

Implementing a new cyber defense paradigm will have two distinct problems. One concerns the paradigm modification, then the redesign and implementation of new informational system, accordingly. This may be the easiest part, if enough resources (measured in time, money and experts) are allocated. The other major problem refers to the involved organizational changes at various departmental levels and also to the gathering of new abilities and procedures by the human security officers. This last problem is more time consuming and, in fact, will strongly decrease the speed of paradigm shift implementation.

In this context, the need for a more complex piece of software that will first help the human to adapt and then will be a common electronic assistant, is obvious (Zaharia, 2016). Therefore, an AI information officer must have the following basic abilities:

- To use direct audio visual interaction with its human partner.
- Each human will have one or more dedicated virtual agents who, in time, will learn to better help the human expert in his work.
- To have minimal auto-programming abilities in terms of modifying the used inference rules at the explicit request of the human.
- To have the proper means to certify that the user is the designated one, not a third undesired party.
- Its credentials must be provided by a third trusted party that will be the only point that can modify those access levels.
- To use highly secured informational channels, according to its existing credentials.
- To have a backup zone that resides in a highly secured zone.
- To send a copy of any data provided to its human partner, to the higher levels of decision.

The higher authority control of the agent should be limited only to suspending its functions or destroying the agent, but without destroying or altering its primary database.

Until the emergence of cloud and big data, this type of software complexity was at least economically unfeasible in order to be implemented, but in the current context, a dedicated layer in the big data mainstream may be designed.

The big data systems already provide all needed tools to assembly this type of agent. In Figure 3 a composition flow for the agent is presented.

For instance, the user can say to the interface agent: "Please initiate a full monitoring over the network communication between the user x and the server y and provide a daily report". As a result the virtual officer will receive the request after the translation receiving from Human Computer Interface Agent. Using an inference engine the rules generated from the user request will be solved. In this particular case a clone of traffic monitoring agent will be created in order to separately handle the traffic between two specified machines. Than the feature extraction agent will extract the rules that define the supervised

Figure 3. Interaction flow among agents

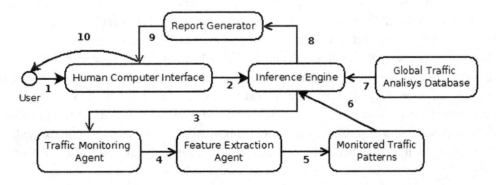

information flow. Full monitoring will be translated by the use of all available sets of rules for vulnerability assessment in the process. The daily report will present a summary of traffic over monitored communication. In case of some anomalies the instant report will be submitted to the security officer.

Customer Satisfaction Evaluation Agent

The problem of automatic evaluation for customer satisfaction is more complex (Wang, Du, Chiu, & Li, 2018). One possibility is based on indirect measurements by the use of information retrieval techniques over public sources, such as social networks. Inhere there are problems of handling the natural language but the most common solution is based on simple associations between brand name and some attributes clustered in bad or good perception. These solutions are also applied in measuring the 'sentiment' or 'emotion' using intelligent agents or not. The approaches provide only simple answers about the general perception, but in many cases they are over evaluated from the correctitude or efficiency point of view (Ragini, Anand, & Bhaskar, 2018).

In the big data context this problem is mostly focused on quality of service or micro-service because the future cyberspace is based on it (Elshawi, Sakr, Talia, & Trunfio, 2018; Sun J., Sun, Li, & Zhao, 2012). As a result, a more detailed measurement process regarding service QoS must be used by measuring various specific factors at different architectural levels of a big data application (Jatoth, Gangadharan, Fiore, & Buyya, 2017).

Measuring service security perception will require the use of direct or indirect measurements. In the case of direct measurements they can be done manually (using experts) or automatically, using AI based solutions. In this case, specific agents can be used in penetration testing. The indirect measurements are based on gathering user community perception. There also are two other possibilities. One is to use dedicated providers. In this case there is an increased economic efficiency, but the measurement area is limited to their offer. In the other case, specific instruments are used in order to gather user satisfaction, especially when some supplementary parameters must be analyzed and there are no external providers. This is, as expected, a solution with higher costs; but choosing it will depend only on the general economic SWOT analysis.

Another important parameter concerns service availability. The fact that cloud guarantees this for its basic services does not automatically apply for custom based services provided by any analyzed application; this is why this investigation must also be done.

The cloud will provide some advantages, as automatic scalability and performance for any hosted service, but at a price. As a result, the parameter concerning the average price – performance must be computed and analyzed, too.

The user perception is also important because not all the users take decisions based only on economic efficiency. This happens only in case of economic actors but there, common clients captive or not may choose based on their internal set of values and perception to use a service or not.

The common user does not take into account in his analysis various components of an application (such as a service or a set of services) but mostly the application as a whole; and sometimes the decision is even simpler and based only on some specific features from the nice to have category.

Gathering user perception can be also done by dedicated market analysis providers or by using specific tools for an application or product evaluation. Unfortunately, when a more complex model for user perception is required, it is dependent on a variable degree on the application specific. In this case, a test must be designed with the help of a team that must enclose at least one psychology and one sociology expert. This may further increase the cost of the solution.

One conclusion is that a more flexible instrument will be an asset. The AI can also help in designing such solution, especially if an inference engine is used because, due to its nature, it is highly customizable by simply adding or changing the used set of rules. If we combine this observation with the use of an agent as design pattern, it can be concluded that an intelligent agent based on inference engine can provide all means to solve the problem. In order to apply this in the big data concept, the agent must be constructed using services, thus naturally integrating into the big data support technology.

Issues, Controversies, Problems

The big data security is still an open problem (Amato, Mazzocca, & Moscato, 2018). The complex infrastructure of services which resides at the cloud base makes possible breaches at any level. Using the proposed system may further increase the system complexity, making a centralized view of the system more difficult. Yet, there are some inherent advantages. Using autonomous service based agents with cognitive abilities to maintain control and system security partially solves the problem of reciprocal check among security parties. For an attacker the system will present itself not as a very well stratified architecture where it is enough to compromise iterative existing security layer, but as a conglomerate of dynamic entities that continuously check one each other or temporary cooperate if it is necessary, making it very hard to attack it.

In case of massive cyber nodes that usually consist of datacenter tier three or four, new dedicated interface security agents must be used in order to continuously interact with their human companions that work in local or external security providers. Moreover, all involved personnel activity must be supervised with dedicated agents but they will also interact with dedicated interface agents that will help on various levels in their work.

Fault Tolerance of the Security System

One of the security problems is cost related (no matter how it is computed). As a result, in most of cases, assuring a fault tolerant security infrastructure is not feasible. So any hacker that manages to disable a specific service may further proceed into the system. The natural solution is to maintain multiple levels of security located on each layer or even tier of the software architecture. The existing software and hardware infrastructure already have, from the original design, implemented various security levels that succeed, with the help of human supervisor, to manage with a reasonable reaction time most of the security breaches. Unfortunately, the cloud and its virtualization support begin to create autonomous systems with higher complexity that cannot be handled manually by human experts. The answer is to further increase the AI involvement on each layer or inside those systems to better model a virtual security officer. It is clear that even that approach cannot harness the wave of problems, but at least with some human supervision (to monitor and change used rules) a significant problem alleviation can be gained with the expected increase in costs.

SOLUTIONS AND RECOMMENDATIONS

The previously proposed solutions conclude that the whole interaction over Internet must be changed beginning with the used security paradigm and ending with the use of a solution consisting of a set of security agents crossing all levels, homogeneously deployed on each part of the big data hardware and software system. In here, the agents are differentiated depending on their role in the global cyberspace. These service based agents can have various sources depending on their producer or owner, so there is a chance that in some areas there may too many different agents doing the same job. This may appear unfeasible form an economic perspective, but as it can be already seen, in the future cyberspace the computer power or communication network may become cheaper when more and more countries will join the global cyberspace. In this context, the security and system tight control will became more important than the associated costs.

AI Associated Security Risks

Manny artificial intelligence (AI) based solutions are used inside Big Data architectural levels (Villaronga, Kieseberg, & Li, 2018; Passalis & Tefas, 2018). The supervised learning can be used in handling the transaction fraud detection problems (Carcillo, et al., 2018).

The simple statistical methods, such as regression, are still efficient in analysis regarding customer lifetime value (Cox, Kartsonaki, & Keogh, 2018).

Of course that using AI without proper analysis (due to the high pressure of needed changes) may drive the global system to a so-called "singularity point" but this problem is over estimated (Bossmann, 2016). The main risk is at the public domain levels where the control of the AI complexity is still weak. A better solution in avoiding this may be found if governments begin to adopt a set of rules that would clearly state the limits that a public AI application must have. This process in not even started so there is serious risk that, without quick and decisive measures at the governmental levels, the free market will produce uncontrollable AI based entities. Unfortunately, such risks already exist at the governmental and military level because many governments already used AI dedicated entities to control the informational market and in some cases the autonomy level of this entities is too high (Fang, 2016). Therefore, the need for a global accepted standard of AI based entity limits is strongly required.

FUTURE RESEARCH DIRECTIONS

The future research regarding the presented solution will involve its testing with the help of a dedicated intelligent framework, based on the cloud specific technologies. As for the domain level, there are many possibilities. One can be the use of quantum based communication that was already tested at satellite level (Liao, et al., 2018). This would provide complete protection in front of the Man in the Middle specific attack (Qin, et al., 2017) due to its properties. In this case the use of cryptographic algorithm may not be necessary or at least the need for new enforced solutions is significantly decreased. Given the fact that this type of communication would be at least one decade prohibitive for most of the economic actors from the global market, some alternative solutions must be proposed, too. Inhere two different main directions emerge. One consists of the continuous improvement at the application architectural level by the introduction of more security related tiers based on technology related design patterns (Dong, Peng,

& Zhao, 2010; Abramov, Sturm, & Shoval, 2012). The other is based on the continuous improvement and replacement of the commonly used cryptographic algorithms. This is required due to the quantum computing that nowadays enters a new era (Chen, et al., 2016). The third less evident problem concerns the effort put in enforcing the specific standards at governmental level. The USA already started this process (Ross, Viscuso, Guissanie, Dempsey, & Riddle, 2016). But, without a strong international cooperation, many security breaches may appear due to the inherent interoperability at the global level that is specific to the information society.

CONCLUSION

In this chapter some solutions regarding new ways of assuring big data cyber defense using intelligent agents as architectural design paradigm were presented. In fact, new general software architecture for big data systems was proposed according to the newly suggested security paradigm change. From architectural point of view the main idea is that the agents can be created, used or destroyed anywhere necessary in the system (the use of AIS solution).

In order to be efficient the system will require agents that will supervise execution at all possible levels (including resource monitoring), agents that will act as information security officers, agents that will be used in interfacing the main system with any human security expert.

This approach may seem very expensive, but in the future cyberspace, computing resources will not be an economical problem. Instead, the problem of maintaining the system under control for security related reasons will became more important. In this context, the proposed solutions may help in solving most of the expected problems.

REFERENCES

Abramov, J., Sturm, A., & Shoval, P. (2012). Evaluation of the Pattern-based method for Secure Development. *Information and Software Technology, 54*(9), 1029–1043. doi:10.1016/j.infsof.2012.04.001

Amato, F., Mazzocca, N., & Moscato, F. (2018). Model driven design and evaluation of security level in orchestrated cloud services. *Journal of Network and Computer Applications, 106*, 78–89. doi:10.1016/j.jnca.2017.12.006

Arnott, D., Lizama, F., & Song, Y. (2017). Patterns of business intelligence systems use in organizations. *Decision Support Systems, 97*, 58–68. doi:10.1016/j.dss.2017.03.005

Ashibani, Y., & Mahmoud, Q. H. (2017). Cyber physical systems security: Analysis, challegnes and solutions. *Computers & Security, 68*, 81–97. doi:10.1016/j.cose.2017.04.005

Badola, V. (2015, October 1). *Cloud migration: benefits and risks of migrating to the Cloud.* Retrieved from http://cloudacademy.com/blog/cloud-migration-benefits-risks/

Bossmann, J. (2016, October 21). *Top 9 ethical issues in artificial intelligence.* Retrieved from https://www.weforum.org/agenda/2016/10/top-10-ethical-issues-in-artificial-intelligence/

Broeders, D., Schrijvers, E., Sloot, B., Brakel, R., Hoog, J., & Ballin, E. H. (2017). Big Data and security policies: Towards a framework for regulating the phases of analytics and use of Big Data. *Computer Law & Security Review, 33*(3), 309–323. doi:10.1016/j.clsr.2017.03.002

Brownlee, J. (2011). *Clever Algorithms: Nature-Inspired Programming Recipes.* Morrisville: LuLu.

Cao, B., Zhao, J., Po Yang, Z. L., Liu, X., Kang, X., Yang, S., ... Anvari-Moghaddam, A. (2018). Distributed parallel cooperative coevolutionary multi-objective. *Future Generation Computer Systems, 82*, 256–267. doi:10.1016/j.future.2017.10.015

Carcillo, F., Pozzolo, A. D., Borgne, Y.-A. L., Caelen, O., Mazzer, Y., & Bontempi, G. (2018). SCARFF: A scalable framework for streaming credit card fraud detection with spark. *Information Fusion, 41*, 182–194. doi:10.1016/j.inffus.2017.09.005

Chen, L., Jordan, S., Liu, Y.-K., Moody, D., Peralta, R., Perlner, R., & Smith, D. (2016). *Report on Post-Quantum Cryptography.* Gaithersburg, MD: National Institute of Standards and Technology. doi:10.6028/NIST.IR.8105

Cox, D., Kartsonaki, C., & Keogh, R. H. (2018). Big data: Some statistical issues. *Statistics & Probability Letters, 136*, 111–115. doi:10.1016/j.spl.2018.02.015 PMID:29899584

Diogo, A. B., & Fernandes, M. M. (2017). Applications of artificial immune systems to computer security: A survey. *Journal of Information Security and Applications, 35*, 138–159. doi:10.1016/j.jisa.2017.06.007

Dong, J., Peng, T., & Zhao, Y. (2010). Automated verification of security pattern compositions. *Information and Software Technology, 52*(3), 274–295. doi:10.1016/j.infsof.2009.10.001

Eggen, A., Hauge, M., Hedenstad, O. E., Lund, K., Legasp, A., Seifert, H., & Simon, P. (2013). *Coalition Networks for Secure Information Sharing (CoNSIS). In MILCOM 2013 - 2013 IEEE Military Communications Conference* (pp. 354–359). San Diego, CA: IEEE. doi:10.1109/MILCOM.2013.68

Elshawi, R., Sakr, S., Talia, D., & Trunfio, P. (2018). Big Data Systems Meet Machine Learning Challenges: Towards Big Data Science as a Service. *Big Data Research*, 1-11.

Erl, T. (2009). *SOA Design Patterns.* New York: Prentice Hall PTR.

Fang, L. (2016, April 14). *The CIA Is Investing in Firms That Mine Your Tweets and Instagram Photos.* Retrieved from The intercept: https://theintercept.com/2016/04/14/in-undisclosed-cia-investments-social-media-mining-looms-large/

Hamon, M. A., & Quintin, J. (2016). Innate immune memory in mammals. *Seminars in Immunology, 28*(4), 351–358. doi:10.1016/j.smim.2016.05.003 PMID:27264334

Hardy, Q. (2016, December 25). *Why the Computing Cloud Will Keep Growing and Growing.* Retrieved from https://www.nytimes.com/2016/12/25/technology/why-the-computing-cloud-will-keep-growing-and-growing.html?_r=0

Harris, S., & Maymi, F. (2016). *CISSP® All-in-One Exam Guide* (7th ed.). New York: McGraw-Hill Education.

Ho, S. M., Kao, D., & Wu, W.-Y. (2018). Following the breadcrumbs: Timestamp pattern identification for cloud forensics. *Digital Investigation*, *24*, 79–94. doi:10.1016/j.diin.2017.12.001

Howarth, F. (2014, September 2). *The Role of Human Error in Successful Security Attacks*. Retrieved from SecurityIntelligence: https://securityintelligence.com/the-role-of-human-error-in-successful-security-attacks/

Hu, L., Wang, Z., Han, Q.-L., & Liu, X. (2018). State estimation under false data injection attacks: Security analysis and system protection. *Automatica*, *87*, 176–183. doi:10.1016/j.automatica.2017.09.028

Inoubli, W., Aridhi, S., Mezni, H., Maddouri, M., & Nguifo, E. M. (2018). An experimental survey on big data frameworks. *Future Generation Computer Systems*, 1–19.

Jatoth, C., Gangadharan, G., Fiore, U., & Buyya, R. (2017). QoS-aware Big service composition using MapReduce based evolutionary algorithm with guided mutation. *Future Generation Computer Systems*, 1–11.

Khana, N., & Al-Yasirib, A. (2016). Identifying Cloud Security Threats to Strengthen Cloud Computing. *Procedia Computer Science*, *94*, 485–490. doi:10.1016/j.procs.2016.08.075

Kozhirbayev, Z., & Sinnott, R. O. (2017). A performance comparison of container-based technologies for the Cloud. *Future Generation Computer Systems*, *68*, 175–182. doi:10.1016/j.future.2016.08.025

Lasconjarias, G., & Larsen, J. A. (2015, December 17). *New Research Division Publication - NATO's Response to Hybrid Threats*. Retrieved from NATO Defence college: http://www.ndc.nato.int/download/downloads.php?icode=471

Liao, S.-K., Cai, W.-Q., Handsteiner, J., Liu, B., Yin, J., Zhang, L., ... Pan, J.-W. (2018). Satellite-Relayed Intercontinental Quantum Network. *Physical Review Letters*, *120*(3), 030501–030505. doi:10.1103/PhysRevLett.120.030501 PMID:29400544

Lord, N. (2017, February 28). *Social Engineering Attacks: Common Techniques & How to Prevent an Attack*. Retrieved from Digital Guardian: https://digitalguardian.com/blog/social-engineering-attacks-common-techniques-how-prevent-attack

Martin, A., Raponi, S., Combe, T., & Pietro, R. D. (2018). Docker ecosystem – Vulnerability Analysis. *Computer Communications*, *122*, 30–43. doi:10.1016/j.comcom.2018.03.011

Mood, D. (2016, February 24). *Post-Quantum Cryptography: NIST plan for the future*. Retrieved from pqcrypto2016.jp: https://pqcrypto2016.jp/data/pqc2016_nist_announcement.pdf

Mourad, A., Laverdiere, M.-A., & Debbabi, M. (2008). An aspect-oriented approach for the systematic security hardening of code. *Computers & Security*, *27*(3-4), 101–114. doi:10.1016/j.cose.2008.04.003

Mumtaz, H., Alshayeb, M., Mahmood, S., & Niazi, M. (2018). An empirical study to improve software security through the application of code refactoring. *Information and Software Technology*, *96*, 112–125. doi:10.1016/j.infsof.2017.11.010

NIST. (2015). *Reports on Computer Systems Technology 1500-5. Big Data Public Working Group*. Gaithersburg, MD: National Institute of Standards and Technology.

NIST. (2017, March 1). *Cybersecurity Framework Overview*. Retrieved from NIST: https://www.nist.gov/file/354081

Passalis, N., & Tefas, A. (2018). Learning bag-of-embedded-words representations for textual information retrieval. *Pattern Recognition, 81*, 254–267. doi:10.1016/j.patcog.2018.04.008

Pekka Pääkkönen, D. P. (2015). Reference Architecture and Classification of Technologies, Products and Services for Big Data Systems. *Big Data Research, 2*(4), 166–186. doi:10.1016/j.bdr.2015.01.001

Qin, B., Huang, J., Wang, Q., Luo, X., Liang, B., & Shi, W. (2017). Cecoin: A decentralized PKI mitigating MitM attacks. *Future Generation Computer Systems*, 1–11.

Ragini, J. R., Anand, P. R., & Bhaskar, V. (2018). Big data analytics for disaster response and recovery through sentiment analysi. *International Journal of Information Management, 42*, 13–24. doi:10.1016/j.ijinfomgt.2018.05.004

Ross, R., Viscuso, P., Guissanie, G., Dempsey, K., & Riddle, M. (2016). *Protecting Controlled Unclassified Information in Nonfederal Systems*. Gaithersburg, MD: National Institute of Standards and Technology. doi:10.6028/NIST.SP.800-171r1

Shao, Y., Li, C., Gu, J., Zhang, J., & Luo, Y. (2018). Efficient jobs scheduling approach for big data applications. *Computers & Industrial Engineering, 117*, 249–261. doi:10.1016/j.cie.2018.02.006

Sharma, C. S. (2016). *Securing Cyberspace: International and Asian Perspectives*. New Delhi: Pentagon Press.

Shrivastavaa, S., Sharmab, A., & Shrivastavac, D. (2015). An Approach for QoS Based Fault Reconfiguration in Service. *Procedia Computer Science, 46*, 766–773. doi:10.1016/j.procs.2015.02.145

Singh, A., & Chatterjee, K. (2017). Cloud security issues and challenges: A survey. *Journal of Network and Computer Applications, 79*, 88–115. doi:10.1016/j.jnca.2016.11.027

Stewart, J. M., Tittel, E., & Chapple, M. (2005). *CISSP: Certified Information Systems Security Professional Study Guide* (3rd ed.). San Francisco: Sybex.

Sun, J., Sun, Z., Li, Y., & Zhao, S. (2012). A Strategic Model of Trust Management in Web Services. *Physics Procedia, 24*(B), 1560-1566.

Sun, Z., Sun, J., & Meredith, G. (2012). Customer Decision Making in Web Services with an Integrated P6 Model. *Physics Procedia, 24*(B), 1553-1559.

Tao, M., Zuo, J., Liu, Z., Castiglione, A., & Palmieri, F. (2018). Multi-layer cloud architectural model and ontology-based security service framework for IoT-based smart homes. *Future Generation Computer Systems, 78*, 1040–1051. doi:10.1016/j.future.2016.11.011

US-CERT. (2017, January 24). *Critical Infrastructure Cyber Community Voluntary Program*. Retrieved from US-CERT: https://www.us-cert.gov/ccubedvp

US Department of Defence. (2015, June). *2015 - The National Military Strategy of the United States of America*. Retrieved from Aquisition Community Connection: http://www.jcs.mil/Portals/36/Documents/Publications/2015_National_Military_Strategy.pdf

Villaronga, E. F., Kieseberg, P., & Li, T. (2018). Humans forget, machines remember: Artificial intelligence and the Right to Be Forgotten. *Computer Law & Security Review, 34*(2), 304–313. doi:10.1016/j.clsr.2017.08.007

Wang, J.-N., Du, J., Chiu, Y.-L., & Li, J. (2018). Dynamic effects of customer experience levels on durable product satisfaction: Priceand popularity moderation. *Electronic Commerce Research and Applications, 28*, 16–29. doi:10.1016/j.elerap.2018.01.002

Zaharia, M. H. (2014). Generalized Demand-Driven Web Services. In Z. Sun, & J. Yearwood (Eds.), Handbook of Research on Demand-Driven Web Services: Theory, Technologies, and Applications (pp. 102-134). IGI Global. doi:10.4018/978-1-4666-5884-4.ch005

Zaharia, M. H. (2016). A Paradigm Shift in Cyberspace Security. In B. A. Hamid & R. Arabnia (Eds.), Emerging Trends in ICT Security (pp. 443-451). Morgan Kaufmann.

Zhang, P., Zhou, M., & Fortino, G. (2018). Security and trust issues in Fog computing: A survey. *Future Generation Computer Systems, 88*, 16–27. doi:10.1016/j.future.2018.05.008

Ziwen, S., Yuhui, L., & Li, T. (2018). Attack localization task allocation in wireless sensor networks based on multi-objective binary particle swarm optimization. *Journal of Network and Computer Applications, 112*, 29–40. doi:10.1016/j.jnca.2018.03.023

Chapter 6
Optimizing and Enhancing Digital Marketing Techniques in Intellectual Big Data Analytics

Vardan Mkrttchian
https://orcid.org/0000-0003-4871-5956
HHH University, Australia

Leyla Gamidullaeva
https://orcid.org/0000-0003-3042-7550
Penza State University, Russia

Svetlana Panasenko
Plekhanov Russian University of Economics, Russia

ABSTRACT

The authors in this chapter show the essence, dignity, current state, and development prospects of avatar-based management using blockchain technology for improving implementation of economic solutions in the digital economy of Russia. The purpose of this chapter is not to review the existing published work on avatar-based models for policy advice, but to try an assessment of the merits and problems of avatar-based models as a solid basis for economic policy advice that is mainly based on the work and experience within the recently finished projects Triple H Avatar, an avatar-based software platform for HHH University, Sydney, Australia. The agenda of this project was to develop an avatar-based closed model with strong empirical grounding and micro-foundations that provides a uniform platform to address issues in different areas of digital economic and creating new tools to improve blockchain technology using the intelligent visualization techniques for big data analytic.

DOI: 10.4018/978-1-5225-7277-0.ch006

INTRODUCTION

Management in Digital Economy is concerned with the design, execution, monitoring, and improvement of business processes. Systems that support the enactment and execution of processes have extensively been used by companies to streamline and automate intra-organizational processes. Yet, for inter-organizational processes, challenges of joint design and a lack of mutual trust have hampered a broader uptake. Emerging blockchain technology has the potential to drastically change the environment in which inter-organizational processes are able to operate. Blockchains offer a way to execute processes in a trustworthy manner even in a network without any mutual trust between nodes. Key aspects are specific algorithms that lead to consensus among the nodes and market mechanisms that motivate the nodes to progress the network. Through these capabilities, this technology has the potential to shift the discourse in management research about how systems might enable the enactment, execution, monitoring or improvement of business process within or across business networks. By using blockchain technology, untrusted parties can establish trust in the truthful execution of the code. Smart contracts can be used to implement business collaborations in general and inter-organizational business processes in particular. The potential of blockchain-based distributed ledgers to enable collaboration in open environments has been successfully tested in diverse fields ranging from diamonds trading to securities settlement (Mendling, J. et al, 2018).

But at this stage, it has to be noted that blockchain technology still faces numerous general technological challenges. In this article, we describe what we believe are the main new challenges and opportunities of blockchain technology for Digital Economy in Russia. A our study in Russia by found that a majority of these challenges have not been addressed by the Russian research community, albeit we note that blockchain developer communities actively discuss some of these challenges and suggest a myriad of potential solutions. Some of them can be addressed by using private or consortium blockchain instead of a fully open network. In general, the technological challenges are limited at this point, in terms of both developer support (lack of adequate tooling) and end-user support (hard to use and understand). Our recent advances on developer support include efforts by of the towards model-driven development of blockchain applications sliding mode in intellectual control and communication, help the technological challenges and created tools (Mkrttchian & Aleshina, 2017).

BACKGROUND

We are the first to identify the application potential of blockchain technology to sliding mode in intellectual control and communication, for help the technological challenges and created tools. A our proposal to support inter-organizational processes through blockchain technology is described by: large parts of the control flow and business logic of inter-organizational business processes can be compiled from process models into smart contracts which ensure the joint process is correctly executed. So-called trigger components allow connecting these inter-organizational process implementations to Web services and internal process implementations. These triggers serve as a bridge between the blockchain and enterprise applications. The concept enables the optional implementation of intellectual control and built-in escrow management at defined points within the process, where this is desired and feasible (Mendling, et al, 2018).

The engineering realization of this advance is still nascent at this stage, although some early efforts can be found in our previous works. For example, intelligent visualization techniques that enforce a process execution in a trustworthy way can be generated from sliding mode process models (Mkrttchian & Aleshina, 2017).

Our study show that blockchain technology and its application to digital economy in Russia are at an important crossroads: engineering realization issues blend with promising application scenarios; early implementations mix with unanticipated challenges. It is timely, therefore, to discuss in broad and encompassing ways where open questions lie that the scholarly community should be interested in addressing. We do so in the sections that follows.

MAIN FOCUS OF THE CHAPTER

Issues, Controversies, Problems, Solutions and Recommendations

In this section, we discuss blockchain in relation to the visualization lifecycle including the following phases: identification, discovery, analysis, redesign, implementation, execution, monitoring, and adaptation. Using this lifecycle as a framework of reference allows us to discuss many incremental changes that blockchains might provide.

Process identification is concerned with the high-level description and evaluation of a company from a process-oriented perspective, thus connecting strategic alignment with process improvement. Currently, identification is mostly approached from an inward-looking perspective [Dumas et al. 2018]. Blockchain technology adds another relevant perspective for evaluating high-level processes in terms of the implied strengths, weaknesses, opportunities, and threats. For example, how can a company systematically identify the most suitable processes for blockchains or the most threatened ones? Research is needed into how this perspective can be integrated into the identification phase. Because blockchains have affinity with the support of inter-organizational processes, process identification may need to encompass not only the needs of one organization, but broader known and even unknown partners.

Process discovery refers to the collection of information about the current way a process operates and its representation as an as-is process model. Currently, methods for process discovery are largely based on interviews, walkthroughs and documentation analysis, complemented with auto-mated process discovery techniques over non-encrypted event logs generated by process-aware information systems [van der Aalst 2016]. Blockchain technology defines new challenges for pro-cess discovery techniques: the information may be fragmented and encrypted; accounts and keys can change frequently; and payload data may be stored partly on-chain and partly off-chain. For example, how can a company discover an overall process from blockchain transactions when these might not be logically related to a process identifier? This fragmentation might require a repeated alignment of information from all relevant parties operating on the blockchain. Work on matching could represent a promising starting point to solve this problem [Cayoglu et al. 2014; Euzenat and Shvaiko 2013; Gal 2011]. There is both the risk and opportunity of conducting process mining on blockchain data. An opportunity could involve establishing trust in how a process or a prospective business partner operates, while a risk is that other parties might be able to understand operational characteristics from blockchain transactions. There are also opportunities for reverse engineering business processes, among others, from smart contracts.

Process analysis refers to obtaining insights into issues relating to the way a business process currently operates. Currently, the analysis of processes mostly builds on data that is available inside of organizations or from perceptions shared by internal and external process stakeholders (Mendling, J. et al, 2018). Records of processes executed on the blockchain yield valuable information that can help to assess the case load, durations, frequencies of paths, parties involved, and correlations between unencrypted data items. These pieces of information can be used to discover processes, detect deviations, and conduct root cause analysis (Mendling, J. et al, 2018), ranging from small groups of companies to an entire industry at large. The question is which effort is required to bring the available blockchain transaction data into a format that permits such analysis.

Process redesign deals with the systematic improvement of a process. Currently, approaches like redesign heuristics build on the assumption that there are recurring patterns of how a process can be improved (Mendling, J. et al, 2018). Blockchain technology offers novel ways of improving specific business processes or resolving specific problems. For instance, instead of involving a trustee to release a payment if an agreed condition is met, a buyer and a seller of a house might agree on a smart contract instead. The question is where blockchains can be applied for optimizing existing interactions and where new interaction patterns without a trusted central party can be established, potentially drawing on insights from related research on Web service interaction. A promising direction for developing blockchain-appropriate abstractions and heuristics may come from data-aware workflows and diagrams. Both techniques combine two primary ingredients of blockchain, namely data and process, in a holistic manner that is well-suited for top-down design of cross-organizational processes. It might also be beneficial to formulate blockchain-specific redesign heuristics that could mimic how Incoterms define standardized interactions in international trade. Specific challenges for redesign include the joint engineering of blockchain processes between all parties involved, an ongoing problem for design (Mendling, J. et al, 2018).

Process implementation refers to the procedure of transforming a to-be model into software components executing the digital economy process. Currently, same processes are often implemented using process-aware information systems or business process management systems inside single organizations. In this context, the question is how the involved parties can make sure that the implementation that they deploy on the blockchain supports their process as desired. Some of the challenges regarding the transformation of a process model to blockchain artifacts are discussed by (Mendling, J. et al, 2018). It has to be noted that choreographies have not been adopted by industry to a large extent yet. Despite this, they are especially helpful in inter-organizational settings, where it is not possible to control and monitor a complete process in a centralized fashion because of organizational borders (Mendling, J. et al, 2018). To verify that contracts between choreography stakeholders have been fulfilled, a trust basis, which is not under control of a particular party, needs to be established. Blockchains may serve to establish this kind of trust between stakeholders.

An important engineering challenge on the implementation level is the identification and definition of abstractions for the design of blockchain-based business process execution. Libraries and operations for engines are required, accompanied by modeling primitives and language extensions of digital economy process.. Software patterns and anti-patterns will be of good help to engineers designing blockchain-based processes. There is also a need for new approaches for quality assurance, correctness, and verification, as well as for new corresponding correctness criteria. These can build on existing notions of compliance the more, dynamic partner binding and rebinding is a challenge that requires attention. Process participants will have to find partners, either manually or automatically on dedicated marketplaces using dedicated look-up services. The property of inhabiting a certain role in a process might itself be a tradable asset.

For example, a supplier might auction off the role of shipper to the highest bidder as part of the process. Finally, as more and more companies use blockchain, there will be a proliferation of smart contract templates available for use. Tools for finding templates appropriate for a given style of collaboration will be essential. All these characteristics emphasize the need for specific testing and verification approaches.

Execution refers to the instantiation of individual cases and their information-technological processing. Currently, such execution is facilitated by process-aware information systems or digital economy process management systems. For the actual execution of a process deployed on a blockchain following the method of (Mendling, J. et al, 2018), several differences with the traditional ways exist. During the execution of an instance, messages between participants need to be passed as blockchain transactions to the smart contract; resulting messages need to be observed from the blocks in the blockchain. Both of these can be achieved by integrating blockchain technology directly with existing enterprise systems or through the use of dedicated integration components, such as the triggers suggested by (Mendling, J. et al, 2018). The main challenge here involves ensuring correctness and security, especially when monetary assets are transferred using this technology.

Process monitoring refers to collecting events of process executions, displaying them in an understandable way, and triggering alerts and escalation in cases where undesired behavior is observed. Currently, such process execution data is recorded by systems that support process execution (Mendling, J. et al, 2018). First, we face issues in terms of data fragmentation and encryption as in the analysis phase. For example, the data on the blockchain alone will likely not be enough to monitor the process, but require integration with local off-chain data. Once such tracing in place, the global view of the process can be monitored independently by each involved party. This provides a suitable basis for continuous conformance and compliance checking and monitoring of service-level agreements. Second, based on monitoring data exchanged via the blockchain, it is possible to verify if a process instance meets the original process model and the contractual obligations of all involved process stakeholders. For this, blockchain technology can be exploited to store the process execution data and handoffs between process participants. Notably, this is even possible without the usage of smart contracts, i.e., in a first-generation blockchain like the one operated by digital economy (Mendling, J. et al, 2018).

Runtime adaptation refers to the concept of changing the process during execution. In traditional approaches, this can for instance be achieved by allowing participants in a process to change the model during its execution. Interacting partners might take a defensive stance in order to avoid certain types of adaptation. As discussed by (Mendling, J. et al, 2018), blockchain can be used to enforce conformance with the model, so that participants can rely on the joint model being followed. In such a setting, adaptation is by default something to be avoided: if a participant can change the model, this could be used to gain an unfair advantage over the other participants. For instance, the rules of retrieving digital process from an escrow account could be changed or the terms of payment. In this setting, process adaptation must strictly adhere to defined paths for it, e.g., any change to a deployed smart contract may require a transaction signed by all participants. In contrast, the method proposed by (Mendling, J. et al, 2018) allows runtime adaptation, but assumes that relevant participants monitor the execution and react if a change is undesired. If smart contracts enforce the process, there are also problems arising in relation to evolution: new smart contracts need to be deployed to reflect changes to a new version of the process model. Porting running instances from an old version to a new one would require effective coordination mechanisms involving all participants ((Mendling, J. et al, 2018).

There are also challenges and opportunities for digital economy process and blockchain technology beyond the classical lifecycle. We refer to the capability areas beyond the methodological support we reflected above, including strategy, governance, information technology, people, and culture.

Strategic alignment refers to the active management of connections between organizational priori-ties and business processes, which aims at facilitating effective actions to improve business performance. Currently, various approaches to digital economy process assume that the corporate strategy is defined first and business processes are aligned with the respective strategic imperatives (Mendling, J. et al, 2018). Blockchain technology challenges these approaches to strategic alignment. For many companies, blockchains define a potential threat to their core digital economy processes. For instance, the banking industry could see a major disintermediation based on blockchain-based payment services. Also lock-in effects might deteriorate when, for example, the banking service is not the banking network itself anymore, but only the interface to it. These developments could lead to business processes and business models being under strong influence of technological innovations outside of companies (Mendling, J. et al, 2018).

The digital economy process governance refers to appropriate and transparent accountability in terms of roles, responsibilities, and decision processes for different digital economy-related programs, projects, and operations (Mendling, J. et al, 2018). Currently, digital economy processes as a management approach builds on the explicit definition of digital economy processes management-related roles and responsibilities with a focus on the internal operations of a company. Blockchain technology might change governance towards a more externally oriented model of self-governance based on smart contracts. Research on corporate governance investigates agency problems and mechanisms to provide effective incentives for intended behavior (Mendling, J. et al, 2018). Smart contracts can be used to establish new governance models as exemplified by (Mendling, J. et al, 2018). It is an important question in how far this idea of Mendling (2018) can be extended towards reducing the agency problem of management discretion or eventually eliminate the need for management altogether. Furthermore, the revolution-ary change suggested by Mendling, (2018) for organization shows just how disruptive this technology can be, and whether similarly radical changes could apply to digital economy processes management. (Mendling, J. et al, 2018).

Digital economy processes management-related information technology subsumes all systems that support process execution, such as process-aware information systems and digital economy process management systems. These systems typically assume central control over the process. Blockchain tech-nology enables novel ways of process execution, but several challenges in terms of security and privacy have to be considered. While the visibility of encrypted data on a blockchain is restricted, it is up to the participants in the process to ensure that these mechanisms are used according to their confidentiality requirements. Some of these requirements are currently being investigated in the financial industry. Fur-ther challenges can be expected with the introduction of the digital economy in Russian Federation. It is also not clear, which new attack scenarios on blockchain networks might emerge. Therefore, guidelines for using private, public, or consortium-based blockchains are required.

A person in this context refers to all individuals, possibly in different roles, who engage with digital economy processes management. Currently, these are people who work as process analyst, process manager, process owner or in other process-related roles. The roles of these individuals are shaped by skills in the area of management, business analysis and requirements engineering. In this capability area, the use of blockchain technology requires extensions of their skill sets. New required skills relate to partner and contract management, software engineering and big data analysts. Also, people have to be willing to design blockchain-based collaborations within the frame of existing regulations to enable adoption. This implies that research into blockchain-specific technology acceptance is needed, extending the established technology acceptance model (Mendling, J. et al, 2018).

Organizational culture is defined by the collective values of a group of people in an organization. Currently, digital economy processes management is discussed in relation to organizational culture from a perspective that emphasizes an affinity with clan and hierarchy culture (Mendling, J. et al, 2018)]. These cultural types are often found in the many companies that use digital economy processes management as an approach for documentation. Blockchains are likely to influence organizational culture towards a stronger emphasis on flexibility and an outward-looking perspective. In the competing values framework by (Mendling et al, 2018), these aspects are associated with an adhocracy organizational culture. Furthermore, not only consequences of blockchain adoption have to be studied, but also antecedents'. These include organizational factors that facilitate early and successful adoption.

By itself, stored data does not generate business value, and this is true of traditional databases, data warehouses, and the new technologies for storing big data. Once the data is appropriately stored, however, it can be analyzed, which can create tremendous value. A variety of analysis technologies, approaches, and products have emerged that are especially applicable to big data, such as in-memory analytics, in-database analytics, and appliances. In our study we are using Intelligent Visualization Techniques for Big Data Analytic, or business intelligence (Mkrttchian et al, 2011-2017). It is helpful to recognize that the term analytics is not used consistently; it is used in at least three different yet related ways. A starting point for understanding analytics is to explore its roots. Decision support systems (DSS) in the 1970s were the first systems to support decision making. DSS came to be used as a description for an application and an academic discipline. Over time, additional decision support applications such as executive information systems, online analytical processing (OLAP), and dashboards/scorecards became popular (Watson, 2014). Then in the 1990s, Howard Dresner, an analyst at Gartner (Watson, 2014), popularized the term business intelligence (BI). A typical definition is that "BI is a broad category of applications, technologies, and processes for gathering, storing, accessing, and analyzing data to help business users make better decisions" (Watson, 2014). With this definition, BI can be viewed as an umbrella term for all applications that support decision making, and this is how it is interpreted in industry and, increasingly, in academia. BI evolved from DSS, and one could argue that analytics evolved from BI (at least in terms of terminology). Thus, analytics is an umbrella term for data analysis applications. BI can also be viewed as "getting data in" (to a data mart or warehouse) and "getting data out" (analyzing the data that is stored). A second interpretation of analytics is that it is the "getting data out" part of BI. The third interpretation is that analytics is the use of "rocket science" algorithms (e.g., machine learning, neural networks) to analyze data. These different takes on analytics do not normally cause much confusion, because the context usually makes the meaning clear (Mkrttchian et al, 2011-2017). It is useful to distinguish between three kinds of analytics because the differences have implications for the technologies and architectures used for big data analytics. Some types of analytics are better performed on some platforms than on others (Watson, 2014). Descriptive analytics, such as reporting/OLAP, dashboards/scorecards, and data visualization, have been widely used for some time, and are the core applications of traditional BI. Descriptive analytics are backward looking (like a car's rear view mirror) and reveal what has occurred. One trend, however, is to include the findings from predictive analytics, such as forecasts of future sales, on dashboards/scorecards (Watson, 2014). Predictive analytics suggest what will occur in the future (like looking through a car's windshield). The methods and algorithms for predictive analytics such as regression analysis, machine learning, and neural networks have existed for some time. Recently, however, software products such as SAS Enterprise Miner have made them much easier to understand and use. They have also been integrated into specific applications, such as for campaign management. Marketing is the target for many predictive analytics applications; here the goal is to better understand customers and their needs and preferences (Watson, 2014). Some people also refer to exploratory or discovery analytics, although these are just other names for predictive analytics. When these terms are used, they normally refer to finding relationships in big data that were not previously known. The ability to analyze new data sources—that is, big data—creates additional opportunities for insights and is especially important for firms with massive amounts of customer data. Golden path analysis is a new and interesting predictive or discovery analytics technique. It involves the analysis of large quantities of behavioral data (i.e., data associated with the activities or actions of people) to identify patterns of events or activities that foretell customer actions such as not renewing a cell phone contract, closing a checking account, or abandoning an electronic shopping cart. When a company can predict a behavior, it can intercede, perhaps with an offer, and possibly change the anticipated behavior (Watson, 2014). Whereas predictive analytics tells you what will happen, prescriptive analytics suggests what to do (like a car's GPS instructions). Prescriptive analytics can identify optimal solutions, often for the allocation of scarce resources. It, too, has been researched in academia for a long time but is now finding wider use in practice. For example, the use of mathematical programming for revenue management is increasingly common for organizations that have "perishable" goods such as rental cars, hotel rooms, and airline seats. For example, Harrah's Entertainment, a leader in the use of analytics, has been using revenue management for hotel room pricing for many years (Watson, 2014). Organizations typically move from descriptive to predictive to prescriptive analytics. Another way of describing this progression is: What happened? Why did it happen? What will happen? How can we make it happen? This progression is normally seen in various BI and analytics maturity models (Watson, 2014). There is no formula for choosing the right platforms; however, the most important considerations include the volume, velocity, and variety of data; the applications that will use the platform; that the users are; and whether the required processing is batch or real time. Some work may require the integrated use of multiple platforms. The final choices ultimately come down to where the required work can be done at the lowest cost (Watson, 2014). For our goal is good Triple H Avatar an Avatar-based Software Platform for HHH University, Sydney, Australia (Mkrttchian et al, 2011-2017).

FUTURE RESEARCH DIRECTION AND CONCLUSIONS

- Blockchains will fundamentally shift how we deal with transactions in general, and therefore how organizations manage their business processes within their network.
- Discussion of challenges in relation to the digital economy processes management lifecycle and beyond points to seven major future research directions. For some of them we expect viable insights to emerge sooner, for others later. The order loosely reflects how soon such insights might appear.
- The digital economy processes management and the Information Systems community have a unique opportunity to help shape this fundamental shift towards a distributed, trustworthy infrastructure to promote inter-organizational processes.

With this article we aim to provide clarity, focus, and impetus for the research challenges in future that are upon us.

1. Developing a diverse set of execution and monitoring systems on blockchain. Research in this area will have to demonstrate the feasibility of using blockchains for process-aware information systems. Among others, design science and algorithm engineering will be required here. Insights from software engineering and distributed systems will be informative.
2. Devising new methods for analysis and engineering business processes based on blockchain technology. Research in this topic area will have to investigate how blockchain-based pro-cesses can be efficiently specified and deployed. Among others, formal research methods and design science will be required to study this topic. Insights from software engineering and database research will be informative here.
3. Redesigning processes to leverage the opportunities granted by blockchain. Research in this context will have to investigate how blockchain may allow re-imagining specific processes and the collaboration with external stakeholders. The whole area of choreographies may be re-vitalized by this technology. Among others, design science will be required here. Insights from operations management and organizational science will be informative.
4. Defining appropriate methods for evolution and adaptation. Research in this area will have to investigate the potential guarantees that can be made for certain types of evolution and adaptation. Among others, formal research methods will be required here. Insights from theoretical computer science and verification will be informative.
5. Developing techniques for identifying, discovering, and analyzing relevant processes for the adoption of blockchain technology. Research on this topic will have to investigate which characteristics of blockchain as a technology best meet requirements of specific processes. Among others, empirical research methods and design science will be required. Insights from management science and innovation research will be informative here.
6. Understanding the impact on strategy and governance of blockchains, in particular regarding new business and governance models enabled by revolutionary innovation based on blockchain. Research in this topic area will have to study which processes in an enterprise setting could be onoverganized differently using blockchain and which consequences this brings. Among others, empirical research methods will be required to investigate this topic. Insights from organizational science and business research will be informative.
7. Investigating the culture shift towards openness in the management and execution of business processes, and on hiring as well as upskilling people as needed. Research in this topic area will have to investigate how corporate culture changes with the introduction of blockchains, and in how far this differs from the adoption of other technologies. Among others, empirical methods will be required for research in this area. Insights from organizational science and business research will be informative.

ACKNOWLEDGMENT

The reported study was funded by RFBR according to the research project No. 18-010-00204_a.

REFERENCES

Bershadsky, A., Bozhday, A., Evseeva, J., Gudkov, A., & Mkrtchian, V. (2017), Techniques for Adaptive Graphics Applications Synthesis Based on Variability Modeling Technology and Graph Theory. In *Proceedings of CIT&DS 2017*, (pp. 169–179). Springer International Publishing AG. DOI: 10.1007/978-3-319-65551-2_33

Bershadsky, A., Evseeva, J., Bozhday, A., Gudkov, A., & Mkrtchian, V. (2015), Variability modeling in the automated system for authoring intelligent adaptive applications on the basis of three-dimensional graphics. In *Proceedings of CIT&DS 2015* (pp. 149–159). Springer International Publishing AG. DOI: 10.1007/978-3-319-23766-4

Glotova, T., Deev, M., Krevskiy, I., Matukin, S., Mkrttchian, V., & Sheremeteva, E. (2015), Individualized learning trajectories using distance education technologies. In *Proceedings of CIT&DS 2015*, (pp. 778–793). Springer International Publishing AG. DOI: 10.1007/978-3-319-23766-4

Mendling, J. (2018). Blockchains for Business Process Management - Challenges and Opportunities. *ACM Trans. Manag. Inform. Syst., 9*.

Mkrttchian, V. (2011). Use 'hhh" technology in transformative models of online education. In G. Kurubacak & T. Vokan Yuzer (Eds.), *Handbook of research on transformative online education and liberation: Models for social equality* (pp. 340–351). Hershey, PA: IGI Global. doi:10.4018/978-1-60960-046-4.ch018

Mkrttchian, V. (2012). Avatar manager and student reflective conversations as the base for describing meta-communication model. In G. Kurubacak, T. Vokan Yuzer, & U. Demiray (Eds.), *Meta-communication for reflective online conversations: Models for distance education* (pp. 340–351). Hershey, PA: IGI Global. doi:10.4018/978-1-61350-071-2.ch005

Mkrttchian, V., & Aleshina, E. (2017). *Sliding Mode in Intellectual Control and Communication: Emerging Research and Opportunities*. Hershey, PA: IGI Global. doi:10.4018/978-1-5225-2292-8

Mkrttchian, V., & Aleshina, E. (2017a). The Sliding Mode Technique and Technology (SM T&T) According to Vardan Mkrttchian in Intellectual Control(IC). In *Sliding Mode in Intellectual Control and Communication: Emerging Research and Opportunities* (pp. 1–9). Hershey, PA: IGI Global. doi:10.4018/978-1-5225-2292-8.ch001

Mkrttchian, V., & Aleshina, E. (2017b). Sliding Mode in Virtual Communications. In *Sliding Mode in Intellectual Control and Communication: Emerging Research and Opportunities* (pp. 10–21). Hershey, PA: IGI Global. doi:10.4018/978-1-5225-2292-8.ch002

Mkrttchian, V., & Aleshina, E. (2017c). Sliding Mode in Real Communication. In *Sliding Mode in Intellectual Control and Communication: Emerging Research and Opportunities* (pp. 22–29). Hershey, PA: IGI Global. doi:10.4018/978-1-5225-2292-8.ch003

Mkrttchian, V., & Aleshina, E. (2017d). Digital Control Models of Continuous Education of Persons with Disabilities Act (IDEA) and Agents in Sliding Mode. In *Sliding Mode in Intellectual Control and Communication: Emerging Research and Opportunities* (pp. 31–62). Hershey, PA: IGI Global. doi:10.4018/978-1-5225-2292-8.ch004

Mkrttchian, V., & Aleshina, E. (2017e). Terms of Adaptive Organization of the Educational Process of Persons with Disabilities with the Use of Open and Distance Learning Technologies (Open and Distance Learning – ODL). In *Sliding Mode in Intellectual Control and Communication: Emerging Research and Opportunities* (pp. 63–69). Hershey, PA: IGI Global. doi:10.4018/978-1-5225-2292-8.ch005

Mkrttchian, V., & Aleshina, E. (2017f). Providing Quality Education for Persons With Disabilities Through the Implementation of Individual Educational Programs Managed by the Intelligent Agents in the Sliding Mode. In *Sliding Mode in Intellectual Control and Communication: Emerging Research and Opportunities* (pp. 70–76). Hershey, PA: IGI Global. doi:10.4018/978-1-5225-2292-8.ch006

Mkrttchian, V., & Aleshina, E. (2017g). Regulation of Discourse in Accordance With the Speech Regulation Factors Creating Conditions for Adaptability to the Situation. In *Sliding Mode in Intellectual Control and Communication: Emerging Research and Opportunities* (pp. 77–85). Hershey, PA: IGI Global. doi:10.4018/978-1-5225-2292-8.ch007

Mkrttchian, V., & Aleshina, E. (2017h). Complex Social, Medical, Psychological, and Educational Support for People with Disability Act (IDEA). In *Sliding Mode in Intellectual Control and Communication: Emerging Research and Opportunities* (pp. 86–90). Hershey, PA: IGI Global. doi:10.4018/978-1-5225-2292-8.ch008

Mkrttchian, V., & Aleshina, E. (2017i). Tolerance as Reflection of Sliding Mode in Psychology. In Sliding Mode in Intellectual Control and Communication: Emerging Research and Opportunities (pp. 91–99). Hershey, PA: IGI Global/ doi:10.4018/978-1-5225-2292-8.ch009

Mkrttchian, V., Amirov, D., & Belyanina, L. (2017). Optimizing an Online Learning Course Using Automatic Curating in Sliding Mode. In N. Ostashewski, J. Howell, & M. Cleveland-Innes (Eds.), *Optimizing K-12 Education through Online and Blended Learning* (pp. 213–224). Hershey, PA: IGI Global. doi:10.4018/978-1-5225-0507-5.ch011

Mkrttchian, V., Aysmontas, B., Uddin, M., Andreev, A., & Vorovchenko, N. (2015). The Academic views from Moscow Universities of the Cyber U-Learning on the Future of Distance Education at Russia and Ukraine. In G. Eby & T. Vokan Yuzer (Eds.), *Identification, Evaluation, and Perceptions of Distance Education Experts* (pp. 32–45). Hershey, PA: IGI Global. doi:10.4018/978-1-4666-8119-4.ch003

Mkrttchian, V., Bershadsky, A., Bozhday, A., & Fionova, L. (2015). Model in SM of DEE Based on Service Oriented Interactions at Dynamic Software Product Lines. In G. Eby & T. Vokan Yuzer (Eds.), *Identification, Evaluation, and Perceptions of Distance Education Experts* (pp. 230–247). Hershey, PA: IGI Global. doi:10.4018/978-1-4666-8119-4.ch014

Mkrttchian, V., Kataev, M., Hwang, W., Bedi, S., & Fedotova, A. (2014). Using Plug-Avatars "hhh" Technology Education as Service-Oriented Virtual Learning Environment in Sliding Mode. In G. Eby & T. Vokan Yuzer (Eds.), *Emerging Priorities and Trends in Distance Education: Communication, Pedagogy, and Technology*. Hershey, PA: IGI Global. doi:10.4018/978-1-4666-5162-3.ch004

Mkrttchian, V., Kataev, M., Hwang, W., Bedi, S., & Fedotova, A. (2016). Using Plug-Avatars "hhh" Technology Education as Service-Oriented Virtual Learning Environment in Sliding Mode. In Leadership and Personnel Management: Concepts, Methodologies, Tools, and Applications (pp. 890-902). Hershey, PA: IGI Global. Doi:10.4018/978-1-4666-9624-2.ch039

Mkrttchian, V., & Stephanova, G. (2013). Training of Avatar Moderator in Sliding Mode Control. In G. Eby & T. Vokan Yuzer (Eds.), *Project Management Approaches for Online Learning Design* (pp. 175–203). Hershey, PA: IGI Global. doi:10.4018/978-1-4666-2830-4.ch009

Mkrttchian, V., & Stephanova, G. (2013). Training of Avatar Moderator in Sliding Mode Control Environment for Virtual Project Management. In Enterprise Resource Planning: Concepts, Methodologies, Tools, and Applications (pp. 1376-1405). Hershey, PA: IGI Global. Doi:10.4018/978-1-4666-4153-2.ch074

Watson, H. J. (2014). Tutorial: Big Data Analytics: Concepts, Technologies, and Applications. *Communications of the Association for Information Systems*, *34*, 65. doi:10.17705/1CAIS.03465

Chapter 7
Using Excel and Excel VBA for Preliminary Analysis in Big Data Research

Paul John Blayney
University of Sydney, Australia

Zhaohao Sun
https://orcid.org/0000-0003-0780-3271
Papua New Guinea University of Technology, Papua New Guinea

ABSTRACT

Can big data research be effectively conducted using spreadsheet software (i.e., Microsoft Excel)? While a definitive response might be closer to "no" rather than "yes," this question cannot be unequivocally answered. As spreadsheet scholars, the authors' inclination is to answer in the positive. To this regard, the chapter looks at how Excel can be used in conjunction with other software and analytical techniques in big data research. This chapter also argues where and how to use spreadsheet software to conduct big data research. A focal argument of this chapter is that the key behind big data driven research is data cleansing and big data driven small data analysis. The proposed approach in this chapter might facilitate the research and development of intelligent big data analytics, big data analytics, and business intelligence.

1. INTRODUCTION

Trained programmers are competent with programming methods and design. They are not generally proficient in Big Data analysis (Raffensperger, 2001, p. 62). On the other hand, Big Data researchers do not necessarily possess programming skills. Spreadsheet software (e.g. Excel) provides a means for the non-programmer to conduct analysis that could previously only performed by a trained programmer or analyst.

DOI: 10.4018/978-1-5225-7277-0.ch007

Most Big Data analysts will be skeptical with the use of Excel for Big Data analysis. They will highlight that the volume, velocity and variety of Big Data far exceeds the capacity of spreadsheet software (Sun, Sun, & Strang, 2018). They're right from several perspectives. However, this chapter attempts to address the following research questions?

1. Have spreadsheets a place in Big Data research?
2. How can programming with Excel VBA contribute?
3. How can the Excel Power Pivot add-in contribute?

This paper does not suggest that spreadsheet software can replace the advanced analytical techniques used for Big Data analytics. However, it does propose that spreadsheets have a place in Big Data in the same way that the apps on your phone have a place in your everyday life. Modern day apps are useful because they're easy to use and readily available. They provide you with useful information on a real-time basis (i.e. when you don't have time to investigate properly or talk to an expert).

The research demonstrates that Excel (especially when supplemented with its Power Pivot add-in) can fill the same role in Big Data analytics. Spreadsheet analysis can provide valuable insights as to what advanced analytics are appropriate.

For example, preliminary testing can be conducted on a subset of the 50 terabytes (TB) of web server logs that an Internet Service Provider CEO wants looked at for the latest trends in customer demands for the company's products (Department of Communication and the Arts, 2018).

Skilled use of Excel will allow better use of the Big Data analyst scarce resource; that valuable analyst time is not wasted exploring "futile" data (i.e. data without significant relationships).

A word of caution is warranted prior to using spreadsheet software for preliminary Big Data (e.g. small data) analysis. While the benefits (in business and other) provided by spreadsheet use are substantial and immeasurable; the costs of spreadsheet errors are also huge and well publicised. For example, see Butler (2018).

To this regard, frightening or entertaining reading (depending on your point of view) is provided by the European Spreadsheet Risks Interest Group (EuSpRIG, n.d.-b). This non-profit organisation of academics and business professionals proclaim their website (www.eusprig.org/) as *"the World's premier site for information, action, conferences and dialogue on Spreadsheet Risk Management"*. One of the links provided on the EuSpRIG homepage is "Horror Stories" (EuSpRIG, n.d.-a).

Many of the spreadsheet errors cited in these stories can be argued to be human error. However, it can also be ascertained that spreadsheet software has been largely responsible for enabling the human error to take place. As elucidated by Ray Panko (1998) most spreadsheets contain errors - "the issue is how many errors there are, not whether an error exists". Therefore, the task for the Big Data analyst is to apply standard organisational programming development principles to their use of spreadsheets.

Much of what Plauger (1993) writes about programming is equally applicable to Big Data analysis. The protocols and regimes described by Plauger are not unique to computer programming. These conventions are general principles that can and should be followed for the successful execution of any complex task; be it organising your daughter's 21st birthday party or conducting Big Data analysis. The Big Data analyst is well advised to follow Plauger's protocols at all times, including the performance of small data analysis with spreadsheet software.

The primary goal of this chapter is a Big Data analyst's version of Plauger's (1993), p. 7) objective with computer programs. It hopes to add the Excel spreadsheet and Excel VBA to the Big Data analysts' repertoire.

"My goal in writing this premiere essay is to convince you that no one tool is best … to introduce you to the many tools … show you where you can use it … show you where it is not at its best or where you should not use it at all."

Plauger (1993, p. 63) reinforces the above assertion later in his book with further support for a multi-tooled analytical approach.

… can't see beyond their favourite tools. What is needed, clearly, is a healthy assortment of methods, plus some guidelines for choosing the right one at the right time.

Excel's low set-up cost for the performance of complex analysis is a double-edged sword. While untrained analysts can produce accurate results with extraordinary efficiency they may also generate output with significant errors with similar efficacy. These analysts will extoll the virtues of spreadsheet use given the ease with which they can adapt their model to deal with new data types or changing user requirements / requests. However, the spreadsheet's adaptability has a downside as a model will tend to grow in complexity and suffer a degradation of structure and integrity.

The Big Data analyst must be aware of not falling into the common trap with spreadsheet use. That is, to have their "scratch pad" of spreadsheet calculations grow into a complex model used to generate important analytics. And because it was a scratch pad proper development protocols have not been followed

This paper provides a description of procedures and methods to achieve the best of both worlds. That is, a world where the analyst does not require months or years of training with analytical procedures and design methodology. The "Excel trained Big Data analyst" will possess skills that emulate the competencies of a trained specialist and eliminate many of the errors that non-programmers tend to make.

The remainder of this chapter is organised as follows. The second section provides an overview of how small data analysis can contribute to Big Data analytics. Section 3 proffers an outline of good spreadsheet methods and the use of Excel's built-in analytical and statistical functions. This section includes Power Pivot. The fourth section delivers an introduction to Excel VBA (Visual Basic for Applications) – the programming language secreted behind the Excel worksheet.

However, data analytics is a new form of data analysis empowered by the current information communication technology (ICT) and Web technology. (Sun, Sun, & Strang, 2018) (Sun & Wang, 2017)

Many recognise Excel as one of the software applications traditionally used for financial analysis (Sun, Sun, & Strang, 2018).

…data analysis has been in the field of business and management for decades. For example, it has been offered as a course with Microsoft Excel or IBM SPSS in undergraduate programs of business for decades worldwide …

2. BIG DATA DERIVED SMALL DATA ANALYSIS

Big data derived small data analysis is important both for a big data approach and for big data analytics as a discipline. There are manifold reasons. First of all, big data has basically been controlled by global data giants such as Facebook, Google, Tencent, Baidu and Alibaba rather than by individual scholars. It is expensive for a scholar to collect and analyse Big Data. It can also be very expensive for a company like Cambridge Analytica to collect data working together with Facebook, e.g. Cambridge Analytica paid a big price through its bankruptcy (Baker, 2018).

Secondly, sampling is the process of collecting some data when collecting it all or analyzing it all is unreasonable (National Research Council, 2013, p. 120). Sampling is a component of any statistical modelling process. The implication from this is that the majority of statistical inferences are based on reasoning from incomplete knowledge or data. Therefore, any statistical modelling or inference is a kind of big data derived small data analysis and reasoning (National Research Council, 2013, p. 120).

From a data processing viewpoint, the largest data analyses will be performed in large data centres of a few global data monopolies running specialized software such as Hadoop over HDFS to harness thousands of cores to process data distributed throughout the cluster (National Research Council, 2013, p. 55). This means that individuals must use big data derived small data analysis to analyse big data.

3. SECTION I: THE ART OF USING EXCEL

This section provides a general description of procedures and methods that are applicable for any serious use of spreadsheet software. Various Excel features that are especially applicable for Big Data analysis are described. A discussion of Excel's Power Pivot add-in is included in this section while Excel VBA (Visual Basic for Applications) is the topic of Section 4.

3.1 Basic Spreadsheet Design and Procedures

Spreadsheet model development is like traditional programming in more than one respect (Walkenbach, 2010, p. 111). Formula creation in Excel is a type of programming.

Virtually every successful spreadsheet application uses formulas. In fact, constructing formulas can certainly be construed as a type of "programming". (Walkenbach, 2002, p. 37)

The typical first step in the software development process is the recognition that all programs can be reduced to IPO [software engineering] - the programming acronym for:

- Inputs
- Processing (steps required to generate the desired outputs)
- Outputs

While spreadsheet models are sometimes criticised by traditional programmers for combining the processing and output components (and thus confusing matters), the IPO model is still a useful starting point in structured systems analysis (Pressman & Maxim, 2014).

Good data is critical for all spreadsheet models. However, expert analysts concentrate their efforts on the structure of their model, not with the search for and analysis of data. Novice analysts will frequently spend a lot of time searching for and analysing data. Better or more accurate data doesn't necessarily mean that the model's outputs will be better. It is essential to remember that modelling is about forecasting the future. Data is past tense (i.e. history) which may be useful for predicting future events but maybe not (Sun, Sun, & Strang, 2018). The analyst should spend most of their time developing an appropriate model structure (e.g. accurate and logical formulas). And less time pursuing that elusive "perfect" data.

3.2 Cell Referenced Formulas (No Hard Coding)

The hard coding of input data or constants into spreadsheet formulas is widely recognised as poor model design (van der Aalst, ter Hofstede, & Weske, 2003, p. 15). However, the importance of avoiding such design defect errors appears to be underestimated as there is not an immediate error and there may never be one. The fact that many models fail to follow this basic software design principle is almost certainly a major contributor to the incidence of spreadsheet errors and the lack of reusability of many models.

Powell and Baker (2004, p. 97) provide an excellent explanation of why it is important to isolate input data or parameters.

A common source of errors in spreadsheets is the tendency to bury parameters in cell formulas and to replicate the same parameter in multiple cells. This makes identifying parameters difficult, because they are not immediately visible. It's also difficult to know whether all numerical values of a parameter have been changed each time an update is required. By contrast, the habit of using a single and separate location considerably streamlines the building and debugging of a spreadsheet.

The problem of hard coding of values into formulae has an equivalence in traditional programming and VBA where a well-constructed program would rarely (never?) enter a value (a number) into a line of executable code. The recommended programming technique is to assign the desired value to a named variable (e.g. RedFont = 3) and use this variable in the program code (Pressman & Maxim, 2014). This can be contrasted to the inferior design that would simply type the value 3 into a line of code. The prevalence of such inferior design practices is caused by the practice being quicker in the short run as the developer avoids to create a variable and assign a value to it. The resulting 'magic number' in the code makes programs more difficult to read, understand, and maintain".

3.3 Logical Functions: IF's, Nested IF's, AND's AND OR's

The Formulas tab provides access to Excel's Function Library – an extensive collection of mathematical, financial, statistical and other ready-made functions. This chapter introduces the extremely powerful and versatile group of Logical functions.

3.4 Modularisation

Powell and Baker (2004) provide a standard set of steps for engineering a spreadsheet model in the typical recommended layout. The basic steps recommended by these authors is use of the concept of modularisation to separate data (inputs), decision variables, detailed calculations (processing) and

Figure 1. Formula tab function library

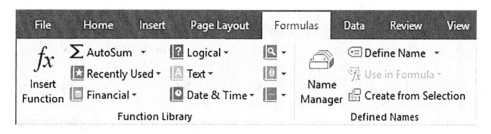

outcome measures (output). They emphasise the importance of isolating input data or input parameters in a specific location in the model (e.g. a designated range of cells for small models or a separate data worksheet in a large model).

Modularisation is an appropriate solution with complex modeling problems because the individual components (modules) are easier to understand and to work with than the whole. The process of modularisation also requires the analyst to plan the overall project and then to focus effort on one area at a time. The experienced analyst will also find that some modules can be used in other models with only minor changes. This reusability of modules can result in huge savings in development time as the experienced analyst doesn't have to start from scratch even with a totally novel modeling job.

The concept of breaking up a complex model into smaller, self-contained bits can also be applied to individual spreadsheet formula (Walkenbach, 2010, p. 54). Poor spreadsheet technique attempts to all components of a complicated formula in a single cell. It is much easier and better to do preliminary calculations in separate cells (Powell & Baker, 2004, p.97). It is good spreadsheet practice to break up your complicated formulas into many simple ones. It is much easier to "debug" such calculations. Debugging is also greatly assisted by a model that has separate areas (e.g. worksheets) for various components of the model.

Reusability of code is certainly one of the basic concepts of traditional programming that is partially achieved by the separation of data inputs from processing and outputs (Pressman & Maxim, 2014).

The idea of breaking up a complicated task into smaller chunks might be seen simply as common sense (Pressman & Maxim, 2014). However, this concept is also strongly supported by considerable research in education in cognitive load theory.

Cognitive load theory identifies the key component of a task's complexity as element interactivity; being the degree to which the task depends on another factor(s) that must be considered simultaneously (Sweller, 2010). Such interactivity is intrinsic to the task and cannot effectively be altered. However, the separation of the overall task into a few less complex components will lessen the difficulty of understanding the overall task.

The applicability of cognitive load theory in this context of this paper is illustrated by Van Merriënboer and Krammer's (1987, p. 256) description of the outcomes provided using a structured programming language.

Especially well-structured languages should make a top-down approach feasible because they facilitate breaking down large programming tasks into smaller subtasks.

3.5 The IF Function

The IF function allows you to ask a question about a value or label on your spreadsheet (e.g. is cell C5 greater than 50) and return a certain result if True (e.g. Pass) or another result if False (e.g. Fail). You must of course get the syntax correct. You can use the IF function dialogue box provided by **Formulas -> Logical -> IF** as shown in Figure 2 or you can simply enter your IF function by typing directly to the desired cell as you would for any other function.

Start with *=IF(* and then the function arguments. Proper syntax for the example described above is *=IF(C5>50,"Pass","Fail")* Note the commas separating the "question" or "logical test" C5>50, the True value "Pass" and the False value "Fail". Also note the opening & closing parentheses and the double quotations around the Pass and Fail results.

3.6 Demonstration of Logical Function With the Balance Sheet

A simple use of the IF function is a check that the balance sheet is in balance. Figure 3 has used the IF function dialogue box to enter such a check. My preference is to type my IF functions directly to cells. However, the dialogue box has a couple of features that you may like.

As you provide entries for each of the three IF function arguments (i.e. Logical test, True value and False value) you are provided with an indicator of the result of your entry. E.g. the Logical test returns a True result as the Total Net Assets value of $128,973 in cell J33 is equal to the Total Owners' Equity value in cell J38.

The True value is set to return the contents of cell H42 which contains the text string *"Great. Balance sheet is in balance"*. The False value has been entered as a text entry to the dialogue box. An indication of the result of the IF function is provided. E.g. *Great. Balance sheet is in balance.* This is what will be displayed in cell I32, the cell where the formula shown here has been entered (via the dialogue box).

Figure 2. IF function dialogue box

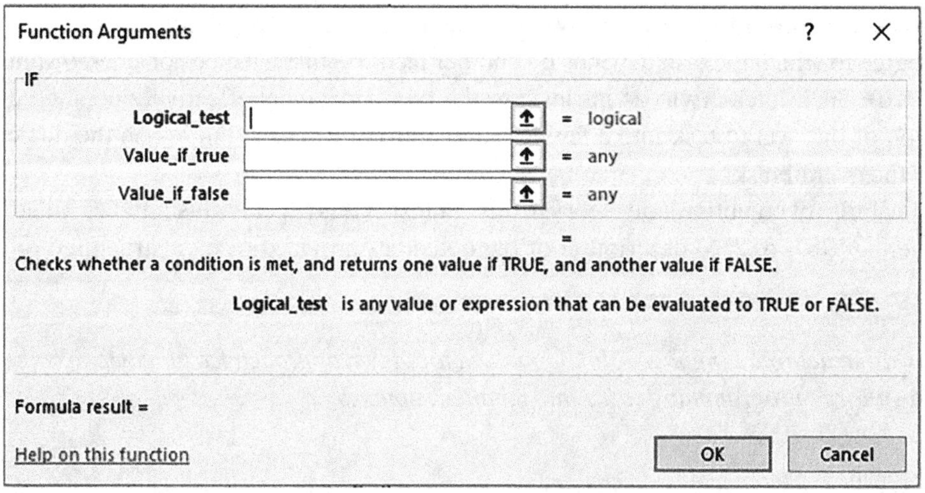

Figure 3. IF function to check that balance sheet is in balance

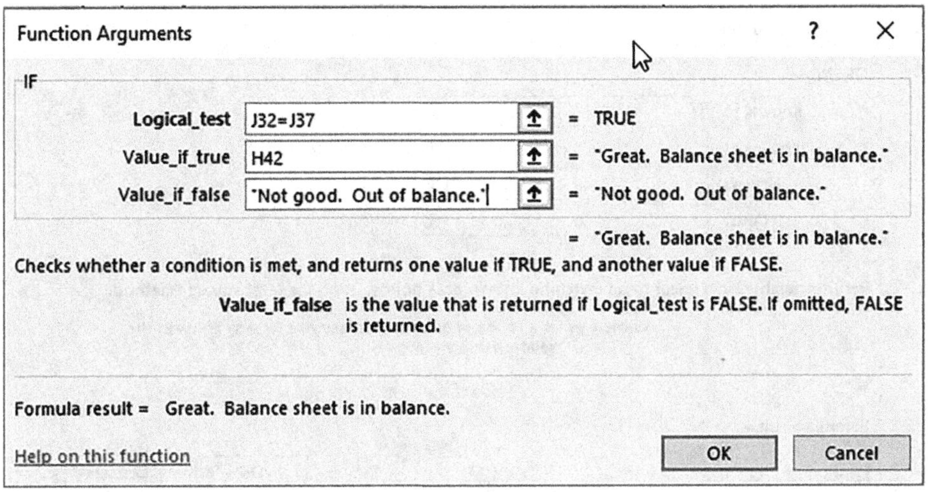

3.7 Excel Statistical Functions

The Excel spreadsheet provides a wide range of statistical functions (more than 100). Big Data analysts are provided with a complete assortment of descriptive statistics (e.g. Average, Maximum, Minimum, Standard Deviation) together with a variety of Inferential statistics (e.g. Least Squares Regression, Chi Square, F Test, T Test).

Excel's built in statistical functions are available to the Big Data analyst through the Formulas menu tab or to the experienced user by typing the name of the statistical function []. For example, typing *=TREND()* accesses an inferential statistical function that "returns numbers in a linear trend matching known data points, using the least squares method".

An advantage of using the Formulas menu tab to access functions is the informational dialogue box provided to assist entry of the various data required for the requested statistic. Figure 4 provides an illustration of the dialogue box provided for the TREND function.

3.8 Using Excel Data Filters

Excel provides some very useful features for filtering information through the Data tab. The "Sort & Filter" options are provided in the middle area of the Data tab (see Figure 5). Each of these methods require the user to highlight the data to be sorted or filtered before selecting Sort or Filter.

The highlighted area in the above figure will work nicely if the user wants to sort the income statement expense categories. With such sorting it is crucial that all relevant columns are included in the sort area, e.g. not good to sort just one column of values.

Use of the Filter option from the Data tab requires inclusion of a "header row" as this option designates the top row of your selection as a header row of titles that will not be filtered. Excel will allow you to specify a blank row for your header. E.g. the row above ... *Selling & marketing expenses 240,100 207,340.*

Figure 4. Dialogue box provided for TREND function

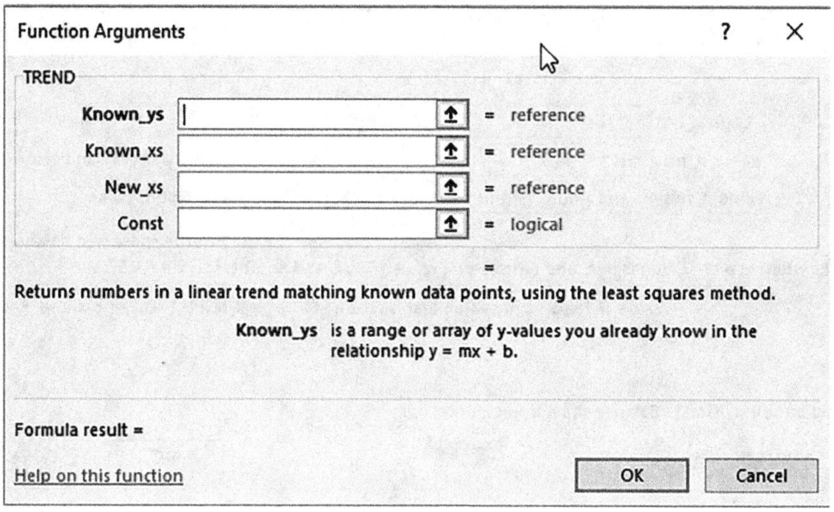

Figure 5. Sort and filter options within the "data" tab with highlighting of range to be sorted

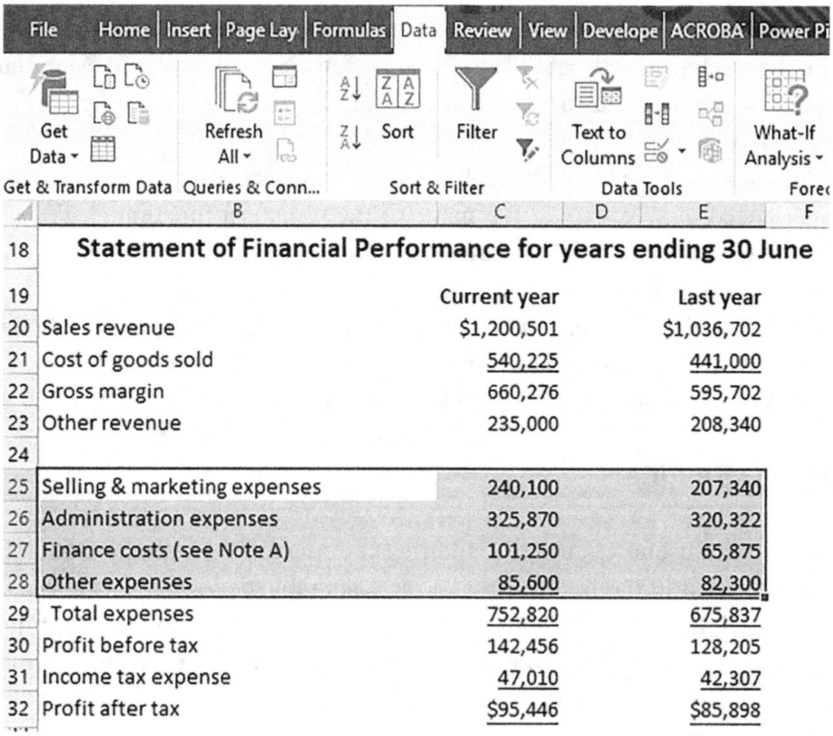

	B	C	D	E	F
18	Statement of Financial Performance for years ending 30 June				
19		Current year		Last year	
20	Sales revenue	$1,200,501		$1,036,702	
21	Cost of goods sold	540,225		441,000	
22	Gross margin	660,276		595,702	
23	Other revenue	235,000		208,340	
24					
25	Selling & marketing expenses	240,100		207,340	
26	Administration expenses	325,870		320,322	
27	Finance costs (see Note A)	101,250		65,875	
28	Other expenses	85,600		82,300	
29	Total expenses	752,820		675,837	
30	Profit before tax	142,456		128,205	
31	Income tax expense	47,010		42,307	
32	Profit after tax	$95,446		$85,898	

The Data Filter output shown in Figure 6 shows the filter drop-downs that are added to each of the header row cells. You may also note that the label "Account names" has been added to cell B9. This is strictly a cosmetic addition to make it more obvious what data are being filtered in this column.

A more important change to the spreadsheet is the insertion of a blank row (row 14) after "Other expenses". This is necessary due to the Data Filter feature that includes data until a blank cell is found in the first column being filtered. Our blank row 14 serves to end the data filter area at row 13. Selection of the drop-down arrow in cell B9 provides the dialogue box shown in Figure 7.

The above figure shows the variety of options provided by the filter method. In addition to sorting alphabetically, reverse alphabetically and by Colour the method provides several options within the Text Filters choice. These options are in addition to the main filter method shown in the lower portion of the Figure 7 dialogue box. In this instance the user has selected two of the available choices (i.e. Administrative expenses and Other expenses). Selecting OK at this point yields the output shown in Figure 8.

Note from the Figure 8 that the non-selected rows have been hidden (i.e. filtered) and that the drop-down arrow in the "Account names" filter header cell has been changed to a "filter" indicator.

3.9 Power Pivot

Good Big Data analysts will use a wide variety of software applications and analytical methods for both preliminary analysis of "small Big Data" and for their full-blown analytics. The Excel spreadsheet will be an excellent and appropriate software choice for performing many small data analytics, to the knowledge of the authors. However, not infrequently the Big Data analyst will be better served by supplementing

Figure 6. Output of data filter method: filter drop-downs added to top row of selection

	A	B	C	E	F
8		Other revenue	235,000	208,340	
9		**Account names** ▼	▼	▼	
10		Selling & marketing expenses	240,100	207,340	
11		Administration expenses	325,870	320,322	
12		Finance costs (see Note A)	101,250	65,875	
13		Other expenses	85,600	82,300	
14					
15		Total expenses	752,820	675,837	
16		Profit before tax	142,456	128,205	
17		Income tax expense	47,010	42,307	
18		Profit after tax	$95,446	$85,898	
19					
20		Note A: These costs relate solely to interest on the long term loan.			
21		**Other available data:**			
22		Credit sales	840,351	704,957	
23		Cash flow from operations	91,500	92,156	
24					

Figure 7. Data Filter dialogue box with filter drop-downs added to top row of selection

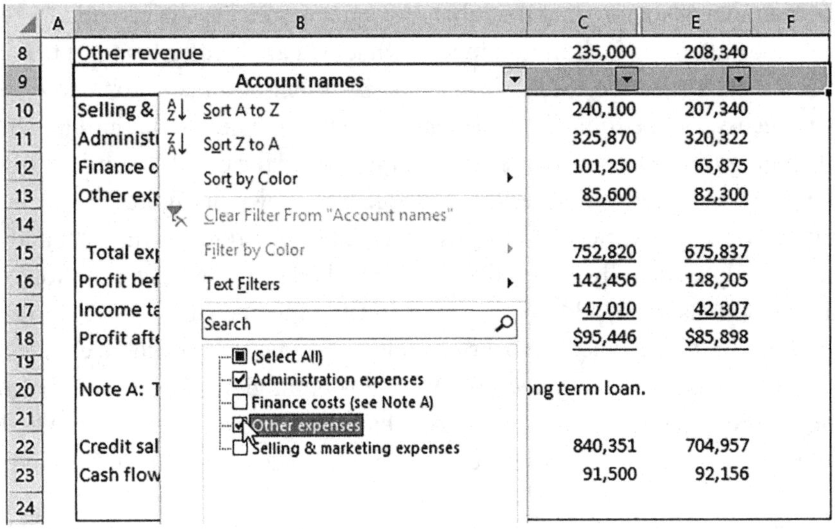

Figure 8. Final output of data filter method with hidden rows

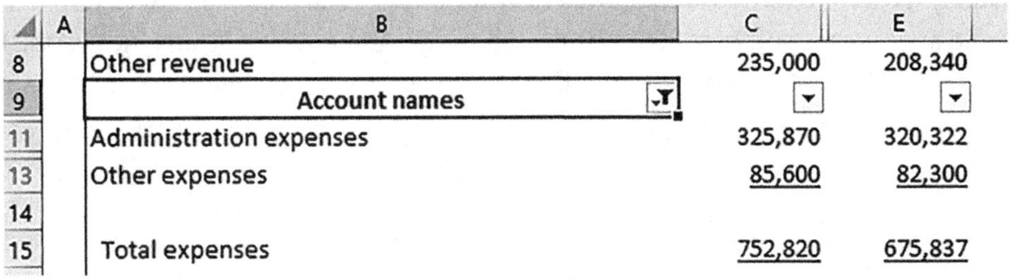

Excel with Power Pivot. Arguably (see below), this add-in provides the means for the Big Data analyst to extend their use of Excel beyond small data analysis.

Following is a summary of Microsoft's on-line description of Power Pivot (Microsoft, n.d.-b).

Power Pivot: Powerful Data Analysis and Data Modeling in Excel

Power Pivot is an Excel add-in you can use to perform powerful data analysis and create sophisticated data models.

In both Excel and in Power Pivot, you can create a Data Model, a collection of tables with relationships.

Top Features of Power Pivot for Excel

- Import millions of rows of data from multiple data sources
  - With Power Pivot for Excel, you can import millions of rows of data from multiple data sources into a single Excel workbook, create relationships between heterogeneous data, create calculated columns and measures using formulas, build PivotTables and PivotCharts, and

then further analyze the data so that you can make timely business decisions—all without requiring IT assistance.

- Enjoy fast calculations and analysis
  - ○ Process millions of rows in about the same time as thousands, and make the most of multi-core processors and gigabytes of memory for fastest processing of calculations.
- Virtually Unlimited Support of Data Sources
  - ○ Provides the foundation to import and combine source data from any location for massive data analysis on the desktop, including relational databases, multidimensional sources, cloud services, data feeds, Excel files, text files, and data from the Web.
- Data Analysis Expressions (DAX)
  - ○ DAX is a formula language that extends the data manipulation capabilities of Excel to enable more sophisticated and complex grouping, calculation, and analysis.

4. SECTION II: THE ART OF PROGRAMMING WITH VBA_

4.1 Introduction

The nature of Big Data provides insurmountable challenges for spreadsheet use by itself. The volume of transactions (e.g. millions of website transactions), the immergence of non-traditional forms of data (e.g. image based, unstructured textual) and the need to link or relate different datasets exceed the capabilities of even the most expert spreadsheeter. That is, for the spreadsheeter who doesn't know how to use Excel VBA. Unknown to most spreadsheet users is the existence of a powerful and user-friendly programming language (VBA or Visual Basic for Applications) sitting behind the Excel spreadsheet.

The competent Excel user can perform a significant amount of Big Data analysis. This amount can be increased exponentially through the mastery of some basic VBA techniques. As Excel VBA advocates the authors would propose that Big Data analysis of virtually any form could be programmed with Excel VBA. In some cases, this may not be efficient. E.g. why write VBA code to relate datasets when SQL does it better.

The answer lies with the expertise of the Big Data analyst. Do they understand SQL? If they do, the solution is obvious. Use SQL. However, other users will need to weigh the costs of learning SQL against using their preferred software (e.g. Excel and Excel/VBA).

This section of the paper describes the procedures required to access the Visual Basic Editor (VBE). Hidden behind the Excel worksheet, the VBE provides access to the VBA programming language. It then describes the Excel VBA provision of the two basic programming structures that will allow the analyst to perform Big Data analysis of virtually any size or form. Common to all programming languages are these structures: (1) Repeating of instructions (e.g. looping) and (2) Making decisions (e.g. If structures).

4.2 Getting Started With Excel VBA

Excel's macro security settings must be dealt with whenever your spreadsheet contains macros (i.e. Visual Basic code). You will receive a security warning advising you to this regard on opening of the file. Indicate your trust of the macro developer by choosing the option to Enable Content to allow you to run the macros. You should not enable macros from unknown sources.

You may have some setup work to do on your PC before you can use Excel VBA. If the DEVEL-OPER tab is displayed on the ribbon that's great. Developer provides access to VBA. If you don't see the Developer tab you need to select the FILE tab and then chose OPTIONS. Select the CUSTOMISE RIBBON option and in the Main Tabs section (right side of the screen) "tick" the box beside DEVEL-OPER. Select OK and your ribbon should now display the Developer tab." The next time you start Excel the Developer tab will be available from your spreadsheet's ribbon.

Macro security settings can be changed through the DEVELOPER tab. Select the MACRO SECU-RITY option (yellow triangle with exclamation mark) from the left side of the ribbon. Select the option to "disable all macros with notification".

In many instances the Big Data analyst will be creating their data analysis spreadsheet from scratch. Excel will allow you to create macros (e.g. write VBA code) in the default workbook file type. However, your programming code cannot be executed from the .xlsx file type. Your Excel file must be saved as a "Macro-enabled workbook".

From the DEVELOPER tab select the VISUAL BASIC option from the far left of the ribbon. The editor can also be opened with the ALT+F11 key combination and once opened can be accessed through its icon on your PC's taskbar (bottom of your monitor's screen). The VBE for a new workbook should look very similar to Figure 9.

The VBE Project Explorer is analogous to the File Explorer in Windows. It allows you to create various VBA programming objects (e.g. modules) and to navigate between them. Clicking the X in its top right corner closes the Project Explorer. You can redisplay with the View menu command (Project Explorer subcommand) or with the *CTRL+r* key combination shortcut.

Before you can write your program, you need somewhere to put your VBA code. Modules are where VBA code is stored and are easily created with the VBE Insert menu as shown in Figure 10.

The result of successfully inserting a new module is shown in Figure 11. The VBE default name of Module1 can be changed if you want through the Properties window (access with View –> Properties Window). As the VBE option to require variable declaration has been selected; the opening line of code (***Option Explicit***) in the Module1 window is automatically inserted by the VBE for all modules. Option Explicit forces you to follow the programming standard of declaring all variables that are used in your program.

Figure 9. The Visual Basic Editor for a new workbook

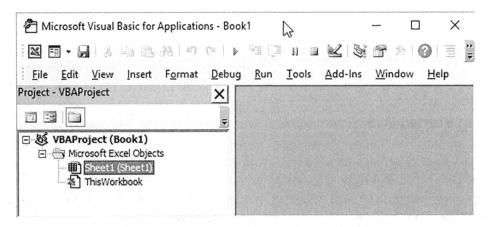

Figure 10. The Visual Basic Editor

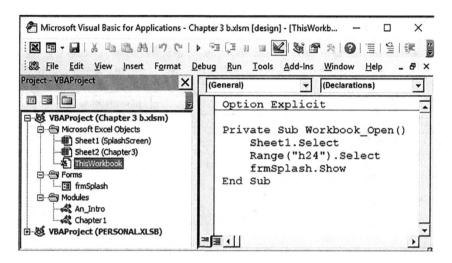

Figure 11. Inserting a module

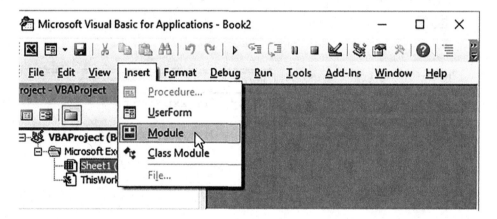

All VBA subroutines begin with the word "sub" followed by the subroutine name and "()". The conclude with the words "end sub" and contain statements or instructions to be executed in order of appearance. Figure 13 shows the creation of a new subroutine. Note that that neither "()" nor "end sub" have been entered. Pressing Enter at the point displayed in Figure 13 results in the addition of "()" and "end sub" to the new subroutine. The VBE has many features like this to aid the programmer in their entering of VBA code.

The declaration of variables is good programming practice which must be followed because of the use of *Option Explicit*. Variables are usually declared at the start of a sub by typing the word Dim as the first line of code followed by one or more variable names. Variable names can consist of both letters and numbers but must begin with a letter. Spaces and special characters are not allowed. The underscore character _ is allowed. The use of mixed case, descriptive names (e.g. VariableCost1) is highly recommended as mixed case variable names are much easier to read. Multiple declarations on the same line of code must be separated by a comma.

Figure 12. Module 1 successfully inserted

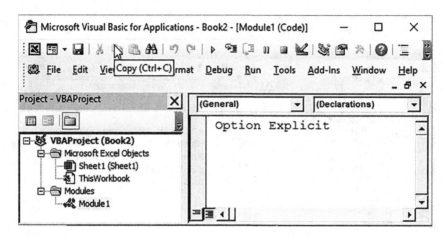

Figure 13. Start of coding for a new subroutine

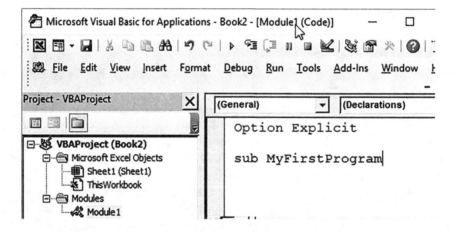

4.3 Repetition Structures: Do Loops

Repetition structures provide the analyst or programmer with a vital tool for Big Data analysis. The volume of Big Data is going to be significant or it wouldn't be Big Data. The programmer or the spreadsheeter will often want to perform identical (or nearly identical) tasks repeatedly. VBA provides several concise and efficient ways in which this can be done, one of these methods being the Do/Loop structure:

```
Do
Statement(s)
Loop
```

The loop starts at the Do. It then executes each statement until it gets to the Loop statement, which transfers execution back to the Do, and the statements are executed again. The Do/Loop can be used in the simple RevenueLoop subroutine as follows:

Figure 14. Declaration of variables

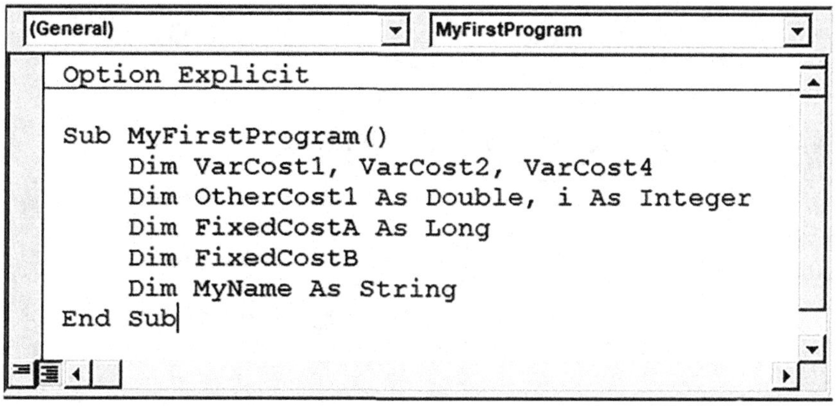

```
(General)                          ▼   MyFirstProgram                    ▼
    Option Explicit                                                      ▲

    Sub MyFirstProgram()
        Dim VarCost1, VarCost2, VarCost4
        Dim OtherCost1 As Double, i As Integer
        Dim FixedCostA As Long
        Dim FixedCostB
        Dim MyName As String
    End Sub                                                              ▼
```

Figure 15. Infinite loop subroutine

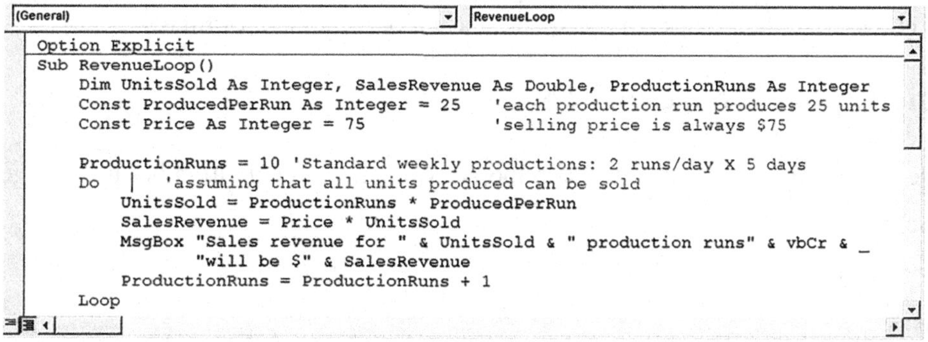

```
(General)                          ▼   RevenueLoop                       ▼
   Option Explicit                                                       ▲
   Sub RevenueLoop()
       Dim UnitsSold As Integer, SalesRevenue As Double, ProductionRuns As Integer
       Const ProducedPerRun As Integer = 25    'each production run produces 25 units
       Const Price As Integer = 75             'selling price is always $75

       ProductionRuns = 10 'Standard weekly productions: 2 runs/day X 5 days
       Do   |    'assuming that all units produced can be sold
           UnitsSold = ProductionRuns * ProducedPerRun
           SalesRevenue = Price * UnitsSold
           MsgBox "Sales revenue for " & UnitsSold & " production runs" & vbCr & _
               "will be $" & SalesRevenue
           ProductionRuns = ProductionRuns + 1
       Loop                                                              ▼
```

The RevenueLoop sub begins by declaring three variables and two constants. Constants may be used in place of variables in situations where the value of an object is not expected to change. The format used is identical to that for declaring a variable with the addition of the equals sign and the constant value. E.g. *Const Price as Integer = 75* as shown in line 4 of Figure 15. The base level of *10 ProductionRuns* is set prior to beginning the Do loop.

The loop begins by multiplying the number of production runs (which is the base level of 10 for the first iteration of the loop) times the units produced per run (i.e. the constant value of 25). The result of 250 (10 * 25) is assigned to the UnitsSold variable. The product of UnitsSold and Price is then assigned to the SalesRevenue variable.

A message box then displays the current values of the UnitsSold and SalesRevenue variables with some explanatory labels. Before getting to the Loop statement and starting all over again, the ProductionRun variable is incremented by one. Figure 16 shows the message displayed after three iterations of the Do Loop.

A somewhat obvious fault of the RevenueLoop subroutine is that it never ends! This is commonly referred to as an infinite loop. To overcome this problem, provisions must be made so that the loop is exited after a finite number of repetitions. Two different approaches are employed to terminate loops.

Figure 16. Output of RevenueLoop subroutine after 3 iterations of loop

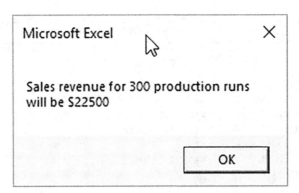

Decision loops can be terminated based on the state of a logical expression (in other words, an expression that is either true or false). In this sense, decision loops are related to decision constructs. Because such loops involve a decision, they may repeat a different number of times on every execution. In contrast, count-controlled loops are pre-set to repeat a fixed number of times.

4.4 Decision Loops (Do/If Exit) Loops

As the name Do/If Exit implies, this decision loops terminates if a condition is true. The general representation is ...

```
Do
Statement(s)
If condition Then Exit Do
Statement(s)
Loop
```

Where condition is a logical condition that tests True or False. Thus, a single-line If statement is used to exit the loop if the condition tests true. Note that, as shown, the exit can be placed in the middle of the loop (that is, with statements before and after it). Such a structure is called a mid-test loop.

If the problem required it, the exit could be placed at the very beginning of the code to create a pre-test loop. An example is:

```
Do
If x < 0 Then Exit Do
x = x - 5
Loop
```

Notice how 5 is subtracted from x on each iteration. This subtraction represents a mechanism that allows the loop to terminate eventually. Every decision loop must have such a mechanism. Otherwise, it would repeat ad infinitum.

Alternatively, the If Exit could be placed at the very end and create a post-test loop:

```
Do
x = x - 5
If x < 0 Then Exit Do
Loop
```

Each of the three loop structures are really the same. The only difference between them is the positioning of the exit; at the beginning, in the middle or at the end. Your choice will depend on the structure of your loop exit statement.

4.5 Count Controlled Loops

Although the Do/If Exit loop is certainly a feasible option for performing a specified number of iterations, such looping operations are so common that a special set of statements is available in VBA for accomplishing the same objective in a more efficient manner. Called the For/Next loop, this set of statements has the general format …

```
For counter = start To finish Step increment
Statement(s)
Next
```

Where *counter* is a numeric variable used as a loop counter, *start* is the initial value of counter, *finish* is the final value of counter, while *Step* increment is the optional argument for to alter the default increment of 1 for each loop.

The For/Next loop operates as follows: the variable counter is set at an initial value, *start*. The program then compares *counter* with the desired final value, *finish*. If counter is less than or equal to *finish*, the program executes the body of the loop. When the *Next* statement that marks the end of the loop is reached, counter is increased by *increment*, and the program loops back to the *For* statement. The process continues until *counter* becomes greater than *finish*. At this point, the loop terminates, and the program continues to the line immediately following the loop's *Next* statement.

Following in Figure 17 is the code for the RevenueLoop subroutine using a For Next loop. The comments provided within the subroutine (e.g. lines beginning with an apostrophe) explain the differences between this subroutine (using the For Next structure) and the previous sub (using the Do Loop structure). The key difference is the specification of a stopping point; in this example 15 runs as specified by the LastProductionRun variable.

Figures 18 and 19 show the message box output for the first and final iterations of the For Next loop in the RevenueLoopUsingForNext subroutine. Operation is identical to the original sub except there is now an ending point. The infinite loop problem is resolved.

4.6 Decision Structures: IF Statements

Excel VBA provides several alternate structures for the programmer to use for making decisions. Discussed here are the different forms of the IF method. Each of the IF method forms are essentially equivalent. In some cases, one of the methods is arguably preferable but essentially it comes down to programmer predilection.

Figure 17. Code for the RevenueLoop sub using a For Next loop

```
(General)                                          RevenueLoopUsingForNext

Sub RevenueLoopUsingForNext()    'same as RevenueLoop using For Next, not Do Loop
    Dim LastProductionRun As Integer
    Dim UnitsSold As Integer, SalesRevenue As Double, ProductionRuns As Integer
    Const ProducedPerRun As Integer = 25   'each production run produces 25 units
    Const Price As Integer = 75            'selling price is always $75

'We've included 'Step 1' at the end of the For statement. This is redundant as 1
' is the default step value.
'Our loop FINISH point is from the new variable LastProductionRun, set below to 15.

    ProductionRuns = 10     'START point for the loop. Also used as COUNTER.
    LastProductionRun = 15  'FINISH point for the loop.

'          Counter          Start            Finish          Step
    For ProductionRuns = ProductionRuns To LastProductionRun Step 1
        UnitsSold = ProductionRuns * ProducedPerRun
        SalesRevenue = Price * UnitsSold
        MsgBox "Sales revenue for " & UnitsSold & " production runs" & vbCr & _
            "will be $" & SalesRevenue
    Next ProductionRuns
End Sub
```

Figure 18. Output after first iteration of loop

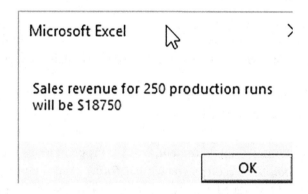

Microsoft Excel

Sales revenue for 250 production runs
will be $18750

OK

Figure 19. Output after final iteration

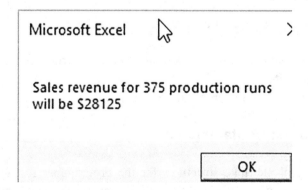

Microsoft Excel

Sales revenue for 375 production runs
will be $28125

OK

The If/Then/Else structure has the syntax

```
If condition Then
TrueStatement(s)
Else
FalseStatement(s)
End If
```

Where condition is a logical expression that evaluates to True or False, *TrueStatement(s)* are one or more statements that are executed if the condition is True, and *FalseStatement(s)* are one or more statements to be executed if the condition is False.

The simplest form of a condition is a single relational expression to compare two values, as in

```
value1 relation value2
```

Where values can be constants, variables, or expressions, and relation is one of the relational operators such as equals (=), greater than (>) or less than (<). Simple examples of conditions are

```
Mark = 100              Mark >= 75              Mark <= 50
```

An example of code that uses the If / Then / Else structure is

```
If Mark >= 50 Then
Grade = "Satisfactory"
Else
Grade = "Fail"
End If
```

You will notice the indentation of the lines of code. While not essential; it is good, standard programming practice. Indenting makes code easier to read and understand.

4.7 If /Then Single Decision Structure

In cases where there is no false alternative, the If/Then/Else structure can be simplified by dropping the Else clause, as in

```
If condition Then
TrueStatement(s)
End If
```

Following is an example using this structure. Suppose you develop a program that requires the user to enter a value for the number of units produced of an object into a worksheet cell, say, B5. The VBA code to fetch this value into your program and assign it to a variable Units can be written as:

```
Range("b5").Select
Units = ActiveCell.Value
```

   or

```
Units = Range("b5").Value                Assigns the value without moving the
cursor.
```

   or

```
Units = Range("b5")                      Relies on Value being the VBA de-
fault for Range.
```

Clearly, the number of units produced cannot be less than zero. Consequently, it would be nice to prevent the user from entering a value that was less than zero. The If/Then structure provides a neat way to detect whether a user's input contains such errors. The following code is illustrative:

```
'Error trap to prevent a negative entry.
If Units < 0 Then
MsgBox "Units cannot be less than zero. Try again."
Range("b5").Select               'moves cursor to cell B5
End                                 'terminates execution of sub
End If
```

If a positive value is entered in cell b5, the program will immediately skip to the End If statement and proceed with the remainder of the program. If an incorrect value (i.e. a negative number or zero) is entered, a message box appears indicating that "Units cannot be less …"

The preceding code does three good things from a programming point of view:

1. It provides the user with constructive feedback in the form of an error message.
2. It places the active cell at the location that needs to be fixed (b5).
3. It terminates execution of the Sub so that the user can correct the mistake and run the program again. Use of the END statement is good programming practice as it prevents further code from running after an error has occurred.

The repetition and decision structure examples have included several assignments of values to VBA variables and spreadsheet cells. Labels or strings of text can also be assigned to variables or cells with the same process. As illustrated where the text string was assigned for ice hockey legend Wayne Gretzky, it's a straightforward process. Your text string needs to be within quotations marks on the right-hand side of your equation. Your VBA variable name or spreadsheet cell is on the left-hand side and assignment is performed with the equals sign, e.g. Range("a99") = "Wayne Gretzky" will input text into cell A99 of the active worksheet of the active workbook.

4.8 Documentation

Our discussion of spreadsheet techniques in Section I is incomplete as it doesn't include a dialogue of the importance of documentation. Appropriate documentation is a critical component of both good spreadsheeting and good programming as it enables the updating of the program / spreadsheet to deal with a changing environment (e.g. new AI technology used by customers) and / or with new statistical outputs required by the analyst or the analyst's boss (e.g. "could you perform a multi-factor regression that simultaneously considers the effect of previous purchases, time of day, phase of the moon and recent success of the customer's favourite sports team as determinants of the likelihood of a current purchase"). In his essay on 'What Tool is Best?' Plauger (1993, p. 67) advises the programmer that they "must know what constitutes adequate documentation both for internal maintenance and for use by the customer".

Documentation is critical but oftentimes it is not given adequate attention. Perhaps you're one of the lucky ones who's forced to provide documentation as your organisation demands it. Or perhaps you've learned the hard way as the authors have and attempted to use a model (or even a complicated formula) a long time after creating it. And spent ages working out how it works.

The authors can speak from experience and promise that a little bit of documentation can go a long way towards increasing the future usability of your model. By someone else or by the modeler themselves. Don't fall into the other trap and convince yourself that your model is so good that it is "self-document-ing". While a well-structured and labelled model will be infinitely more usable than a "spaghetti code" abomination it will almost certainly still benefit from a few words of precise documentation.

And when's the best time to document your work? Immediately as the model is completed is alright but it is still going to be more difficult to do than if you add bits of documentation as you are creating the model. Hopefully it's extremely clear to you when you're writing the formula or line of code. It will be much less obvious in an hour/day/week. Do yourself a favour and write your documentation as you're building the model. You'll certainly thank yourself when you need to make changes in a year's time and perhaps even when you're doing the final debugging.

5. USING EXCEL, EXCEL VBA AND POWER PIVOT FOR PRELIMINARY ANALYSIS IN BIG DATA RESEARCH: A CASE STUDY OF BANKRUPTCY PREDICTION

This section uses corporate bankruptcy prediction to illustrate the use of Excel, Excel VBA and Power Pivot for performing data cleansing and small data analysis. Bankruptcy prediction is an ideal case study for our illustration in several respects.

Traditional bankruptcy research has relied on the calculation and analysis of various financial vari-ables such as current ratio, acid test and debt to equity. Determination of values for these variables for a longitudinal analysis of 10 years, 20 years or more can be efficiently conducted by any competent spreadsheet user. Previously (e.g. before Big Data) the entire analysis component of a bankruptcy re-search study could arguably have been effectively performed using spreadsheet software. Not so in the twenty-first century with the arrival of Big Data.

The arrival of Big Data and advancement in the scope of bankruptcy predictors (beyond financial variables) has caused virtually all serious bankruptcy researchers to abandon their spreadsheets for the use of statistical packages such as SPSS, SAS and R. The data provided from advanced analytical techniques such as support vector machines, neural networks and AdaBoost will initially be viewed as being inappropriate (too voluminous or varied) for spreadsheet analysis. However, this case study will illustrate that spreadsheet software still has a valuable role to play with bankruptcy prediction and in other areas.

Even without advanced data (e.g. AdaBoost) the volume and variety of information available (e.g. from stock exchange databases) for bankruptcy research is immense. Figures 20 and 21 provide a snapshot of 12 rows from an ASX database comprised of over 800,000 rows of data.

The spreadsheet trained Big Data analyst might decide that analysis for such a database might begin with use of the Data Filter method described in section 3.8. Small data analysis could then include the use of the custom auto-filter from the numbers filter option. Figure 22 illustrates the analyst's extraction of extreme data for the "Price or Bid/Ask Average" variable; i.e. prices above $120 or below $8.

Figure 23 shows an extract of the filtered data from the Figure 22 number filter. As expected the Price values in column N are either less than $8 or greater than $120. The analyst may extract this data for further analysis in another statistical package or choose to conduct further investigation within the spreadsheet model.

Preliminary spreadsheet analysis such as that just described allows the analyst (i.e. the bankruptcy researcher in this case) to quickly obtain indications of where further "serious analysis" should be focused. Just as important, the spreadsheet analysis may indicate areas of analysis that should be avoided. Appropriate preliminary analysis in Big Data research will go a long way towards at least partially solving the problem of TMI (i.e. too much information).

Small data analysis could also include the use of Power Pivot as described in Section 3.8. Most spreadsheet users and business analysts are aware of pivot tables as an efficient means of summarizing data and highlighting desired information. The Excel spreadsheet by itself provides for the creation of pivot tables. However, the limitations of Excel (e.g. 1,048,576 rows) may come into play for the Big

Figure 20. ASX (Australia Stock Exchange) data – bottom 12 rows – columns A-N

	A	B	C	D	E	F	G	H	L	M	N
1	PERMNO	Names Date	Exchange Code	Ticker Symbol	Company Name	Primary Exchange	Trading Status	CUSIP Header	Bid or Low Price	Ask or High Price	Price or Bid/Ask Average
803348	10026	04/11/2016	3	ABCD	ABCD Ltd	Q	A	46603210	102.81	117.13	113.99
803349	10026	07/11/2016	3	ABCD	ABCD Ltd	Q	A	46603210	113.195	116.83	116.59
803350	10026	08/11/2016	3	ABCD	ABCD Ltd	Q	A	46603210	115.8	117.9	115.99
803351	10026	09/11/2016	3	ABCD	ABCD Ltd	Q	A	46603210	112.9	117.6	116.85
803352	10026	10/11/2016	3	ABCD	ABCD Ltd	Q	A	46603210	105.06	116.77	116.21
803353	10026	11/11/2016	3	ABCD	ABCD Ltd	Q	A	46603210	114.69	119.16	119.01
803354	10026	14/11/2016	3	ABCD	ABCD Ltd	Q	A	46603210	118.34	120.18	119.32
803355	10026	15/11/2016	3	ABCD	ABCD Ltd	Q	A	46603210	118.535	120.115	119.32
803356	10026	16/11/2016	3	ABCD	ABCD Ltd	Q	A	46603210	118.1	122	120.8
803357	10026	17/11/2016	3	ABCD	ABCD Ltd	Q	A	46603210	120.34	122.78	122.19
803358	10026	18/11/2016	3	ABCD	ABCD Ltd	Q	A	46603210	122.47	124.5	124.17
803359	10026	21/11/2016	3	ABCD	ABCD Ltd	Q	A	46603210	122.09	124.65	123.87

Figure 21. ASX (Australia Stock Exchange) data – bottom 12 rows – columns O-Y

	O	P	Q	R	S	T	U	V	W	X	Y
1	Volume	Returns	Bid	Ask	Shares Outstd'g	Price Alternate	Returns without Dividends	Value-Weighted Return-incl. dividends	Value-Weighted Return-excl. dividends	Equal-Weighted Return-incl. dividends	Equal-Weighted Return-excl. dividends
803348	127953	-0.02155	113.89	113.9	18668	114.89	-0.021545	-0.001239	-0.00128	0.000762	0.000692
803349	88091	0.022809	116.48	116.57	18668	114.44	0.022809	0.020921	0.020898	0.016048	0.015996
803350	69622	-0.00515	115.98	116.07	18683	115.87	-0.005146	0.003886	0.00353	0.002824	0.002656
803351	78725	0.007414	116.9	116.99	18683	114.75	0.007414	0.012049	0.011949	0.01576	0.015604
803352	88979	-0.00548	116.2	116.21	18683	115.8	-0.005477	0.001947	0.001836	0.006012	0.005822
803353	113433	0.024094	118.93	119.01	18683	116.54	0.024094	0.000248	0.000248	0.008794	0.008794
803354	81004	0.002605	119.23	119.32	18683	120.01	0.002605	0.002364	0.002254	0.005859	0.005792
803355	79049	0	119.21	119.32	18683	119.57	0	0.007917	0.00774	0.007791	0.007712
803356	58147	0.012404	120.8	120.9	18683	119.31	0.012404	-0.001509	-0.001714	0.001924	0.001801
803357	50253	0.011507	122.15	122.19	18683	121.26	0.011507	0.004593	0.004543	0.002985	0.002921
803358	59927	0.016204	124.19	124.33	18683	122.47	0.016204	-0.001348	-0.001473	0.001528	0.001467
803359	46620	-0.00242	123.86	123.87	18683	123.98	-0.002416	0.007775	0.007747	0.006578	0.006461

Figure 22. Custom number filter dialogue box

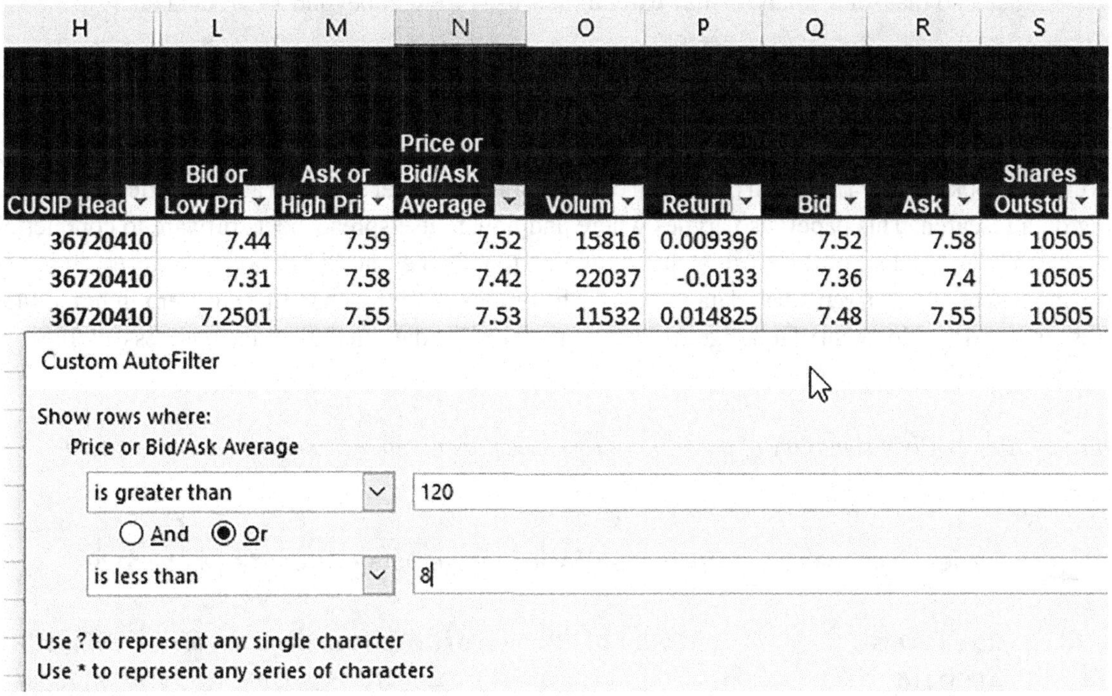

H	L	M	N	O	P	Q	R	S
CUSIP Head ▼	Bid or Low Pri ▼	Ask or High Pri ▼	Price or Bid/Ask Average ▼	Volum ▼	Return ▼	Bid ▼	Ask ▼	Shares Outstd ▼
36720410	7.44	7.59	7.52	15816	0.009396	7.52	7.58	10505
36720410	7.31	7.58	7.42	22037	-0.0133	7.36	7.4	10505
36720410	7.2501	7.55	7.53	11532	0.014825	7.48	7.55	10505

Custom AutoFilter

Show rows where:
Price or Bid/Ask Average

| is greater than | ∨ | 120 |

○ And   ⦿ Or

| is less than | ∨ | 8| |

Use ? to represent any single character
Use * to represent any series of characters

Data analyst. As described in this earlier section, Power Pivot expands the use of pivot tables to accommodate data tables that cannot be handled by Excel alone. Most spreadsheet users know all to well they are limited to much less than the maximum number of rows. Frequent crashes and calculation updates that take several minutes or longer become the norm when the analyst pushes their spreadsheet boundaries too much.

Figure 23. Extract of data filtered with custom number filter (col N) <8 or >120

	A	B	C	D	E	F	G	H	L	M	N
1	PERMNO	Names Dat	Exchange Code	Ticker Symb	Company Name	Primary Exchang	Trading Status	CUSIP Header	Bid or Low Pri	Ask or High Pri	Price or Bid/Ask Averag
584065	10001	15/01/2016	2	EGAS	GAS NATU	A	A	36720410	7.8201	8.12	7.99
584066	10001	15/01/2016	2	EGAS	GAS NATU	A	A	36720410	7.8201	8.12	7.99
584067	10001	15/01/2016	2	EGAS	GAS NATU	A	A	36720410	7.8201	8.12	7.99
584068	10026	01/11/2016	3	EGAS	J & J SNAC	Q	A	46603210	119.76	122.485	120.05
584069	10026	01/11/2016	3	EGAS	J & J SNAC	Q	A	46603210	119.76	122.485	120.05
584070	10026	01/11/2016	3	EGAS	J & J SNAC	Q	A	46603210	119.76	122.485	120.05
584071	10026	01/11/2016	3	EGAS	J & J SNAC	Q	A	46603210	119.76	122.485	120.05

As described in Section 3.8, Power Pivot provides for the analysis of millions of rows of data (from multiple data sources if desired) in a single workbook. The analyst can create relationships between heterogeneous data, calculated columns and measures using formulas. Figure 23 provides an illustration of a summary information table created using Power Pivot with the previous bankruptcy data set.

Figure 24 provides a rudimentary illustration of the power that Power Pivot adds to the Excel spreadsheet. In truth, the Big Data analyst's capabilities are dramatically extended through the use of Power Pivot. So much so that some analysts may extend their use of Excel beyond small data analysis.

6. CONCLUSION

This chapter looks at how Excel can be used in conjunction with other software and analytical techniques in big data research. This paper also argues where and how to use spreadsheet software to conduct big data research. A focal argument of this chapter is that the key behind big data driven research is data cleansing and big data driven small data analysis. The proposed approach in this chapter might facilitate the research and development of intelligent big data analytics, big data analytics, and business intelligence.

Figure 24. Power Pivot summary of data filtered with custom number filter (col N) <8 or >120

	A	B	C	D	E	F	G
1		Power Pivot analysis of Price or Bid/Ask Average Data - Filter of < $8 or > $120					
2							
3		Row Labels	Count of Pric	Sum of Price	Average	Max of Pri	Min of P
4		ABCD Ltd	4	$491.03	$122.76	$124.17	$120.80
5		GAS NATURAL INC	167,504	$1,231,571.51	$7.35	$7.99	$6.88
6		J & J SNACK FOODS CORP	62,810	$7,637,426.89	$121.60	$124.17	$120.05
7		**Grand Total**	**230,318**	**$8,869,489.43**	**$38.51**	**$124.17**	**$6.88**

It is the authors' firm opinion that the humble spreadsheet has a significant role to play in making Big Data analysis available to the masses. The global data giants (e.g. Google, Amazon, etc) will still be the key players. However, small data analysis with Excel will provide an invitation to the Big Data party for academics and business (i.e. non-global data giant companies). The use of Excel VBA and Power Pivot are the keys for turning Excel into a Big Data analyst's first choice for analysis.

REFERENCES

Baker, S. (2018, May 9). *Cambridge Analytica Won't Be Revived Under New Company Name*. Retrieved from Bloomberg: https://www.bloomberg.com/news/articles/2018-05-08/cambridge-analytica-won-t-be-revived-under-new-company-name

Butler, S. (2018, March 22). Bargain Booze owner Conviviality must raise £125m to halt bankruptcy. *The Guardian*. Retrieved from https://www.theguardian.com/business/2018/mar/21/bargain-booze-owner-conviviality-must-raise-125m-to-halt-bankruptcy

Department of Communication and the Arts. (2018, February 27). *Future trends in bandwidth demand*. Retrieved from https://www.communications.gov.au/departmental-news/future-trends-bandwidth-demand

European Spreadsheet Risks Interest Group (EuSpRIG). (n.d.a). *Horror stories*. Retrieved from http://www.eusprig.org/horror-stories.htm

European Spreadsheet Risks Interest Group (EuSpRIG). (n.d.b). *Welcome*. Retrieved from http://www.eusprig.org/index.htm

Jones, S. (2017). Corporate bankruptcy prediction: a high dimensional analysis. *Review of Accounting Studies, 22*(3), 1366.

Jones, S., Johnstone, D., & Wilson, R. (2016). Predicting Corporate Bankruptcy: An Evaluation of Alternative Statistical Frameworks. *Journal of Business Finance & Accounting, 44*, 1–2. doi:10.1111/jbfa.12218

Microsoft. (n.d.b). *Power Pivot: Powerful data analysis and data modeling in Excel*. Retrieved from https://support.office.com/en-us/article/Power-Pivot-Powerful-data-analysis-and-data-modeling-in-Excel-A9C2C6E2-CC49-4976-A7D7-40896795D045

National Research Council. (2013). *Frontiers in Massive Data Analysis*. Washington, DC: The National Research Press.

Panko, R. (1998). What we know about spreadsheet errors. *Journal of Organizational and End User Computing, 10*(2), 15–21. doi:10.4018/joeuc.1998040102

Plauger, P. J. (1993). *Programming on purpose: Essays on software design*. Englewood Cliffs, NJ: Prentice Hall.

Powell, S. G., & Baker, K. R. (2004). *Management science: The art of modeling with spreadsheets*. Hoboken, NJ: Wiley.

Pressman, R., & Maxim, B. (2014). *Software engineering: A practitioner's approach.* Boston: McGraw-Hill.

Raffensperger, J. F. (2001). New guidelines for spreadsheets. *Proceedings of the European Spreadsheet Risks Information Group (EuSpRIG),* 61-76.

Sun, Z., Sun, L., & Strang, K. (2018). Big data analytics services for enhancing business intelligence. *Journal of Computer Information Systems, 58*(2), 162–169. doi:10.1080/08874417.2016.1220239

Sun, Z., & Wang, P. (2017). Big Data, Analytics and Intelligence: An Editorial Perspective. *Journal of New Mathematics and Natural Computation, 13*(2), 75–81. doi:10.1142/S179300571702001X

Sweller, J. (2010). Element interactivity and intrinsic, extraneous, and germane cognitive load. *Educational Psychology Review, 22*(2), 123–138. doi:10.100710648-010-9128-5

van der Aalst, W. M. P., ter Hofstede, A. H. M., & Weske, M. (2003). Business process management: A survey. In W.M.P van der Aalst, & M. Weske (Eds.), Business Process Management. Lecture Notes in Computer Science (vol. 2678). Berlin: Springer. doi:10.1007/3-540-44895-0_1

Van Merriënboer, J. J. G., & Krammer, H. P. (1987). Instructional strategies and tactics for the design of introductory computer programming courses in high school. *Instructional Science, 16*(3), 251–285. doi:10.1007/BF00120253

Walkenbach, J. (2002). *Microsoft Excel 2000 power programming with VBA.* Foster City, CA: IDC Books.

Walkenbach, J. (2010). *Microsoft Excel 2010 power programming with VBA.* Hoboken, NJ: Wiley. doi:10.1002/9781118257616

Chapter 8
Census Data Analysis and Visualization Using R Tool:
A Case Study

Veena Gadad
Rashtreeya Vidyalaya College of Engineering, India

Sowmyarani C. N.
Rashtreeya Vidyalaya College of Engineering, India

ABSTRACT

As a result of increased usage of internet, a huge amount of data is collected from variety of sources like surveys, census, and sensors in internet of things. This resultant data is coined as big data and analysis of this leads to major decision making. Since the collected data is in raw form, it is difficult to understand inherent properties and it becomes just a liability if not analyzed, summarized, and visualized. Although text can be used to articulate the relation between facts and to explain the findings, presenting it in the form of tables and graphs conveys information effectively. Presentation of data using tools to create visual images in order to gain more insights into data is called as data visualization. Data analysis is processing and interpretation of data to discover useful information and to deduce certain inferences based on the values. This chapter concerns usage of R tool and understanding its effectiveness for data analysis and intelligent data visualization by experimenting on data set obtained from University of California Irvine Machine Learning Repository.

INTRODUCTION

R is an open source programming language whose main purpose is to deliver an user friendly way to perform data analysis, statistics and data visualization. The survey performed by IEEE spectrum on "The top programming languages of 2017" (Cass, 2018) tells that the R language is on the sixth position and python on first position among top 48 programming languages used by data scientists for analysis. As of June 2018, R ranks 10th in TIOBE index, a measure of popularity of programming languages (TIOBE The software Quality Company, 2018)The reason that R is used popularly is:

DOI: 10.4018/978-1-5225-7277-0.ch008

1. R is a open source programming language- There is no limit with respect to subscription costs or license management. The libraries of the language are freely accessible.
2. R is best statistical analysis tool- Data can be accessed in variety of format and many operations can be performed on the data with several functionalities useful for modern statistician. "dplyr" and "ggplot2" are examples for data manipulation and plotting.
3. R provides best data visualization tools to create graphs, bar charts, multi panel lattice charts, scatter plots and custom designed graphics.
4. R has consistent online support- The language being open source has a loyal support from statisticians, scientists and engineers.

Big data has potential to revolutionize the operational and strategic impacts, however there is paucity of empirical research. (Wamba, S. F, 2015). Big data as it is difficult to describe data without performing data analysis and visualization. In this article the important features of R to manage big data are discussed, relevant examples are articulated by carrying out experiments on UCI repository adult data set. The following are the main objectives of this article:

1. Performing descriptive analysis for quantitative describing or summarizing the properties of the collected data. This includes examining the mean, standard deviation, minimum, maximum and median for numeric data or frequency of observation for nominal data.
2. Intelligent data visualization for descriptive analysis with graphs like histograms, scatter plots and QQ plots.
3. Exploratory data analysis is used to understand the properties and find patterns in the data set with visual methods (R, pp. 10-50). R provides number of functions useful for exploratory data analysis like box plot, histograms, scatter plot, violin plot etc..
4. To perform statistical tests to perform statistical inferences and to draw some conclusions about the data. R provides functions to determine p-value and alpha to test the null hypothesis.
5. Generation of dynamic documents using R Markdown and R programming language.

ORGANIZATION OF THE PAPER

The initial part of the paper presents managerial perspective of big data, description of the dataset used to understand the R tool, existing proprietary and open source tools to perform data analysis and visualization. In the rest of paper, usage of important R - libraries are discussed which can be used to perform effective data analysis and data visualization using census data as part of case study. Generation of reports using R markdown is discussed in the last part of the paper.

MANAGERIAL PERSPECTIVE OF BIG DATA

In digital era, huge amount of data is collected through surveys. The intension of any survey is to perform statistics, derive implications and to make decisions. Carrying out surveys is a reliable method to get feedback directly from the source/individuals/data owners. Some of survey examples are: customer satisfaction survey, employee survey, product survey, market research survey, website feedback survey, real time data from sensors etc. The data collected should be managed and utilized for analysis. The steps involved in managing any survey data remains the same as shown in Figure 1.

- **Planning:** This is a crucial stage of the entire process, various issues are to be addressed such as objectives of data collection, determining the type of data collection, sample design and sample unit size.
- **Data Collection:** Once the planning phase is completed and the decision on what data had to be collected is decided, either a software or hardware are deployed to collect the data. The questionnaire needs to be prepared to collect the data appropriately.
- **Processing:** The data collected is in the raw form, it has to be processed which involves data cleaning and transformations as per the requirements. R tool provides various functions like separate, gather, merge etc. for tidying the messy data.
- **Analysis:** The data just becomes liability if not analysed appropriately. R provides library dplyr. This provides various functions to perform data analysis.
- **Dissemination:** Since the data is collected for a purpose it should be disseminated as per the requirements of the concerned user.
- **Evaluation:** The process ends with evaluation of the processed data and user consultation.

DATASET DESCRIPTION

In this paper, analysis of census data which is obtained from University of California Irvine (UCI) machine learning repository (C. Blake, C. Merz, 1998) is used. The dataset is multivariate with 15 variables.

The total number of records are 32561, out of which variables type_ employer has 1836 records, occupation has 1843 records and country has 583 records. The description of the attributes in the data set is shown in table 1.

BACKGROUND

Big data has variety of data structures and the number of attributes is much larger. Many tools both commercial and open source are used by industries to exploit the hidden structure of the data. In this section popularly used commercial and open source data analysis tools their specific use and advantage is discussed.

Figure 1. Managerial perspective of big data

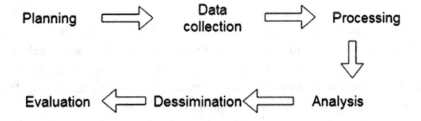

Table 1. Description of adult data set

Sl.No	Attribute Name	Data type	Description	Possible Values
1	age	Numeric	Age of the individual	10,11,12......39,40,41.
2	workclass	categorical	class of work	"Private, Self-emp-not-inc, Self-emp-inc, Federal-gov, Local-gov, State-gov, Without-pay, Never-worked
3	fnlwgt	Continous	Final weight determined by census org	Numeric
3	education	Ordered Factor	Education of the individual	Bachelors, Some-college, 11th, HS-grad, Prof-school, Assoc-acdm, Assoc-voc, 9th, 7th-8th, 12th, Masters, 1st-4th, 10th, Doctorate, 5th-6th, Preschool
4	education-num	continous	Number of years of education	Numeric
5	maritial-status	categorical	marital status of the individual	Married-civ-spouse, Divorced, Never-married, Separated, Widowed, Married-spouse-absent, Married-AF-spouse
6	occupation	categorical	Occupation of the individual	Tech-support, Craft-repair, Other-service, Sales, Exec-managerial, Prof-specialty, Handlers-cleaners, Machine-op-inspct, Adm-clerical, Farming-fishing, Transport-moving, Priv-house-serv, Protective-serv, Armed-Forces
8	relationship	categorical	Present relationship	Wife, Own-child, Husband, Not-in-family, Other-relative, Unmarried
9	race	categorical	Race of the individual	White, Asian-Pac-Islander, Amer-Indian-Eskimo, Other, Black
10	gender	categorical	gender of the individual	Male, Female
11	capital-gain	Continuous	Capital gain made by the individual	Numeric
12	capital-loss	Continuous	Capital loss made by the individual	Numeric
13	hours-per-week	Continuous	Average number of hours spent by the individual on work	Numeric.
14	native-country	categorical	Native country of the individual	United-States, Cambodia, England, Puerto-Rico, Canada, Germany, Outlying-US(Guam-USVI-etc), India, Japan, Greece, South, China, Cuba, Iran, Honduras, Philippines, Italy, Poland, Jamaica, Vietnam, Mexico, Portugal, Ireland, France, Dominican-Republic, Laos, Ecuador, Taiwan, Haiti, Columbia, Hungary, Guatemala, Nicaragua, Scotland, Thailand, Yugoslavia, El-Salvador, Trinadad & Tobago, Peru, Hong, Holand-Netherlands
15	income level	categorical	income level of an individual	"<=50k",">=50k"

Commercial Big Data Analysis Tools

SAS (Statistical Analysis System) is a suite of software tool that facilitates data analysis, reporting, data mining, predictive modelling, business intelligence, data management etc. It supports powerful visualization and interactive dashboards (SAS - https://www.sas.com/en_in/software/access.html). SAS can mine, alter, manage and retrieve data from a variety of sources and perform statistical analysis on it. It also provides a graphical point-and-click user interface for non-technical users and more advanced options through the SAS language. The other advantages of SAS are ability to handle large databases, easy to debug, tested algorithms, data security etc. The disadvantage associated with this tool is that it is not an open source software therefore algorithms used in SAS are not made public for common use. Other disadvantages include cost, lack of graphical representation, needs to learn SAS language etc.

Another such software is Tableau (Tableau - https://www.tableau.com/products/prep) It is a tool for visually analysing and exploring the data, it can combine multiple databases easily. Tableau queries relational databases, OLAP cubes, cloud databases, and spreadsheets and then generates a number of graph types. It has mapping functionality and is able to plot latitude, longitude coordinates and connect to spatial files. The products can also extract data and store and retrieve from its in-memory data engine. The tool does not require any complex scripting and after analysis the reports can be shared easily by publishing the reports to Tableau server. Other advantages of the software are ease of implementations, quickly create interactive visualizations, can handle large amounts of data, use of other scripting languages in tableau etc, however the limitations are that the software can be used only on static data extracts and the libraries are not open source. Tableau does not provide the feature of automatic refreshing of reports with the scheduling.

Qlik View is another commercial data analysis tool that is used for searching, visualizing and analyzing the data with in depth insight on the data (Qlik View- https://www.qlik.com/us/products/qlikview). It provides better value to existing data stores with clean and simple user interface. The feature of in-memory data processing, gives superfast result to the users also the aggregations are calculated on the fly and data is compressed to 10% of original size. The software has data volume limitations and hence may not be suitable for big data analysis. The other limitations include it cannot be OLTP (OnLine Transaction Processing Tool).

Splunk- is a proprietary software platform used to search, analyze and visualize the machine generated data gathered from websites, applications, sensors, devices etc. It is also used for system performance analysis, monitor business metrics and provides a dashboards to visualize and analyze results.(Splunk -https://www.splunk.com/en_us/resources.html). Splunk captures, indexes, and correlates real-time data in a searchable repository from which it can generate graphs, reports, alerts, dashboards, and visualizations. The main advantage of the tool is its real time data processing, the input data can be in any format (.csv, json or other), can configure the tool to give alerts/ event notifications, create knowledge objects for operational intelligence. The main limitation of the software is it is not open source software.

Open Source Big Data Analysis Tools

There are few open source Big data analysis tools such as R it is an open source language developed for data analysis, it is used mainly for statistical analysis and data visualization. R is open source and easy to install locally and has rich libraries to serve the purpose(R -https://www.r-project.org). The ggplot2 library provides visualization functionality, dplyr library provides necessary functions to perform data analysis. R also has libraries for linear and non linear modelling, time series analysis, clustering and graphical representation. It provides the most comprehensive statistical analysis package that incorporates all standard statistical tests, models and analysis.

Another data analysis tool is Python, itis a multi purpose programming language that has support for data analysis, visualization a machine learning and building models (Eubank, 2015). It provides functionalities through libraries like NumPy and pandas. The package Pandas makes importing and analysing the data much easier. NumPy is a general purpose array-processing package. It provides high performance multidimensional array object and tools for working with these arrays.

Google Fusion Tables is another open source tool used for data analysis, mapping and large dataset visualization(Google Fusion Tables-https://sites.google.com/site/fusiontablestalks/home). It is the web service provided by google for data management. Fusion can filter and summarize many rows, combining multiple databases, generate single visualization that includes sets of data. Data are stored in multiple tables that Internet users can view and download. Google fusion table is designed such that it can handle hundreds and thousands of tables with diverse schemas, sizes and query load characteristics. (Gonzalez, H., Halevy, A., Jensen, C. S., Langen, A., Madhavan, J., Shapley, R., & Shen, W, 2010) The limitation of the tool is its scalability (Balakrishnan, 2017).

Table 2 and Table 3 summarizes the commercial data analysis tools and open source data analysis tools.

Table 2. Commercial big data analysis tools

Sl.No	Name	Specific Use	Advantage	Disadvantage
1	SAS (Statistical Analysis System)	Statistical Analysis, Business Intelligence, data mining, predictive modelling, data management.	Easy to learn and use. Ability to handle large data base. Tested algorithms. SAS GUI.Data Security	SAS is not open source. Cost inefficient, lack of graphical representation.
2	Tableau	Data discovery and data exploration. Data visualization	Get connected to different data sources from files and server. Quickly create data visualization, can handle large amount of data.	The software can be used only on static data extracts and the libraries are not open source. It does not provide the feature of automatic refreshing of reports with the scheduling.
3	Qlikview	Data discovery and decision making. Data analysis and visualization	Flexibility in access, fast analysis, quick time to value, user centric interactivity.	Requires trained developer, not open source.
4	Splunk	Analyze machine generated data.	It can pull data from multiple systems in real time. The input data can be in any format. The tool can be configured to generate alerts and notifications.	Not an open source tool

Table 3. Open source big data analysis tools

Sl.No	Name	Specific Use	Advantage
1	R	Statistical analysis Data visualization	Built in data analysis functionality. Core libraries are well maintained by the CRAN and key programmers Open source.
2	Python	Prototyping, visualization and data analysis on small and medium sized data sets. Machine learning and building tools.	Easy to learn and use Less code and large work. Open source Libraries for handling large multi dimensional arrays and matrices.
3	Google Fusion Tables	Summary with simple aggregate statistics, variety of charts.	Scalability

Growing Popularity of Open Source Tools

Recently open source software, applications and projects are commonly used than the closed source software also known as proprietary software. In proprietary software only the author has a legal copy and he only can modify, distribute, inspect or alter the software. Some of the proprietary softwares are Apple iOS mobile operating system, Microsoft Office suite, Adobe Photo shop etc. To use such softwares the end user must purchase the software and agree to some specific terms set forth by the owner. Open source software can be altered, shared by anyone. Open source software is equal to or more capable than professional proprietary software. The benefits and popularity of open source software is extremely high mainly because the software is free to use, modify and distribute. This software are more secured and accessible to everyone. The main advantage of such software tools is, it is free from complex licensing issues and do not need anti-piracy measures such as product activation and serial number. Some of the examples of open source softwares are Libre Office, Linux operating system and its flavours, VLC media player, Android mobile operating system etc. With Big data it is possible to enhance decision making and organizational perspective with the help of many available tools, technologies and management as discussed in (Storey, 2017).

MAIN FOCUS OF THE CHAPTER

The main aim of the article is to describe important libraries in R that can be used to perform effective data analysis, data visualization and generate reports. The applications of relevant functions is discussed taking census data as a case study. Various graphs are demonstrated using examples.

DATA MANAGEMENT LIFE CYCLE

The data management life cycle consists of various phases from data collection to generation of information from the data, figure 2 depicts various stages of data management systems.

1. Data Collection

Data collection is a process of gathering information in a systematic fashion which subsequently allows for data analysis to be performed on the collected information. In this first step the data is collected from various sources to get complete and accurate picture of an area of interest, the data is stored in form of a tables. Accurate data collection is essential for maintaining integrity of research, making business decisions and ensuring quality assurance. A formal data collection process is necessary as it ensures that the data gathered are both defined and accurate and that subsequent decisions based on arguments embodied in the findings are valid(Sapsford, R., & Jupp, V, 2006)

2. Over Viewing the Data

Collected data is over viewed to understand the number and nature of variables, number of rows/columns in the data. This can be done by using various commands in R shown in table 4.

Figure 2. Data management life cycle

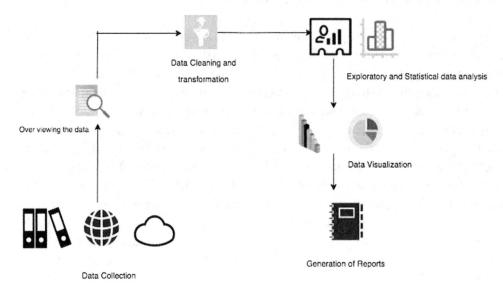

Table 4. Over viewing data using R

Sl.No	Command Name	Usage	Description
1.	dim() Example: dim(db.adult) 32561 db.adult is the data frame.	dim(x) dim(x) =value where x is an object and value is either NULL or numeric vector	Retrieve or sets number of observations of an object
2	names()	names(x) or names(x)= value	Retrives or sets names of an object
3	head() and tail()	head(x), tail(x)	Displays first/last few rows of the object
4	str()	str(x)	Compactly displays the internal structure of the object x
5	levels()	levels(x)	provides access to the factors of the categorical attributes.
6	factor()	factor(x)	Used to encode a vector as a factor
7	length()	length(x)	To retrieve length of vectors and factors.

3. Data Cleaning and Transformations

This process deals with detecting bad or missing values and shaping the data for efficient analysis. Before proceeding with any type of analysis the collected data should be cleaned by detecting and removing corrupt or inaccurate records from the data set. The bad values are NA, NaN or Inf, there can be invalid values like negative number for age attribute or values beyond the range. In R the function complete. cases() on the data frame returns TRUE for the observation where there is no NA's otherwise FALSE.

For Example:

```
TotalRows=nrow(db.adult)
CompleteRows=sum(complete.cases(db.adult))
TotalRows/CompleteRows
```

Based upon this value decision may be take to either drop or not to drop the invalid /missing observation. In R the process of transforming and mapping data from one form to another form with the intent of making it more appropriate and valuable for analysis is called data wrangling (Boehmk, 2016). It can be carried out using the functions in library tidyr and dplyr. The tidyr package makes it easy to "tidy " the data, so that it becomes appropriate to manage, visualize and model. tidyr provides four main functions for tidying the messy data (Wickham H, 2014). The description of these functions is discussed in table 6. dplyr package is used for data manipulation. The functions provided are used for performing exploratory data analysis and manipulation (Wickham. H., Francois. R,2015). The description and use of functions of dplyr is presented in table 5.

4. Exploratory and Statistical Analysis

Given any data set the variables can be classified as numeric and categorical. The numeric variables can further be classified as continuous and discrete. The categorical variables can be further classified as ordinal and nominal variables. The figure 3 explains the possible ways of performing analysis on the data.

Table 5. Description of functions in dplyr library

Sl.No	Function Name	Description	Usage
1.	glimpse	Provide summary of each column of the dataset.	glimpse(dataset)
2.	summary	If the data is numeric or integer, the summary distribution of the column including minimum and maximum, mean is displayed	summary(dataset)
3.	Filter	Returns the rows that satisfy certain condition	filter(dataframe, condition)
4.	Summarise	Used to summarise multiple value into a single value.	summarize(dataframe, expression)
4.	Group By	Used to group the data by one or more variables.	group_by(dataset, grouping attributes)
5.	Count	Used to tally the observations based on a group.	count(dataframe, expression)
6.	Arrange	For sorting data in ascending or descending order (ascending is default)..	arrange(dataframe, col_name)
7.	select	used to take a subset of a data frame by columns	select(Dataframe,col_name)

Table 6. Description of functions in tidyr

Sl.No	Function	description	usage
1	gather	Takes multiple columns, and gathers them into key-value pairs: it makes "wide" data longer	gather(variable name/s)
2	separate	Separate one column into several.	separate(variable name/s)
3	spread	Takes two columns (a key-value pair) and spreads them in to multiple columns, making "long" data wider.	spread(variable name/s)
4	unite	unite several columns into one	unite(variable name/s)

Figure 3. Variable analysis

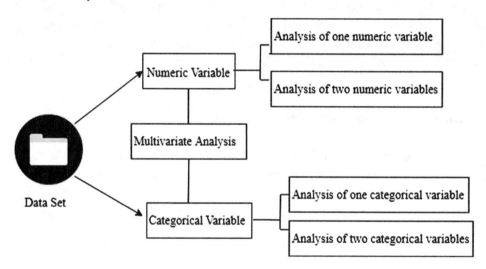

Analysis of One Numeric Variable

This includes finding mean, standard deviation, median, central tendency, dispersion and finding five number summary. Most of the functions used for this analysis are from basic packages that are loaded by default in R. Table 7 lists the functions and their usage to perform analysis of numeric variables.

Analysis of One Categorical Variable

This can be done using frequency tables and using proportion. The useful functions are listed in the table 8.

Analysis of Two Categorical Variables

A contingency table also called as cross tabulation is often used to analyze the relationship between two or more categorical variables. In R xtabs function is used to construct contingency table. For example, the contingency table for work class and gender is given below.

Table 7. Functions for analysis of numeric variable

Sl.no	Function	Description	Usage
1	mean()	Calculates the arithmetic mean of the numeric data	mean(data)
2	median()	Calculates the midpoint of frequency distribution of observed values or quantities.	median(data)
3	sd()	Calculates standard deviation of the data	sd(data)
4	range()	Calculating measures of dispersion	range(data)- Gives the minimum and maximum value.
5	cv()- defined in raster package	Computing coefficient of variation- standard deviation/mean	cv(data)
6	summary()	overall description of the data- Minimum, 1st Quartile, Median, Mean, 3rd Quartile, Maximum value of the data	summary(data)
7	describe()- defined in psych package	overall description of data including standard deviation, sample size, skewness and kurtosis.	describe(data)

Table 8. Useful functions for analyzing categorical variables

Sl.No	Function	Description	Usage
1	table()	To determine occurrences of each type of categorical variable	mytable=table(data)
2	prop.table()	To determine the proportions	prop.table(mytable)
3	margin.table()	To compute the sum of table entries for a given index.	margin.table(x, margin = NULL) x- data object margin- index number
4	ftable()	To generate multidimensional tables based on 3 or more categorical variables	mytable =table(A, B, C)) ftable(mytable)

```
xtabs(~ workclass + sex, data=adultfull)
   workclass                sex
                    Female   Male
   Federal-gov        309    634
   Local-gov          824   1243
   Private           7642  14644
   Self-emp-inc       126    948
   Self-emp-not-inc   392   2107
   State-gov          484    795
   Without-pay          5      9
```

The table shows the number of observations that are associated with work class and gender combinations. The association can also be performed on more than two categorical variables. Most commonly used approach is to use graphical summaries to understand the relationship between two categorical variables, this will be discussed in intelligent visualization section.

Analysis of Two Numeric Variables

This is to determine the association between the pairs of numerical variables in a sample. The analysis is also called as bivariate associations. Pearson's Correlation coefficient is used to determine association between the variables (Benesty J., 2009). The mathematical formula for Pearson's correlation coefficient is:

$$rxy = \frac{1}{N-1}\left(\sum_{i=1}^{N} \frac{Xi - Xmean}{Sx} \frac{Yi - Ymean}{Sy}\right)$$

Xi and Yi are two different variables in a sample. Sx and Sy denote the standard deviation of each sample. Xmean and Ymean denote the sample mean. N is sample size. The coefficient is designed to summarize the strength of linear association, if the result is 0 then the two variables are not correlated, if the value is +1 or -1 they are related. In R cor is used used to compute Pearson's correlation coefficient.

For example, the Pearson correlation coefficient between age and hours per week is 0.068, this indicates that they are not correlated.

Analysis of One Numeric Variable Grouped by a Categorical Variable or Multivariate Analysis

Box plot is commonly used approach to explore the relationship between categorical-numerical variables. This is discussed in detail in intelligent visualization section.

Examples Using Census Data to Understand Exploratory and Descriptive Analysis

This type of analysis is performed to describe or characterize the data prior to any complex analysis or modelling. For example in the case study computing the mean, calculation of average of distribution, determining the range to characterize its variability constitutes descriptive analysis. Using R tool computing the mean, standard deviation, minimum, maximum and median for numeric data or frequency of observation for nominal data is much easier. This section discusses the descriptive analysis on census data using R tool

Inspecting the Census Data Set

1.   ls(adultfull) – Lists all the variables in the dataset.

```
"age"           "capital_gain"   "capital_loss"   "education"        "edunum"
"fnlwt"         "hours_week"     "marital_status" "native_country" "occupation"
"race"          "relationship"   "salary"         "sex"        "workclass"
```

2.   str(adultfull)- Structure of the dataset

```
$ V1:int   39 50 38 53 28 37 49 52 31 42 ...
$ V2: Factor w/ 9 levels " ?"," Federal-gov",..: 8 7 5 5 5 5 5 7 5 5 ...
$ V3:int   77516 83311 215646 234721 338409 284582 160187 209642 45781 159449
...
$ V4: Factor w/ 16 levels " 10th"," 11th",..: 10 10 12 2 10 13 7 12 13 10 ...
$ V5:int   13 13 9 7 13 14 5 9 14 13 ...
$ V6: Factor w/ 7 levels " Divorced"," Married-AF-spouse",..: 5 3 1 3 3 3 4 3
5 3 ...
$ V7: Factor w/ 15 levels " ?"," Adm-clerical",..: 2 5 7 7 11 5 9 5 11 5 ...
$ V8: Factor w/ 6 levels " Husband"," Not-in-family",..: 2 1 2 1 6 6 2 1 2 1
...
$ V9: Factor w/ 5 levels " Amer-Indian-Eskimo",..: 5 5 5 3 3 5 3 5 5 5 ...
$ V10: Factor w/ 2 levels " Female"," Male": 2 2 2 2 1 1 1 2 1 2 ...
$ V11: int   2174 0 0 0 0 0 0 0 14084 5178 ...
$ V12: int   0 0 0 0 0 0 0 0 0 ...
$ V13: int   40 13 40 40 40 40 16 45 50 40 ...
$ V14: Factor w/ 42 levels " ?"," Cambodia",..: 40 40 40 40 6 40 24 40 40 40
...
$ V15: Factor w/ 2 levels " <=50K"," >50K": 1 1 1 1 1 1 1 2 2 2 ...
```

The dataset contains 6 numeric variables and 9 categorical/factor variables. Mean, median, standard deviation and variance can be determined on numeric variables. The numeric variables can be extracted from the large dataset using subset() and select function. Let the resultant dataset be stored in test. data variable.

```
test.data=subset(adultfull,select=c("age","fnlwt","edunum","capital_
gain","capital_loss","hours_week"))
str(test.data)
$ age        : num  39 50 38 53 28 37 49 52 31 42 ...
$ fnlwt      : num  77516 83311 215646 234721 338409 ...
$ edunum     : num  13 13 9 7 13 14 5 9 14 13 ...
$ capital_gain: num  2174 0 0 0 0 ...
$ capital_loss: num  0 0 0 0 0 0 0 0 0 ...
$ hours_week:num  40 13 40 40 40 40 16 45 50 40 ...
```

Computing Mean of Variables

```
mean(test.data$age) -38.4379 - The average age of the population is 38 yrs.
mean(test.data$hours_week)40.93124 - The average working hours is 41 hrs.
mean(test.data$capital_gain) -1092.008 - The average capital gain of the popu-
lation is $1092
mean(test.data$capital_loss) -88.37249-The average capital loss of the popula-
tion is $88
```

```
mean(test.data$edunum) -10.12131 - The average education number is 10.
```

To understand the relation between edunum and education group_by function of dplyr library is used as follows.
```
A=adultfull[,c("edunum","education")]
library(dplyr)
B=group_by(unique(A),"education")
```

Variable B now has mapping of edunum and education. This is shown in the table 9
    Average edunum 10 shows that the minimum education of the population is some college.

Computing Standard Deviation of the Variables

Standard deviation is a number that indicates how measurements of a population are spread out from the mean. Lower this value means most of the numbers are close to mean, higher value indicates the spread of the numbers. In R sd(VAR) function is used to determine the standard deviation. For example:

```
sd(test.data$age) -13.13
sd(test.data$hours_week) -11.97
sd(test.data$capital_gain) -7406.346
sd(test.data$capital_loss) -404.29
```

Table 9. Mapping of edunum and education variables

edunum	Education
1	Preschool
2	1st-4th
3	5th-6th
4	7th-8th
5	9th
6	10th
7	11th
8	12th
edunum	Education
9	HS-grad
10	Some College
11	Assoc-voc
12	Assoc-acdm
13	Bachelors
14	Masters
15	Prof-School
16	Doctorate

Computing Median of the Variables

In a population the mean of the variables is influenced by the outliers. Median is another way to measure the centre of the numeric variable. In R the function median(VAR) is used to compute the median.
   For example

```
median(test.data$age) -37
median(test.data$hours_week) -40
median(test.data$capital_gain) -0
median(test.data$capital_loss) -0
```

Summary of the Observation

In R the summary of the observation is obtained by using a function fivenum(VAR). It is the most useful function as it gives the five number summary- minimum value, 1st Quartile, median, 3rdQuartile and maximum value. A quartile describes division of observations into four defined intervals based upon values of data. A boxplot gives the graphical representation of median and quartiles explained later.

5. Intelligent Data Visualization Using R

Bigdata means large and complex datasets, processing them with traditional data processing applications is difficult. Data analysis followed by intelligent data visualization yeilds a better aesthetic to Bigdata that is easily understood by the analyst. Any visualization presented, has to represent quantitative and qualitative information of the data, data graphics(also called as data visualization) instruments the former and information graphics instruments the later. These presents intense as sophisticated information on certain subjects in a planned and comprehensible manner (Dur, 2014). In R, ggplot2 library provides most elegant graphics framework to design for any type of data graphics. The graphs can be created on both univariate and multivariate numerical and categorical data in a straightforward manner. ggplot2 is based on the grammar of graphics, every graph is built from few components like data set, set of geoms(visualization marks that represent the data points) and the coordinate system. To display values, map variables in the data to visual properties of the geom(aesthetics) like size, color and x and y locations. The main features of ggplot2 are: it is consistent underlying grammar of graphics, plot specification at a high level of abstraction, theme system for polishing plot appearance, mature and complete graphics system. This library does not support 3-dimensional graphics, Graph-theory type graphs igraph package and interactive graphics. The useful functions contained in the library are described in the table 10.
   The ggplot() function of ggplot2 library that creates a basic plot object requires dataframe as the argument and this data frame has all necessary features to generate a plot. The aesthetic mappings are specified by using aes() inside ggplot like X and Y axis that are respective variables from the dataset. The graph is then added with layers, scales and facets.
   A layer (is also called as geom) is added using geom_function that combines data, aesthetic mapping, geometric object, statistical transformation and position adjustment. (Prabhakaran, 2017) illustrates many graphs with a primary purpose, some of them are as listed in table. The scales control the details of how data values are translated to visual properties. Facets generates a multiples of different subset of the data.

Usage of Proposed Managerial Perspective for Census Data Analysis With Examples

1. **Workclass analysis for gender based on age group:** The various workclasses are: Federal-gov, Local-gov,Private, Self-Employed, State-gov, Without pay. The figure 4 shows gender analysis with their age in various workclasses.

Inference from figure 4:

- Maximum population works for private workclass
- Female and male population equally work in local government.
- There are people below age 15 and above 70 who work without pay.
- Female population is less in self-employed workclass.

Table 10. Description of useful functions in ggplot library

Sl.no	Function	Description	Usage
1	ggplot()	Create basic plot object that will display something	ggplot(data=df, aes(x=xcol_name,y=ycol_name))
2	geom_point()	Creates scatter plot on top of blank ggplot using a geom layer.	geom._point(col="steelblue", size=3) // Specifies color and size of the points. geom._point(aes(col="col_name"),size=3) //Set the points to reflect categories in another column.
3	ggtitle()	To add titles and lables to the chart	ggtitle("Main title", subtitle="Sub title Name")
4	xlab()	To add label to x axis	xlab("x-axis label")
5	ylab()	To add label to y axis	ylab("y-axis label")
6	coord_cartesian()	To change X and Y axis text and its location	coord_cartesian(xlim=c(0,max_limit), ylim=0,max_limit)) // To set the limit.
7	geom._encircle()	used to encircle certain group of points or region in the chart, to draw the attention to those peculiar cases.	

Table 11. Various types of graphs in R using ggplot()

Sl. No	Primary purpose	Types of Graphs
1.	Correlation between two variables	Scatter plot, Jitter plot, Bubble plot, Box plot
2.	Deviation	Diverging bar, lollipops, dot graph and slope chart
3.	Ranking	Bar chart, Dot Plot, slope chart etc.
4.	Composition	Pie chart, Bar chart, tree map etc..
5.	Distribution	Histogram, boxplot, density plot, violin plot, etc..

2.   **Workclass analysis for age based on gender:** The figure 5 shows the age of male and female population working for different workclasses.

Inference from figure 5:

- Maximum population is engaged in working between age group 25 to 30.
- There is gradual decrease in working population after age of 50.
- There are male and female population working even after age of 75.

3.   **Total working hours based on age:** The figure 6 shows how many people with different age group work for how many hours per week.
Inference from figure 6:

- Age group 30-40 works for maximum hours per week.
- There is gradual decrease in the working hours for age group 50-75.
- There are people at age 80 who works for few hours per week.

Figure 4. Workclass analysis for gender based on age group

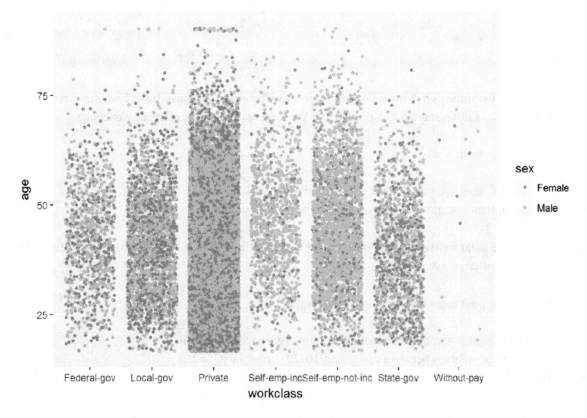

Figure 5. Workclass analysis for age based on gender

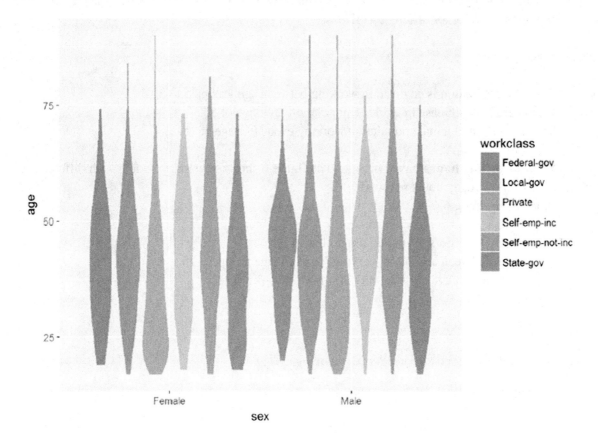

4. **Analysis of population with different race in different workclass based on age group:** The figure 7 shows different races of people and their age working for different workclass.

    Inference from figure 7:

    *   All types of races are into federal govt and private workclass.
    *   Americ-Indian-Eskimos are not involved in self-employment.

5. **Analysis of salary earned by people under different age group:** The figure 8 shows the salary earned by different age group.

    The following inferences can be drawn from figure 8:

    *   40% of the population between age group 30-40 earn salary >=50k.
    *   20% of the population between age group 10-20 earn salary <=50k.
    *   70% of the population between 65-75 earn salary >=50k.

Figure 6. Total working hours based on age

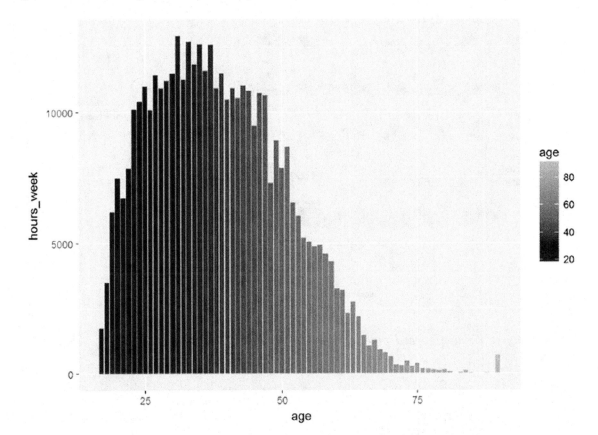

6. **Analysis of Income based on qualification:** The figure 9 shows the visualization.

Inference from figure 9:

- 76% of people earn salary >=50k and 24% of people earn <=50k with doctorate.
- 50% of people with bachelor and master earn equally.

6. Generation of Reports Using R

Using R Mark down and R programming language dynamic documents can be created. It supports dozens of static and dynamic output formats including HTML, PDF, MS word, HTML5 slides, scientific articles, websites etc. An R Markdown document is written in markdown (an easy-to-write plain text format) consists of chunks of embedded R code with .rmd extension. R Markdown uses markdown syntax. It provides an easy way of creating documents.

The documents produced by R markdown can be converted into many other file types. The documents that R Markdown provides are fully reproducible and support a wide variety of static and dynamic output formats. It is also possible to analyze the data into high quality documents, reports and presentations using R Markdown. There are a large number of tasks that can be done using R Markdown:

Figure 7. Different race in different workclass based on age

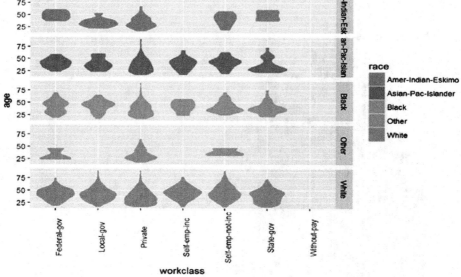

Figure 8. Analysis of salary earned under different age group

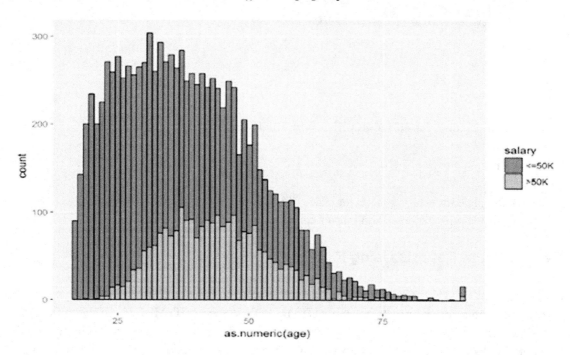

Figure 9. Income level analysis based on qualification

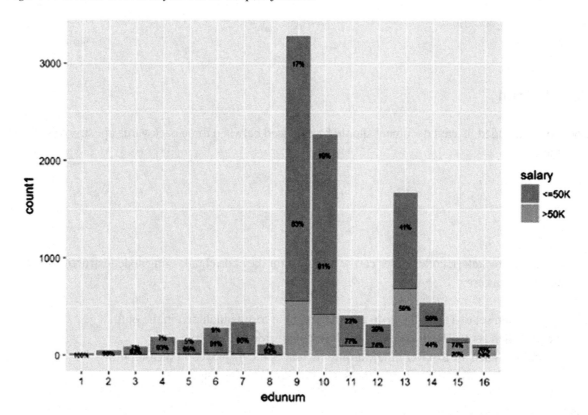

- Create a report in different formats like as PDF, HTML, or Word.
- Design notebooks with code snippet.
- Write journal articles.
- Write books of multiple chapters.
- Design attractive websites and blogs.

R Markdown file contents are discussed below.

The Header Section

At the top of any R Markdown file there is always the header section. The header section includes a title, author, date and the file type that appears in the output.

```
---
title: "BOOK CHAPTER"
author: "Veena Gadad"
```

```
date: "4 November 2018"
output: html_document
---
```

Code Section

Code to be included in .rmd document should be enclosed between three backwards apostrophes ``` for example:

```
```{r}
summary(adult)
```
```

    Within the brackets{r, code}, rules can be assigned for the code chunk using code instructions. Some of the instructions are:

1. eval: When set to TRUE the code executed and the results included in the output.
2. echo: When set to TRUE the code displayed alongside the results.
3. warning: When set to TRUE the warning messages are displayed in the output.
    4.error: When set to TRUE error messages displayed in the output.

Inserting Figures

To insert the figures in the output, there are instructions to set the figure dimensions, the instructions can be inserted as:

```
```{r,fig.width=5, fig.height=5,echo=FALSE}
plot(cars)
```
```

Inserting Tables

Using code instructions in R Markdown it is easy to print the contents of a data frame by enclosing the name of the data frame in a code chunk..

```
```{r,echo=FALSE}
dataframe
```
```

    A better solution is to use the table formatting function kable() in the knitr package. For example,

```
```{r,echo=FALSE}
library(knitr)
kable(dataframe,digits=1)
```
```

Formatting Text

Commands in Markdown can also be used to change the appearance of the output file, some of the common formatting commands are:

```
To include header of style1: # header 1
To include header of style1 header 2: ## header 2
To include header of style1 header 3: ### header 3
To include header of style1 header 4: #### header 4
To include bold text: **bold** text
To include italics text: *italics* text
To include code text: `code` text
To inlcude a link: [link](www.rvce.edu.in)
To include  a picture: R Studio Logo ![R Studio Logo](img/R Studio Logo.png)
To include LaTeX equation syntax: $A = \pi \times r^{2}$
```

Compiling an R Markdown File

The file in R Markdown can be transformed in two ways:

1. **knit-** This is a compiler that runs the part of R code in the document and appends the results of the code to the document, so that the document can consists of the graphs by actually running the R code. R Markdown file contains the code it needs to make its own graphs, tables and numbers, also the document can be updated by re-knitting it.
2. **convert-** Using "pandoc" it is possible to transform the R Markdown file into any new format like HTML, PDF or MS word, preserving the code results and formatting in the original .rmd file.

CONCLUSION

Data analysis and visualization are essential to understand and present the data systematically, understand the hidden patterns. As Big data is getting bigger and bigger in this digital age proper data management tools become very much essential. A systematic representation of data helps in understanding the marketing strategies, comparisons of results, decision making, estimating the targets etc. Among many of the available open source data analysis tools, R is one such open source tool using which the data management can be done efficiently. The article discusses various libraries and functions to carry out data analysis, intelligent visualization and generation of reports using R. The dplyr and ggplot2 libraries of R provides number of features using which any data can be analysed. Using R markdown and R programming language dynamic documents can be created. As a part of future work, this work can be extended to understand the libraries and functions in R to perform statistical analysis, preserving the privacy of the data and to apply data analysis using R for the data sets stored in cloud environment.

This research received no specific grant from any funding agency in the public, commercial, or not-for-profit sectors.

REFERENCES

About us: Splunk Software. (n.d.). Retrieved from https://www.splunk.com/en_us/resources.html

Balakrishnan, S. J.-A. (2017). Google Fusion Tables. Encyclopedia of GIS, 788-797.

Benesty, J. C. J. (2009). Pearson Correlation Coefficient. In *Noise Reduction in Speech Processing. Springer Topics in Signal Processing* (Vol. 2). Berlin: Springer. doi:10.1007/978-3-642-00296-0_5

Björn Berg, S. G. (n.d.). Retrieved from Qlik Technologies, Inc.: https://www.qlik.com/us/products/qlikview

Blake & Merz. (1998). *UCI repository of machine learning databases.* Academic Press.

Boehmk, B. C. (2016). *Data Wrangling with R.* Springer. doi:10.1007/978-3-319-45599-0

Cass, S. (2018). *The 2017 Top Programming Languages.* Retrieved from https://spectrum.ieee.org/computing/software/the-2017-top-programming-languages

Dur, B. I. (2014). Data visualization and infographics in visual communication design education at the age of information. *Journal of Arts and Humanities, 5,* 39–50.

Eubank, N. (2015). *Data Analysis in Python.* Retrieved from http://www.data-analysis-in-python.org/

Gentleman, R. I. (n.d.). *About R. Introduction to R.* Retrieved from https://www.r-project.org/

Gonzalez, H., Halevy, A., Jensen, C. S., Langen, A., Madhavan, J., Shapley, R., & Shen, W. (2010, June). Google fusion tables: data management, integration and collaboration in the cloud. In *Proceedings of the 1st ACM symposium on Cloud computing* (pp. 175-180). ACM. 10.1145/1807128.1807158

Google. (n.d.). *Tutorials.* Retrieved from https://sites.google.com/site/fusiontablestalks/home

Institute, S. (n.d.). *Products & Solutions A- Z.* Retrieved from SAS/ACCESS® Software: https://www.sas.com

Pat Hanrahan, C. C. (n.d.). *Combine, shape, and clean your data for analysis with Tableau Prep.* Retrieved from https://www.tableau.com/products/prep

Prabhakaran, S. (2017). *Top 50 ggplot2 Visualizations - The Master List.* Retrieved from r-statistics.co: http://r-statistics.co/Top50-Ggplot2-Visualizations-MasterList-R-Code.html

R, P. R. (n.d.). *Understanding statistics in the behavioral sciences.* Cengage Learning.

Sapsford, R., & Jupp, V. (Eds.). (2006). *Data collection and analysis.* Sage. doi:10.4135/9781849208802

Storey, V. C., & Song, I. Y. (2017). Big data technologies and management: What conceptual modeling can do. *Data & Knowledge Engineering, 108*, 50–67. doi:10.1016/j.datak.2017.01.001

TIOBE The software Quality Company. (2018, June). Retrieved from https://www.tiobe.com/tiobe-index/

Wamba, S. F., Akter, S., Edwards, A., Chopin, G., & Gnanzou, D. (2015). How 'big data' can make big impact: Findings from a systematic review and a longitudinal case study. *International Journal of Production Economics, 165*, 234–246. doi:10.1016/j.ijpe.2014.12.031

Wickham, H. (2014). Tidy data. *Journal of Statistical Software, 59*(10), 1–23. doi:10.18637/jss.v059. i10 PMID:26917999

Wickham, H., Francois, R., Henry, L., & Müller, K. (2015). dplyr: A grammar of data manipulation. *R package version 0.4, 3.*

Section 3
Applications of Intelligent Big Data Analytics

Chapter 9
Remote Patient Monitoring for Healthcare:
A Big Challenge for Big Data

Andrew Stranieri
Federation University, Australia

Venki Balasubramanian
Federation University, Australia

ABSTRACT

Remote patient monitoring involves the collection of data from wearable sensors that typically requires analysis in real time. The real-time analysis of data streaming continuously to a server challenges data mining algorithms that have mostly been developed for static data residing in central repositories. Remote patient monitoring also generates huge data sets that present storage and management problems. Although virtual records of every health event throughout an individual's lifespan known as the electronic health record are rapidly emerging, few electronic records accommodate data from continuous remote patient monitoring. These factors combine to make data analytics with continuous patient data very challenging. In this chapter, benefits for data analytics inherent in the use of standards for clinical concepts for remote patient monitoring is presented. The openEHR standard that describes the way in which concepts are used in clinical practice is well suited to be adopted as the standard required to record meta-data about remote monitoring. The claim is advanced that this is likely to facilitate meaningful real time analyses with big remote patient monitoring data. The point is made by drawing on a case study involving the transmission of patient vital sign data collected from wearable sensors in an Indian hospital.

INTRODUCTION

Continuous remote monitoring of patients using wearable sensors and Cloud processing is emerging as a technology that promises to lead to new ways to realize early detection of conditions and increased efficiency and safety in health care systems (Chan, Estève, Fourniols, Escriba, & Campo, 2012). The approach combines body area wireless sensor networks (BSN) with systems that are designed to pro-

DOI: 10.4018/978-1-5225-7277-0.ch009

cess and store the data for the purpose of raising alarms immediately or for data analytics exercises at a later point in time (Balasubramanian, Stranieri, & Kaur, 2015). Real time remote monitoring systems have been described for a number of remote monitoring applications including: continuous vital signs monitoring (Balasubramanian & Stranieri, 2014; Catley, Smith, McGregor, & Tracy, 2009), arrhythmia detection (Kakria, Tripathi, & Kitipawang, 2015), regulating oxygen therapy (Zhu et al., 2005), monitoring of pregnant women (Balasubramanian, Hoang, & Ahmad, 2008), fall detection (Thilo et al., 2016), chemotherapy reaction (Breen et al., 2017) and glucose monitoring(Klonoff, Ahn, & Drincic, 2017). Ultimately, a multitude of condition specific applications, each using different subsets of each patient's health data commissioned by diverse healthcare practices can be expected to emerge in the near future. For instance, a rehabilitation clinic may be interested in tracking a patient's gait, while a counselling service may be interested in tracking heart rate variability to detect suicidal depression (Carta & Angst, 2016) and a hospital may be interested in detecting post-operative sepsis (Brown et al., 2016).

Remote patient monitoring (RPM) applications often generate high volumes of data with great velocity and variety to produce valuable diagnostic information. For instance an ECG wearable sensor alone can produce 125 to 8000 samples per second (Shimmer, 2018), that can be used to predict various heart conditions in real time. In many occasions, a RPM application uses more than one wearable sensor to monitor vital signs, such as ECG, body temperature, blood pressure, oxygen saturation (SpO_2) and respiratory rate, to analyze and predict the health condition of the patient. This leads to large data repositories that present serious challenges for Big Data analytics algorithms (Kalid et al., 2018). A review by (Mikalef, Pappas, Krogstie, & Giannakos, 2017) reveals that Big Data is characterized in terms of the five main 'Vs:' volume, velocity, variety, veracity and value. Although a great deal has been written about the Big Data explosion, little is known of the conditions under which Big Data Analysis (BDA) leads to the generation of value for an organization (Wang, Kung, & Byrd, 2018).

In this chapter, the observation is first made that BDA for remote patient monitoring is difficult to perform due to the volume, velocity, veracity and diversity of data. Consequently, few electronic health records include RPM data despite the increasing prevalence of data from continuous monitors because electronic health records were designed for structured and less variable health data. In addition, explicit decisions about the way in which RPM data is collected, processed and interpreted in practice are rarely made by analysts acting in isolation in health care, but by diverse stakeholders working in teams in sociopolitical contexts. For instance, in the data analytics exercise with an Australian hospital described by (Sharma, Stranieri, Ugon, Vamplew, & Martin, 2017), the problem, and interpretation of analytics results depended on stakeholder priorities at the executive, management and operational levels of the hospital. The data analytics process model CRISP-DM (Shearer, 2000) cannot readily accommodate diverse stakeholder priorities and also cannot easily be adapted for continuous analytics with RPM data.

The openEHR (open Electronic Health Record pronounced open A'yr) standard that depicts the pragmatics of health care concepts described by (Kalra, Beale, & Heard, 2005) provides an important precursor to facilitate the application of Big Data analytics for RPM data. The use of openEHR has the potential to ensure data is correctly interpreted in analytics exercises and facilitate diverse stakeholder priorities and views. The next section in this chapter outlines the background literature, describes RPM research and provides an overview of the openEHR standard. Following that, the way in which openEHR can facilitate RPM Big Data analytics is described.

BACKGROUND

In general, an application system consists of a group of related application programs designed to perform certain functions. The RPM is an application system made up of two related applications, the healthcare application (HA) and the body area wireless sensor network (BAWSN), the monitoring application component. A BAWSN consists of a number of wireless sensors located on or in close proximity to the human body, such as on the clothing. The low-power sensors, such as medical sensors, wearable sensors, mobile sensors and fixed sensors, depending on the disease or needs of those aged and other patients, are equipped with a wireless interface and are capable of sensing the required intrinsic health data of that person over an extended period of time. In addition, these sensors can transmit the data to a monitoring application in a Local Processing Unit (LPU), generally a smartphone, for pre-processing. The distinct functions of a BAWSN are to authenticate the patient for continuous monitoring, to sense the vital health data from the patient, to pre-process the health data of the patient for sending any alert messages in the case of an emergency and to send the pre-processed data to the HA for further medical diagnoses. The HA is a sophisticated application assisting the doctors/care staff to monitor the patients' health condition and consult with the patient 'on the fly', regardless of where they are located. It is evident from early work by (Soini, Nummela, Oksa, Ukkonen, & Sydänheimo, 2008; Van Halteren et al., 2004; Van Laerhoven et al., 2004; Venkatasubramanian et al., 2005), the HA depends heavily on its monitoring component, the BAWSN, for the continuous generation of the health data. One of the pioneer RPM applications by (Balasubramanian et al., 2008), Active Care Loop Framework consist of Assistive Maternity Care application and a BAWSN capable of continuously monitor the Blood Pressure of a pregnant women and raise alarms using an SMS gateway is shown in Figure 1.

Although the BAWSN achieves the critical function of gathering trustworthy health data from the patient, the HA provides the visualisation of the patients' progress to the doctor and can have many functionalities. Examples are maintaining the electronic health records (EHR) in the database, alerting the concerned clinicians about the condition of the patients, the ability to provide a common ground for the patients and the care staff to discuss their needs in detail and in private; it can have an intelligent algorithm to predict any forthcoming emergency.

Figure 1. Active care loop framework for monitoring pregnant women

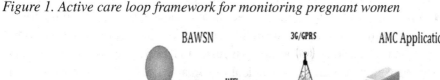
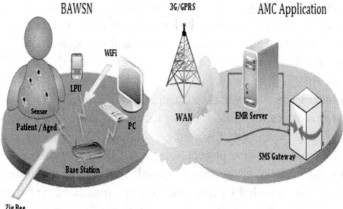

The general functionalities mentioned above are under the perspective of the user of this application. However, from the application developers' perspective, the specific implementation of these functionalities differs considerably depending on the health care requirements. For instance, the design of the electronic health records differs considerably for patients who are suffering from lymphoma and heart disease, and for those with other functionalities associated with an intelligent algorithm to predict any situation(Balasubramanian Appiah, 2012).

Therefore, the development of electronic health records requires a very high level of interoperability between diverse computer systems and extensive use of standards (Sitton & Reich, 2016). Government led electronic health record systems development tends to be enormously expensive and few countries have successfully implemented EHR systems despite the promise of potential efficiency gains and healthcare improvements that arise from access to so much data (Séroussi & Bouaud, 2016)(Garavand, Samadbeik, Kafashi, & Abhari, 2016). (Allen-Graham et al., 2018) outline the benefits and deficiencies of an electronic health record system introduced by the Australian government for a cost of well over $AUD 1 billion.

The standards essential for electronic health records include Open Systems Interconnection (OSI) network communication standards, messaging standards such as HL7 (Schloeffel, Beale, Hayworth, Heard, & Leslie, 2006) and medical vocabulary standards such as SNOMET-CT ((IHTSDO), 2018). Each standard maintained and kept up to date by worldwide communities engaging thousands of contributors. A great deal of importance on the benefits of having standardized terminologies for data mining exercises some years ago was emphasized by (Ramakrishnan, Hanauer, & Keller, 2010), when SNOMED-CT and Big Data were in their infancy. However, perhaps contrary to early expectations, the emergence of SNOMED-CT has not automatically facilitated Big Data analytics (BDa) (Benson & Grieve, 2016).

Reasons for this include the observation that coding of conditions, events, and test results to the appropriate SNOMED-CT code requires expertise and, in practice is often not done precisely or consistently, resulting in ambiguous data. For example: a variable "systolic blood pressure" may appear in a dataset with no indication of whether this refers to inter-arterial blood pressure measured with an intravenous device or the more common, around the cuff blood pressure. Relating blood pressures measures over time for the same patient is likely to result in very misleading analyses if the different kinds of blood pressure measures are confused. In addition, as (Matney et al., 2017) found, physiological variables used by diverse providers needed to be manually mapped to SNOMED-CT concepts in order to create a minimum data set of variables that could be used for data mining exercises. The concept of "patient height" may appear to be terminologically unique and well defined as the distance between the top of the head and the bottom of the feet, however this concept is inappropriate if the patient cannot stand straight or is an infant. Height data collected inappropriately is likely to hamper analytics exercises. Issues related to understanding the data is recognized as critical for BDa or Data mining exercise and is a key phase of the CRISP-DM reference model used to guide the execution of Data Mining exercises (SmartVision, Accessed 2017).

The CRISP-DM standard sets out six phases illustrated in *Figure 2*.

The first CRSIP-DM phase, *business understanding* focuses on understanding organizational objectives and identifying a data mining problem that is in alignment with the business objectives. The outcome is a preliminary plan designed to achieve project objectives. The next phase is the *data understanding* phase which provides understanding of the data that needs to be analysed. In the understanding phase, the data mining expert becomes familiar with the meaning and quality of the data. Following that phase, data needs to be prepared for modelling. The *data preparation* phase includes deciding what needs to

Figure 2. The CRISP-DM process model (adapted from (Chapman et al., 2000)

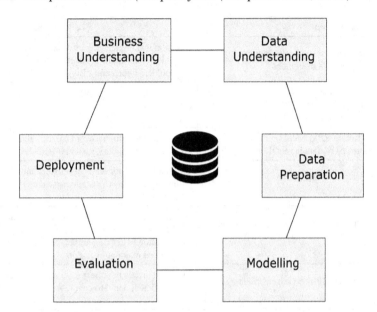

be included in the dataset, cleaning the data and all other activities that need to be done to process the data, which serves as an input to the modelling step. In the *modelling* phase, a classification, prediction, association or clustering technique is applied on the data set and a model is generated. In the evaluation phase, the model is evaluated and results are analysed in relation to the business success criterion. If the model and the results are not in alignment with the organisational objectives, a new cycle of CRISP-DM is initiated otherwise, the model is deployed.

CRISP-DM has limited applicability for remote patient monitoring data because the temporal nature of RPM data requires additional abstraction as noted in (Catley et al., 2009). A patient's blood pressure measured continuously every 20 minutes over 24 hours may fluctuate between 140/70 mmHg and 110/90 mmHg for a particular patient. This level of fluctuation is not usually clinically significant so can be abstracted to a label like "Normal blood pressure". Conversely, a sudden drop in blood pressure from 150/80 mmHg to 90/60 mmHg in minutes warrants concern even if both measures are not clinically concerning in their own right.

Another limitation inherent in the CRISP-DM approach was raised in (Sharma et al., 2017). In their case study of a data analytics exercise in a hospital setting, they report that every aspect of the exercise required decisions and collaboration amongst groups of stakeholders within the organization. However, the way in which groups reason toward making decisions in an analytics exercise is not described or prescribed in the CRISP-DM process. This is paradoxical because major decisions including the specification of business objectives, the selection of a problem to focus on, the identification of relevant variables, and the ultimate interpretation of Big Data Analysis findings are rarely made by a single decision maker but involve a complex interplay between and within staff at operational, management and executive levels.

This chapter outlines challenges for Big Data Analytics that specifically arise in the presence of Remote Patient Monitoring data. *Table 1* provides an outline of the main challenge which are elaborated on in subsequent sections. A key feature of the chapter involves the assertion that many Big Data challenges inherent in remote patient monitoring can be reduced with the use of standards. The openEHR standard outlined in the next section, is sufficiently expressive for this.

Table 1. Overview of big data analysis challenges for remote patient monitoring

Phenomena	Challenge
The interpretation of Big Data Analyses in health requires input from many individuals across multiple disciplines	Decision making techniques designed to support groups to reach decisions are rarely used to facilitate consensus between stakeholders interpreting Big Data Analytics exercises in healthcare
The extent to which Big Data Analyses realise business objectives is a recommended evaluation criteria by CRISP-DM, however this is not an effective criteria to evaluate BDA using RPM data.	The challenge is to discover criteria for the evaluation of BDA exercises on RPM data that do not rely on abstract statements of business objectives.
BDA is difficult to perform live on RPM because few analytics algorithms can operate on streams of data in real time	The challenge is to discover analytics algorithms that can operate quickly on partial data, then revise analyses as new data streams in.
RPM data cannot easily be integrated into electronic health records.	The challenge is for RPM developers and EHR developers to use common standards to encode meta-data that will facilitate inter-operability of health information.
Existing standards for inter-operability of health data including HL7 are not well suited to encoding meta-data from RPM datasets.	The challenge is to adapt the openEHR standard so that RPM data can be readily encoded. The openEHR standard requires minor modification to existing archetypes compared with HL7 which would need major adjustments.
The meaning of each variable in an RPM exercise is often difficult to ascertain	The challenge is to collect meta-data that describes each variable with sufficient detail to enable Analysts to correctly interpret RPM data.

Outline of openEHR

The demands of interoperability between health care provider computer systems has driven the development of standards in addition to OSI network standards. The openEHR standard (Kalra et al., 2005) (www.openehr.org) was proposed over a decade ago as an attempt to model the pragmatics of health care knowledge. This was considered to be critical for the design of electronic health records systems and the achievement of the interoperability required.

The archetype is a core primitive in the openEHR standard. An archetype models a concept in use within health care with the following elements: concept name, description, purpose, use and misuse. For example, the archetype named "Blood pressure" listed in the openEHR clinical knowledge base (http://openehr.org/ckm/) is linked to SNOMED-CT Concept 16307200007. In the "Blood pressure" openEHR archetype, the blood pressure concept is described as the local measurement of arterial pressure as a surrogate for pressure in systemic circulation. The purpose of the concept is to record an individual's blood pressure. The appropriate use and misuse are listed. For instance, the concept is not to be used to refer to intravenous blood pressure. The openEHR archetype for "Blood pressure" also includes a description of the data associated with the measurement of blood pressure. This includes definitions and units of measure for systolic, diastolic, mean arterial pressure and pulse pressure. The state of the individual when the "Blood pressure" is measures is also specified in the archetype; for instance the assumed position is sitting but "Blood pressure" can also be taken standing or reclining. Descriptors relevant for a protocol for the measure of "Blood pressure" including cuff size, location on the body, various formulas and the type of device used are also specified in the archetype. Version 1.1.1 of the "Blood pressure" archetype was attributed to an originator, Sam Heard in 2006 (openEHR, 2018). A community comprised of over 30 contributors whose names are listed in the archetype is also included.

In the next section of this chapter, the way in which the openEHR standard can facilitate data analytics with Big Data that derives from remote patient monitoring will be outlined. The approach accommodates the group reasoning amongst diverse stakeholders inherent in most data mining exercises despite not being made explicit in the CRSIP-DM process model. The innovations will be described with reference to a case study involving remote monitoring of vital signs amongst patients in an Indian Hospital.

OPENEHR FOR RPM ANALYTICS

RPM Trial

An architecture was designed and implemented by (Balasubramanian & Stranieri, 2014) that enables the transmission of patient data to Cloud-based repositories, as shown in Figure 3, where software services invoked by health care providers can be instantiated, executed and terminated readily to securely and efficiently process all or part of a patient's data collected continuously with wearable sensors. The prototype of the architecture was trialed in a Medical College Hospital, Coimbatore, India in 2016. Consenting patients in a general medical ward at the hospital were fitted with wearable sensors capable of monitoring ECG, blood pressure, temperature, respiratory rate and heart rate. The sensors were configured to continuously transmit data to a nearby Android Tablet running prototype software developed by (Balasubramanian & Stranieri, 2014).

Twelve patients were selected to participate in the trial over a three-week period. The data was streamed by room and bed number only so that the patient privacy was maintained. Nurses who volunteered for the trial were trained to recharge sensors, locate them on the patients, and check that data transmission

Figure 3. Architecture Design for Assistive Patient monitoring cloud Platform for active healthcare Applications (AppA)

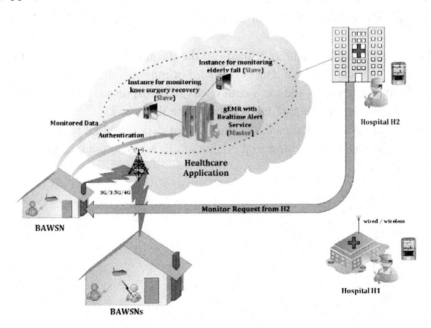

had commenced. *Table 2* illustrates sample raw data for blood oxygen (SPO2), diastolic blood pressure (DiaPress), systolic blood pressure (SysPress), pulse rate and respiratory rate. *Table 1* presents data collected from one patient for 27 seconds during the trial. A "0" was entered into the array between sensed episodes. The device did not broadcast any meta-data so the units of measurement for each variable were only understood from the manufacturer's technical manuals. A value for the body temperature seemed to be included in every second's transmission except when the SPO2 and pulse was recorded.

During the trial, the nurses had to remove the sensors an average of two times per day per patient, to help the patient to use the restroom or to have lunch. States such as active, paused, disconnected, are not identified in a standard way and rarely captured in RPM devices but become very important for RPM Analytics exercises.

The transfer of data from the tablet to the cloud server used a TCP/IP connection with the total payload of 26 Bytes, the TCP packet sent every second from a sensor will be less than 100 Bytes which includes the maximum TCP header size of 60 Bytes. Therefore, the total amount of data produced for one patient will not be more than 300 Megabytes every month. However, one hundred patients monitored in this way generates 360 Gbytes of data per year. The vast majority of this data is not of direct clinical interest for treating physicians, however once collected in digital form, health record legislation in most jurisdictions mandate that digital health data be stored and only deleted following onerous procedures. Most hospital information systems are not designed to store RPM data so storage must be done outside these systems with safeguards in place to ensure privacy and security.

The data was processed in real time by software executing on the Tablet and in the Cloud to raise SMS alarms to nurses and doctors mobile phones during the trial. Data regarding the status of the messages was not captured for the trial however this can be regarded as useful data for future data analysis exercises as discussed further below. Data relating to remote physician login such as the login duration, delays, and outcomes was not collected but can also be expected to be useful for future analyses.

The Trial illustrated that remote and continuous patient monitoring can be seen as technology that has recently arisen that enables a great deal of data to be generated continuously. However, as RPM continues to be adopted by healthcare systems, problems for data analytics exercises can be expected to emerge that dramatically reduce the utility of the data. Two challenges include:

- **Meta-Data:** Describing the data generated, on the fly, that includes units of measure needs to be associated with each bucket of data collected. For interoperability with other systems such as hospital information systems, the meta-data needs to be expressed using the openEHR standard though some extensions are required to accommodate RPM.
- **Real Time Analytics:** The incremental acquisition of data from real time sensors raises the possibility of real time analytics. Automated raising of alarms is an obvious application of real time analytics for RPM.

Table 2. Sample data for 27 seconds RPM

SPO2	SysPress	DiaPress	PulseRate	RespRate	Temp1	SensorId	PatientId	CreatedDate
0	0	0	0	0	37.1	5	4	17/10/2016 4:22
0	0	0	0	0	37.1	5	4	17/10/2016 4:22
0	0	0	0	0	37.1	5	4	17/10/2016 4:22
95	0	0	80	0	37.1	5	4	17/10/2016 4:22
0	0	0	0	0	37.1	5	4	17/10/2016 4:22
0	0	0	0	0	37.1	5	4	17/10/2016 4:22
0	0	0	0	0	37.1	5	4	17/10/2016 4:22
0	0	0	0	0	37.1	5	4	17/10/2016 4:22
0	0	0	0	0	37.1	5	4	17/10/2016 4:22
0	0	0	0	0	37.1	5	4	17/10/2016 4:22
0	0	0	0	0	37.1	5	4	17/10/2016 4:22
0	0	0	0	0	37.1	5	4	17/10/2016 4:22
0	0	0	0	0	37.1	5	4	17/10/2016 4:22
95	0	0	81	0	0	5	4	17/10/2016 4:22
0	0	0	0	0	37.0	5	4	17/10/2016 4:22
0	0	0	0	0	37.0	5	4	17/10/2016 4:22
0	0	0	0	0	37.0	5	4	17/10/2016 4:22
0	0	0	0	0	37.0	5	4	17/10/2016 4:22
0	0	0	0	0	37.0	5	4	17/10/2016 4:22
0	0	0	0	0	37.0	5	4	17/10/2016 4:22
0	0	0	0	0	37.0	5	4	17/10/2016 4:22
0	0	0	0	0	37.0	5	4	17/10/2016 4:22
95	0	0	81	0	0	5	4	17/10/2016 4:22
0	0	0	0	0	37.1	5	4	17/10/2016 4:22
0	0	0	0	0	37.1	5	4	17/10/2016 4:22
0	0	0	0	0	37.1	5	4	17/10/2016 4:22
0	140	90	0	0	37.1	5	4	17/10/2016 4:22

SOLUTIONS AND RECOMMENDATIONS

Meta-Data

The sample data illustrated in *Table 2* can be imagined to be useful for real time processing to raise alarms that the patient is deteriorating. If the vitals signs are not alarming, the data does not need to be stored beyond its collection. Indeed, the vast majority of static patient monitoring devices currently in use in hospitals do not store data after its collection and simply provide an optional print out facility. However, RPM data is collected digitally so there is a legislative requirement in most jurisdictions to store the data (Swire, 2013). For instance, the Health Records Act in Victoria, Australia prescribes detailed processes for the archiving of health records and deletion is only permissible to correct errors.

The storage of RPM data such as that in *Table 2* can be seen to be of use for future, off-line analytics purposes in addition to real time purposes. For example, associations between features can be used for predictions, particularly if linked with other data. Lee et al (2010) present an example of the potential that data mining can bring to monitoring by integrating environmental data including weather information with patient bio-data to predict an asthma attack. Data such as that presented in *Table 2* can be linked to medication and demographic information about patients across multiple hospitals for outcomes such as the early detection of adverse reactions to medications. If the data was linked to staffing data in hospital information systems, a raft of analyses to do with workplace efficiencies can be readily imagined.

Linking data collected at different times and places across diverse repositories becomes extremely labor intensive unless meta-data describing the data collected is included with the data. Without the meta-data, the "Understanding Data" phase in the CRISP-DM process involves discovering what each feature is, the unit of measure, the collection method and many more meta-data concepts. This kind of exercise with RPM data cannot be imagined to be successfully performed by data analysts without clinical knowledge. For example, in *Table 2* the temperature occasionally drops from 37.1 degrees to 0 degrees for a second then returns to 37.0 degrees. Clinical knowledge is required to understand that this is not a real drop in body temperature but an indication that the temperature was not sensed at that instance. Similarly, clinical knowledge is required to know that the temperature feature may refer to surface temperature, core temperature, temperature at extremities or other commonly used temperature measures and that each measure of temperature ought not be confused with other measures.

Meta-data stored with the RPM data enables the "Understanding Data" phase to be performed far more easily. However, this is likely to be the case only to the extent that the Meta-data conforms to a common standard. The contention advanced here is that the openEHR standard is sufficiently expressive to capture the semantics and pragmatics of RPM data with some expansion. An archetype currently exists for each feature listed in *Table 2* such as the blood pressure archetype described above. That archetype clearly distinguishes between systolic and diastolic blood pressure and defines units of measure. An archetype can be used as a rich template whenever RPM data is initialized for storage to enable clear and comparable descriptions of the data later when RPM Analytics exercises are performed.

Additional fields that are required for RPM include the status of the monitoring (e.g. active, off, paused), the status and history of the remote access, and feature based interpretation (e.g. 0 means no data is sensed). (Robles-Bykbaev, Quisi-Peralta, López-Nores, Gil-Solla, & García-Duque, 2016) demonstrate that meta-data expressed as openEHR archetypes can lead to a great deal of automation in the development of decision support system knowledge bases from data mining.

Real Time Analytics

Data streams pose unique space and time constraints on the computation process (Aggarwal & Philip, 2007). Unlike conventional data mining, stream mining approaches must occur in real time, which challenges computational processing efficiency. Further, most machine learning algorithms have been developed assuming all data is available to the algorithm. (Sanila, Subramanian, & Sathyalakshmi, 2018) reviews real time mining techniques to reveal the adaptation of algorithms for use when data streams incrementally in, is a pressing research problem. One approach to deal with this involves data summarisation where data is typically segmented into windows and reduced using filters. For instance, (Allami, Stranieri, Balasubramanian, & Jelinek, 2016) presents a low computational resource algorithm for reducing ECG data without losing key data points critical for diagnoses. Another approach involves incrementing subsequence counts (Abadia, Stranieri, Quinn, & Seifollahi, 2011) as each new data streams in. Sub-sequence counts can be directly used in classification algorithms advanced by (Quinn, Stranieri, Yearwood, Hafen, & Jelinek, 2008). Frequency counts profiles of interbeat heart rate variability has been shown by (Allami, Stranieri, Balasubramanian, & Jelinek, 2017) to predict future heart rate variability and some heart conditions.

Real time analytics with data streams is enhanced when it is linked with other data. The data stream exemplified in *Table 2* can be enhanced with links to the patient's conditions, medication, demographic or other relevant data. However, accessing static data stored in other repositories during a real time analysis of the stream presents severe computational complexity challenges. Setting up processes to perform analyses that link stream data with static data requires a great deal of labor intensive work and challenges in the "Understanding Data" phase as alluded to above.

Analytics with Big Data in practice requires that many decisions in the analytics process be made by a group of stakeholders who often have competing priorities. This is particularly the case in the business understanding, data understanding and evaluation phases of a CRISP-DM process. The pilot study (Sharma et al., 2017) revealed three main categories of decisions that were made by groups in a hospital data mining exercise; decisions about what problem to focus on, how to interpret data, and how to resource the data mining exercise.

Decision made by groups involve characteristics that render the decision making process quite different than decisions made by individuals. A group, deliberating toward a decision has been called a Reasoning Community by (Yearwood & Stranieri, 2010) who advance a process for ensuring that some of the deficiencies of group reasoning including groupthink (Janis, 1972), shared information bias (Wittenbaum, 2000) and argument fallacies are contained. A Reasoning Community refers to any group of participants that reason individually, communicate with each other, and attempt to coalesce their reasoning in order to reason collectively to perform an action or solve a problem. Reasoning communities are viewed as broader and more encompassing than communities of practice(Lave & Wenger, 1998).

The process for ideal deliberation advanced by (Yearwood & Stranieri, 2010) includes tasks to be performed in four key phases illustrated in *Figure 4* and include: Engagement, Individual reasoning, Coalesced Reasoning and Decision making described below.

Figure 4. Group reasoning in the CRISP-DM process

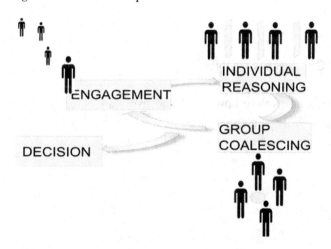

The Engagement phase for an RPM Analytics exercise involves the selection and recruitment of the people who participate in the decision making process. An RPM Analytics process can be expected to involve clinicians along with data analysts but may also require Internet of Things (IOT) experts. This phase also involves the articulation of the issue to be resolved. RPM Analytics is new and emerging, so articulating the issue that could be resolved except at a very high and abstract level such as "increase efficiency" may be difficult.

In the individual reasoning phase of a Reasoning Community process, each participant establishes facts, makes inferences from facts to draw conclusions and, by so doing contributes reasons to a pool of reasons for the community. A key part of individual reasoning involves an individual's coalescing of reasoning. This is the process of juxtaposing background knowledge with reasons advanced by other participants in order to understand the issue and position his or her claims amidst the others. A participant's coalescing of reasoning involves making sense of reasons in order to assert their own claims or to understand the claims of others. Following the Reasoning Community model, each participant of an RPM Analytics process will initially analyse the data independently from others. Initially, there is no interaction or exchange of thoughts/ideas between the group members in order to avoid negative consequences of group interactions such as groupthink (Janis, 1972).

Group coalescing of reasoning involves organizing the analyses advanced by each participant into an explicit, coherent representation. This is important for shared and democratic decision-making where decisions are made on the basis of reasoned debate. Further, group coalescing enables communities in the future to adopt coalesced reasoning as a starting point for their own deliberations in what Stranieri and Yearwood (Stranieri & Yearwood, 2012) call re-use of reasoning. Most analytics exercises perform individual reasoning but do not systematically perform group coalescing.

Finally, the decision making phase of a Reasoning Community depicts the stage when participants must decide on an ultimate interpretation from the RPM Analyses. Many patterns noticed in an analytics exercise are deemed to be spurious or uninteresting. Conclusions that are reached as a result of the RPM Analytics are typically determined to be worthwhile by the entire team including clinicians, data analyst and management.

The recognition that any Analytics exercise is not performed in isolation by an analyst but occurs in a socio-political context where a group of interacting individuals performs at each phase of the CRISP-DM process. RPM Analytics exercises, currently in their infancy, are likely to require a more diverse group of stakeholders that each initially arrive at diverse conclusions that must be assimilated into an agreed analytics outcome.

FUTURE RESEARCH DIRECTIONS

Future research is required to explore how RPM endeavors are actually established and conducted as their prevalence emerges. Work is also required to validate the difficulties inherent in the use of the openEHR standard to specify meta-data needs of RPM data.

CONCLUSION

Remote patient monitoring systems collect data from patients, typically with wearable sensors, and transfer the data to servers so that health care professionals can remotely log in to view the data in real time. Although these systems are emerging, to date little attention has been placed on the challenges inherent in analyzing data collected from remote patient monitoring systems. In this chapter, the openEHR standard was presented as an important standard for specifying the variables and context for the data collected so that data collected from diverse RPM systems or at different times can be more readily compared and analysed. The view that *openEHR* can be used to describe meta-data inherent in collecting RPM data. The chapter also advanced the notion that RPM analytics exercises, like any analytics process is not performed by an analyst in isolation but involves a group of stakeholders who have diverse interests, expertise and background. Real time analytics is challenging because data streams need to be analysed in real time and ideally linked with static data stored in electronic health records. Analyses reached by individuals need to be validated and confirmed by stakeholders for analyses to be accepted. Remote patient monitoring in a Big Data era has the potential to add another dimension to health care, however many technical, organizational and clinical challenges need to be addressed before useful outcomes of analyses emerge.

ACKNOWLEDGMENT

This research received no specific grant from any funding agency in the public, commercial, or not-for-profit sectors.

REFERENCES

Abadia, R., Stranieri, A., Quinn, A., & Seifollahi, S. (2011). Real time processing of data from patient biodevices. *Proceedings of the Fourth Australasian Workshop on Health Informatics and Knowledge Management-Volume 120.*

Aggarwal, C. C., & Philip, S. Y. (2007). *A survey of synopsis construction in data streams. In Data Streams* (pp. 169–207). Springer.

Allami, R., Stranieri, A., Balasubramanian, V., & Jelinek, H. F. (2016). *ECG Reduction for Wearable Sensor.* Paper presented at the Signal-Image Technology & Internet-Based Systems (SITIS), 2016 12th International Conference on. 10.1109/SITIS.2016.88

Allami, R., Stranieri, A., Balasubramanian, V., & Jelinek, H. F. (2017). A count data model for heart rate variability forecasting and premature ventricular contraction detection. *Signal, Image and Video Processing*, 1–9.

Balasubramanian, V., Hoang, D. B., & Ahmad, N. (2008). *SOAP based Assistive Care Loop using wireless sensor networks.* Paper presented at the IT in Medicine and Education, 2008. ITME 2008. IEEE International Symposium on. 10.1109/ITME.2008.4743897

Balasubramanian, V., & Stranieri, A. (2014). *A scalable cloud Platform for Active healthcare monitoring applications*. Paper presented at the e-Learning, e-Management and e-Services (IC3e), 2014 IEEE Conference on. 10.1109/IC3e.2014.7081248

Balasubramanian, V., Stranieri, A., & Kaur, R. (2015). AppA: assistive patient monitoring cloud platform for active healthcare applications. *Proceedings of the 9th International Conference on Ubiquitous Information Management and Communication*. 10.1145/2701126.2701224

Balasubramanian Appiah, V. (2012). *Dependability of body area wireless sensor networks in assistive care loop framework (PhD)*. University Technology Sydney.

Breen, S., Kofoed, S., Ritchie, D., Dryden, T., Maguire, R., Kearney, N., & Aranda, S. (2017). Remote real-time monitoring for chemotherapy side-effects in patients with blood cancers. *Collegian (Royal College of Nursing, Australia)*, *24*(6), 541–549. doi:10.1016/j.colegn.2016.10.009

Brown, S. M., Jones, J., Kuttler, K. G., Keddington, R. K., Allen, T. L., & Haug, P. (2016). Prospective evaluation of an automated method to identify patients with severe sepsis or septic shock in the emergency department. *BMC Emergency Medicine*, *16*(1), 31. doi:10.118612873-016-0095-0 PMID:27549755

Carta, M., & Angst, J. (2016). Screening for bipolar disorders: A public health issue. *Journal of Affective Disorders*, *205*, 139–143. doi:10.1016/j.jad.2016.03.072 PMID:27442457

Catley, C., Smith, K., McGregor, C., & Tracy, M. (2009). *Extending CRISP-DM to incorporate temporal data mining of multidimensional medical data streams: A neonatal intensive care unit case study*. Paper presented at the Computer-Based Medical Systems, 2009. CBMS 2009. 22nd IEEE International Symposium on. 10.1109/CBMS.2009.5255394

Chan, M., Estève, D., Fourniols, J.-Y., Escriba, C., & Campo, E. (2012). Smart wearable systems: Current status and future challenges. *Artificial Intelligence in Medicine*, *56*(3), 137–156. doi:10.1016/j.artmed.2012.09.003 PMID:23122689

Chapman, P., Clinton, J., Kerber, R., Khabaza, T., Reinartz, T., Shearer, C., & Wirth, R. (2000). *CRISP-DM 1.0 Step-by-step data mining guide*. Academic Press.

IHTSDO. (2018). *SNOMED-CT*. Retrieved from https://www.snomed.org

Janis, I. L. (1972). *Victims of groupthink: a psychological study of foreign-policy decisions and fiascoes*. Academic Press.

Kakria, P., Tripathi, N., & Kitipawang, P. (2015). A real-time health monitoring system for remote cardiac patients using smartphone and wearable sensors. *International Journal of Telemedicine and Applications*, *2015*, 8. doi:10.1155/2015/373474 PMID:26788055

Kalid, N., Zaidan, A. A., Zaidan, B. B., Salman, O. H., Hashim, M., & Muzammil, H. (2018). Based Real Time Remote Health Monitoring Systems: A Review on Patients Prioritization and Related "Big Data" Using Body Sensors information and Communication Technology. *Journal of Medical Systems*, *42*(2), 30. doi:10.100710916-017-0883-4 PMID:29288419

Kalra, D., Beale, T., & Heard, S. (2005). The openEHR foundation. *Studies in Health Technology and Informatics*, *115*, 153–173. PMID:16160223

Klonoff, D. C., Ahn, D., & Drincic, A. (2017). Continuous glucose monitoring: A review of the technology and clinical use. *Diabetes Research and Clinical Practice*, *133*, 178–192. doi:10.1016/j.diabres.2017.08.005 PMID:28965029

Lave, J., & Wenger, E. (1998). *Communities of practice*. Academic Press.

Matney, S. A., Settergren, T., Carrington, J. M., Richesson, R. L., Sheide, A., & Westra, B. L. (2017). Standardizing Physiologic Assessment Data to Enable Big Data Analytics. *Western Journal of Nursing Research*, *39*(1), 63–77. doi:10.1177/0193945916659471 PMID:27435084

Mikalef, P., Pappas, I. O., Krogstie, J., & Giannakos, M. (2017). Big data analytics capabilities: A systematic literature review and research agenda. *Information Systems and e-Business Management*, 1–32. doi:10.100710257-017-0362-y

openEHR. (2018). *Clinical Knowledge Manager*. Retrieved from http://openehr.org/ckm/

Quinn, A., Stranieri, A., Yearwood, J., Hafen, G., & Jelinek, H. F. (2008). AWSum-Combining Classification with Knowledge Aquisition. *Int. J. Software and Informatics*, *2*(2), 199–214.

Robles-Bykbaev, V., Quisi-Peralta, D., López-Nores, M., Gil-Solla, A., & García-Duque, J. (2016). *SPELTA-Miner: An expert system based on data mining and multilabel classification to design therapy plans for communication disorders*. Paper presented at the Control, Decision and Information Technologies (CoDIT), 2016 International Conference on.

Sanila, S., Subramanian, D. V., & Sathyalakshmi, S. (2018). Real-Time Mining Techniques: A Big Data Perspective for a Smart Future. *Indian Journal of Science and Technology*, *10*(42), 1–7. doi:10.17485/ijst/2017/v10i42/120344

Schloeffel, P., Beale, T., Hayworth, G., Heard, S., & Leslie, H. (2006). The relationship between CEN 13606, HL7, and openEHR. *HIC 2006 and HINZ 2006: Proceedings, 24.*

Sharma, V., Stranieri, A., Ugon, J., Vamplew, P., & Martin, L. (2017). An Agile Group Aware Process beyond CRISP-DM: A Hospital Data Mining Case Study. *Proceedings of the International Conference on Compute and Data Analysis*. 10.1145/3093241.3093273

Shearer, C. (2000). The CRISP-DM model: The new blueprint for data mining. *Journal of Data Warehousing*, *5*(4), 13–22.

Shimmer. (2018). Retrieved from http://www.shimmersensing.com/products/shimmer3-ecg-sensor#specifications-tab

Sitton, M., & Reich, Y. (2016). Enterprise Systems Engineering for Better Operational Interoperability. *Systems Engineering*.

SmartVision. (n.d.). *CRSP-DM*. Retrieved from http://crisp-dm.eu

Soini, M., Nummela, J., Oksa, P., Ukkonen, L., & Sydänheimo, L. (2008). Wireless body area network for hip rehabilitation system. *Ubiquitous Computing and Communication Journal*, *3*(5), 42–48.

Stranieri, A., & Yearwood, J. (2012). The Case for a Re-Use of Community Reasoning. In J. Yearwood & A. Stranieri (Eds.), *Approaches for Community Decision Making and Collective Reasoning* (pp. 237–249). IGI Global.

Swire, P. (2013). Finding the best of the imperfect alternatives for privacy, health it, and cybersecurity. *Wisconsin Law Review*, (2): 649–669.

Thilo, F. J., Hürlimann, B., Hahn, S., Bilger, S., Schols, J. M., & Halfens, R. J. (2016). Involvement of older people in the development of fall detection systems: A scoping review. *BMC Geriatrics*, *16*(1), 42. doi:10.118612877-016-0216-3 PMID:26869259

Van Halteren, A., Bults, R., Wac, K., Konstantas, D., Widya, I., Dokovsky, N., ... Herzog, R. (2004). Mobile patient monitoring: The mobihealth system. *The Journal on Information Technology in Healthcare*, *2*(5), 365–373.

Van Laerhoven, K., Lo, B. P., Ng, J. W., Thiemjarus, S., King, R., Kwan, S., ... Needham, P. (2004). Medical healthcare monitoring with wearable and implantable sensors. *Proc. of the 3rd International Workshop on Ubiquitous Computing for Healthcare Applications.*

Venkatasubramanian, K., Deng, G., Mukherjee, T., Quintero, J., Annamalai, V., & Gupta, S. K. (2005). Ayushman: A wireless sensor network based health monitoring infrastructure and testbed. *Proceedings of the First IEEE international conference on Distributed Computing in Sensor Systems.* 10.1007/11502593_39

Wang, Y., Kung, L., & Byrd, T. A. (2018). Big data analytics: Understanding its capabilities and potential benefits for healthcare organizations. *Technological Forecasting and Social Change*, *126*, 3–13. doi:10.1016/j.techfore.2015.12.019

Wittenbaum, G. M. (2000). The bias toward discussing shared information: Why are high-status group members immune. *Communication Research*, *27*(3), 379–401. doi:10.1177/009365000027003005

Yearwood, J., & Stranieri, A. (2010). *Technologies for Supporting Reasoning Communities and Collaborative Decision Making: Cooperative Approaches: Cooperative Approaches*. IGI Global.

Zhu, Z., Barnette, R. K., Fussell, K. M., Michael Rodriguez, R., Canonico, A., & Light, R. W. (2005). Continuous oxygen monitoring—A better way to prescribe long-term oxygen therapy. *Respiratory Medicine*, *99*(11), 1386–1392. doi:10.1016/j.rmed.2005.03.010 PMID:15878655

ADDITIONAL READING

Stranieri, A., & Yearwood, J. (2012). The Case for a Re-Use of Community Reasoning. In J. Yearwood & A. Stranieri (Eds.), *Approaches for Community Decision Making and Collective Reasoning* (pp. 237–249). IGI Global Press.

KEY TERMS AND DEFINITIONS

CRISP-DM: A process model for performing data mining exercises.

Electronic Health Record: A virtual record of major health related events for an individual from before birth to after death.

openEHR: A standard that describes clinical concepts and their use.

Reasoning Community: A model of how individuals reason together to solve a problem. This model can be applied to describe how analysts and other stakeholders interact to analyze data from remote patient monitoring systems.

Remote Patient Monitoring: Monitoring patients physiological signs. This is typically performed with wearable, implantable or digestible sensors but may be done at a distance with camera surveillance.

Chapter 10

Credit Rating Forecasting Using Machine Learning Techniques

Mark Wallis
Bond University, Australia

Kuldeep Kumar
Bond University, Australia

Adrian Gepp
Bond University, Australia

ABSTRACT

Credit ratings are an important metric for business managers and a contributor to economic growth. Forecasting such ratings might be a suitable application of big data analytics. As machine learning is one of the foundations of intelligent big data analytics, this chapter presents a comparative analysis of traditional statistical models and popular machine learning models for the prediction of Moody's long-term corporate debt ratings. Machine learning techniques such as artificial neural networks, support vector machines, and random forests generally outperformed their traditional counterparts in terms of both overall accuracy and the Kappa statistic. The parametric models may be hindered by missing variables and restrictive assumptions about the underlying distributions in the data. This chapter reveals the relative effectiveness of non-parametric big data analytics to model a complex process that frequently arises in business, specifically determining credit ratings.

INTRODUCTION

The notion of credit rating has been present in financial markets since 1860, where H.V. Poor began publishing financial statistics about railroad companies to attract public investments (Standard & Poor's, 2016). After this development, in 1909 J. Moody, founder of Moody's Investors Service, expanded on this idea by classifying these statistics into categories represented by letters of the alphabet. This methodology was mostly used on railway bonds. After the Great Depression in the late 1930's, the bond rating system became institutionalized in the United States. The repetitive nature of strong markets followed

DOI: 10.4018/978-1-5225-7277-0.ch010

by crashes increased the need for a measure of risk and uncertainty for investors. Nowadays, 100 percent of all commercial papers and 99 percent of corporate bonds have been rated by at least one credit rating agency in the United States. These credit rating agencies have expanded across the globe to aid the needs of investors and corporate borrowers.

Credit ratings for companies have evolved to become an integral source of information for the financial sector. This information has a range of financial and economic benefits to society. These benefits can be categorized into three groups: benefits to investors, the company and the economy. The investors benefit from this information because it is a convenient and cost-effective source of information that allows for calculated risk. Furthermore, it encourages market confidence and entices retail investors to invest their savings into corporate securities and receive higher returns. For companies, credit ratings allow them to enter the market more confidently and raise funds at a lower cost. Companies may also use credit ratings as a means for brand repair or improvement. Lastly, with regard to the overall economy, consistent and accurate credit ratings fuel public investment in the corporate sector, which in-turn stimulates economic growth. These credit rating systems can facilitate the formation of public policy guidelines on institutional investors. They also play a vital role in investor protection by encouraging ethical behavior among corporate borrowers without putting a larger burden on the government.

Although they are not perfect, it is clear that credit ratings offer a plethora of benefits to society and are necessary to sustain strong economic growth and prosperity. These ratings are formed by incorporating a range of quantitative and qualitative variables that are gathered through public information and on-site research. However, these ratings take a substantial amount of labor and time to develop, making it a very costly process. This means it is difficult for management at many companies to afford regular credit rating updates. As a result, credit rating modelling has become a large area of research due to the economic and financial benefits associated with making credit ratings more efficient and cost-effective. With the expansion of machine learning and big data analytics over the past decade, there has been an influx of credit rating models in academic literature. As machine learning is one of the foundations of intelligent big data analytics, this chapter presents a comparative analysis of both traditional statistical models and popular machine learning models for the prediction of Moody's long term corporate debt ratings for top companies in the United States.

Moody's Rating System

Moody's, alongside Standard & Poor's and Fitch Group, is one of the three largest credit rating agencies in the world. The agencies all provide international finance research on bonds that are issued by both government and commercial entities. Moody's focuses on rating a borrower's creditworthiness based on a range of factors and rating scales that are designed to estimate the expected loss suffered by an investor in the event of a default and the probability of that event occurring. These rating systems are universally comparable, meaning they can be compared across different currencies, industries and countries. Moody's provide eight main categories of credit ratings (Moody's Investor service, 2017):

1. Moody's Long-Term Ratings
2. Moody's Short-Term Ratings
3. Moody's Bank Deposit Ratings
4. Moody's Bank Financial Strength Ratings
5. Moody's Mutual Fund Ratings

6.   Moody's Insurance financial strength Ratings
7.   Moody's issuer Ratings
8.   Moody's management quality ratings for US affordable housing provider and National Scale Ratings

For the purpose of this chapter, the main focus will be placed on Moody's Long-Term Ratings. Moody's Long-Term Ratings are assigned to a range of fixed income instruments including bonds, debentures and preferred stocks. This rating system is a reflection of two major areas of the company. First, it reflects the credit risk of the company and how likely an issuer of debt is to meet its obligation. Secondly, it reflects the indenture protection, which represents the level of legal protection of the security. Some factors that may be included in the determination of this rating may include the seniority of the bond, negative pledge clauses and guarantees.

The following ratings are possible with Moody's Long-Term Ratings:

1.   **Investment-Grade:** Aaa, Aa1, Aa2, Aa3, A1, A2, A3, Baa1, Baa2, Baa3, and
2.   **Speculative-Grade:** Ba1, Ba2, Ba3, B1, B2, B3, Caa1, Caa2, Caa3, Ca and C.

In this chapter, these ratings are grouped into six categories as shown in Table 1, which is consistent with the earlier work of Kumar and Bhattacharya (2006). This categorization was used to ensure that a broad range of companies and credit ratings would be analyzed.

BACKGROUND

This section presents a brief review of reviewing the academic literature on credit rating forecasting with a focus on modelling techniques used to predict long-term credit ratings of corporate debt.

Studies about modelling credit rating have increased substantially over the past decade, likely because of the Global Financial Crisis and the realized importance of credit rating agencies in financial markets. Prior research identifies two main benefits gained from modelling credit ratings. First, it is very costly to employ a credit rating agency to provide long-term debt ratings more frequently than once a year, particularly for smaller companies who wish to improve their financial image in the market. Companies with good credit ratings enter the market with higher confidence and can raise funds at a cheaper rate (Kumar & Bhattacharya, 2006). On the other hand, for lending institutions and investors who create debt portfolios, it is important to have a regular indication of the riskiness of that portfolio. This also encour-

Table 1. Categories of Moody's ratings used in this chapter

Codes	Categories	Moody's Ratings
X1	High Grade	Aaa, Aa1, Aa2, Aa3
X2	Investment Grade	A1, A2, A3
X3	Upper Medium Grade	Baa1, Baa2, Baa3
X4	Medium Grade	Ba1, Ba2, Ba3
X5	Lower Medium Grade	B1, B2, B3
X6	Speculative Grade	Caa1, Caa2, Caa3, Ca and C

ages economic growth through investment in the corporate sector. As a result, credit rating forecasting has become a popular area of study.

The credit rating forecasting literature is split into research using traditional statistical methods, machine learning techniques and ensemble techniques. The traditional statistical techniques used include logistic regression (Stepanova & Thomas, 2001; Steenackers & Goovaerts, 1989), linear discriminant analysis (Kumar & Bhattacharya, 2006; Khemakhem & Boujelbene, 2015) and Bayesian networks (Hajek, Olej, & Prochazka, 2016). These techniques were found to produce an average accuracy range of only 60 to 70% using financial statements ratios and other financial statement data. There was a consensus that accuracy could not be meaningfully increased further without gathering qualitative information such as that used by Moody's. As an extension to this hypothesis, Hajek, Olej & Prochazka (2016) explored the effect that news sentiment has on credit ratings. It was found that positive sentiment in the company's reports and negative words in news articles were statistically significant in predicting credit ratings.

Consistent with other areas of business modelling, there has been increased popularity in the application of non-parametric approaches to credit rating forecasting. The idea is to capture the non-linear relationships between variables and increase the predictive accuracy of the models without incorporating the qualitative variables used by Moody's. The most common techniques used include decision trees (e.g. Yobas & Crook, 2000) and k-nearest neighbors (KNN) (e.g. Henley & Hand, 1997). The performance of decision trees was found to outperform KNN when evaluated on imbalanced datasets with either a majority of low credit ratings or majority high credit ratings (Abdou & Pointon, 2011). However, there are often discrepancies in conclusions about the relative performance of these techniques when data sets of varying degrees of imbalance (skewness) (Abdou & Pointon, 2011; Henley & Hand, 1997). Overall, it is recognized that non-parametric approaches perform better than traditional statistical approaches (Abdou & Pointon, 2011).

Kernel classifiers and other modern machine learning techniques have also been applied to credit rating forecasting, encouraged by the success of other non-parametric approaches. A broad range of techniques applied and the most successful include Artificial Neural Networks (ANNs) (Kumar & Haynes, 2003; Kumar & Bhattacharya, 2006), Support Vector Machines (SVM) (Cristianini & Scholkopf, 2002) and a Gaussian Process Classifier (GPC) (Shian-Chang, 2011). Overall, SVMs have had the most success. SVMs are a popular model in this field because it is believed that the formulation of the SVM embodies the structural risk minimization principle. This means that the SVM produces an optimal trade-off between complexity and the empirical accuracy (Sewell, 2008). Despite these attractive features, many practitioners believe that SVMs ability to handle sparse data has potentially been overstated. For example, it has been shown that SVMs are not always able to construct parsimonious models in system identification and financial forecasting (Huang, Chuang, Wu, & Lai, 2010). It is also argued that SVM's underperform in their predictions because of the big data nature of the financial data used in credit rating forecasting – the curse of dimensionality (Huang et al., 2010).

This weakness in SVMs has sparked the use of many probability kernel classifiers such as the Gaussian process based classifiers (Girolami & Rogers, 2006). This technique has been prominent in statistics for decades and has outperformed ANNs on smaller datasets (Lilley & Frean, 2005). Huang (2011) explored the use of Gaussian processes in predicting credit ratings compared to using SVMs for prediction. GPCs were found to outperform conventional SVMs, even when enhanced by true selection and dimensionality reduction schemes, as tested on the Taiwanese banking sector (Shian-Chang, 2011). This is due to GPCs robustness when dealing with the high dimensionality of data using a fast-variational Bayesian algorithm proposed by Girolami & Rogers (2006) to reduce the computational loading of predictions.

Other modern research about modelling credit ratings uses ensemble techniques such as Random Forest (Wu & Wu, 2016) and Gradient Boosted Machines (GBM) (Abdou & Pointon, 2011). The resulting models are more difficult to interpret and some deem them to be similar to *black box* models. Nevertheless, they have produced high predictive performance and have a robust variable importance feature that partially explains the relationships between credit rating output and the input predictor variables (Imad, 2017).

Overall, the literature consists of a range of modelling techniques used to forecast long-term credit ratings. These techniques all have their own strengths and limitations and have all been tested on different data with diverse economic characteristics and distributions of credit ratings. There have been a range of papers claiming to produce the most accurate modelling technique; however, there has been a lack of comparisons between traditional statistical, non-parametric, ensembles and machine learning techniques on the same data set. Without such a comparison there is no solid evidence to suggest what technique results in the highest accuracy. The remainder of this chapter presents the findings from such a comparison.

DATA AND MODELLING TECHNIQUES

Data

Moody's Investor Service typically model credit ratings based on certain financial ratios. Financial ratios are often deemed to be good indicators of the company's financial health and security of the company (Ganeshalingam & Kumar, 2001). However, Moody's deems that the variables used to formulate these ratings are part of the company's intellectual property and so do not disclose these inputs (Moody's Investor service, 2017). As a result of this, financial ratios and other variables that are important in predicting the profitability, liquidity, and capital gearing of the company were gathered. The following 27 variables were considered when creating and formulating the credit rating models:

1. Operating Margin,
2. Pre-tax Margin,
3. Return on Invested Capital,
4. Return on Assets,
5. Current Ratio,
6. Quick Ratio,
7. Current Asset to Total Assets,
8. Operating Income to Net Sales,
9. Retained Earnings to Total Assets,
10. Accounts Receivable to Sales,
11. Inventory to Sales,
12. Sales to Total Assets,
13. Net Fixed Assets to Total Assets,
14. Long-Term Debt to Total Assets,
15. Total Liabilities to Total Liabilities and Equity,
16. Number of Employees,

17.   Disposal of Fixed Assets,
18.   Best Sales,
19.   Total Assets,
20.   Inventory to Current Assets,
21.   Total Debt to Total Equity,
22.   Total Debt to Total Capital Expenditure,
23.   Cash Ratio,
24.   Cash to Total Assets,
25.   Asset Turnover,
26.   Equity to Total Capital, and
27.   Equity to Total Asset.

The above data were collected for 308 companies of the United States S&P 500 from Bloomberg with an examined time-period of January 2016 to November 2017. The companies were chosen such that Moody's Long-term Debt Ratings were available within the past five years, which resulted in useful data set for modelling. This data set also spans a range of industries and sectors, making it adequate to conduct a broad comparative evaluation.

Parametric Modelling Techniques

As mentioned in the literature review, credit rating modelling was initially conducted using parametric models such as multinomial logistic regression and linear discriminant analysis. These models are the best possible modelling techniques if the assumptions of the underlying data are satisfied. This section discusses the parametric models evaluated in this chapter.

Multinomial Logistic Regression

There are three main assumptions behind Multinomial Logistic Regression (MLR): observations are independent of one another, outcomes follow a categorical distribution derived from the covariates via a link function and there is a linear relationship between the covariates and the link-function-transformed outcome (Miyamoto, 2014). MLR is an extension from logistic regression in the sense that it produces a probability that an outcome belongs to a particular category. The link function used remains as logit, which is the logarithm of the odds – this correctly restricts the probability between 0 and 1. Other link functions are possible. For example, the probit model uses the inverse normal distribution function.

Linear and Regularized Discriminant Analysis

Observations are still assumed to be independent of one another by Linear Discriminant Analysis (LDA). In addition, data categories are assumed to be normally distributed (or at least symmetric), the covariance matrix is assumed to be the same for all categories and model accuracy is multicollinearity problems. LDA looks for linear combinations of variables that explain the data, where it focuses on attempting to model the differences between the categories of data and makes use of Bayes Theorem to estimate the probability of the output category given each input. Quadratic Discriminant Analysis (QDA) relaxes the assumption of a common covariance matrix. An extension to these modelling techniques is Regularized Discriminant Analysis (RDA) (Guo, Hastie, & Tibshirani, 2007), which is a weighted average of LDA and QDA. It introduces regularization in the modelling process to empirically determine a balance between a common covariance structure (LDA) and different covariance structures for each category (QDA). That is, RDA will automatically become more weighted towards QDA if the covariance matrix is not common to all categories. This model is the most statistically powerful and efficient technique if the data is a multivariate normal and homoscedasticity is present. In this chapter, both LDA and RDA will be evaluated.

Non-Parametric and Machine Learning Modelling Techniques

It is often argued that, particularly in smaller companies, there are not enough companies seeking financing to gain a full understanding of the population distribution of credit rating data. Therefore, it is not conclusive that the credit rating data meets the assumptions of parametric models (Guotai & Zhipeng, 2017). In fact, after a comprehensive review of such parametric assumptions, Elliot & Kennedy (1988) found that these assumptions often do not hold true for financial data. As a result, the following non-parametric modelling techniques are used in this chapter.

Artificial Neural Networks

As mentioned, Artificial Neural Networks (ANNs) have frequently been used to model credit rating. ANNs are soft computing techniques that are based on the neural structure of human brains. ANNs are able to model complexities that traditional quantitative methods used in finance and economics cannot due to the complexity in translating the system into precise functions. ANNs consist of three main layers: input, hidden and output, whereby more hidden layers are used to model more complex relationships in the data. Initially the neural connections within and between layers are set with random weights and then the model adjusts the weights during the learning process. If the prediction is correct, the ANN adjusts the weights in a positive way, whereas they are adjusted in a negative way if the outcome is negative. This modelling technique is useful when the underlying model structure is unknown, as the model has the ability to learn a wide variety of patterns from the data. ANNs have been shown to be effective at classification of groups and short-term predictions. They are also robust in the sense that they deal well with missing data and correlations between input variables (multicollinearity). However, ANNs are seen to be a *black box* technique because it is difficult to understand why the model makes the predictions it does. ANNs have also been known to over-fit the data used for training, which results in low accuracy for future predictions, particularly long-term predictions. Chapter 6 of Negnevitsky (2011) provides a more detailed introduction into ANNs.

Support Vector-Machines

Support Vector Machines (SVMs) are another type of supervised machine learning technique. They have increased in popularity in the literature in recent years (see Provost and Fawcett (2013, p. 89-94) for a brief introduction to SVMs). The SVM produces hyperplanes that divide data into the different categories. The hyperplanes are chosen such that they maximize the distance (margin) between the nearest data points of different categories. If data cannot be linearly separated, a kernel can be added to transform the data to assist separation by the SVM. This method often works effectively when there is a large number of variables (high dimensionality) and with low sample data. However, SVMs take a large amount of time to train and do not deal well with noisy data, which is data with inaccuracies.

Gaussian Process Classifier

Another non-parametric method that has been applied to credit rating forecasting is the Gaussian Process Classifier (GPC). This process is founded upon a Bayesian methodology. It assumes a prior distribution on the probability densities using the underlying mean and covariance of each variable (Shian-Chang, 2011). It assumes that each variable is drawn from a Gaussian distribution with the respective mean and variance and observing new elements creates a posterior distribution. The data is transformed using a squared-exponential kernel and parametrized using two parameters- sigma and L. Sigma (or L) dictates the height (or length) of the distribution that a point can be drawn from without being classified as an outlier. Predictions are formed by drawing from these collective underlying distributions and categorized into its appropriate category (Girolami & Rogers, 2006).

Random Forest (Ensemble)

Random Forest (Breiman, 2001) is an ensemble technique that has been applied to credit rating data with success in recent years. Random Forest utilizes multiple decision trees and bootstrapping to estimate an outcome. These decision trees are formed by recursively splitting data in two. The aim is that each one of the resulting number of groups identifies with a single category; it is common for multiple groups to be assigned the same category. One of the features of Random Forests is that only a random subset of variables is considered at each split. The other main feature is that each tree is grown to its maximum size, which means individually they are overly-complex, over-fit and will be poor future predictors. However, the accuracy is usually greatly improves then the individual predictions are combined. The way the combination is done is that each individual tree makes a separate prediction and then the category with the most votes (predictions) is assigned. This modelling technique is robust in large datasets with a large number of variables (high dimensionality), deals well with missing data and noise being present in the data, and has methods for adjusting to imbalanced data.

Gradient Boosted Machines (Ensemble)

Boosted machines combine multiple weak models together to form an accurate model. In the case of decision trees, a Gradient Boosted Machine (GBM) (Friedman, 2001; Friedman, 2002) first estimates an overly-simple decision tree (with shallow depth). The GBM then slightly improves the model based on the its prediction error. This process of gradual improvement is then repeated a large number of times to ideally achieve a substantially higher accuracy. This ensemble technique has been less popular than ANNs, but it has often produced higher accuracy (Imad, 2017).

PROCEDURE AND RESULTS

This section outlines the process behind selecting the parameters for the different models and an analysis of the predictive accuracy of each model. It also outlines the most important variables for each model.

The two measures for evaluating accuracy are the overall accuracy (percentage of correct classifications) and Cohen's Kappa statistic (Kappa). Kappa is an accuracy measure that considers both the observed accuracy of the model and the expected accuracy. It is calculated as

$$\frac{Observed\ Accuracy - Expected\ Accuracy}{1 - Observed\ Accuracy}.$$

The inclusion of the expected accuracy allows the statistic to adjust to imbalanced data sets that do not have an equal number of data points in each category. This is particularly important given that credit rating forecasting often involves imbalanced data, as mentioned earlier in the Background. A more detailed explanation of Kappa is provided in the Appendix.

In the literature, the predictive performance of models is commonly compared using hold-out or test data. This process involves training models on a random subset of the data (typically 70%) and then measuring its predictive performance on a hold-out testing set (30%); thus, obtaining a real-world estimate of model performance using new data unseen by the model. However, the resulting single estimate of accuracy can be greatly influenced by precise data split that occurred. Although very big data sets mitigate this problem, it is possible that very different results could be obtained if a different split were randomly chosen. To avoid this issue, the analysis presented in this chapter uses repeated 10-fold cross-validation, where the number 10 is a standard through modelling literature. 10-fold cross validation involves randomly splitting the data into 10 approximately equal partitions, then training the model on 9 of the data subsets and evaluating the model on the final subset. This train-evaluate process is repeated for all 10 possibilities for the subset that is used for evaluation. Further, this whole 10-fold process is then repeated 5 times, each time with a different randomly chosen 10 subsets. This results in a total of 50 accuracy measures per model. These 50 figures can be averaged to obtain a more stable estimate of model performance. Moreover, the 50 different estimates allows for the variability in model performance to be assessed and confidence intervals for both to be estimated for both overall accuracy and the Kappa statistic. It is widely understood that compared to single point estimates, confidence intervals can greatly enhance the interpretability from a managerial perspective.

Importantly, the repeated cross-validation process is common to all models. That means that the data splits are identical for all models, which enables comparison between models to be fair and valid.

Multinomial Logistic Regression

The top 20 most important variables are shown in Figure 1. This ranking was determined by determining the Area Under the receiver operating characteristic Curve (AUC) for each category pair (i.e. High Grade vs Investment Grade, Investment Grade vs Upper Medium Grade and so on). For a specific category, the maximum AUC for all the relevant pairs is used as the variable importance measure (Abdou & Pointon, 2011). The top three most important variables are long-term debt, retained earnings to assets and return on assets.

Figure 1. Variable importance ranking according to multinomial logistic regression

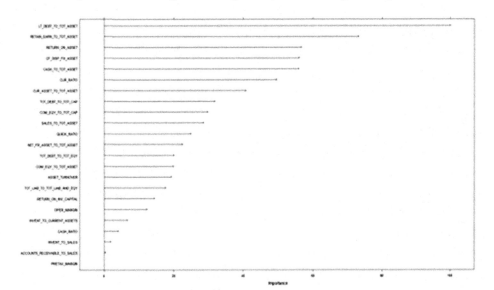

Linear and Regularized Discriminant Analysis (LDA and RDA)

The choice of model parameters can have a large influence on model accuracy; consequently, the main parameters for each model are empirically optimized using cross-validation. As with MLR, LDA does not require any parameters to be set. However, as RDA is a weighted average of LDA and QDA, the relative weights for each are determined by maximizing accuracy using cross-validation. Interestingly, the resulting RDA model weighted LDA at 100% and QDA at 0%, indicating that the same covariance structure is common to all rating categories.

In this case, LDA and RDA have the same variable importance. Similar to most machine learning techniques, discriminant analysis considers variable importance for each rating category separately. Figure 2 shows these rankings. Return on Assets is the most important predictor for all ratings except for X3 and X4, where the most important predictor is Total Assets. It is interesting to note that discriminant analysis ranks pre-tax margin as the second most important variable out of all the variables, whereas MLR ranked it last. The most important variable in multinomial logistic regression was Long-term debt to total assets and this was the 8th most important variable in LDA and RDA.

Artificial Neural Network (ANN)

The main parameters set for the ANN include the number of hidden layers and the weight decay. Weight decay is a weight update rule that causes the hidden layer weights to exponentially decay to zero if no other update is issued. Up to three hidden layers were trialed and again cross-validation was used to determine the optimum. The training tolerance was also set to 0.01 to ensure a balance between accuracy and over-fitting. The optimal model was found to be an ANN with 2 hidden layers and a weight decay of 0.1.

As shown in Figure 3, the variable importance rankings appear to be similar to RDA across all rating categories except for Debt to Assets, Number of Employees and Best Sales. The importance across the categories shift in order compared to RDA.

Figure 2. Variable importance ranking according to discriminant analysis

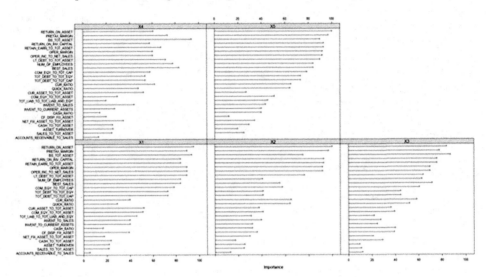

Figure 3. Variable importance ranking according to artificial neural network

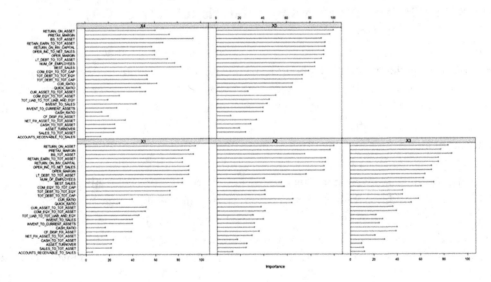

Support Vector Machine (SVM)

SVMs can be tuned using two variables in the freely available R programming language. These variables are Sigma and Cost and together they control the trade-off between the accuracy on the training data and the risk of over-fitting (resulting in poor future predictions). The settings that yielded the highest cross-validated accuracy were a Sigma of 0.03125 and Cost of 5.

The variable importance for the SVM is calculated by computing the AUC. As shown by 8, the variable importance rankings of the SVM have remained relatively similar to that of the ANN. There is only one material changes that occur in the variable importance rankings. First, Return on Invested Capital overtook Retained Earnings to Total Assets for 4th most important variable.

Figure 4. Variable importance ranking according to support vector machine

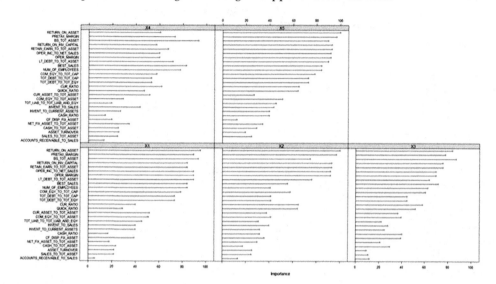

Gaussian Process Classifier (GPC)

The GPC in the R programming language can be tuned using one parameter when modelled using the popular Radial Basis kernel function-sigma. This sigma is a hyper-parameter for the kernel; it indicates the width of the Radial Basis of the kernel function and the Laplacian kernel (Shian-Chang, 2011). In essence, it represents how far away a data point needs to be before it is deemed an outlier. A higher sigma may lead to a more accurate model, but it also makes the model susceptible to over-fitting. This is essentially the same trade-off between accuracy and over-fitting. The optimal model was found to have a sigma of 0.135, chosen based on cross-validated accuracy.

The variable importance for a GPC is generated according to the technique specified by Linkletter, Bingham, Hengartner, Higdon, & Ye (2006). This methodology uses a Bayesian approach whereby it analyses the effects on the posterior distribution. As shown in Figure 5, the variable importance is essentially the same as for the SVM.

Random Forest (RF)

RF is controlled by two main parameters: the number of trees in the ensemble and the number variables to be randomly selected at each split point for each tree. 500 trees were grown based on the size of the data set. The number of variables to randomly choose is often chosen as the square root of the number of variables ($\sqrt{27} \approx 5$). However, it is prudent to empirically verify the optimum setting using cross-validation. This resulted in a setting of four, similar to the square root heuristic that suggested five.

The variable importance of the RF model is ranked using the standard metric: mean decrease in node impurity. This allows an overall ranking to be calculated, rather than a different ranking for each category. As shown in Figure 6, the variable importance is notably different to all other models. The most important variable is Best Sales, which is typically ranked around 4th in SVM and GPC and did not even make it into the top 20 most important variables for MLR. This difference is likely because

Figure 5. Variable importance ranking according to a Gaussian process classifier

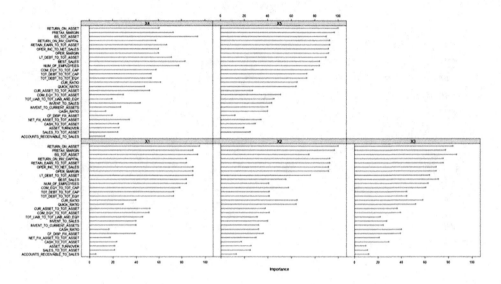

unlike the other models, Random Forest is an ensemble of multiple models and so its predictions can arguably be considered more stable.

Gradient Boosted Machines (GBMs)

GBMs can be parametrized using three main variables: the number of trees, the shrinkage (or learning) factor and the size of each individual tree. The number of trees represents the amount of weak learning predictors that will be grown in the simulation and the shrinkage factor represents the learning rate of the algorithm. The learning rate determines the rate at which it shrinks the impact of incorrect predictors. Using cross-validation, the optimal settings are 1000 trees, shrinkage of 0.005 and a minimum of 30 nodes per tree.

The variable importance method used is similar to the method used for Random Forest. The importance is measured based on the mean decrease in impurity. As shown in Figure 7, the most important variable is Return on Assets followed by Best Sales. This is similar to Random Forest, the other ensemble model, but different to all the other models.

Comparison

Table 2 shows the average results for all models, while Figure 8 shows the distribution of overall accuracy and Kappa statistic results. Based on Figure 8, an overall ranking is obtained and is shown in Table 2. All modelling techniques appeared to produce relatively similar mean average accuracy, but the top three techniques produced the largest improvement above guessing (Kappa statistic). The focus of this chapter is the comparison between models.

In general, the lowest ranked models are the parametric techniques. This makes sense as these modelling techniques make a range of assumptions that are likely not satisfied by financial data. The multinomial logistic regression is the poorest performing modelling technique in terms of average accuracy

Figure 6. Variable importance ranking according to Random Forest

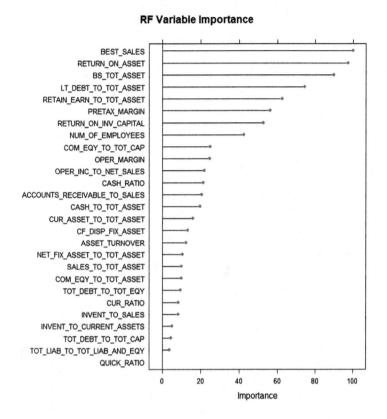

and the second worst in terms of Kappa, with a mean accuracy of 59.6% and a mean Kappa statistic of 22.6%. It is interesting to note that RDA performs worse than LDA. The two models are similar, but the RDA includes a gamma penalty parameter (optimized by cross-validation) that appears to reduce the accuracy of the model.

The ANN performed the best in terms of the Kappa statistic, suggesting it had the largest improvement compared to guessing the credit rating by chance. However, the overall accuracy was only the 6th best. The GPC performed relatively poorly compared to what was reported in Shian-Chang (2011), performing the worst in terms of Kappa and 5th in overall accuracy. The best overall performer was Random Forest, producing the highest overall accuracy and second highest Kappa statistic. This was followed closely by SVM, which produced the second highest overall accuracy and the third highest Kappa.

CONCLUSION

This chapter presented a comparative study of some of the most popular modelling techniques used to model credit ratings. These models were evaluated on 308 of the S&P 500 companies to predict the Moody's long-term credit rating. It was found that non-parametric techniques usually outperformed parametric techniques, likely because the underlying assumptions were not met by financial data. The top three performing modelling techniques were Random Forest, Artificial Neural Networks and Support Vector Machines. They produced models with an average accuracy of 64.6%, 63.6% and 60.1% respectively.

Figure 7. Variable importance ranking according to Gradient Boosted Machine

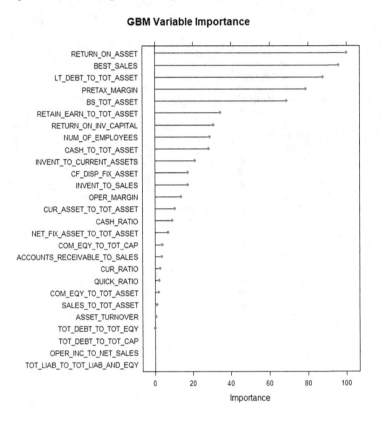

GBM Variable Importance

Table 2. Comparison of model accuracy

Method	Overall Ranking	Average Accuracy	Average Kappa
RF	1	64.6%	31.3%
SVM	2	63.6%	30.6%
ANN	3	60.8%	31.5%
GBM	4	62.3%	27.4%
LDA	5	61.7%	28.8%
RDA	6	60.4%	25.3%
MLR	7	59.6%	22.6%
GPC	8	61.6%	20.6%

Credit rating forecasting is an example of an important business process that is better modelled by flexible machine learning models that, unlike traditional parametric techniques, do not make restrictive assumptions about the data. The machine learning techniques are also better able to handle collinearity between variables in the model that can cause serious problems in traditional models. Overall, as machine learning is a key component of big data analytics, credit rating forecasting is a clear example of the value and importance of big data analytics in the future business world.

Figure 8. Box plot of model performance

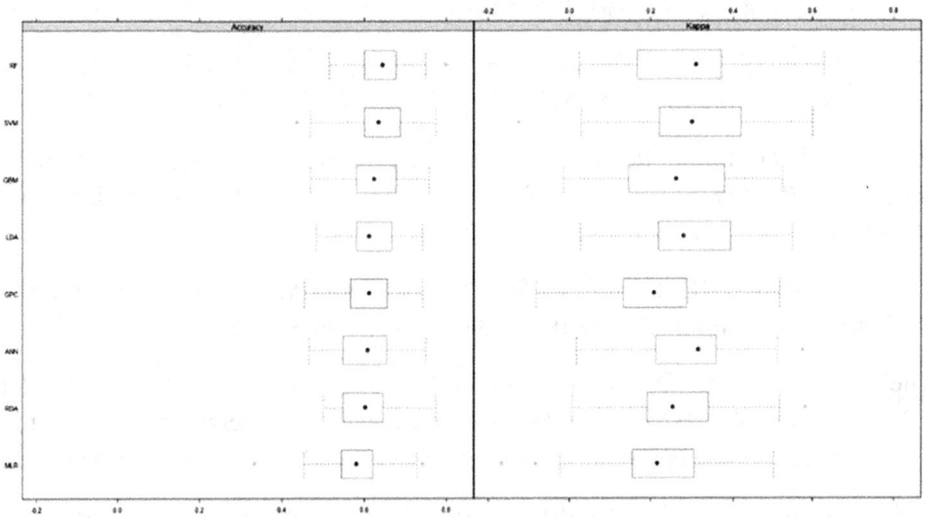

An advantage of big data analytics is its adaptability to non-traditional data sources. One such example is automated sentiment analysis that determines whether there is positive or negative sentiment in text, such as annual reports or business news. Future research could incorporate the sentiment score output from big data analytics into the credit ratings models presented in this chapter. This has the potential to substantially increase accuracy given that Hajek et al. (2016) found credit ratings were affected by positive words in the relevant company's reports and negative words in associated news articles.

REFERENCES

Abdou, H., & Pointon, J. (2011). Credit scoring, statistical techniques and evaluation criteria: A review of the literature. *Intelligent Systems in Accounting, Finance & Management, 18*(2-3), 59–88. doi:10.1002/isaf.325

Breiman, L. (2001). Random Forests. *Machine Learning, 45*(1), 5–32. doi:10.1023/A:1010933404324

Cristianini, N., & Scholkopf, B. (2002). Support Vector Machines and Kernel Methods: The New Generation of Learning Machines. *AI Magazine, 23*(3), 31–41.

Elliot, J. A., & Kennedy, D. B. (1988). Estimation and prediction of categorical models in accounting research. *Journal of Accounting Literature, 7*, 202–242.

Friedman, J. H. (2001). Greedy function approximation: A gradient boosting machine. *Annals of Statistics, 29*(5), 1189–1232. doi:10.1214/aos/1013203451

Friedman, J. H. (2002). Stochastic gradient boosting. *Computational Statistics & Data Analysis, 38*(4), 367–378. doi:10.1016/S0167-9473(01)00065-2

Ganeshalingam, S., & Kumar, K. (2001). Detection and prediction of financial distress. *Managerial Finance, 27*(4), 45–55. doi:10.1108/03074350110767132

Girolami, M., & Rogers, S. (2006). Variational Bayesian multinomial probit regression with Gaussian process priors. *Neural Computation, 18*(8), 1790–1817. doi:10.1162/neco.2006.18.8.1790

Guo, Y., Hastie, T., & Tibshirani, R. (2007). Regularized linear discriminant analysis and its application in microarrays. *Biostatistics (Oxford, England), 8*(1), 86–100. doi:10.1093/biostatistics/kxj035 PMID:16603682

Guotai, C., & Zhipeng, Z. (2017). Multi Criteria Credit Rating Model for Small Enterprise Using a Nonparametric Method. *Sustainability, 9*(10), 1834. doi:10.3390u9101834

Hajek, P., Olej, V., & Prochazka, O. (2016). Predicting Corporate Credit Ratings Using Content Analysis of Annual Reports – A Naïve Bayesian Network Approach. In S. Feuerriegel & D. Neumann (Eds.), Enterprise Applications, Markets and Services in the Finance Industry (pp 47-61). Springer.

Henley, W. E., & Hand, D. J. (1997). Construction of a k-nearest neighbour credit-scoring system. *IMA Journal of Management Mathematics, 8*(4), 305–321. doi:10.1093/imaman/8.4.305

Huang, S.-C. (2011). Using Gaussian process based kernel classifiers for credit rating forecasting. *Expert Systems with Applications, 38*(7), 8607–8611. doi:10.1016/j.eswa.2011.01.064

Huang, S.-C., Chuang, P. J., Wu, C. F., & Lai, H. J. (2010). Chaos-based support vector regressions for exchange rate forecasting. *Expert Systems with Applications, 37*(12), 8590–8598. doi:10.1016/j.eswa.2010.06.001

Imad, B.-H. (2017). Bayesian credit ratings: A random forest alternative approach. *Communications in Statistics. Theory and Methods, 46*(15), 7289–7300. doi:10.1080/03610926.2016.1148730

Khemakhem, S., & Boujelbene, Y. (2015). Credit Risk Prediction: A comparative study between discriminant analysis and the neural network approach. *Accounting and Management Information Systems, 14*(1), 60–78.

Kumar, K., & Bhattacharya, S. (2006). Artificial neural network vs linear discriminant analysis in credit ratings forecast. *Review of Accounting and Finance, 5*(3), 216–227. doi:10.1108/14757700610686426

Kumar, K., & Haynes, J. D. (2003). Forecasting credit ratings using an ANN and statistical techniques. *International Journal of Business Studies, 11*(1), 91-108.

Lilley, M., & Frean, M. (2005) Neural Networks: A Replacement for Gaussian Processes? In Intelligent Data Engineering and Automated Learning - IDEAL 2005 (pp. 195-212). Springer. doi:10.1007/11508069_26

Linkletter, C., Bingham, D., Hengartner, N., Higdon, D., & Ye, K. Q. (2006). Variable selection for Gaussian process models in computer experiments. *Technometrics, 48*(4), 478–490. doi:10.1198/004017006000000228

Miyamoto, M. (2014). Credit risk assessment for a small bank by using a multinomial logistic regression model. *International Journal of Finance and Accounting, 3*(5), 327–334.

Moody's Investor service. (2017). *Moody's rating system in brief.* Retrieved from https://www.moodys. com/sites/products/ProductAttachments/Moody's%20Rating%20System.pdf

Negnevitsky, M. (2011). *Artificial intelligence: a guide to intelligent systems.* Harlow, UK: Addison Wesley/Pearson.

Provost, F., & Fawcett, T. (2013). *Data science for business.* Sebastopol, CA: O'Reilly Media.

Sewell, M. (2008). *Structural Risk Minimization.* Technical Report: Department of Computer Science, University College London. Retrieved from http://www.svms.org/srm/

Shian-Chang, H. (2011). Using Gaussian process based kernel classifiers for credit rating forecasting. *Expert Systems with Applications, 38*(7), 8607–8611. doi:10.1016/j.eswa.2011.01.064

Standard & Poor's. (2016, October 12). *Standard & Poor's History.* Retrieved from https://www.isin. net/standard-poors/

Steenackers, A., & Goovaerts, M. J. (1989). A credit scoring model for personal loans. *Insurance, Mathematics & Economics, 8*(1), 31–34. doi:10.1016/0167-6687(89)90044-9

Stepanova, M., & Thomas, L. C. (2001). PHAB scores: Proportional hazards analysis. *The Journal of the Operational Research Society, 52*(9), 1007–1016. doi:10.1057/palgrave.jors.2601189

Wu, H.-C., & Wu, Y.-T. (2016). Evaluating credit rating prediction by using the KMV model and random forest. *Kybernetes, 45*(10), 1637–1651. doi:10.1108/K-12-2014-0285

Yobas, M. B., & Crook, J. N. (2000). Credit scoring using neural and evolutionary techniques. *IMA Journal of Management Mathematics, 11*(2), 111–125. doi:10.1093/imaman/11.2.111

APPENDIX

Cohen's Kappa statistic is best explained using an example. The following example is related to 50 events, each which is either *Yes* or *No*. The goal of the model is to predict the *Yes/No* result of each event. The accuracy of the result is derived from the underlying truth of the variable. As shown by Table 3, out of the 50 events, 20 were correctly predicted *yes* and 15 were correctly predicted *no*. That means the observed accuracy is (20+15)/50=0.70 or 70%.

This accuracy however does not consider the expected accuracy based on the fact that, in truth, there are more *Yes* events than *No* events. Using the following equation, the Kappa statistic considers the expected chance of agreement between the truth and the model.

$$K = \left(P_o - P_e\right) / \left(1 - P_e\right),$$

where P_o represents the observed agreement and P_e represents the expected agreement.
The observed agreement is the accuracy calculated in the example above; in this case, 70%. The expected accuracy is calculated by summing the probability that the truth and the model agree on yes and agree on no:

- The model predicted *Yes* 25 (20+5) times and *No* 25 (10+15) times, which means the model predicts *Yes* 50% of the time;
- In truth, *Yes* occurs 30 (20+10) times, which represents 60% (30/50);
- Therefore, the probability that, at random, the model correctly predicts *Yes* is $0.5 \times 0.6 = 0.3$. The same calculation for *No* events is $\left(1 - 0.5\right) \times \left(1 - 0.6\right) = 0.2$. This process is then continued if there are more than two categories. Finally, the sum of these two figures is calculated as the expected accuracy, which is in this case $0.3 + 0.2 = 0.5$.

The Kappa can then be calculated, as

$$K = \frac{0.7 - 0.5}{1 - 0.5} = 0.4$$

Table 3. Visits to public libraries

		Truth	
		Yes	**No**
Model Prediction	**Yes**	20	5
	No	10	15

Chapter 11
Analysis of Cutting–Edge Regression Algorithms Used for Data Analysis

Indivar Mishra
KIIT University, India

Ritwik Bandyopadhyay
KIIT University, India

Sourish Ghosh
KIIT University, India

Aleena Swetapadma
KIIT University, India

ABSTRACT

Considering the growing applications of big data analytics in the various fields such as healthcare, finance, e-commerce, and web services, it is essential to continuously develop techniques useful for big data. Among various techniques used for big data analytics, regression analysis is very important. In this chapter, an attempt is made to take a detailed look into some of the main regression algorithms and their origin that are used for big data analytics. In this study, some of very famous works related to regression along with some latest research are analyzed. Regression is the process of deducing a predictive model for real-world information based on verified information that is already received. It is used for making predictions, optimizing solutions to complex problems, and understands trends in large and big data analytics. The goal of this study is to promote and facilitate a better understanding of regression algorithms that are in use in the real world for big data analytics.

DOI: 10.4018/978-1-5225-7277-0.ch011

INTRODUCTION

With advancement of technology the amount of data is increasing exponentially which makes it difficult for data scientists to retrieve much of useful information out of it. Classical data analysis techniques focus on data collection followed by the imposition of a model, analysis, estimation and testing that depends on the parameters of that model. This type of analysis is not suitable for all types of data as it is a hectic job to explicitly program the system with respect to new datasets. This is where big data analytics comes in to the picture. Big data analytics uses various techniques for analysis such as rule-based systems, machine learning, multi-agent systems techniques, neural networks systems, fuzzy logic systems, cased-based reasoning techniques, genetic algorithms techniques, data mining algorithms, cognitive computing, natural computing, intelligent agents etc. Among these techniques for big data analytics, regression is an important method which is focused in this study.

In this study various types regression algorithms has been described in brief and its importance in big data analytics has been explored. Various types of regression algorithm that has been used for big data analytics are linear regression, polynomial regression, support vector machine regression, decision tree regression, ensemble learning regression, neural network regression, pattern aided regression etc. Above described regression algorithms and its relation with respect to big data analytics will be described in the next section.

BACKGROUND

Before diving into regression and methods to implement it, first it must be mentioned clearly basics and importance of a dataset in big data analytics. Data as the formal definition goes are unprocessed facts, in predictive modeling data has two parts dependent and independent data/variable/feature, goal is to build relation for dependent variable with respect to one or more independent variables. Dependent variables are those variables whose scalar/vector magnitude value depend on independent variables and can be found through some relation among independent variables, on the other hand independent variables are the variables which are not dependent or have any relation with other variables in the dataset. Datasets can be discrete data or continuous data (Pasta, 2009).

Regression algorithms are used to predict continuous variables/data on the basis of one or more independent variables (Rawlings, Pantula, & Dickey, 1998). Attempts at regression date back to the days of the legendary Isaac Newton and Joseph-Louis Lagrange. The crudest attempt at this was interpolation- where, given (n+1) points on a 2-D plane, a polynomial of degree n satisfying all those points can be derived. Then the values at all other points by using this polynomial can be predicted. Unfortunately, such a simple solution cannot be applied in the fabrication of an intelligent device. This method is used for mathematical purposes with purely academic ambition.

The solution relies overly on the training data supplied to it. This is called over-fitting. In Figure1, the red line shows a curve that uses a method like interpolation and exhibits the problem of over-fitting. The green line does not touch each point given, but it is a better predictive model because the total error is less. It shows the difference between a useful regression model and a curve obtained by interpolation which goes through each given data point. At the point labeled 0.9, the approximate error for the red line

Figure 1. A simple example demonstrating over-fitting

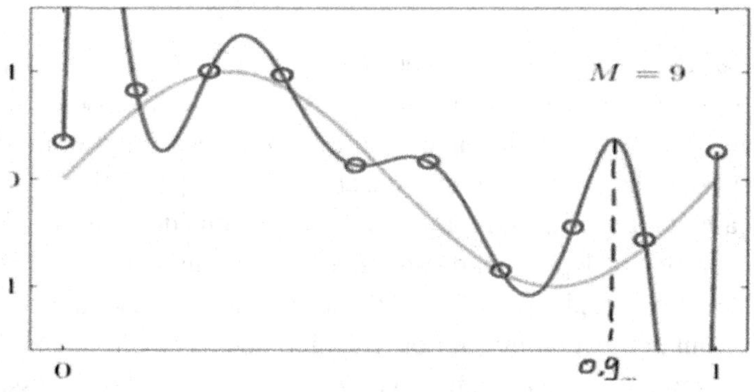

is much higher than that for the green line. This means, that the green line is a much more accurate predictive model- as mentioned earlier. This is achieved through some of the methods discussed in this study.

REGRESSION TECHNIQUES

Above described problems paved the way for mathematicians, who eventually evolved into computer scientists, to chalk up algorithms for regression. The ultimate objective of these attempts was to find a way to fashion a predictive model which is neither too reliant on the data provided, nor overly generalized (Umam, n.d.). This optimization between bias and variance is the main challenge of regression algorithms. This has many approaches giving weight-age to certain points, using error functions to determine the usefulness of a data point or even using simple conditional statements. There are various types of regression algorithm which are being used in big data analytics such as linear regression, polynomial regression, support vector machine regression, decision tree regression, ensemble learning regression, neural network regression, pattern aided regression etc. Some of the regression methods have been discussed below.

Linear Regression

It is a very basic and popularly used algorithm to find a linear relation between dependent and independent variables. If there is only one independent variable then it is called simple linear regression as shown in (1),

$$Y = A_0 + A_1 X_1 + E \tag{1}$$

Similarly there is one more type of regression called as multiple linear regressions. Multiple regressions are the relationship between several independent or predictor variables and a dependent or criterion variable (Su, Gao, Li, & Tao, 2012). If a relation is to be built from more than one independent variables then it's called multiple linear regressions as shown in (2).

$$Y = A_0 + A_1 X_1 + A_2 X_2 + \ldots + A_n X_n + E \qquad (2)$$

Here the variables X_1, X_2, ..., X_n are the independent variables and Y is the dependent variable and E is the error related to prediction. The coefficients A_0, A_1, ..., A_n are chosen such that the line drawn through these equations have minimum distance from each point causing minimum error.

Figure 2 shows the example graph of simple linear regression prediction line with corresponding errors. In Figure 2, a case of simple linear regression has been considered in which the red dots are dependent value on y-axis which is dependent on an independent value on x-axis. When some dataset to the algorithm is provided it will find coefficients A0 and A1 such that the line using these coefficients will be closest to each point of the training dataset. The blue line represents equation shown above. The magnitude of green line shows the error related to each prediction. If all the possible error with every possible coefficient from the equation will plotted it will always form out to be a convex contour plot as show in Figure 3.

In Figure 3 the two horizontal axes are the two coefficients (in case for simple linear regression) and corresponding vertical axis gives error associated with those coefficients. Coefficients of linear equation mentioned above are calculated by using cost function. The very purpose of the cost function is to find the coefficients of equation such that the magnitude of error is minimal. This algorithm is known as gradient descent algorithm (Hall'en, 2017) as shown in (3).

$$J\left(a\right) = 1/2m \sum_{i=1}^{m} \left(h(x^i) - y^i \right)^2 \qquad (3)$$

The above formula is repeated until convergence with arbitrary coefficients usually (0, 0). For every iteration, coefficients are chosen such that the resulting value of the cost function is minimum, and the coefficients are updated after everyone complete execution. In Cervellera & Macciò (2014) a method has been suggested for linear regression which concludes that the estimation improves as the discrepancy of the observation points becomes smaller. It allows to treat indifferently the cases in which the samples come from a random external source and the one in which the input space can be freely explored. Lasso is a popular technique for joint estimation and continuous variable selection for sparse linear regression problems. In Mateos, Bazerque, & Giannakis (2010), an algorithm had been developed to estimate the

Figure 2. Graph of simple linear regression prediction line with corresponding errors

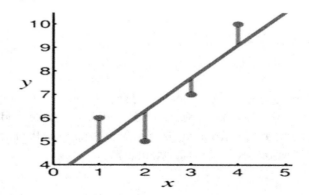

Figure 3. Contour plot

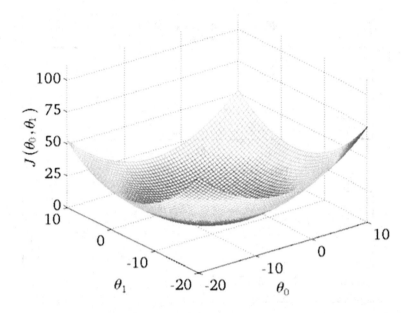

regression coefficients via Lasso when the training data are distributed across different agents, and their communication to a central processing unit is prohibited. Other than linear regression there is one more type of linear regression called polynomial linear regression which will be explored in the subsection below.

Polynomial Linear Regression

Linear regression as discussed above is a good method for data fitting when there is a linear relation among the variables. But when dataset is concerned about growth of population, tissues etc., where there is exponential increase in dependent variable over small change in independent variable, then the linear models fail to show a good fit/prediction. In these cases polynomial linear regression come in handy. Polynomial linear regression is capable of fitting non linear data. Generalized equation for linear model with one independent variable is shown in (4) and generalized equation for polynomial model with one independent variable is shown in (5),

$$Y = A_0 + A_1.X_1 \tag{4}$$

$$Y = A_0 + A_1.X_1 + A_2.X_2^2 \tag{5}$$

Figure 4 shows two plots, first line is fitted using linear regression and latter is fitted using polynomial regression. It is clear from Figure4 that polynomial model is far better fitted than linear model. It's the X_2^2 factor that gives the curve parabolic effect and hence covering most of the points in the plot with minimum error. Like linear regression, polynomial linear regression also works on the concept of

Figure 4. Comparison of fit between simple linear and polynomial fit

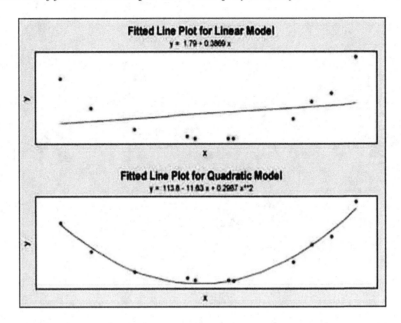

ordinary least square method. Generalized polynomial equation for one independent variable is shown in (6),

$$Y = A_0 + A_1.X_1 + A_2.X_2^2 + A_3.X_3^3 + ... + A_n.X_n^2 \tag{6}$$

Depending on the highest power used in an equation they are named as quadratic, cubic, quadratic and so on. Polynomial models are still called linear models as there coefficients which are known are have linear dependency i.e. a0, a1, a2... an, hence polynomial linear is a special case of multiple linear regression.

Support Vector Machines Regression (SVR)

Now that there is a general idea about regression and its importance in classifying dataset by generating decision boundaries. But the problem arises when a dataset is classified where the two or more classes of data are not linearly separable (Osuna, Freund, & Girosi, 1997). This is where the idea of SVM, championed by Vladimir Vapnik in Statistical Learning Theory (1998), comes in which can generate a non linear decision boundary by drawing hyper-planes with the help of kernels as shown in Figure 5 (Lin, Huang, & Chiueh, 1998).

SVM, a supervised learning algorithm, is a large margin learner that is it chooses such a decision boundary where there is maximum distance between the hyper-plane and the corresponding classes of data or the best line that can fit the training data keeping a maximum margin. Classification is the process by which an algorithm analyzes the decision boundary taking help from the training data containing known observations. Likewise in regression, it estimates the relationship among one or more

Figure 5. A typical case of support vector machine

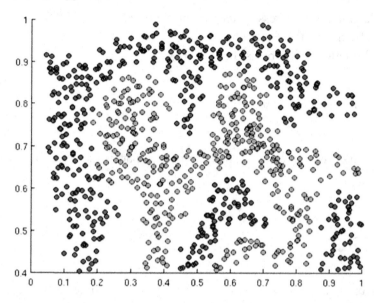

independent variables. SVM works on empirical risk minimization which leads us to an optimization function as given in (7).

$$minimum of \omega \sum \ell \left(x_i, y_i, \omega\right) + \lambda \cdot r \left(\omega\right) \tag{7}$$

where l is the hinge loss function and r is the regularization function. In case of support vector regression (SVR), where the output takes on continuous values, it becomes very difficult to predict the best fit line. A loss function is defined that ignores the errors, which are situated at certain distance of the true value. This function is known as Epsilon (ξ) intensive loss function (Cherkassky & Ma, 2002), which is a

Figure 6. A support vector regressor mode forming the best line between the 2 dotted lines

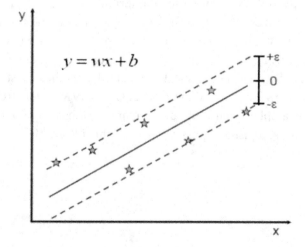

margin of tolerance. However, the main idea is to minimize error while individualizing the hyperplane which maintains a large-margin regressor, keeping in mind that a part of the error has to be tolerated. The SVR model has been shown in Figure 6.

Thus, the general solution would be as shown in (8),

$$min \frac{1}{2} \mid \|\omega\| \mid^2 \text{ with constraint } y_i - \omega x_i - b \leq \varepsilon \tag{8}$$

where $\|\omega\|$ is the length of the vector $\vec{\omega}$. Another important part is the error minimization as shown in (9),

$$\frac{1}{2} \mid \|\omega\| \mid^2 + c \sum_{i=1}^{N} \left(\xi i + \xi' i \right) \tag{9}$$

When moving from non-linear SVR where no best line is possible to fit the data it is needed to transform that data into a much higher dimensional feature vector. This is achieved with the help of kernel functions (Smola & Schölkopf, 1998). There are mainly 2 types of kernel functions that are used mostly. Those are polynomial function and Gaussian radial basis function which are given in (10) and (11) respectively.

$$k\left(xi, xj \right) = \left(xi \cdot xj \right)^d \tag{10}$$

$$k\left(xi, xj \right) = exp\left(-\frac{\mid \|xi - xj\| \mid^2}{2\sigma^2} \right) \tag{11}$$

SVR have been very successful in pattern recognition and function estimation problems for crisp data. In (Hong & Hwang, 2005), a new method to evaluate interval linear and nonlinear regression models combining the possibility and necessity estimation formulation with the principle of quadratic loss SVR has been proposed. It utilizes quadratic loss function, unlike the traditional SVM. When function approximation in SVR is non-stationary the single kernel approach may be ineffective. In (Bellocchio, Ferrari, Piuri, & Borghese, 2012), a hierarchical SVR model has been presented which aims to provide a good solution. It consists of a set of hierarchical layers, each containing a standard SVR with Gaussian kernel at a given scale. However with all these advantages, SVR suffers from a basic disadvantage. When number of training examples is much more than number of features, SVR can take up a lot of time to train. In such circumstances, logistic regression is preferable over SVR.

Decision Tree Regression

Decision tree as name suggests works on the principles of traditional data structures tree (Mohamed & Robert, 2010). Decision tree, also known as CART (Breiman, Friedman, Olshen, & Stone, 1987), is a powerful tool to predict dependent variables compared to other algorithms, the basic/generalised idea behind working of decision trees are to keep splitting the dataset to smaller homogeneous groups, and then check if a data belongs to that particular group. Consider the plot shown in Figure 7 (a). Suppose it is required to predict a dependent variable with two independent variables x1 and x2, so the dependent variable will be perpendicular to the plane (x1, x2). Now if a point in this plane say (x01, x02) is placed then and its corresponding value which is the average of the data points in the plane, which will give a very poor prediction if we apply this idea to our machine learning algorithm. Ironically decision tree uses somewhat similar approach the algorithm divides the plane into sub planes (nodes) until each plane has considerable homogeneity, or maximum features/depth is reached (leaf nodes). For decision tree regression the splits in the regions are made taking those independent variables first which have minimum value of cost function i.e. error, and it keeps dividing the recursively until a criterion like maximum splits/maximum depth is reached.

Figure 7 (c) shows decision making tree model to predict the value given dependent variable in our case x1 and x2, the small triangles are decision-making nodes and rectangular boxes are the predicted values of particular x1,x2 model also called leaf node of tree which basically contain average value of the split region in Figure 7 (b). Suppose x1 = 0.6 and x2 = 0.6, now from Figure 7 (c) it can be observed that x2 is not smaller than 0.55 therefore move to the right child (decision node) of tree which gives another condition clearly x1 is not smaller than 0.23 therefore again move to right child of the decisive node where next condition is satisfied so move to left child node of the decisive node and apparently reach leaf node which will contain average value of data points in the region 4 in Figure 7 (b).

Figure 7a. A random data set scattered in 2-D plane

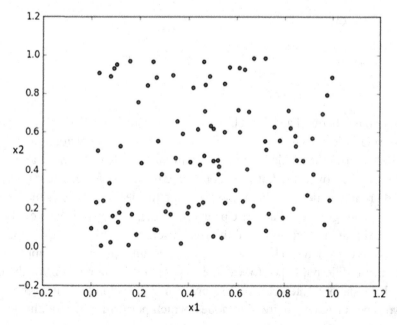

Figure 7b. After applying Decision tree algorithm 2-D plane with virtual/imaginary lines

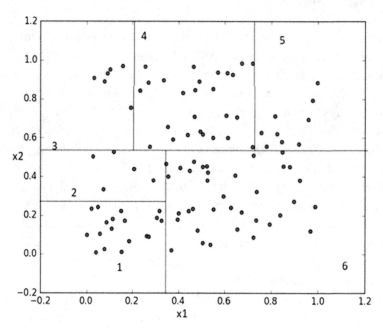

Figure 7c. Decision tree graph of said dataset

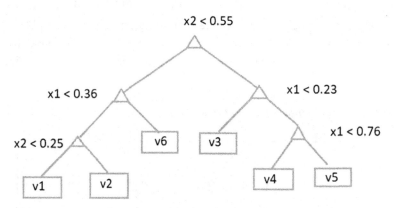

Decision tree are much better than other classifiers as they give an intuitive tree from which one can understand how the classification is done and which feature has most contribution in the problem. They are one of the powerful tool for predictive modelling in machine learning arsenal but still it has some drawbacks like it easily gets over fitted, it works on a greedy approach etc. These problems are handled by a method called pruning which simply means removing the decisive nodes which have less contribution to the classification/regression (Patel & Upadhyay, 2012). In Gey & Nedelec (2005), performance of the regression trees pruning algorithm and the final discrete selection by test sample as a functional estimation procedure is considered. The validation of the pruning procedure is applied to Gaussian and bounded regression. In Malerba, Esposito, Ceci, & Appice (2004) a method for the data-driven construction of model trees is presented called as stepwise model tree induction method. Main feature of the method is two types of nodes: regression nodes, which perform only straight-line regression, and splitting nodes, which partition the feature space. The multiple linear models associated with each leaf are then built stepwise by combining straight-line regressions reported along the path from the root to the leaf. Internal regression nodes contribute to the definition of multiple models which have global effect. Straight-line regressions at leaves have local effects. These trees are simple and easily interpretable and their analysis often reveals interesting patterns.

Ensemble Learning Regression

Sometimes, these predictive models by themselves are not very effective. That is where ensemble learning comes in. In Freund & Schapire (1999), a bottom-up approach where a number of weak learners are given and a better predictive model is obtained by combining them. A weak learner is defined as a learning algorithm that has an error rate less than a half. In this paper, we come across the concept of AdaBoost. In this algorithm, a weak learner is trained on the training dataset for T times. Every time, the training data has a distribution of weight over itself and after every round of training, the weight is increased for samples with higher error rate. Which means, as the number of rounds of training increases, the error keeps going down. The maximum training error and the generalisation error are also calculated.

Similar algorithms include Gradient tree boosting and XGBoost. These are basically ways to improve the basic weak learner used and then incorporate them to the simple AdaBoost processing that is discussed in Freund & Schapire (1999). In simpler words, the difference between them is similar, in a manner, to the difference between simple and compound interest on a fixed sum of money. Another widely used type is bootstrap aggregating or bagging. In this, the training dataset is divided into subsets. Then the learner is trained on each of these training data subsets. Then average all the learning models derived and do not score. Figure 8 shows the plot of error and round for training and testing.

This gives a much better predictive model than others. This is better than the other regression models because the models that are biased due to over-fitting have very little effect. In ensemble learning regression, due to repetitive use of the algorithms, the generalization error is very hard to remove.

Figure 8. Lower curve for training and upper curve for testing

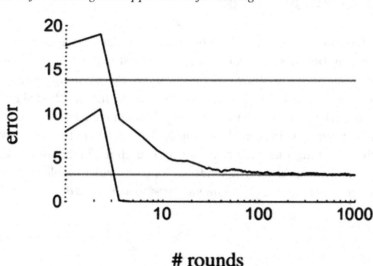

APPLICATIONS OF REGRESSION IN BIG DATA ANALYTICS FRAMEWORK

The above described regression algorithms are used most frequently in big data analytics framework. Some of the applications of regression algorithm in big data analytics will be discussed here. In Berberidis, Kekatos, & Giannakis (2016), a method was suggested for identifying and omitting less informative observations in an online and data-adaptive fashion. Here the maximum-likelihood estimator is sequentially found using first- and second-order stochastic approximation algorithms. These schemes are well suited when data are inherently censored or when the aim is to save communication overhead in decentralized learning setups.

In Lin, Chen, & Tsai (2016), a novel robust non-contact technique has been suggested for the evaluation of heart rate variation. Here ensemble empirical mode decomposition of the Hilbert-Huang transform has been used to acquire the primary heart rate signal. The instantaneous frequencies from intrinsic mode functions are implemented by the multiple-linear regression model to evaluate heart rates. Predicting the bug number of a software system is important for project managers and software end-users. In Zhang, Du, Yoshida, Wang, & Li (2018), a method called SamEn-SVR has been proposed to combine sample entropy and support vector regression (SVR) to predict software bug number. Template vectors are used with the smallest complexity as input vectors for SVR classifiers to ensure predictability.

Transmission lines are one of the major components of the electrical power system. With the growing demand of the power the number of transmission lines is increasing day by day. With increase in transmission lines the type and volume of the data are also increasing. To efficiently manage this type big data in electrical power system various data analytics techniques has been used. In Swetapadma & Yadav (2017), a decision tree regression based fault distance estimation scheme for double-circuit transmission lines has been presented. Here decision tree regression was chosen because it requires less training time, offers greater accuracy with a large data set, and robustness than all other techniques like artificial neural networks, support vector machines, adaptive neuro-fuzzy inference systems, etc. The scheme is relatively simple and easy in comparison with complex equation-based fault-location estimation methods.

CONCLUSION AND FUTURE WORK

Big data analytics is the most interesting topic of the data science due to the increasing and large data in today's world in almost all fields. Regression is one of the most important techniques used in big data among various other techniques. In this study, concept of various regression algorithms has been presented. It was observed that there is no best algorithm for regression. The ones mentioned are the primary types of regression algorithms. These are used based on the application intended and the constraints imposed by the nature of training data. Algorithms implementing other learners to keep working on a problem are called auto machine learning which the next stage of everything in this study is. However, there is no algorithm to determine the optimal method needed for a particular problem. That would need a algorithm coupled with natural language processing to come to a credible decision for big data analytics.

REFERENCES

Bellocchio, F., Ferrari, S., Piuri, V., & Borghese, N. (2012). Hierarchical Approach for Multi-scale Support Vector Regression. *IEEE Transactions on Neural Networks and Learning Systems*, *23*(9), 1448–1460. doi:10.1109/TNNLS.2012.2205018 PMID:24807928

Berberidis, D., Kekatos, V., & Giannakis, G. (2016). Online Censoring for Large-Scale Regressions with Application to Streaming Big Data. *IEEE Transactions on Signal Processing*, *64*(15), 3854–3867. doi:10.1109/TSP.2016.2546225 PMID:28042229

Breiman, L., Friedman, J., Olshen, R., & Stone, C. (1987). Classification and Regression Trees. *Cytometry*, *8*, 534–535.

Cervellera, C., & Macciò, D. (2014). Local Linear Regression for Function Learning: An Analysis Based on Sample Discrepancy. *IEEE Transactions on Neural Networks and Learning Systems*, *25*(11), 2086–2098. doi:10.1109/TNNLS.2014.2305193 PMID:25330431

Cherkassky, V., & Ma, Y. (2002). *Selecting of the Loss Function for Robust Linear Regression*. Academic Press.

Freund, Y., & Schapire, R. (1999). A Short Introduction to Boosting. *Proceedings of the 16th international joint conference on Artificial intelligence*, *2*, 1401-1406.

Gey, S., & Nedelec, E. (2005). Model selection for CART regression trees. *IEEE Transactions on Information Theory*, *51*(2), 658–670. doi:10.1109/TIT.2004.840903

Hall'en, R. (2017). *A Study of Gradient-Based Algorithms*. Mathematical Statistics, Lund University Libraries.

Hong, D., & Hwang, C. (2005). Interval regression analysis using quadratic loss support vector machine. *IEEE Transactions on Fuzzy Systems*, *13*(2), 229–237. doi:10.1109/TFUZZ.2004.840133

Lin, K., Chen, D., & Tsai, W. (2016). Face-Based Heart Rate Signal Decomposition and Evaluation Using Multiple Linear Regression. *IEEE Sensors Journal*, *16*(5), 1351–1360. doi:10.1109/JSEN.2015.2500032

Lin, S., Huang, R., & Chiueh, T. (1998). A tunable Gaussian/square function computation circuit for analog neural networks. *IEEE Transactions on Circuits and Systems. 2, Analog and Digital Signal Processing*, *45*(3), 441–446. doi:10.1109/82.664259

Malerba, D., Esposito, F., Ceci, M., & Appice, A. (2004). Top-down induction of model trees with regression and splitting nodes. *IEEE Transactions on Pattern Analysis and Machine Intelligence*, *26*(5), 612–625. doi:10.1109/TPAMI.2004.1273937 PMID:15460282

Mateos, G., Bazerque, J., & Giannakis, G. (2010). Distributed Sparse Linear Regression. *IEEE Transactions on Signal Processing*, *58*(10), 5262–5276. doi:10.1109/TSP.2010.2055862

Mohamed, H., & Robert, P. (2010). *Dynamic Tree Algorithms*. arXiv:0809.3577 [math.PR]

Osuna, E., Freund, R., & Girosi, F. (1997). An Improved Training Algorithm for Support Vector Machines. *Proceedings of the IEEE Signal Processing Society Workshop on Neural Networks for Signal Processing VII*, 276-285. 10.1109/NNSP.1997.622408

Pasta, D. (2009). *Learning When to Be Discrete: Continuous vs. Categorical Predictors*. San Francisco, CA: ICON Clinical Research.

Patel, N., & Upadhyay, S. (2012). Study of Various Decision Tree Pruning Methods with their Empirical Comparison in WEKA. *International Journal of Computers and Applications*, 60(12), 20–25. doi:10.5120/9744-4304

Rawlings, J., Pantula, S., & Dickey, D. (1998). *Applied Regression Analysis: A Research Tool*. Springer. doi:10.1007/b98890

Smola, A., & Schölkopf, B. (1998). *A Tutorial on Support Vector Regression NeuroCOLT Technical Report*. NC-TR-98-030, Royal Holloway College, University of London, UK.

Su, Y., Gao, X., Li, X., & Tao, D. (2012). Multivariate Multilinear Regression. *IEEE Transactions on Systems, Man, and Cybernetics. Part B, Cybernetics*, 42(6), 1560–1573. doi:10.1109/TSMCB.2012.2195171 PMID:22677310

Swetapadma, A., & Yadav, A. (2017). A Novel Decision Tree Regression-Based Fault Distance Estimation Scheme for Transmission Lines. *IEEE Transactions on Power Delivery*, 32(1), 234–245. doi:10.1109/TPWRD.2016.2598553

Umam, A. (n.d.). *Ardian Umam Blog*. Retrieved from https://ardianumam.wordpress.com/tag/regression/ArdianUmam Blog.

Vapnik, V. (1998). *Statistical Learning Theory*. New York: Wiley-Interscience Publication.

Zhang, W., Du, Y., Yoshida, T., Wang, Q., & Li, X. (2018). SamEn-SVR: Using sample entropy and support vector regression for bug number prediction. *IET Software*, 12(3), 183–189. doi:10.1049/iet-sen.2017.0168

ADDITIONAL READING

Baesens, B. (2014). *Analytics in a Big Data World: The Essential Guide to Data Science and Its Applications*. North Carolina, USA: Wiley.

Cady, F. (2017). *The Data Science Handbook*. New Jersy, USA: Wiley. doi:10.1002/9781119092919

Dasgupta, N. (2018). *Practical Big Data Analytics*. Birmingham, United Kingdom: Packt Publishing.

Dhiraj, A., Minelli, M., & Chambers, M. (2012). *Big Data, Big Analytics*. New Jersy, USA: Wiley CIO Series.

Marr, B. (2015). *Big Data: Using SMART Big Data, Analytics and Metrics To Make Better Decisions and Improve Performance*. USA: Wiley.

Mayer-Schonberger, V., & Cukier, K. (2013). *Big Data: A Revolution That Will Transform How We Live, Work and Think*. London: John Murray.

Zikopoulos, P., & Eaton, C. (2011). *Understanding Big Data: Analytics for Enterprise Class Hadoop and Streaming Data*. USA: McGraw-Hill.

KEY TERMS AND DEFINITIONS

Big Data: It is a massive volume of both structured and unstructured data that is difficult to process using traditional techniques.

CART: It is the classification and regression trees which work on decision tree algorithms that can be used for classification or regression predictive modelling.

Data Analytics: It is the process of examining data to draw conclusions about the information they contain.

Ensemble Learning: It uses multiple learning algorithms to obtain better predictive performance than could be obtained from any of the constituent learning algorithms alone.

Linear Regression: It is an approach to modelling the relationship between a scalar response and explanatory variables.

Regression: It is a statistical measure used to determine the strength of the relationship between one dependent variable and a series of other changing variables.

SVM Kernels: SVM algorithms use a set of mathematical functions called kernel which take data as input and transform it into the required form.

Chapter 12
Proactive Information Security Strategy for a Secure Business Environment

Ionica Oncioiu
Titu Maiorescu University, Romania

Anca Gabriela Petrescu
Valahia University, Romania

Diana Andreea Mândricel
Titu Maiorescu University, Romania

Ana Maria Ifrim
Titu Maiorescu University, Romania

ABSTRACT

Taking into consideration the competitive market, the protection of information infrastructure for a company means competitive advantage. The protected information along with risk analysis are the underlying decision making in the company: either development, positioning on new markets, expansion on emerging markets, exit markets, or acquisitions. At the same time, the protection of information together with operational business intelligence systems are the keys for the decisions of CEOs. Implementing appropriate security measures to counter threats such as attacks can be blocked, or its effects can be mitigated. In this context, this chapter intends to be a thorough reflection on the awareness of potential threats and vulnerabilities, as well as a preoccupation towards cooperation in countering them with well-established rules and mechanisms created at a national and organizational level. The results are relevant to better understand how the actors involved in information and communication technologies could develop new models of information systems and risk management strategies.

DOI: 10.4018/978-1-5225-7277-0.ch012

INTRODUCTION

Today it is considered that information is secured (protected) by ensuring a balanced availability, confidentiality, integrity, authenticity and non-repudiation of them, so far as is necessary entity created it or who uses it (Baskerville, 2010; Martinez-Caro et al., 2018; Tropina & Callanan, 2015).

Risks can impact organizations in the short, medium or long (Andress, 2003; Da Veiga, 2016; Stepchenko & Voronova, 2015). These risks are operational, tactical and respectively strategically (Gandotra, Singhal & Bedi, 2012). Strategy sets the long-term objectives of the organization; the term typically is approximately 3-5 years (Hong, Kim & Cho, 2010). Tactics is how organizations intend to achieve change (Hiller & Russel, 2013; Tutton, 2010).

Therefore, the risks generally associated tactical projects, mergers, acquisitions, product development, and so on (Bojanc & Jerman-Blažic, 2012). Operations are routine activities of the organization, having, in turn, associated operational risks (Gkioulos et al., 2017). Implementing appropriate security measures to counter threats such as attacks can be blocked or its effects can be mitigated (McQuade, 2006).

Prevention means that the attack will be prevented (Baskerville, Spagnoletti & Kim, 2014; Renaud et al., 2018). Typically, prevention involves implementation of mechanisms that users not be able to counteract and are implemented correctly, unaltered, so the attacker cannot alter those (Singer & Friedman, 2014). Prevention mechanisms are cumbersome and often interfere with the use of the system to the point that, sometimes hamper normal use thereof (Winkler, 2010). But some simple preventive mechanisms with as passwords (which are designed to prevent unauthorized users from using the system) have become widely accepted plan (Banker, Chang, & Kao, 2010; Sveen, Torres & Sarriegi, 2009). Once implemented, the resources protected by mechanisms not are monitored to identify any security issues, at least in theory (Ruževičius & Gedminaitė, 2007).

At the same time, this process requires a division of responsibilities clearly delineated within the organization, creating a culture of risk prevention at all levels of the organization (Landoll, 2010).

Organizational culture has also impact on the level of risk tolerance, reflected in opening the organization to adopt cutting-edge high technology (Da Veiga, 2016). For example, it is expected to open such organizations that are engaged in research and development (Ahmad, Maynard & Park, 2014; Flowerday & Tuyikeze, 2016). These organizations are prepared to adopt new technologies and, therefore, more likely to see these technologies in terms of the potential benefits against the potential disadvantages (Karim, 2007).

In contrast, organizations that are involved in activities related to information security can be more conservative, their appetite for new technologies being booked, especially if the products are developed less known entities or unreliable (Clarke-Sather et al., 2011). These types of organizations are often reluctant to adopt new technologies and are more inclined to look at new products rather in terms of the damage it can cause. Another example is the cases of organizations customize their software and services or develop applications or services solely for them (Shamala, Ahmad, Zolait & Sahib, 2015). Other organizations may be reluctant to use software or services developed by other entities (Dor & Elovici, 2016). This reluctance may result in other risks. On the other hand, there are organizations seeking maximize the benefits of modern technologies such as cloud computing, service oriented architectures, calling for it to external entities (Mohammed, Ibrahim, & Ithnin, 2016; Renwick & Martin, 2017). Given that the organization typically has no control over how external entity performing the analysis and handling of information security risks, additional risks may concerns the organization (Peltier, 2010).

Therefore, recognition and acceptance of the significant influence that organizational culture has on managerial decisions on the approach to information security risk is a key factor in enabling effective risk management process (Chai, Kim &. Raoc, 2011; Bojanc, Jerman-Blaic & Tekavcic, 2012). For all that, understanding the impact that organizational culture has on treatment programs for risk analysis and information security is important given the fact that these processes may involve major changes throughout the organization these changes must be managed effectively and understanding culture embedded in an organization plays an important role in bringing about the changes that affect the entire organization (Flores, Antonsen & Ekstedt, 2014). Implement processes analysis, treatment and monitoring of information security risks requires a major change throughout the organization (Soomro, Hussain Shah & Ahmed, 2016).

This change involves the alignment of personnel, processes and organizational culture with the new objectives of the organization, strategy and approach to risk communication mechanisms for risk-related information between the entities concerned (Anderson & Choobineh, 2008). To effectively manage these changes, organizations can use the considerations of organizational culture as a key component in their strategic thinking and decision-making processes such as strategy development approach for risk (Baskerville, 2010). If the manager is aware of the importance of organizational culture has increased opportunities to achieve the organization's strategic objectives through proper risk management (Eloff & Von Solms, 2000). When several organizations are working together to fulfill common objectives might appear different approaches that can lead to different risk management strategies, which would create new risks and determine the tendency to accept more readily the risks (Fenz, 2014).

Besides the fact that the staff is directly responsible for the risk analysis takes on a heightened awareness of the risks to the security of information managed by the organization, all staff of the organization is accountable about threats and vulnerabilities resulting from the use communications and information systems processing, storing and transmitting information (Chen, Ge & Xie, 2015). Resuming regular risk analysis process security is a good opportunity to involve all staff who manages sensitive information. In this way, the staff will be aware of the importance and sensitivity of the actions we take and will be less reluctant to comply with the security requirements sometimes constitutes barriers to timeliness (Hausmann et al., 2014).

In addition, as we pointed out previously, management vision must change radically, from a passive or reactive management style to a proactive style, ready at any moment to face the challenges of achieving the objectives of the organization (Gandino, Celozzi & Rebaudengo, 2017).

However, the protection of information infrastructure implies that no access, modification, deletion or otherwise denial of access to data or network resources or services is performed by unauthorized persons or entities (Chou, Seng-Cho & Tzeng, 2006). Cyber security incidents recorded in recent years are likely to demonstrate that while policies and technology are critical components of any system of data protection, they alone can not provide effective protection of information (Ahmad, Hadgkiss & Ruighaver, 2012; Yar, 2006). Risk awareness information security is the first line of defense personnel is true perimeter security computer networks, and their behavior is critical to the protection of information handled by these systems (Choi et al., 2014).

In this context, this chapter intends to be a thorough reflection on the awareness of potential threats and vulnerabilities, as well as a preoccupation towards cooperation in countering them with well-established rules and mechanisms created at a national and organizational level. This chapter is also relevant to better understand how the actors involved in information and communication technologies could develop new models of information systems and risk management strategies.

This chapter is structured as follows: the first section introduces the dynamics of the information technology security threat; in the second section, research methodology is discussed; in the third section, the results of the study and statistics analysis are shown; in the last section, the conclusions and limitations are covered.

BACKGROUND

Detection is particularly useful where an attack cannot be prevented, but can also indicate the effectiveness of preventive mechanisms (Malatras, Geneiatakis & Vakalis, 2016). Detection mechanisms accepts that an attack may occur; the goal is to determine if an attack is about to occur or has occurred, and to report this procedure. However, the attack can be monitored to collect data on the nature, severity, and results (Arukonda & Sinha, 2015). Typical detection mechanisms monitor various aspects of the system, looking for action and information indicating an attack (Krombholz et al., 2015). An example of such mechanisms is providing an alarm when the user enters the wrong password more than three times. The procedure for obtaining access to the system can be continued, but history records system audit report an unusually high number of erroneous input passwords (Collins & McCombie, 2012). Detection mechanisms do not prevent compromise of parts of the system, which is a serious drawback (Lin, Lin & Pei, 2017). Protected resources detection mechanisms must be monitored continuously or periodically to identify any security issues (Wang & Hu, 2014).

This is why, security mechanisms have to be properly designed and commensurate with the specific threats for the specific types of information (Agrawal & Tapaswi, 2017). Organizations have to expand and deepen their current information security risk frameworks to address these key threats (Smith, 2005). This process implies a more profound understanding of the risks associated with each threat, and a better capacity of tailoring the security framework to align with the organization's identified risks, regulatory requirements and perhaps most important – the increasing dependencies on information technology.

Over the time, a large number of methodologies for identifying information security risks were proposed and adopted and simplified approach to different methodologies has led to their classification in quantitative and qualitative, especially in terms of metrics used to quantify risk (Friedberg et al., 2016; Kesan & Hayes, 2012).

A qualitative method using words or descriptive scales and the form a hierarchical structure that alternates between "rarely" and "almost certainly" (Singh & Fhom, 2017). Such a method is intended to prioritize the likelihood and the consequences of which can range from insignificant to moderate to severe.

Quantitative analysis is based criteria to establish the possibility of producing an event and its consequences. The possibility of the occurrence probability is expressed as, not in the form of frequency, thereby ensuring that the risks were compared to a similar base (Liaudanskienel, Ustinovicius & Bogdanovicius, 2009). When we speak of the possibility of occurrence of similar events small possibility of this happening can be treated as a single event.

Method OCTAVE (Operationally Critical Threat, Asset and Vulnerability Evaluation - Evaluation Threats, Assets and Organizational Vulnerability Critical) based on the definition of complex, systematic and contextual essential components of an information system, using a three-stage organization to determine the risks associated with privacy, integrity and availability of information assets critical to the proper performance of the organization considered (Karim, 2007). Measuring losses or impact severity level of risk can be both qualitative and quantitative, depending on available resources collective organizational and risk management information security system.Determination of information security risks is generally difficult because information about threats and asset values are generally more difficult to obtain and quantify and risk factors are constantly changing (Tu et al., 2018). OCTAVE risk analysis based on the methodology involves the use of risk scenarios associated with each critical asset of the organization (Gaidelys & Valodkiene, 2011).

Another mixed method (qualitative and quantitative risk assessment, known as VaR (Value Risk) based on the identification of the most severe effects of the production risks could have on the objectives of the organization, in a horizon type and a given confidence interval and aims to achieve optimal balance between the risks assumed and necessary expenses of minimizing them. The four steps proposed by the VAR methodology includes identifying threats, estimating the probability of these threats, the calculation VAR (value risk) and determining controls to prevent or minimize the effects of identified risks (He et al., 2012).

As such, concern continues to diminish the effect of unwanted influence involving a compulsory dedication of resources which, if prolonged, neglect can radically affect the overall level of resources of an organization and, therefore, the quality of its task (Mittelman, 2011).

Among the most important factors of disruptive impact on the activities of an organization, risk factors are by far the most significant (Yang, Wu & Wang, 2014). Risk, as defined in the western socio-economic and military environments, can occur anywhere: within the organization, structure, and decision-making process, the relationship with the external environment, the management, and policies of the organization (Campbell, Gordon, Loeb & Zhou, 2003; Sá-Soares, Soares & Arnaud, 2014).

Choosing an effective strategy development organization should consider the risks and vulnerabilities exposed to treatment solutions adapted to the needs of each organization's risk and reduce costs, both short- and long-term (Broadbent & Schaffner, 2016). Meanwhile, the adoption of certain measures that contribute to risk management is conditioned by the nature of the organization and the costs incurred for these measures (Hjortdal, 2011). To identify, analyze, and organize organizational risk assessment activities to reiterate the importance of the organizational concepts of systems theory perspective (Xu et al., 2018). Risk treatment is the second important step in risk management organizational stage where management organization has the key role in the adoption of the most appropriate decision in terms of the balance between the need to fulfill the performance indicators proposed and costs (Hadžiosmanović, Bolzoni & Hartel, 2012).

Stage security risk treatment is based entirely on the results of the risk analysis phase, the risks have been identified, and ranked in terms of the impact that their implementation can have on the organization's mission (Okamoto & Takashima, 2015). This is why security mechanisms must be properly designed and commensurate with the specific threats for the specific types of information (Tropina & Callanan, 2015).

The proposed research framework consists of nine independent constructs (past crimes and threats, facility characteristics (static and dynamic), current security measures, existing vulnerabilities, reducing consequences, procedures and training, security personnel, virtual infrastructure security, corporate security policy), one dependent variable (security management framework) within two different characteristics (technological and organisational) and build research hypotheses.

Current security measures is defined as the degree in which a new technology or innovation is consistent with current technologies and addresses the needs of the company (Willems, 2011). It is especially important for companies to make sure that all changes in their infrastructure, services and / or technologies are compatible with their existing vulnerabilities (Hoang & Ruckes, 2017).Therefore, the following hypotheses is defined for this study:

Hypothesis One ₐ: Perceived advantages of adopting current security measures have a positive effect on the information security strategy of companies

Hypothesis One ᵦ: Review of past crimes and threats with existing company technologies has a positive effect on the information security strategy of companies

Hypothesis One ᵧ: Observability of existing vulnerabilities has a positive effect on the information security strategy of companies

Virtual infrastructure security is the level at which the existence and availability of technology are visible to others (Tiago, Manoj & Espadanal, 2014). Empirical data shows a direct relationship between the virtual infrastructure security and their effects on companies' information security strategy. Accordingly, the following hypothesis is proposed in this research:

Hypothesis One ₔ: Availability of virtual infrastructure security has a positive effect on the information security strategy of companies

Procedures and training combine the necessary people, space and business processes which support the formation and development of companies (Fischbacher-Smith, 2016). One of the major purposes of a security personnel programme is stimulating employees by creating an environment for supporting the development and survival of new technologies (Khan et al., 2016). In the same manner, the availability of corporate security policy may affect the information security strategy of companies as hypotheses in the following:

Hypothesis Two ₐ: Availability of procedures and training has a positive effect on the information security strategy of companies

Hypothesis Two ᵦ: Availability of security personnel has a positive effect on the information security strategy of companies

Hypothesis Two ᵧ: Availability of reducing consequences has a positive effect on the information security strategy of companies

Hypothesis Two ₔ: Availability of the facility characteristics (static and dynamic) has a positive effect on the information security strategy of companies

Hypothesis Two ₑ: Availability of corporate security policy has a positive effect on the information security strategy of companies

RESEARCH METHODOLOGY

In order to obtain an image of the Romanian organizations' attitude towards information security strategy for a secure business environment, the authors performed a detailed survey using questionnaires. The major objective of this research is to identify those factors affecting the information security strategy of companies. More specifically, we are trying to detect if there is any significant relationship between two sets of characteristics (technologica and organisational) and the information security strategy of businesses. The findings suggest positive effects of technological and organisational characteristics on the information security strategy of businesses.

The survey was performed during the first trimester of 2018. The questionnaires were forwarded to 385 Romanian companies were randomly selected and contacted in two rounds.

The responding were representing different fields of activity: industry, commerce, transportation, finance, education, ICT, constructions, public administration, and non-governmental organizations. Considering the diversity of fields of activity and bearing in mind that the questionnaires were voluntarily completed, we estimate the findings of this research activity reflect in a good manner the attitude of the Romanian companies towards information security strategy.

In this study, a seven-point Likert-type scale ranging from ('1 = strongly disagree' to '7 = strongly agree') were utilized for measuring responses. In addition, ordinal or nominal scales were used to gain a more accurate response in a few questions. Normal distribution of variables is the most fundamental assumption in any multivariate analysis including SEM (Kaplan, 2000). Skewness and Kurtosis values were used to reflect a normal distribution of all variables in this research. Table 1 shows, for each research construct, its alpha value, mean, standard deviation and normality.

Responses were collected using questionnaires processed using the Scientific Package for Social Sciences (SPSS) 17.0 and the making of the database structure was achieved by defining variables in Variable View. It is also important to note that all completed questionnaires were checked in terms of background completeness and usefulness of data and using the statistical program previously mentioned, data analysis was materialized through frequency tables and histograms for each item, and the centralization of all items. In this research, Principal Components Analysis (PCA) and the orthogonal method with Varimax rotation along with Exploratory Factor Analysis (EFA) were employed through Statistical Package for Social Sciences (SPSS) version 21. The results of Bartlett's test (Table 2) were significant with $\chi^2 = 10279.6$ and p<0.05. Therefore, the factor analysis technique seems to be an appropriate analysis method for this study. The Kaiser-Meyer-Olkin (KMO) value for this research was 0.927 which is very close to 1 which indicates the appropriateness of factor analysis technique for this study. Following this, the path analysis process was used to investigate direct and indirect structural relationships between research variables.

Since all variables had a factor loading of 0.6 or better they were suitable for CFA testing. Evaluation of goodness-of-fit indices and other parameters estimates of the hypothesized structural model suggested that ten out of thirteen hypothesised paths were significant, hence supported. As a general rule, all vari-

Table 1. Variable reliabilities and descriptive statistics

	Alpha	Mean	Std Dev	Skewness	Kurtosis
Past Crimes and Threats (PCT)	0.850	5.33	1.372	-.290	-.838
Facility Characteristics (static and dynamic) (FC)	0.904	5.17	1.485	-.008	-1.134
Current Security Measures (CSM)	0.871	5.18	1.397	.133	-.905
Existing Vulnerabilities (EV)	0.921	5.18	1.484	-.104	-1.035
Reducing Consequences (RC)	0.911	5.19	1.392	-.220	-1.101
Procedures and Training (PT)	0.839	5.22	1.372	-.207	-.756
Security Personnel (SP)	0.897	5.26	1.367	-.093	-.738
Virtual Infrastructure Security (VIS)	0.797	5.21	1.407	-.604	.133
Security Management Framework (SMF)	0.931	5.16	1.408	-.111	-1.290
Corporate Security Policy (CSP)	0.876	4.48	1.538	-.465	-.474

Table 2. KMO statistics and Bartlett's Test of Sphericity

Kaiser-Meyer-Olkin Measure of Sampling Adequacy		.927
Bartlett's Test of Sphericity	Approx. Chi-Square	10279.647
	Df	1485
	Sig.	.000

ables with less than 0.05 factor loading should be removed. Also, as shown in Table 3, AVE estimates of each construct of this research is larger than Squared Inter-construct Correlation (SIC) estimate and so supports discriminate validity for each construct of this study.

A parameter estimate is significant at the .05 level when its Critical Ratio (CR) is more than 1.96. Moreover, the structural model fit was used to quantify each and every hypothesis as shown in Table 4.

According with the results it can be concluded that perceived advantage of adopting current security measures ($\beta = 0.273$) is the most influential construct on the information security strategy of companies followed by the facility characteristics (static and dynamic) ($\beta = 0.203$), past crimes and threats ($\beta = 0.198$), corporate security policy ($\beta = 0.189$), security personnel ($\beta = 0.149$), reducing consequences ($\beta = 0.140$), existing vulnerabilities ($\beta = 0.123$), and virtual infrastructure security ($\beta = 0.229$).

Moreover, the hypotheses analysis summary of this research is represent in Table 5.

SOLUTIONS AND RECOMMENDATIONS

Modern society is constantly subjected to during its development, the action of a multitude of disturbing factors (Xu et al., 2018). The influence can not be neglected because, over time, may increase up to the actual situation where the obstacles are sometimes insurmountable (Charki, Josserand & Boukef, 2017). As such, concern continues to diminish the effect of unwanted influence involves a compulsory,

Table 3. Inter-construct correlations

	PCT	FC	CSM	EV	RC	PT	SP	VIS	SMF	CSP
Past Crimes and Threats (PCT)	1.000									
Facility Characteristics (static and dynamic) (FC)	.567	1.000								
Current Security Measures (CSM)	.556	.565	1.000							
Existing Vulnerabilities (EV)	.629	.552	.501	1.000						
Reducing Consequences (RC)	.599	.504	.553	.563	1.000					
Procedures and Training (PT)	.575	.519	.534	.548	.564	1.000				
Security Personnel (SP)	.529	.392	.320	.335	.279	.396	1.000			
Virtual Infrastructure Security (VIS)	.656	.624	.634	.609	.643	.626	.414	1.000		
Security Management Framework (SMF)	.637	.503	.449	.579	.550	.644	.391	.641	1.000	
Corporate Security Policy (CSP)	.531	.479	.416	.471	.410	.403	.402	.489	.488	1.000

** Correlation is significant at the 0.01 level (2-tailed)

Table 4. Structural path analysis result

Dependent variables		Independent variables		Estimate	S.E.	C.R.	P
SMF	<---	CSM	0.273	0.075		3.640	***
SMF	<---	PCT	0.198	0.087		2.267	*
SMF	<---	EV	0.123	0.042		2.928	**
SMF	<---	VIS	0.229	0.06		0.488	0.626
SMF	<---	PT	0.351	0.082		4.254	***
SMF	<---	SP	0.149	0.066		2.244	*
SMF	<---	RC	0.140	0.059		2.372	*
SMF	<---	FC	0.203	0.056		3.625	***
SMF	<---	CSP	0.189	0.065		2.907	**

***$p<.000$, **$p<.01$, *$p<.05$, NS $p>.05$

Table 5. Hypotheses analysis summary

No		β	Findings
H1$_a$	Perceived advantages of adopting current security measures have a positive effect on the information security strategy of companies	0.273***	Significant
H1$_b$	Review of past crimes and threats with existing company technologies has a positive effect on the information security strategy of companies	0.198*	Significant
H1$_c$	Observability of existing vulnerabilities has a positive effect on the information security strategy of companies	0.123**	Significant
H1$_d$	Availability of virtual infrastructure security has a positive effect on the information security strategy of companies	0.229	Significant
H2$_a$	Availability of procedures and training has a positive effect on the information security strategy of companies	0.351***	Significant
H2$_b$	Availability of security personnel has a positive effect on the information security strategy of companies	0.149*	Significant
H2$_c$	Availability of reducing consequences has a positive effect on the information security strategy of companies	0.140*	Significant
H2$_d$	Availability of the facility characteristics (static and dynamic) has a positive effect on the information security strategy of companies	0.203***	Significant
H2$_e$	Availability of corporate security policy has a positive effect on the information security strategy of companies	0.189**	Significant

***$p<.000$, **$p<.01$, *$p<.05$, NS $p>.05$

dedication of resources which, if prolonged neglect can radically affect the overall level of resources of an organization and therefore, the quality of its task. Among the most important factors of disruptive impact on the activities of an organization, risk factors are, by far the leading place.

The goal of information security is to be able not only to implement measures to detect and mitigate attacks, but also to preemptively predict attacks, deter attackers from attacking, and thus defend the systems from attack in the first place (Arukonda & Sinha, 2015). In order for information security measures to have the capacity to deter conventional attacks, both due to aggression by external parties and those caused by internal sources, policies must be developed within each organization to parallel those developed at the governmental level.

Between the concepts of risk, organizational culture and trust there is a direct relationship (Kolkowska, Karlsson & Hedström, 2017). Changing an organization's operational needs as determined for example by changing mission requirements and exchange information with other entities may involve changing risk tolerance level, above the level set by the management of the organization. These measures lead to building confidence in the organization long term.

The interaction between trust in organization and organizational culture can also be observed when there is overlapping responsibility or uncovered areas between various parts of an organization may impact on the ability to undertake operative.

Developing a risk management process and its proper procedures are likely to enhance the credibility of the organization and the capital trust with its partners and investment. Demonstrating that the organization has structures and procedures to ensure effective protection of information that circulates determines both the organization's external partners (suppliers, customers, entities whose business depends on the organization in question) and to staff the faith that the organization operates in a consistent manner based on clear rules and procedures, which leaves no room for chaos and bias.

Limiting to a reactive management style is not a viable option for an efficient management. No organization can be managed on the basis of the "seeing and doing" principle. Equally important is the identification of possible threats before they materialize and produce adverse consequences to the objectives. This means adopting a proactive management style. Proactive management is based on the principle "it is better to prevent than to note a fact".

Many organizations adopt the practice of updating the risk management policy annually. This practice ensures that the overall approach to risk management is in line with the latest practices. At the same time, it offers the organization the opportunity to focus on future goals, on the identification of priorities in terms of risk management and to identify emerging risks.

In a stage where, as we pointed out above, information has become a basic resource of any organization, making the best decisions to protect this resource must be based on a coherent analysis.

FUTURE RESEARCH DIRECTIONS

Future research is important because certain events with a negative impact on the objectives to be transformed into opportunities if they are identified early. One of the limitations of this study is that the collected data was cross-sectional, and all hypotheses were examined for a particular period. In addition, the data in this study was collected within particular urban areas in Romania. Hence, special care should be taken when generalizing our findings to other country's businesses. Furthermore, the effects of demography are not included in this study, but some demographic factors may have more explanatory power than others which can be investigated in future research. Best practices will consist of technical and procedural security measures whose effectiveness in combating specific threats and vulnerabilities has been proven.

CONCLUSION

Big data was the relatively new way of conducting business by providing new insight (Yeow, Soh & Hansen, 2018). The two types of uses were categorized into either user facing or business facing (Lowry & Wilson, 2016). The business facing applications tended to provide system infrastructure and details analytics to either streamline internal practices or improve business decision making.

The manager of an organization should not be limited to treating each time, the consequences of events that have occurred, showing a passive management style, or respond to negative punctual events that may affect the organization's objectives, proving a reactive management style. Treating the consequences does not eliminate the causes and, therefore, already materialized risks will occur in the future, usually with greater frequency and with an increased impact on the objectives. Managers must adopt a proactive management style, which means that it is necessary to design and implement measures to mitigate risks manifestation. Future-oriented response allows the organization to master, within acceptable limits, the past risks, which is the same as increasing the chances to achieve its objectives.

From another perspective, a better integration of data analysis and use of open data sources into design curriculums could prove to be invaluable to new designers who may benefit from exposure to new methods of research. A strong connection to the importance of alternate data collection methods as a source of design innovation and creativity could bring designers to big data to use in future projects.

Bearing in mind the conclusions outlined above, the organizations benefiting from an efficient management, "scrutinizing the horizon" is not limited to the immediate future, but consider further perspective, the trends projected for the external environment of the organization. In these situations, proactive management becomes a prospective management, in which the management tries to identify those risks that may arise due to changes in strategy or environment. The organization must be prepared to accept the change.

In order to consolidate and improve the information security posture, efforts should be based on a series of few principles that we consider to be essential bricks towards a building trust and credibility:

- Coordination, meaning that all policies approved and actions taken to be circumscribed to a unitary concept, according to convergent plans of action towards attaining information security, according to responsibilities and competencies of each organizational department within the organization; a team-oriented approach is vital in fighting against information security threats;
- Cooperation, meaning that all entities having responsibilities (either public institutions or private companies or non-governmental organizations) should collaborate at international, national and organizational level, in order to ensure an adequate response to information technology threats and to possible successful information security attacks;
- Efficiency, meaning that all resources, either financial, human, material, have to be correctly allocated and managed in order to address the primary needs and priorities;
- Prioritization, meaning that the efforts have to be focused on the protection of those communication and information systems supporting critical functions of the society and, respectively, of the organization;
- Dissemination, meaning that a proper transfer and sharing of information, expertise and best practices have to be ensured among persons with responsibilities in the field of protecting communication and information systems handling sensitive information or supporting critical functions.

Like any factor in a complex system, the benefits of information security are weighed against their total cost (including the additional costs incurred if the system is compromised). If the data or resources cost less, or are of less value, than their protection, adding security mechanisms and procedures is not cost-effective because the data or resources can be reconstructed more cheaply than the protections themselves. Unfortunately, this is rarely the case.

Residual risk is the risk that remains after security measures are implemented in a computer system and communications, as a consequence of the fact that not all threats can be countered and not all vulnerabilities can be eliminated or reduced to zero.

As we have seen, for safety information required increasingly more stringent use of cryptographic mechanisms that make information become inaccessible to unauthorized persons. On the other hand, there is concern becoming more serious on the use of cryptography by criminals in order to escape police observation.

Strategy to restore services and resources information system provides a quick and effective way to restore the operability of a system in case of interruption of its operation. The strategy should be linked to the impact on information security objectives in case of disruption of its operation and the maximum time allowed for the decommissioning of the system, as we have previously defined.

Overlapping benefits are also a consideration. Suppose the integrity protection mechanism can be augmented very quickly and cheaply to provide confidentiality. Then the cost of providing confidentiality is much lower. This shows that evaluating the cost of a particular security service depends on the mechanism chosen to implement it and on the mechanisms chosen to implement other security services. The cost-benefit analysis should take into account as many mechanisms as possible. Adding security mechanisms to an existing system is often more expensive (and, incidentally, less effective) than designing them into the system in the first place.

REFERENCES

Agrawal, N., & Tapaswi, S. (2017). Defense schemes for variants of distributed denial-of-service (DDoS) attacks in cloud computing: A survey. *Information Security Journal: A Global Perspective, 26*(1), 1-13.

Ahmad, A., Hadgkiss, J., & Ruighaver, A. B. (2012). Incident Response Teams–Challenges in Supporting the Organisational Security Function. *Computers & Security, 31*(5), 643–652. doi:10.1016/j.cose.2012.04.001

Ahmad, A., Maynard, S. B., & Park, S. (2014). Information security strategies: Towards an organizational multi-strategy perspective. *Journal of Intelligent Manufacturing, 25*(2), 357–370. doi:10.100710845-012-0683-0

Anderson, E., & Choobineh, J. (2008). Enterprise information security strategies. *Computers & Security, 27*(1-2), 22–29. doi:10.1016/j.cose.2008.03.002

Andress, A. (2003). *Surviving Security: How to Integrate People, Process, and Technology.* Boca Raton, FL: Auerbach Publications. doi:10.1201/9780203501405

Arukonda, S., & Sinha, S. (2015). The innocent perpetrators: Reflectors and reflection attacks. *Advanced Computer Science, 4,* 94–98.

Banker, R., Chang, H., & Kao, Y.-C. (2010). Evaluating Cross-Organizational Impacts of Information Technology – an Empirical Analysis. *European Journal of Information Systems*, *19*(2), 153–167. doi:10.1057/ejis.2010.9

Baskerville, R. (2010). Third-Degree Conflicts: Information Warfare. *European Journal of Information Systems*, *19*(1), 1–4. doi:10.1057/ejis.2010.2

Baskerville, R., Spagnoletti, P., & Kim, J. (2014). Incident-Centered Information Security: Managing a Strategic Balance between Prevention and Response. *Information & Management*, *51*(1), 138–151. doi:10.1016/j.im.2013.11.004

Bojanc, R., Jerman-Blaic, B., & Tekavcic, M. (2012). Managing the Investment in Information Security Technology by Use of a Quantitative Modeling. *Information Processing & Management*, *48*(6), 1031–1052. doi:10.1016/j.ipm.2012.01.001

Bojanc, R., & Jerman-Blažic, B. (2012). Quantitative Model for Economic Analyses of Information Security Investment in an Enterprise Information System. *Organizacija*, *45*(6), 276–288. doi:10.2478/v10051-012-0027-z

Broadbent, A., & Schaffner, C. (2016). Quantum cryptography beyond quantum key distribution. *Designs, Codes and Cryptography*, *78*(1), 351–382. doi:10.100710623-015-0157-4

Campbell, K., Gordon, L. A., Loeb, M. P., & Zhou, L. (2003). The Economic Cost of Publicly Announced Information Security Breaches: Empirical Evidence from the Stock Market. *Journal of Computer Security*, *11*(3), 431–448. doi:10.3233/JCS-2003-11308

Chai, S., Kim, M., & Raoc, R. (2011). Firms' information security investment decisions: Stock market evidence of investors' behaviour. *Decision Support Systems*, *50*(4), 651–661. doi:10.1016/j.dss.2010.08.017

Charki, M. H., Josserand, E., & Boukef, N. (2017). The paradoxical effects of legal intervention over unethical information technology use: A rational choice theory perspective. *The Journal of Strategic Information Systems*, *26*(1), 58–76. doi:10.1016/j.jsis.2016.07.001

Chen, H., Ge, L., & Xie, L. A. (2015). User Authentication Scheme Based on Elliptic Curves Cryptography for Wireless Ad Hoc Networks. *Sensors (Basel)*, *15*(7), 17057–17075. doi:10.3390150717057 PMID:26184224

Choi, Y., Lee, D., Kim, J., Jung, J., Nam, J., & Won, D. (2014). Security Enhanced User Authentication Protocol for Wireless Sensor Networks Using Elliptic Curves Cryptography. *Sensors (Basel)*, *14*(6), 10081–10106. doi:10.3390140610081 PMID:24919012

Chou, T.-Y., Seng-Cho, T. C., & Tzeng, G.-H. (2006). Evaluating IT/IS Investments: A Fuzzy Multi-Criteria Decision Model Approach. *European Journal of Operational Research*, *173*(3), 1026–1046. doi:10.1016/j.ejor.2005.07.003

Clarke-Sather, A. R., Hutchins, M. J., Zhang, Q., Gershenson, J. K., & Sutherland, J. W. (2011). Development of social, environmental, and economic indicators for a small/medium enterprise. *International Journal of Accounting and Information Management*, *19*(3), 247–266. doi:10.1108/18347641111169250

Collins, S., & McCombie, S. (2012). Stuxnet: The emergence of a new cyber weapon and its implications. *Journal of Policing. Intelligence and Counter Terrorism*, *7*(1), 80–91. doi:10.1080/18335330.2012.653198

Da Veiga, A. (2016). Comparing the information security culture of employees who had read the information security policy and those who had not: Illustrated through an empirical study. *Information & Computer Security*, *24*(2), 139–151. doi:10.1108/ICS-12-2015-0048

Dor, D., & Elovici, Y. (2016). A Model of the Information Security Investment DecisionMaking Process. *Computers & Security*, *63*, 1–13. doi:10.1016/j.cose.2016.09.006

Eloff, M. M., & Von Solms, S. H. (2000). Information Security Management: An Approach to Combine Process Certification and Product Evaluation. *Computers & Security*, *19*(8), 698–709. doi:10.1016/S0167-4048(00)08019-6

Fenz, S., Heurix, J., Neubauer, T., & Pechstein, F. (2014). Current challenges in information security risk management. *Information Management & Computer Security*, *22*(5), 410–430. doi:10.1108/IMCS-07-2013-0053

Fischbacher-Smith, D. (2016). Breaking bad? In search of a (softer) systems view of security ergonomics. *Security Journal*, *29*(1), 5–22. doi:10.1057j.2015.41

Flores, W. R., Antonsen, E., & Ekstedt, M. (2014). Information Security Knowledge Sharing in Organizations: Investigating the Effect of Behavioral Information Security Governance and National Culture. *Computers & Security*, *43*, 90–110. doi:10.1016/j.cose.2014.03.004

Flowerday, S. V., & Tuyikeze, T. (2016). Information security policy development and implementation: The what, how and who. *Computers & Security*, *61*, 169–183. doi:10.1016/j.cose.2016.06.002

Friedberg, I., McLaughlin, K., Smith, P., Laverty, D., & Sezer, S. (2016). STPA-SafeSec: Safety and security analysis for cyber-physical systems. *Journal of Information Security and Applications*, *29*, 1–12.

Gaidelys, V., & Valodkiene, G. (2011). The Methods of Selecting and Assessing Potential Consumers Used of by Competitive Intelligence. *Inzinerine Ekonomika-Engineering Economics*, *22*(2), 196–202.

Gandino, F., Celozzi, C., & Rebaudengo, M. (2017). A Key Management Scheme for Mobile Wireless Sensor Networks. *Applied Sciences*, *7*(5), 490. doi:10.3390/app7050490

Gandotra, V., Singhal, A., & Bedi, P. (2012). Threat-Oriented Security Framework: A Proactive Approach in Threat Management. *Procedia Technology*, *4*, 487–494. doi:10.1016/j.protcy.2012.05.078

Gkioulos, V., Wangen, G., Katsikas, S. K., Kavallieratos, G., & Kotzanikolaou, P. (2017). Security Awareness of the Digital Natives. *Information*, *8*(2), 42. doi:10.3390/info8020042

Hadžiosmanović, D., Bolzoni, D., & Hartel, P. H. (2012). A log mining approach for process monitoring in SCADA. *International Journal of Information Security*, *11*(4), 231–251. doi:10.100710207-012-0163-8

Hausmann, V., Williams, S. P., Hardy, C. A., & Schubert, P. (2014). Enterprise Information Management Readiness: A Survey of Current Issues, Challenges and Strategy. *Procedia Technology*, *16*, 42–51. doi:10.1016/j.protcy.2014.10.066

He, D., Chen, C., Chan, S., & Bu, J. (2012). Secure and efficient handover authentication based on bilinear pairing functions. *IEEE Transactions on Wireless Communications*, *11*(1), 48–53. doi:10.1109/TWC.2011.110811.111240

Hiller, J., & Russel, R. (2013). The challenge and imperative of private sector cybersecurity: An international comparison. *Computer Law & Security Review*, *29*(3), 236–245. doi:10.1016/j.clsr.2013.03.003

Hjortdal, M. (2011). China's use of cyber warfare: Espionage meets strategic deterrence. *The Journal of Strategic Studies*, *4*(2), 1–24.

Hoang, D., & Ruckes, M. (2017). Corporate risk management, product market competition, and disclosure. *Journal of Financial Intermediation*, *30*, 107–121. doi:10.1016/j.jfi.2016.07.003

Hong, J., Kim, J., & Cho, J. (2010). The trend of the security research for the insider cyber threat. *International Journal of Future Generation Communication and Networking*, *3*(2), 31–40.

Karim, H. V. (2007). *Strategic security management: a risk assessment guide for decision makers*. Amsterdam: Elsevier.

Kesan, P. J., & Hayes, M. C. (2012). Mitigative counterstriking: Self-defense and deterrence in cyberspace. *Harvard Journal of Law & Technology*, *25*(2), 474–529.

Khan, S., Gani, A., Wahab, A. W. A., Shiraz, M., & Ahmad, I. (2016). Network forensics: Review, taxonomy, and open challenges. *Journal of Network and Computer Applications*, *66*, 214–235. doi:10.1016/j.jnca.2016.03.005

Kim, S. H., Wang, Q.-H., & Ullrich, J. B. (2012). A Comparative Study of Cyberattacks. *Communications of the ACM*, *55*(3), 66. doi:10.1145/2093548.2093568

Kolkowska, E., Karlsson, F., & Hedström, K. (2017). Towards analysing the rationale of information security non-compliance: Devising a Value-Based Compliance analysis method. *The Journal of Strategic Information Systems*, *26*(1), 39–57. doi:10.1016/j.jsis.2016.08.005

Krombholz, K., Hobel, H., Huber, M., & Weippl, E. (2015). Advanced social engineering attacks. *Journal of Information Security and Applications*, *22*, 113–122. doi:10.1016/j.jisa.2014.09.005

Landoll, D. J. (2010). *The security risk assessment handbook: a complete guide for performing security risk assessment* (2nd ed.). New York: CRC Press.

Liaudanskienel, R., Ustinovicius, L., & Bogdanovicius, A. (2009). Evaluation of Construction Process Safety Solutions Using the TOPSIS Method. *Inzinerine Ekonomika-Engineering Economics*, *64*(4), 32–40.

Lin, Z., Lin, D., & Pei, D. (2017). Practical construction of ring LFSRs and ring FCSRs with low diffusion delay for hardware cryptographic applications. *Cryptography and Communications*, *9*(4), 431–440. doi:10.100712095-016-0183-8

Lowry, P. B., & Wilson, D. (2016). Creating agile organizations through IT: The influence of internal IT service perceptions on IT service quality and IT agility. *The Journal of Strategic Information Systems*, *25*(3), 211–226. doi:10.1016/j.jsis.2016.05.002

Malatras, A., Geneiatakis, D., & Vakalis, I. (2016). On the efficiency of user identification: A system-based approach. *International Journal of Information Security*, *15*(1), 1–19.

Martinez-Caro, J.-M., Aledo-Hernandez, A.-J., Guillen-Perez, A., Sanchez-Iborra, R., & Cano, M.-D. (2018). A Comparative Study of Web Content Management Systems. *Information*, *9*(2), 27. doi:10.3390/info9020027

McQuade, S. (2006). *Understanding and Managing Cybercrime*. Boston: Allyn & Bacon.

Mittelman, J. H. (2011). Global (in) security: The confluence of intelligence and will. *Global Change, Peace & Security*, *23*(2), 135–139. doi:10.1080/14781158.2011.580954

Mohammed, F., Ibrahim, O., & Ithnin, N. (2016). Factors influencing cloud computing adoption for e-government implementation in developing countries: Instrument development. *Journal of Systems and Information Technology*, *18*(3), 297–327. doi:10.1108/JSIT-01-2016-0001

Okamoto, T., & Takashima, K. (2015). Achieving short ciphertexts or short secret-keys for adaptively secure general inner-product encryption. *Designs, Codes and Cryptography*, *77*(2), 725–771. doi:10.100710623-015-0131-1

Peltier, T. R. (2010). *Information security risk analysis* (3rd ed.). New York: CRC Press, Auerbach Publications.

Renaud, K., Flowerday, S., Warkentin, M., Cockshott, P., & Orgeron, C. (2018). Is the responsibilization of the cyber security risk reasonable and judicious? *Computers & Security*, *78*, 198–211. doi:10.1016/j.cose.2018.06.006

Renwick, S. L., & Martin, K. M. (2017). Practical Architectures for Deployment of Searchable Encryption in a Cloud Environment. *Cryptography*, *1*(3), 19. doi:10.3390/cryptography1030019

Ruževičius, J., & Gedminaitė, A. (2007). Business Information Quality and its Assessment. *Inzinerine Ekonomika-Engineering Economics*, *52*(2), 18–25.

Sá-Soares, F., Soares, D., & Arnaud, J. (2014). Towards a Theory of Information Systems Outsourcing Risk. *Procedia Technology*, *16*, 623–637. doi:10.1016/j.protcy.2014.10.011

Shamala, P., Ahmad, R., Zolait, A. H., & Sahib, S. (2015). Collective information structure model for Information Security Risk Assessment (ISRA). *Journal of Systems and Information Technology*, *17*(2), 193–219. doi:10.1108/JSIT-02-2015-0013

Singer, W. P., & Friedman, A. (2014). *Cyber Security and Cyber War: What Everyone Needs to Know*. New York: Oxford University Press.

Singh, A., & Fhom, H. C. S. (2017). Restricted usage of anonymous credentials in vehicular ad hoc networks for misbehavior detection. *International Journal of Information Security*, *16*(2), 195–201. doi:10.100710207-016-0328-y

Smith, D. (2005). Dancing with the mysterious forces of chaos: Issues around complexity, knowledge and the management of uncertainty. *Clinician in Management*, (3/4), 115–123.

Soomro, Z., Hussain Shah, A. M., & Ahmed, J. (2016). Information security management needs more holistic approach: A literature review. *International Journal of Information Management, 36*(2), 215–225. doi:10.1016/j.ijinfomgt.2015.11.009

Stepchenko, D., & Voronova, I. (2015). Assessment of Risk Function Using Analytical Network Process. *Inzinerine Ekonomika-Engineering Economics, 26*(3), 264–271.

Sveen, F., Torres, J., & Sarriegi, J. (2009). Blind Information Security Strategy. *International Journal of Critical Infrastructure Protection, 2*(3), 95–109. doi:10.1016/j.ijcip.2009.07.003

Tiago, O., Manoj, T., & Espadanal, M. (2014). Assessing the determinants of cloud computing adoption: An analysis of the manufacturing and services sectors. *Information & Management, 51*(5), 497–510. doi:10.1016/j.im.2014.03.006

Tropina, T., & Callanan, C. (2015). *Self- and Co-regulation in Cybercrime, Cybersecurity and National Security*. New York: Springer International Publishing. doi:10.1007/978-3-319-16447-2

Tu, C. Z., Yuan, Y., Archer, N., & Connelly, C. E. (2018). Strategic value alignment for information security management: A critical success factor analysis. *Information & Computer Security, 26*(2), 150–170. doi:10.1108/ICS-06-2017-0042

Tutton, J. (2010). Incident Response and Compliance: A Case Study of the Recent Attacks. *Information Security Technical Report, 15*(4), 145–149. doi:10.1016/j.istr.2011.02.001

Wang, W., & Hu, L. (2014). A secure and efficient handover authentication protocol for wireless networks. *Journal of Sensors, 14*(7), 11379–11394. doi:10.3390140711379 PMID:24971471

Willems, E. (2011). Cyber-terrorism in the process industry. *Computer Fraud & Security, 3*(3), 16–19. doi:10.1016/S1361-3723(11)70032-X

Winkler, I. (2010). *Justifying IT Security – Managing Risk & Keeping your network Secure*. Qualys Inc.

Xu, R., Chen, Y., Blasch, E., & Chen, G. (2018). BlendCAC: A Smart Contract Enabled Decentralized Capability-Based Access Control Mechanism for the IoT. *Computers, 7*(3), 39. doi:10.3390/computers7030039

Yang, C. N., Wu, C. C., & Wang, D. S. (2014). A discussion on the relationship between probabilistic visual cryptography and random grid. *Information Sciences, 278*, 141–173. doi:10.1016/j.ins.2014.03.033

Yar, M. (2006). *Cybercrime and Society*. London: Sage.

Yeow, A., Soh, C., & Hansen, R. (2018). Aligning with new digital strategy: A dynamic capabilities approach. *The Journal of Strategic Information Systems, 27*(1), 43–58. doi:10.1016/j.jsis.2017.09.001

ADDITIONAL READING

Agrawal, N., & Tapaswi, S. (2017). Defense schemes for variants of distributed denial-of-service (DDoS) attacks in cloud computing: A survey. *Information Security Journal: A Global Perspective, 26(1)*, 1-13.

Karanja, E. (2017). The role of the chief information security officer in the management of IT security. *Information & Computer Security*, *25*(3), 300–329. doi:10.1108/ICS-02-2016-0013

Kurosawa, K., Ohta, H., & Kakuta, K. (2017). How to make a linear network code (strongly) secure. *Designs, Codes and Cryptography*, *82*(3), 559–582. doi:10.100710623-016-0180-0

Lee, C., Lee, C. C., & Kim, S. (2016). Understanding information security stress: Focusing on the type of information security compliance activity. *Computers & Security*, *59*, 60–70. doi:10.1016/j.cose.2016.02.004

Lee, W., & Kim, N. (2017). Security Policy Scheme for an Efficient Security Architecture in Software-Defined Networking. *Information*, *8*(2), 65. doi:10.3390/info8020065

Zangeneh, V., & Shajari, M. (2018). A cost-sensitive move selection strategy for moving target defense. *Computers & Security*, *75*, 72–91. doi:10.1016/j.cose.2017.12.013

KEY TERMS AND DEFINITIONS

Availability: Ensuring the conditions necessary for easy retrieval and use of information and system resources, whenever necessary, with strict conditions of confidentiality and integrity.

Cost: The money form of all material and labor expenses made by the company to produce and market material goods, execution works and service works.

Cyber Physical Systems: They are being set up by the internet of things that are machines, employees, products and products facilities being digitally interconnected by the internet.

Integrity: The prohibition amendment—by deleting or adding—or the unauthorized destruction of information; integrity refers to confidence in the data and resources of a system by which to manage information.

Organizational Culture: Values and behaviors that contribute to creating a social and psychological environment of an organization.

Prevention: Implementation of mechanisms that users not be able to counteract and are implemented correctly, unaltered, so the attacker cannot alter them.

Risk Management: The implementation and updating of methods and tools to minimize risks associated with the information system of an organization, such as the Information Security policies, procedures and practices associated formalized and adopted other means in order to bring these risks to acceptable levels.

SEM: Structural equation modeling.

Threats: The possibility of accidental or deliberate compromise of information security, the loss of confidentiality, integrity, or availability or impaired functions that provide authenticity and non-repudiation of information.

Vulnerabilities: Gaps or weaknesses in the design and implementation of safety or security measures which could be exploited accidentally or intentionally by a threat.

Chapter 13

The Impact of Creating a Business Intelligence Platform on Higher Education:
The Case of the American University in Cairo

Sherif H. Kamel

https://orcid.org/0000-0002-2758-3766

The American University in Cairo, Egypt

Iman Megahed

The American University in Cairo, Egypt

Heba Atteya

The American University in Cairo, Egypt

ABSTRACT

In today's ever-changing global environment, the higher education industry is facing many diversified and evolving challenges and its landscape is becoming more competitive, dynamic, and complex. To proactively operate in such a changing and complicated environment, innovation, creativity, information, and knowledge represent key competitive edges that need to be introduced, cultivated, and managed effectively. The American University in Cairo (AUC) is a leading institution of higher education in the Middle East North Africa (MENA) region that recognized early on the power of knowledge and the need for a paradigm shift in management that capitalizes on innovative information and communication technologies. Accordingly, the university embarked on an ambitious journey as the first higher education institution in Egypt to build a state-of-the-art business intelligence (BI) platform that would support proactive, informed decision-making as a distinctive and sustainable competitive advantage.

DOI: 10.4018/978-1-5225-7277-0.ch013

INTRODUCTION

In an age where organizations are constantly in quest of competitiveness through innovation and transformation, business intelligence (BI) becomes mandatory for organizational effectiveness. This is true for organizations of all forms, sizes and industries, profit and non-profit, small, medium and large, as well as different types including government, private and public sector organizations, including academic and higher education institutions such as university settings. Moreover, it is invaluable for all organizational levels whether strategic, operational and/or tactical. The reason being the impact BI has on the quality of the organization's decision-making process. BI creates a conducive organizational context to make better and more rational decisions by availing a comprehensive view of organizational data that would allow executives, middle managers and others to be more informed and build their decision making processes on timely and analyzed data to be more certain and accurate of the decisions made (Rouhani, Asgari, & Mirhosseini, 2012).

The role of BI is to create an informational environment with supporting processes by which operational data is gathered from transactional systems and enterprise resource planning (ERP) systems to be analyzed for strategic business and organizational insights. This is where the concept of an *"intelligent organization"* appears as one that deploys BI to enable faster and smarter decisions than its competition to create a sustainable competitive advantage. Accordingly, the *"intelligence"* element results from the transformation of huge volumes of data into information and knowledge through mechanisms for filtering, analysis and visualization, in support of the decision making process and corporate strategy tracking and progress (Gupta & Singh, 2014).

Despite the significant impact BI has in supporting informed decision making, strategy management and organizational success, the literature shows that there is a lack of agreement on the definition and real and effective implications of BI (Shollo, 2013). Based on the literature review conducted, following are some key definitions stand out and help illustrate the nature and scope of BI. For example, BI was defined as extracting the information deemed central to the business, and presenting or manipulating that data into information that is useful for managerial decision support (Gibson, Arnott, & Jagielska, 2004). Another definition suggests to perceive BI as combining data from operational systems with analytical front-ends to deliver timely information when decisions need to be made (Negash, 2004). However, in 2008, Baars and Kemper generalized the definition to encompass all components of an integrated management support infrastructure. Moreover, in 2010 Wixom and Watson defined BI as a broad category of technologies, applications, and processes for gathering, storing, accessing, and analyzing data to help its users make better decisions.

In 2011, according to Fitriana, Djatna, & Eriyatno in their analysis of the progress of BI systems, they defined BI as a process for extracting, transforming, managing and analyzing large data to gain information and knowledge that can support decision-making; and in 2014 Uma and Sankarasubramanian identified BI to be the ability to collect and analyze huge amounts of data pertaining to the customers, vendors, markets, internal processes, and the business environment. Therefore, from these various key definitions one can conclude that BI was initially used as a collective term for data analysis abilities, tools, techniques, technologies and solutions used in transforming data into knowledge. However, this understanding with time was broadened to include all the various components and processes associated in using information and analyzing them in order to create an integrated decision support infrastructure. It is important to note that the objective of all BI infrastructures and systems is defining the fundamental direction of an organization by supporting the decision-making process and helping different organizations to forecast the behavior of competitors, suppliers, customers and environments to differentiate themselves, and compete in the global economy (Wieder & Ossimitz, 2015).

The evolution of BI and its dynamic and iterative nature makes it more agile, invaluable and increasingly demanded by various organizations given the added-value it brings to each organization's different constituents. In many ways, the definition that mostly represents the true nature of BI is the one offered by Garner Group which indicates that "business intelligence is an umbrella term that includes the applications, infrastructure and tools, and best practices that enable access to and analysis of information to improve and optimize decisions and performance" (Gartner, n.d.).

The experience of the American University in Cairo (AUC) BI platform to date demonstrates a set of lessons learnt that could be of invaluable use to organizations in the space of higher education and the objective is to understand the implications of business intelligence on academia. The early added-value demonstrates that on a strategic level, the availability of a cutting-edge BI platform unleashed the power, depth and magnitude information can have in transforming and positively impacting a non-profit institute in higher education that is celebrating its centennial in 2019 into a modern information-based and technology-driven university that is passionate, eager and has the appetite to explore, discover and capitalize on all forms of knowledge creation and dissemination in the decision-making process both academically and administratively. This includes the ability to have a timely, accurate and efficient platform that can enable decision makers both faculty and staff to manipulate the data, better understand the organizational dynamics, and develop predictive scenarios to mention a few and accordingly, take better decisions.

These decisions can relate to every academic and non-academic aspect on campus in the form of a variety of dashboards covering different data elements including, but not limited to, campus demographics, budgeting, planning, procurement, students' enrolment, faculty evaluations, staff assessment, performance appraisal, research output, teaching records, and different services offered. In other words, at a time where BI is growing in use and impact, the volume, velocity and variety of data have changed and continues to change reflecting elements that relate to governance, privacy and security challenges which are generating a new level of concerns from faculty, staff and administrators, AUC included (Boutlon, 2013).

The journey started by assessing the university's current status on BI maturity curve, defined its goals and targets and set out a strategic plan to accomplish it expeditiously and efficiently. The journey was faced with challenges such as settling on the most suitable landscape, identifying the technical specifications and sizing of the solution, selecting the architecture (full stack, multi-vendor, on-premise, on-cloud or a hybrid solution); selecting the right tools that fit the university's needs from a wide pool of tools currently available in the market; identifying the best practice project management implementation; regularly tracking and assessing the progress for improvement and most importantly identifying, recruiting and preparing the much needed human capital to transform the space of decision-making. This represented the technology side of the project but the real challenges were represented by a series of elements inherited in the university's environment and culture which required a clear strategy supported by the university leadership, a suitable governance structure; excavating for the suitable talents from within the university to help build a knowledgeable BI team; and finally availing an understanding of BI as a journey and managing the different stakeholders' expectations.

Two fundamental challenges that faced AUC included the readiness of the university population to understand the power and advantages that could be offered through the BI platform as well as the data cleansing effort across campus to reflect the most timely and accurate data infrastructure possible and integrate it with BI. Both elements represented challenges that required several orientation sessions and workshops for faculty and staff across campus and representing different units, departments and schools to understand how BI can affect their work. As for the data infrastructure, it is still work-in-progress and needs a regular and rigorous maintenance given the constant changes in the various data elements.

THE EVOLUTION OF BUSINESS INTELLIGENCE

The diversity in BI definitions reflects its long history and evolution. Looking back, it is clear that BI grew out of the concepts and technology initiated by decision support systems (DSS) in the 1950s and still deployed today in many organizations to support individual and group decision making leading to competitive advantage (Heang, 2017; Kamel, 2008; 2013).

In 1958, Hans Peter Luhn, an IBM researcher in his paper "a BI system", was the first to describe an "automatic method to provide current awareness services to scientists and engineers" (Shollo, 2013) in support of researchers to cope with the expanding scientific and technical needs. These concepts continued to evolve until the 1990s when the term became widely adopted. To fully understand the concepts of BI, a review of the historical background and evolution of DSS to BI is necessary (Shollo, 2013). The introduction of the mainframe computer in 1950s was the starting point for all data processing systems and, eventually led to the evolution to management information systems (MIS). In the mid 1960s, DSS came into the scene. Until that point, MIS reports were basically large data lists and reports with no interactivity or visualization tools that would support executives and managers in their decision-making (Kamel, 1992). DSS were more accommodating in their ability to support decisions in a more interactive manner. The late 1970s witnessed the introduction and wide adoption of relational databases and stronger modeling practices which allowed the capture of larger quantities of data and the arrival of executive information systems (EIS) with more advanced support of decision-making for executives (Shollo, 2013; El-Sherif & El-Sawy, 1998).

Despite the presence of EIS and DSS as decision support tools, the amount of manual intervention needed to transform and upload data from multiple sources led to limited adoption and exacerbated the need for more advanced information infrastructures (Shollo, 2013). Consequently, by the 1990s, data warehousing concepts appeared with their on-line analytical processing (OLAP) and extract transform and load (ETL) tools. These tools were integrated under one umbrella term introduced by Howard Dresner of the Gartner Group in 1989 to include the set of concepts and methods used in enhancing decision making (Rouhani et al., 2012). Accordingly, BI replaced EIS as well as DSS as the primary decision-making platforms. BI, as we know it today, can initially be attributed to the extensive research behind decision support systems (Kowalczyk, Buxmann, & Besier, 2013). This research shaped BI to become the umbrella that integrates all relevant techniques, processes and technologies. It extends beyond internal and structured data to external and unstructured data needed for decision making (Shollo, 2013).

Business Intelligence and The Impact on Organizational Performance

Today, organizations around the world are facing many unprecedented challenges alongside continuously shortening business cycles. To gain competitive advantage, their need for good, reliable, accurate and timely data, information and knowledge has become a necessity for decision-making at different organizational levels including strategic, operational and tactical (Turban, Sharda, & Delen, 2010; Karen Loch et al., 2003).

With the improvement and emergence of innovative information technologies, the BI infrastructure has been able to provide this set-up through effective data collection, transformation, representation and analysis. Using BI managers can sift through massive quantities of data and only be exposed to knowledge and insights to identify key patterns and historic trends quickly (Raisinghani, 2004). BI has become one of the vital technological and innovative developments to impact modern organizations and a cornerstone in business decision making mainly through stimulating the diffusion of knowledge (Heang, 2017). S. and W. Williams addressed the impact of BI on organizational functions. Accordingly, the main quantifiable impact they pursued was the "change in value added", basically a return on investment (ROI) of BI implementations (Williams & Williams, 2003).

To be able to quantify this impact, in 2006 T. H. Davenport and J. G. Harris conducted a survey among 371 large and medium-sized organizations and found that "a high level of analytical competence had a positive impact on organizations' financial results" (Tunowski, 2015). The literature reports many potential advantages of successful BI implementations such as: having a single point of access to data; timeliness and reliability of the data results; customer-centric approach applicable to different organizational levels and departments; leveraging investments in ERPs; well-informed human capital; and ultimately better decision-making. These elements eventually lead to improving operational efficiency; reduction of waste and costs; effective relationship management with customers, suppliers and key stakeholders; improved stakeholders' communication; and enhanced market analysis, more profits and improved overall performance. All these elements and more represented some of the items in the initial action plan that AUC worked on in order to kick-start the BI experience on campus with the most relevant and effective ecosystem possible.

On a wider scope, the real and indirect potential of BI implementations is that it triggers a "series of changes that involves the entire company – from strategic to tactical structures – and penetrates into operational work, improving and increasing the efficiency and effectiveness of the organization" (Williams & Williams, 2003; Ludoslaw & Remigiusz, 2013). In the context of AUC, the changes were many and different including developing new processes, hiring human resources with the required expertise, redefining the data owners, and restructuring the Data Analytics and Institutional Research (DAIR) unit on campus to cater for the evolving mandate, objectives and targets of the BI platform. This powerful yet hidden transformation is the true force successful BI implementations have on organizations with no exceptions. These organizational developments emphasize the importance and impact of effective and well-thought BI infrastructures on organizations. However, it is worth noting that to date BI implementations are complicated and expensive in nature with high failure rates reported (Gartner, 2005).

Business Intelligence Implementation Critical Success (Enabling) Factors

In 2012, according to Gartner "less than 30% of BI initiatives will align analytic metrics completely with enterprise business drivers by 2014" (Gartner, 2012). As organizations must learn from failures to ensure success, a review of critical success factors mostly associated with BI implementations was imperative (Tunowski, 2015). The literature has an abundance of success factors, but some are more critical than others to the success of a BI project. These factors include organization readiness for transformation and change, culture for information-based decision making, BI implementation goals, strategy and project planning, human capital availability, leadership support, and quality of data and data governance. These factors need to be in harmony and alignment with the BI project for a successful implementation.

Business Intelligence Applications With a Focus on the Higher Education Industry

BI has been widely applied to many industries, businesses and economic sectors to capitalize on the positive results and improved decision-making through enhanced forecasting and planning; customer and market analysis; channel analysis and product profitability analysis. These industries include (a) banking and financial institutions where BI is used in the identification and clustering of the customer base. BI informs marketing strategies, aids in preparing performance metrics and benchmarks and tracking performance; (b) fast moving consumer goods (FMCGs) and retailing where BI harnesses the power of predictive analysis to forecast demand fluctuations through understanding consumer behavior; optimize manufacturing and supply chain processes and enhances stakeholder relationships; (c) distribution and logistics where BI has the ability to improve communication with stakeholders and business partners resulting in more efficient and effective operations; and (d) services where BI plays a key role in managing human capital, a critical resource for performance in this particular industry. It also enhances stakeholders' relationships in general as well as render organizations more effective and efficient.

CASE STUDY: THE AMERICAN UNIVERSITY IN CAIRO

The American University in Cairo (AUC) was founded in 1919 by a group of Americans devoted to education and service in the Middle East. Its founding president, Dr Charles R. Watson, wanted to create an English-language university based on high standards of conduct and scholarship and to contribute to the intellectual growth, discipline and character of the future leaders of Egypt and the region. AUC was located on a nine-acre campus in the heart of downtown Cairo, a city of more than 18 million people and the largest urban area in the Middle East and North Africa. In 2008, AUC relocated to a new suburb of the capital "New Cairo" where it established a new 260-acre, state-of-the-art "city of learning", designed to embody the university's liberal arts tradition and provide room for growth.

AUC is an independent, not-for-profit, equal-opportunity institution offering American-style liberal arts and professional undergraduate and graduate education to students from Egypt, the region and the world. In Egypt, AUC is licensed to grant degrees and is incorporated within the State of Delaware and accredited by Middle States Commission on Higher Education (MSCHE). Its academic program enrollment has grown to over 5,474 undergraduates and 979 graduate students (DAIR, 2017). Adult education has expanded and now serves more than 24,000 participants each year in non-credit courses and contracted training programs. 95% of students are Egyptian; the remaining 5% comprised of 49 different nationalities. The university academic endeavors are led by 475 full-time faculty members, 55% are international.

AUC Infostructure

AUC has been heavily investing in building its information infrastructure "infostructure" and in introducing a state-of-the-art enterprise resource planning systems since 1988. This emphasis on technology was to ensure that mission critical and precious data was stored in well-structured formats and to facilitate the automation of its various business processes. Over time, these systems have continued to amass large amounts of data. However, leveraging this humongous amount of data to generate insights has constantly been side tracked due to the following factors which, combined, paved the way for inconsistencies, redundancies and many different versions of the truth. Some of the lessons learnt in the case of AUC includes;

- The lack of an institutional strategic information technology roadmap resulting in multiple, non-integrated systems.
- Data scattered in separate silos and a term-based, off-line data snapshot called *"census"* is the only source used for official reporting.
- Ambiguous and conflicting data governance rules, data definitions and best practice business processes to regulate data standardization and cleanliness.
- Integration across the different systems not accounted for in ERP implementations posing a major challenge for consolidated data views.
- Immature organizational culture in terms of data sharing, transparency and evidence-based decision making.
- Data gaps preventing a holistic view of key stakeholders' records including students, faculty and staff.
- Spreadmarts became prevalent culture for reporting on all levels.
- No leadership in terms of information management, organizational development, information for business; looking only at technological issues through technical expertise.

However, AUC had a strong Data Analytics and Institutional Research (DAIR) team that was aware of the problem and its implications on effectiveness, agility and competitiveness of the university. DAIR was established in 1991 to support the university in strategic planning, assessment, data and analytics functions to advance the university's mission, promote institutional effectiveness and informed-based decision making. As the clearing house for the university data, the office is committed to a process of transparency, a culture of evidence and open communication in which information is made widely available to the campus community, as well as facilitating the flow of information between the central administration and campus units. In 2016, the office started its BI journey to further advance its mission and was rebranded as *"strategy management and institutional effectiveness"* to reflect its active strategic role. DAIR continuously advocated for the need of a BI infrastructure as an initial step in a journey to transform the universities information infrastructure and harness the opportunities this transformation can bring AUC.

Business Intelligence Issues: Challenges and Opportunities in Higher Education

The higher education sector is rather late adopter of BI. However, its abundance of data and emerging challenges necessitated that it too embarks on this journey. BI has since found many cases where it can help support decision making in this invaluable, dynamic, demanding, and growing sector. This has also been reflected in the increasing number of academic and executive programs and courses that defines and explains the notion of BI (Wixom et al, 2014). Among the key elements of the higher education sector that can benefit from the depth and breadth of BI are the following:

Enrollment Management

The management of the enrollment process from start to finish is a huge concern for higher education institutions. Enrollment management starts as early in the student journey as students' recruitment. Universities allocate huge budgets for costly school visits, college fairs and hosting special events on campus to reach out to the largest population of potential qualifying and best applicants. BI using data mining and predictive analytics have helped universities in identifying those potential applicants with maximum likelihood of becoming actual admits. Universities, such as Baylor University in Texas, in the United States, raised their number of new applications from 15,000 to 26,000 in Fall 2005 after using data mining to develop a model of the different student profiles who are most likely to be admitted and concentrated their recruitment efforts to target those students (Campbell, DeBlois, and Oblinger, 2007). In the context of AUC, using BI helped better identify the enrolment targets year-on-year including the quality and diversity of the students as well as clearly identify their performance and retention rates.

Course Planning

Effective course planning and schedule building is a major challenge that higher education institutions have to overcome to ensure high completion rates. In this context, BI can be used as analytical tools to help both students and advisors in selecting and prioritizing courses (Shatnawi et al, 2014). It mines student registration records of previous semesters to identify patterns in courses registered and uses them to recommend courses for new students and future terms (Atteya, 2017). In the context of AUC, with four undergraduate degrees' granting schools on campus including a school of business (BUS) and a school of sciences and engineering (SSE) where the majority of the students want to go; BI has been instrumental in more efficiently allocate resources in terms of faculty and staff to maintain the university's ratio of 1:11 of faculty to students as well as make sure that the other schools get on a semester-basis the required number of students needed per class which is 15 through elective courses.

Major "Discipline" Selection

Selecting the suitable major/discipline is key to student' success and a major challenge facing advisers. BI analytics tools have been used to support advisers in this process. In 2013, Nagy, Aly and Hegazy proposed a framework that uses classification and clustering to recommend a specific major or track for a student. Clustering is based on a multitude of student-related variables including students' academic level before university enrollment, students' major of interest and his/her first year grades (Atteya, 2017). The framework is then used to compare new students with these clusters and aid in predicting the most suitable major for the student. Similarly in 2014, Slim et al, presented a framework that predicts the performance of students early in their academic careers and advise them into their best-fit majors (Atteya, 2017).

Identifying and Predicting At-Risk Students

Identifying students who are academically at-risk early on during their educational journey is another application of BI that enables institutions to intervene in a timely manner. The definition of academically at-risk students differs from one university to another (Krase & Nyatepe-Coo, 2012). Intervention can be through one-on-one advising or providing remedial courses for those lagging behind academically as well as counseling sessions for those with psychological concerns. An institution that is proactively pursuing student success will yield higher retention and completion rates and consequently ranking and reputation (Atteya, 2017). There are a large number of researchers and academics who addressed this problem through exploring the techniques and innovative solutions that BI and analytics techniques offer (Al-Sarem, 2015; Lauría et al, 2012; Romero & Ventura, 2010).

Predicting Student Performance and Student Success

Similar to best-fit majors and students at-risk, BI analytics techniques are able to predict university student graduation performance based on high school scores and grades in first and second year courses without having to check any socioeconomic or demographic information (Asif, Merceron, & Pathan, 2015). The researcher reported the highest performance prediction accuracy of 83.65% by the Naive Bayesian classifier. The findings were also confirmed that students' grades in courses closer to graduation are better predictors of their performance than pre-university or first-year courses (Zimmermann et al., 2007). In the case of AUC, early adoption of BI across campus helped understanding the trends associated with students' performances and accordingly students advising for courses, and scheduling of courses throughout their studies have greatly improved. However, it is important to say that AUC is still scratching the surface when it comes to BI implementation, there is a lot more to be learn, adopt, diffuse and adapt. BI is a continuous journey and not a destination.

In 2013 the research conducted by Rusk and Song, the authors were able to identify the factors that serve as good indicators of engineering student's program drop-out or failure. They focused their study on electrical and computer engineering students only and used their first academic year information only to predict the student classified as satisfactory for those who completed their degree without ever being put on probation. They identified the three foundational courses that were the most informative predictors of engineering students' academic performance. Moreover, in 2012 Yadav et al, used decision trees to predict student's performance, probable drop-outs, students who need special attention based on past student's performance in Purchanval University from 2008 to 2011. For every student, his previous semester grades, average of current semester grades, student's performance in the seminar class, assignments submission, student's attendance and completion of lab work are used to predict his overall performance.

These are sample examples that most academic institutions are facing and the evolution of BI simply provides a platform to deal efficiently and timely with most of these issues offering decision makers an opportunity to provide the best students-centered experience based on thoroughly captured and analyzed data from different sources, including social media, and providing predictive analysis and scenarios. Following is the case of the American University in Cairo in introducing BI into its ecosystem and accordingly positively affecting the decision-making process with implications on the management style of the campus at large with its multifaceted resources and the learning experience of its different constituents both on and off campus.

The Business Intelligence and Data Analytics Journey at AUC

Building on years of information and communication technology and information infrastructure investments, it was time for AUC to take this whole realm to the next level. The massive and growing importance of data analytics and knowledge management was increasingly becoming invaluable for the university as a platform for agility and competitiveness as it celebrates in the academic year 2019-2020 (Rizk and Kamel, 2013).

University Administration Vision and Buy-In Is Key

The actual transformation process from deploying state-of-the-art information technology infrastructure into using BI started in 2016 with the creation of a new position at the university leadership level in the form of a "vice president of information management". Fortunately, the holder of the position was a visionary and strongly believed in the power of data to any institution let alone AUC where he has been an administrator and a faculty member since 1992, and more importantly with a market experience in IT projects in both government and the private sector for more than 30 years. Following a few months of deliberations and regular brainstorming, the data analytics team represented by DAIR realized that it was the right time to present to the university leadership a comprehensive proposal that demonstrates their vision to unleashing the power and opportunities behind BI, predictive analytics and big data and its associated implications to AUC.

The objective of the proposal was to provide decision-makers across campus with a visual, easy to use, powerful, dynamic platform for decision-making that has the ability to predict trends, generate insights and provide directions based on extensive analysis of historical data and recorded trends. The DAIR team was fortunate to secure the full support and endorsement of the vice president of information management in terms of budget but more importantly, in introducing on campus the much-needed cultural change, transformation of the mindset and the legacy systems when it comes to using data, taking decisions, and effectively managing it from start to finish.

AUC Gets Down to Real Business With BI

Knowing ahead of time that naturally BI projects were associated with high failure rates, the DAIR team researched a variety of diversified BI implementations to learn from their failures and successes. This helped them identify the critical ingredients to a successful BI recipe and enabled them to plan well before embarking on the actual project. This was not going to be a one size fits all venture, it needed adaptation and customization to the conditions on campus and the nature of the decision-making process at AUC in specific. The key critical success factors identified at this stage can be summarized as follows:

Project Structure, Strategy, and Human Capital

Identifying and setting a clear project vision, mission and established goals aligned with AUC strategy and business directions and objectives. The BI project had a clear mandate from the start as well as solid reporting line to the business side of the university – the DAIR team – to ensure complete alignment and ownership of business needs with BI goals and milestones. According to Boris Evelson, vice president and principal analyst at Forrester Research, "one of the essential components of a successful BI strategy is ensuring business ownership over BI" (Pratt, 2017).

Assigning a strong and capable management team with effective project management skills and a clearly defined, flexible and agile project plan. Due to the nature of the BI project that was more of a continuous effort and the expected resistance to change that accompanies any transformation effort.

Therefore, a solid project organization structure was mandatory. Consequently, the project organization was very conductive and composed of the following:

- **Project Sponsor:** The project reported directly to the vice president for information management to reflect its priority institutionally, ensure timely progress and that any organizational issues were handled in a timely and effective manner. Weekly reports were submitted from the project manager followed by lengthy and productive meetings. The vice president for information management also appointed an advisor with expertise in BI and big data analytics to guide the project team in the early phases of the project.
- **Project Manager:** To ensure consistency, sustainability and a positive launch of this campus-wide mega data-driven project, the executive director of the office of DAIR was appointed as project manager due to the need for regular monitoring, accountability and expert project management skills.
- **Functional and Technical Project Managers:** The project manager was supported in this role by a functional BI project manager and a technical IT project manager. Each was responsible in their respective domains to harness resources and drive progress.
- **Project Team Members:** The team was composed of a diversified set of skillsets needed by the project and reflective of its complexity. From security officers, database administrators and network staff to data governance and BI skills were assigned to the team. Weekly team meetings and updates were carried out to ensure that the whole team remained motivated, informed and aligned. Figure 1 demonstrates the project management team without any reporting lines or segregation to enhance alignment and a common mission.

Forming a strong and motivated purple BI team with the right mix of technical and business knowledge and expertise that brings the best out of the two worlds business (blue) and IT (red). A key success factor of any BI project lies in the competence and drive of the BI human capital to deliver solutions and get things done effectively and efficiently. Once the budget was approved, the daunting mission of excavating for the right talents that can help AUC make the best and the highest returns out of its massive investment was unlocked. This was one of the most challenging steps in the project, due to the scarceness of BI resources in Egypt and the restricted compensation AUC had to offer in comparison to other industries in the local and regional markets.

Even though there is no absolute right or wrong, AUC used some general guidelines and best practices when building the BI team. In formulating the team, it was necessary to make sure that people were not just hired because they know a specific programming language or had previous experience of any of the tools; organizational fitting, and understanding the nature of the higher education landscape were other key important factors. Although some foundational technical knowledge was needed, people were also evaluated based on their belief in the power of data and information in transforming an organization like AUC. The selection and filtering processes were based on tests to ensure the right expertise, attitude and aptitude followed by one-on-one interviews to assess fit and drive.

AUC started with a small team of five, including the project manager (Figure 2). This meant that it had to go with the multiple-hats approach in which every team member had more than one role to play, in many ways, it was a multi-disciplinary mode of operation. For example, the project manager served as a solution architect and a requirements analyst, a data modeler was also expected to build ETL codes and a data scientist also performed quality assurance checks. It was necessary to make sure that team

Figure 1. BI project team

members are capable of wearing the multiple hats whenever needed and regularly experience a daily multi-tasking routine. Multi-disciplinary teams work collaboratively and effectively in finding solutions to the problems without having to face the bureaucratic problems of the different groups of specialists. The groups of specialists work in isolation where one group throws its output to the next group in the BI assembly line without having one group holding the full ownership of the final result, this proves to be inefficient when both the business perspective and customer satisfaction is brought into focus. Multi-disciplinary groups think and work iteratively together to address the business needs and requirements. In doing that, they learn more and transfer more knowledge to each-others.

Having these two essential selection criteria in mind, AUC received more than 100 applications for the five positions needed for the BI team, which were evaluated and filtered until the five positions were

Figure 2. BI organization structure

fulfilled by the best calibers available who were able to follow an aggressive implementation roadmap, and in some areas where ahead of it.

A well-communicated campus-wide BI roadmap that addresses the institutional priorities and sets the expectations of the different stakeholders. After completing the first phase of BI in May 2017, which addressed students' admissions, enrollment, and graduation, and releasing the related dashboards to the community, it was necessary that the BI team manages the expectations of the different stakeholders. Therefore, the team started to develop different alternatives to the BI roadmap for the following year and discussed the roadmap at the university cabinet level (including the president, provost, and university counsellor and vice presidents) to gather feedback, thoughts and reactions. After several refinements to address the different priorities of the various stakeholders, the team was able to seek final approval of the roadmap and locked it for implementation. The appendix has a sample of the most recent BI roadmap (Figure 3). This gap analysis will be used to inform the new BI roadmap for the academic year 2018-2019.

Organizational Readiness

Community Endorsement, Buy-In and Wise Change Management Strategy for Informed Decision-Making

The university senior administration endorsement was key to the success of the project. In addition to the support of the vice president for information management, the team needed key business champions across campus to help the BI team spread the word and act as role models for adopting the change. Accordingly, an impact assessment matrix was prepared and was shared with all cabinet and senior administration executives for prioritizing the different milestones of the project as shown in Table 1.

Figure 3. Sample of the 2018 BI roadmap

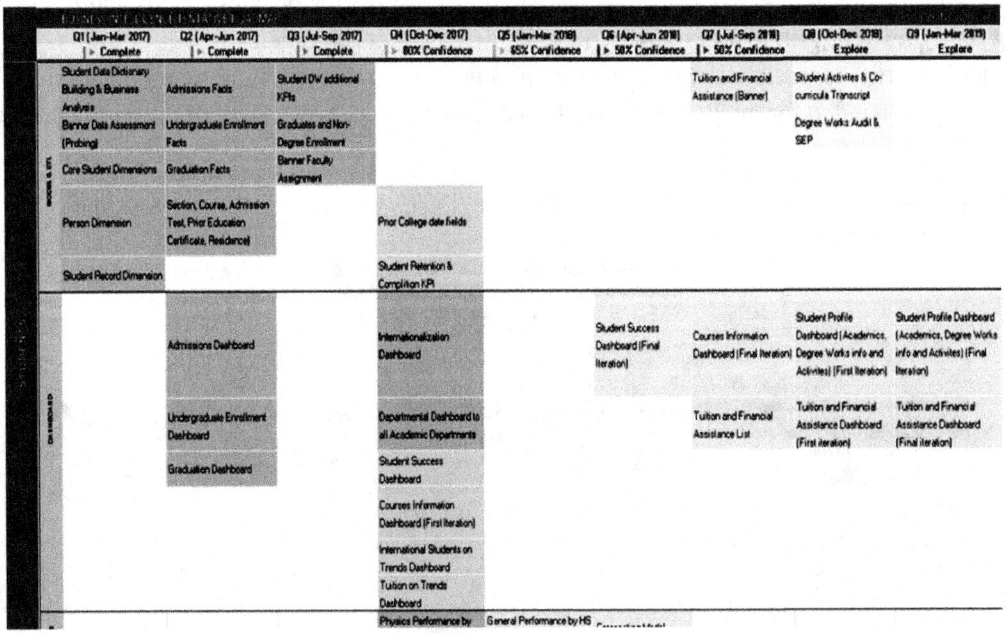

Table 1. BI impact assessment matrix

Business Processes	Academic School Deans	Academic Department Chairs	Registrar	Provost	Financial Area	Human Resources	Enrollment Management	Student Development	Research and Sponsored Programs
Enrollment Analysis & Forecasting	X	X	X	X	X		X	X	
Student Pipeline Analysis	X	X	X	X			X	X	X
Faculty Load Assessment	X	X	X	X		X			
Financial Analysis	X	X		X	X				
Contracts and Grants Analysis	X	X		X	X				X
Financial Aid Analysis	X	X				X	X		
Alumni Demographics/Tracking	X	X							
Human Resources	X			X					

According to the impact assessment matrix, student's academic information came in as the top priority and constituted the first of the project. Accordingly, key champions of this area were selected to be part of the early process of requirements gathering and dashboard designing. The university senior administration involvement was further strengthened after the completion of the first phase of the project where reviews and signing-off on BI project roadmap on an annual basis was introduced to make sure it aligns with the university's overall strategy and directions. Moreover, clear and progressive change management rules and procedures were formulated to make sure that the project had sufficient stability to complete milestones on time and effectively.

Laying Grounds for Data Governance Rules, Data Standards, and Enforcing the Related Policies

One of the biggest challenges for institutions implementing BI is the quality of its data and AUC is no exception. After the launch of the BI Project, the need for data governance rules, data definitions and standards became crystal clear to the BI team and to the university senior administration. Consequently, a committee for information management was formulated with a clear assignment of writing up the first data governance policy at AUC. The data governance policy manages the quality, consistency, usability, security, accessibility, and availability of administrative data. The governance platform covers staff, policies, processes, best practices, awareness and technologies required to manage the university's administrative data as an institutional asset, and focuses on university administrative data maintained by administrative and academic offices.

After several iterations of refinement to the policy, it was communicated and shared with all stakeholders such as the university cabinet, university senate, provost council and other stakeholders. The policy was then released and published on AUC website to be accessible by all the AUC community. According to the policy, the data analytics and institutional research team became responsible for working with the appropriate data stewards to develop standard definitions of commonly used terms; define how official university metrics are calculated; work to discover data discrepancies, inconsistencies and gaps and report such to the appropriate data steward for resolution. Having this authority granted to the DAIR team, with the BI team part of it, made it easier to request access to the source systems, report data inconsistencies and access the data definitions and standards for KPIs calculation and reporting.

Revisiting Ambiguous Business Processes for Optimization Based on Best-Practices: AUC Has Constantly Had an Issue With Its, or Lack of, Business Processes

This was exaggerated with the BI implementation. One of the challenges faced in the implementation was the integration of faculty data from the students' information system (running on banner) and the human resource ERP (running on SAP). Faculty members did not have unique identification on both systems. They also had multiple identities on the same system and their records were usually inconsistent. This was due to the ambiguous business process of faculty records' creation and maintenance and the non-alignment of the two constituents owning the faculty records on the two separate systems.

Ambiguous business processes like these usually hinder smooth progression of BI projects and add more complexity to understanding the data behind it. On this note, it was a good wake-up call for AUC to revisit its business processes for re-engineering and optimization. The business process witnessed massive transformation and still work-in-progress to adapt to the new culture and requirements of BI. The presence of the two functions of business process improvement (BPI) and BI within the same team was actually beneficial and rewarding to the university. Not only that improving business processes will enhance the data quality for the BI platform, it is in the team's vision to use BI to inform different decision points in the business processes and enhance the overall efficiency of operations on campus.

Technology: Vendors and Tools Selection

Selecting the Tools That Satisfy the Business Needs as Well as the Implementation Partner Who Is Technically Capable of Building an Environment That Is Scalable and Easy to Maintain

At the earliest stages of the project, the DAIR team realized the need for formulating a standing committee, which included, in addition to the DAIR team, IT members covering the different functions of the infrastructure, networks and security for the technical assessment of the tools available in the market. The team had a consensus on favoring a single-vendor full-stack solution over the best-of-breed option for a number of reasons including; working with one vendor makes things easier for everyone involved, communication is much easier where sharing the requirements and/or problems with one vendor without having to repeat the same message with multiple vendors and risking lack of adaptation or matching across multiple vendors. Working with one vendor means an intrinsic synergy between the different tools used, and a single focal point of support leading to a more seamless and effective implementation process. The team's mission was to find that single vendor whose different tools were innovative, and that can support all the university's needs and requirements. The team started to assess the tools provided by the market leaders; which according to Gartner Magic Quadrant of 2016 (Figure 4) included IBM, Microsoft, Teradata, SAP, and Oracle.

All vendors were invited for a proof of concept (PoC) which was an actual exercise to demonstrate the expertise and quality of each vendor and their associated implementation partner. Vendors who completed the PoC were short-listed and were further evaluated based primarily on the technical features of their solution then based on their financial quotations. The technical comparison addressed multiple dimensions with different weighting scores for mandatory and preferable criteria as demonstrated in Table 2.

After thorough deliberations and discussions, the final evaluation resulted in selecting IBM Egypt as the local implementation partner.

Figure 4. Gartner magic quadrant of 2016

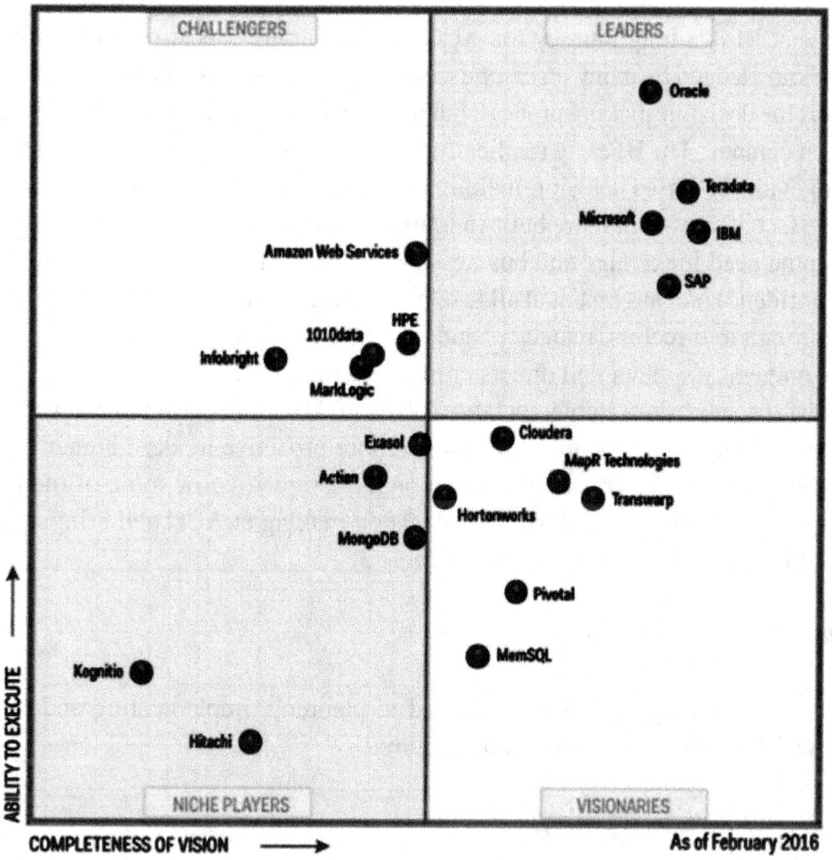

Table 2. Vendor selection process

Mandatory Criteria	Preferable Criteria
- Ease of connecting their tools to the university's ERP system for data extraction. - Capabilities of the reporting and visualization tools. - Solution compliance with the university's security requirements. - Existence of audit logs provided by the tools for troubleshooting. - The university's previous experience with vendor support and responsiveness. - Expertise of vendor-recommended implementation partners. - Steepness of the learning curve.	- **Previous experience in implementing BI platforms in other higher education institutions in the MENA region and beyond.** - **Existence knowledge of the vendors' tools within the university team.** - **Previous projects' experience with the university, if any.** - **The availability of professional expertise through the vendor and/or the implementation partner.**

Reaping the Early Fruits of Success "Just Scratching the Surface"

Despite the fact that BI is a long journey for AUC, the beginning was strong and promising and was celebrated and acknowledged by many on campus. Not only did it address the need for an effective infostructure to support the decision-making process, but it also had several indirect effects on the performance of several units on campus. The BI early implications included; (a) gradually shifting the organizational culture to a more evidence-based decision-making process; (b) enhancing data quality, governance and diminishing the effect of silos with more built-in transparency; (c) transforming the university at its core and emphasizing the need for change and business process documentation and re-engineering; and (d) increasing the confidence and alignment at all levels of management from the board of trustees to senior administrators through to directors, managers and first-line officers by creating one point of truth that consolidates the university's views and directs common action.

Fundamentally, the successful implementation of BI at AUC has played a significant role in transforming a 100-year old university to move towards a more proactive modern higher education institution in every aspect of its management and operation. A compilation of some of the key institutional dashboards designed with the aim of supporting decision making at AUC and bringing unusual events to the attention of the administrators are listed in Table 3.

Lessons Learnt

To capitalize on the university experience acquired in planning, implementing and managing the BI infrastructure, the following lessons need to be captured.

Planning for Agility and Scalability

Having a clear vision from the outset on the scope of the BI, type of users and estimate of data sources is key. However, only a few implementations have these details at the start. Hence planning for agility, flexibility and scalability are essential for adoption and effective use. In the case of AUC, the DAIR team was keen from the beginning to select a BI infrastructure that would allow scalability in terms of data sources. However, at the start the target user group was senior administration; shortly after, and with the reveal of BI's true potential, stakeholders at various levels demonstrated a clear appetite to use it. This was later handled by acquiring more information distribution mechanisms.

Deploying Best Practices in Project Management

The quality of project management skills in a BI implementation is critical due to their complex, non-traditional nature. Preparing high-level and detailed project plans led to a more proactive implementation enabling effective and timely allocation of resources from across the university. Decisions were made early on to initiate and maintain strong partnerships with business and IT stakeholders which proved to be of paramount importance. Business stakeholders were involved in the implementation through extensive needs analysis sessions to secure buy-in and adoption. Solid partnership with IT was critical in streamlining access, securing resources, learning about integration points and much more.

Table 3. BI dashboards

Dashboard	Description
AUC trends	Trends in the university admissions, enrollment, graduation and tuition fees KPIs while allowing decision makers to compare AUC to other peers for evaluation and improvement.
Internationalization	Focuses on the international student's population and provides decision makers with information regarding their academic level, majors, nationalities, payment mode and more.
Admissions	Provides daily updates on the number of applicants, accepted and newly enrolled students broken down by their demographical information, prior institutions certificates, and more highlighting the university's selectivity and yield KPIs at a given semester.
Enrollment	Focuses on the students enrolled and addresses their demographical information, academic performance, distribution across the different schools and majors, double majoring patterns, major-minor preferences and migration patterns between the different majors.
Graduation	Focuses on the graduating cohort in a specific semester broken down by demographics, primary and secondary majors and the time to complete their degrees.
AUC and school's partnership	Describes the student journey at AUC triggered by students' high school while analyzing their schools, focuses on their behaviors starting with their freshman year, major declaration and tracks them until graduation.
Human resources	Describes the university staff demographics, headcount analysis with different breakdowns and classifications.
Human resources trends	Tracks the trends of new hires, voluntary and involuntary separations, turnover rates and total headcounts.
Faculty	Describes the faculty demographics per school and department, breaks them down by their rank and tenure status.
Financial assistance	Provides information about the number financial assistance opportunities offered by the university broken down by their different types and need/merit classification as well as showing the distribution of offerings per school, major, gender and nationalities.
AUC coin	The university has recently gone cashless with a new system that enables students, staff and faculty to top-up their ID cards with cash and use it on campus for purchasing food, reserving events and more. Accordingly, the dashboard tracks the number of transactions and their amounts performed by the different community members and integrates information from the AUC Coin and the demographical information of the users from the different ERPs showing purchasing patterns, peak times of the day, most active group of users and more.
Cash position	Designed to help the university chief financial officer (CFO) track the university cash position on a weekly basis, showing its accounts balance in the different banks, the interest rates and more.

Selecting and Investing in BI Human Capital

Investing time and resources in selecting and training the suitable skills set was an essential ingredient for success. Scarcity of competent BI human resources in the market along with restricted budgets of higher education institutions in comparison to telecom and banking institutions made this more of a challenging task. Therefore, the focus was on building a team with certain competencies that ensured future project sustainability, drive, willingness to learn, agility, commitment, passion and knowledge to handle timely information. The team was made integral to the implementation process from the early stages where they shadowed the implementation consultants and participated in the actual implementation to gain concrete knowledge and hands-on expertise. This led to a smooth transition from the consultants to the

BI team and enabled them to add data sources and continue the BI journey. While this strategy implied additional initial costs, it proved to be very effective on the long run.

Maintaining a Clear Business Orientation and Coupling BI With Business Process Management, Strategy Management and ERP Systems

BI aims at supporting institutional strategy management and enhancing organizational performance. This necessitates clear business orientation, reporting and ownership to align the project with institutional business goals. It also leverages existing business process management (BPM) initiatives and enterprise resource planning systems. According to Janiesch, Matzner, and Müller (2012), the application of measurement methods to process specific data is referred to as process intelligence and process mining. The AUC team experience shows that *"process-centric"* BI has the potential to track the execution of processes and yield invaluable insights with consolidated views on operations and customers (Nofal and Yusof, 2013). AUC realized the significant value behind this integration at a later stage and steps were taken to address this through restructuring. Similarly, AUC invested heavily in ERP and BI systems ensuring a tight link between ERP and BI powers this investment to improve decision making and optimize the use of both platforms. Accordingly, AUC had an effective organizational structure where the vice president for information management oversaw both functions and endorsed the value of information (Popovič, Vukšić, and Bach, 2013).

Business Intelligence Realistic Expectations and Strong Change Management Practices

BI is a tool to aid business stakeholders and managers to improve decision making. It also requires strong top management support and buy-in. This was clear at AUC and demonstrated in the senior administrations' shift in expectations to more realistic ones. Furthermore, clear change management practices were established to counteract the effects of turbulent environments and their potential implications on roadmap completion. BI roadmaps were built in alignment with institutional strategy, and were signed off by the university senior administration and shared with all the AUC community.

Assessment of Institutional Data Quality

The success of a BI implementation is highly associated with the quality of its data, data standards and data governance mechanisms. On campus, the discussions on poor data quality had significantly delayed the implementation of a BI infrastructure and little progress to tackle the quality issue was made. Deciding to implement the BI platform, led to a strong and clear mobilization of institutional resources to address data quality and governance at a profound level. Both elements worked in parallel with each solidifying and supporting the other. BI was used to detect and report on data anomalies which decreased with every cycle and emphasized the importance of data standards and governance. Data governance supported BI by providing functional and technical definitions and standards to follow as well as clarifying data ownership and access rights.

Future Vision and Strategy

It is worth noting that moving forward, the BI team at AUC aspires to realize the strategic objective where all their tools and processes continue to effectively support the open access to accurate and timely data and introduce new advancements in promoting the culture of evidence-based decision making at the university. Accordingly, the BI team envisions the use of BI on campus as follows:

- Users will have access to the data they need to efficiently execute their job functions.
- Users will gradually not suffer from data silos and will have an integrated data hub that provide information and analytics that span multiple systems through a one-stop-shop "the BI system".
- A well-trained and powered BI user will be secured for every administrative area/academic school to cater for customized data requests that require adjusting reports and dashboards parameters.
- A series of "train-the-trainer" sessions will be conducted to all BI users in the different departments across campus to educate them on the wealth of information currently available in the BI system and how to access it and use it effectively and efficiently.
- A set of automated data quality and governance reports based on business rules will be availed through the BI system to the governance team once a business process is reviewed and approved by the business processes team to enable prompt capturing of quality issues on the source systems.
- Data definitions and dictionaries will be linked to the BI dashboards and reports, whenever possible.
- The BI system will continue to provide the decision-makers across campus with data that was difficult to access through integrating data from external sources and systems other than the main ERPs
- The BI system will start to address "Big data" sources and predictive analytics more seriously to take the decision-making process to another level

The BI team recognizes that a future data warehouse strategy should consider both a penetration strategy and a datawarehouse expansion strategy.

Penetration Strategy

When the BI first started its journey at AUC, the university senior administrators' vision positioned the BI project as a strategic-decision making supporting tool. The BI team's experience is that it is crucial to align operational and strategic decision-making to reach the true state of having one version of the truth. Accordingly, it was inevitable that the BI team includes in the 2019 roadmap a penetration strategy that would enable and empower department assistants and operational teams across campus to access the information they need for running smooth and efficient operational business processes.

In light of that, the BI team opted for a type of license that would enable unlimited number of users' access to restricted reporting features to cater for the large number of users who would be using BI for operational purposes. In addition to that, the BI team needs to secure a larger number of power user licenses to enable one power user per each administrative department and academic school. This power user should be able to run more sophisticated reports and dashboards in which they can change default parameters and filtering options. In preparation for this, the team has chosen the *"school of business"* as a pioneer BI user and started to gather their strategic and operational reporting needs. The school of business dashboards and reports will be used as a template to be extended to other schools and departments. Moreover, a *"train-the-trainer"* plan has to be set and periodically provided as part of the human resources orientation sessions held on a yearly-basis to disseminate the much-needed know-how of running the reports and dashboards, understanding the different KPIs and reaching out to the correct definitions of the reported figures. There is a cost to expanding the activity of the BI platform in terms of financial cost of added licenses and needed effort to support the increase in the number of BI users. However, coupled with sound project management and highly skillful BI teams with customer-oriented behavior, this challenge should be rocking waters but wreaking havoc.

Datawarehouse Expansion Strategy

The datawarehouse strategy has to address expanding the data sources of the datawarehouse to new sources of information that was hard to retrieve in the past. Therefore, the BI team decided to try to integrate the data from the alumni system into the datawarehouse such that users can access a fully integrated students/alumni record seamlessly. The alumni system has data about the university alumni who voluntarily opted of providing this information which introduces a new challenge of dealing with large portions of missing information of those who did not. In order to overcome this problem, the BI team will disembark a new challenge of addressing external data sources to retrieve LinkedIn profiles for AUC graduates. The aim of addressing the alumni information is to start providing the university senior administrators with information related to where do AUC graduates get employed and when, whether they pursue post-graduate degrees elsewhere and identify graduates of specific majors who prefer to switch careers and get employed in different industries. This wealth of unprecedented information is going to add a new perception to how the university envisions its students and alumni.

The BI team is planning to integrate the data from the academic degree evaluation system into the data warehouse to answer business questions addressing building a schedule of offerings that accommodates the registration needs of students. This can be achieved by studying the gap between the actual demand and supply of courses, the optimal number of sections to offer of each course given the number of students, the percentage degree completion of each student and whether the students adhere or deviate from their advising plans. Among the BI priorities set for this year, the team intends to complement factual data collected from the main information systems with data addressing students' perceptions. AUC has a rich calendar of institutional surveys providing a wealth of information about students' opinions, satisfaction levels, aspirations and future-plans.

Blending factual and perceptual information will give us another depth of knowledge that would support informed decision-making. The plan also includes addressing extracurricular activities data to assess student engagement. This wealth of information will contribute to providing a 360° view of the students at AUC that extends beyond students' academic information. It is also crucial that the BI team invests more time in practicing predictive modeling to answer key business questions like students at-risk of dropping out, students who are best-fit for specific major declarations and students who are most-likely to graduate on-time. The team is aware that aspired high accuracy of predictive modeling will always be hard to achieve from the first round of analytics and is intending to pursue continuous enhancements to these models as more and more information becomes available in the datawarehouse. Working on these two strategies in parallel will have a significant impact on nurturing a culture of evidence-based decision-making that the BI team thinks that AUC truly deserves and that is long overdue.

FUTURE RESEARCH

Moving forward it is recommended that further research is conducted on the experience of AUC and other higher education institutions in integrating and blending business intelligence platforms into their decision-making processes. The implications, challenges and opportunities of implementing such platforms in the context of higher education will continue to bring new insights and perceptions of the power of innovative information management and data analytics and will undoubtedly have positive implications on the students' learning experience and the management of campuses at large.

CONCLUSION

Business intelligence is a term used to describe applications and technologies which are used to gather, provide access to and analyze data and information about the organization, to help make better business decisions. The objective of BI is to provide "actionable insight" that support informed-based decision making (Wu, Liya, and Bartolini, 2007). The power of BI platforms stem from the enhanced quality it brings to the decision-making table and its impact on organizational performance. As an established 100-year old institution, The American University in Cairo was undergoing extensive management transformation to align with its ever changing and dynamic environment. However, the lack of quality, comprehensive data was crippling its advancement resulting in gut-feeling and best guess decision making. A courageous decision was made by the university senior administration to invest in and implement a state-of-the-art BI platform to tackle this weakness.

The decision was supported and endorsed by the leadership of the information management area and supported by effective project management, and competent newly established business intelligence team. This decision was a profound game changer in the university's performance and decision-making platform. The BI project proved once again that AUC is a leader and trend setter in the higher education industry in the MENA region. The implementation was challenging and complicated especially being faced with the extensive resistance to change that initially impeded the transformation initiatives typical in traditional and legacy organizations.

The challenge was exacerbated by the existing fragmented IT landscape; information silos, organizational culture; lack of data governance or clear ownership and poor business performance management practices. However, even at this early stage of the BI journey at AUC, the results were promising and gradually the BI platform started to transform one area after the other at the university. Accordingly, it was widely endorsed by many key stakeholders on campus. However, BI is a journey and AUC remains in the initial steps of building its infostructure with an aggressive penetration and expansion strategy laid out to take AUC into its centennial with solid information tools imperative for strong decision making.

ACKNOWLEDGMENT

I would like to acknowledge the work of the Data Analytics and Institutional Research (DAIR) team at the American University in Cairo for their hard work, commitment, dedication, resilience and determination to introduce and effectively and efficiently integrate the culture of data-driven decision-making using advanced and innovative information technology tools and applications into the campus.

REFERENCES

Al-Sarem, M. (2015). Building a decision tree model for academic advising affairs based on the algorithm C4-5. *Intenational Journal of Computer Science Issues*, *12*(5), 33–37.

Asif, R., Merceron, A., & Pathan, M. K. (2015). Predicting student academic performance at degree level: A case study. *Intelligent Systems and Applications*, *1*, 49–61.

Atteya, H. (2017). *Visualization as a guidance to classification for large datasets*. The American University in Cairo. Retrieved from http://dar.aucegypt.edu/handle/10526/5132

Baars, H., & Kemper, H. G. (2008). Management support with structured and unstructured data— An integrated business intelligence framework. *Information Systems Management*, *25*(2), 132–148. doi:10.1080/10580530801941058

Boutlon, C. (2013). How much Hadoop about nothing. *CIO Journal*. Retrieved from http://blogs.wsj.com/cio/2013/01/25/much-hadoop-about-nothing/

Campbell, J. P., DeBlois, P. B., & Oblinger, D. G. (2007). Academic analytics: A new tool for a new era. *EDUCAUSE Review*, *42*, 40–57. Retrieved from http://net.educause.edu/ir/library/pdf/ERM0742.pdf

Davenport, T. H., & Harris, J. G. (2006). *Inteligencja analityczna w biznesie: nowa nauka zwyciężania*. Warszawa: MT Biznes. (in Polish)

El-Sherif, H., & El-Sawy, O. (1998). Issue-based decision support systems for the Cabinet of Egypt. *Management Information Systems Quarterly*, *12*(4), 551–569. doi:10.2307/249131

Fitriana, R., & Djatna, T., & Eriyatno. (2011). Progress in business intelligence system research : A literature review. *International Journal of Basic and Applied Sciences*, *11*(3), 96–105.

Gartner, I. (2005). *Gartner says more than 50 percent of data warehouse projects will have limited acceptance or will be failures through 2007* [Press Release]. Retrieved from https://www.gartner.com/newsroom/id/492112

Gartner, I. (2012). *Gartner says fewer than 30 percent of business intelligence initiatives will align analytic metrics completely with enterprise business drivers by 2014* [Press Release]. Retrieved from https://www.gartner.com/newsroom/id/1891515

Gartner. (n.d.). *Business intelligence (BI)*. Retrieved from https://www.gartner.com/it-glossary/business-intelligence-bi

Gibson, M., Arnott, D., & Jagielska, I. (2004). *Evaluating the intangible benefits of business intelligence: review and research agenda*. Academic Press.

Gupta, V., & Singh, J. (2014). A review of data warehousing and business intelligence in different perspective. *International Journal of Computer Science and Information Technologies*, *5*(6), 8263–8268.

Heang, R. (2017). *Literature review of business intelligence*. Academic Press.

Janiesch, C., Matzner, M., & Müller, O. (2012). Beyond process monitoring: A proof-of-concept of event-driven business activity management. *Business Process Management Journal, 18*(4), 625–643. doi:10.1108/14637151211253765

Kamel, S. (1992). The governorates information and decision support centers project. *Proceedings of the United Nations Seminar on Urban Information Systems and their Applications in Developing Countries.*

Kamel, S. (1993). Decision support in the governorates level in Egypt. *Proceedings of the 4th Information Resources Management Association International Conference (IRMA) on challenges for information management in a world economy,* 390–398.

Kamel, S. (2008). DSS experience in Africa – cases from Egypt. In Handbook on Decision Support Systems 2. Springer-Verlag.

Kowalczyk, M., Buxmann, P., & Besier, J. (2013). *Investigating business intelligence and analytics from a decision process perspective: a structured literature review - analytics from a decsion process perspective.* ECIS. Retrieved from http://aisel.aisnet.org/ecis2013_cr/126

Krase, H., & Nyatepe-Coo, E. (2012). *Identifying and supporting academically at-risk students in Canadian universities.* Retrieved from http://www.uky.edu/ie/sites/www.uky.edu.ie/files/uploads/BP_Identifying%26 SupportingAcademically At Risk Students . . .pdf

Lauría, E. J. M., Baron, J. D., Devireddy, M., Sundararaju, V., & Jayaprakash, S. M. (2012). Mining academic data to improve college student retention: an open source perspective. *Proceedings of the Second International Conference on Learning Analytics and Knowledge,* 139–142. 10.1145/2330601.2330637

Li, K. F., Rusk, D., & Song, F. (2013). Predicting student academic performance. *Seventh International Conference on Complex, Intelligent, and Software Intensive Systems Predicting,* 27–33.

Loch, K., Straub, S., & Kamel, S. (2003). Diffusing the internet in the Arab world: The role of social norms and technological culturation. *IEEE Transactions on Engineering Management, 50*(1), 45–63. doi:10.1109/TEM.2002.808257

Ludoslaw, D., & Remigiusz, L. (2013). Methodological aspects and case studies of business intelligence application tools in knowledge management as corporations' strategy development. *Proceedings of the Management, Knowledge and Learning International Conference,* 1461–1468.

Luhn, H. P. (1958). A Business intelligence system. *IBM Journal of Research and Development, 2*(4), 314–319. doi:10.1147/rd.24.0314

Nagy, H. M., Aly, W. M., & Hegazy, O. F. (2013). An educational data mining system for advising higher education students. *International Journal of Computer, Electrical, Automation Control and Information Engineering, 7*(10), 622–626.

Negash, S. (2004). Business intelligence. *Communications of the Association for Information Systems, 13,* 177–195. doi:10.17705/1CAIS.01315

Nofal, M. I., & Yusof, Z. M. (2013). Integration of business intelligence and enterprise resource planning within organizations. *Procedia Technology, 11,* 658–665. doi:10.1016/j.protcy.2013.12.242

Popovič, A., Vukšić, V. B., & Bach, M. P. (2013). Supporting performance management with business process management and business intelligence: A case analysis of integration and orchestration. *International Journal of Information Management*, *33*(4), 613–619. doi:10.1016/j.ijinfomgt.2013.03.008

Pratt, M. (2017). *7 keys to a successful business intelligence strategy*. Retrieved August 1, 2018, from https://www.cio.com/article/2437838/business-intelligence/7-keys-to-a-successful-business-intelligence-strategy.html

Raisinghani, M. S. (2004). *Business intelligence in the digital economy : opportunities, limitations, and risks*. Hershey, PA : Idea Group Pub. Retrieved from http://services.igi-global.com/resolvedoi/resolve.aspx?doi=10.4018/978-1-59140-206-0

Rizk, N., & Kamel, S. (2013). ICT and building a knowledge society in Egypt. *International Journal of Knowledge Management*, *9*(1), 1–20. doi:10.4018/jkm.2013010101

Romero, C., & Ventura, S. (2010). Educational data mining: A review of the state-of-the-art. *Transactions on Systems. Man and Cybernetics - Part C: Applications and Reviews*, *40*(6), 601–618. doi:10.1109/TSMCC.2010.2053532

Rouhani, S., Asgari, S., & Mirhosseini, S. (2012). Business intelligence concepts and approaches. *American Journal of Scientific Research*, *50*, 62–75.

Shatnawi, R., Qlthebyan, Q., Ghalib, B., & Al-Maolegi, M. (2014). *Building a smart academic advising system using association rule mining*. arXiv:1407.1807

Shollo, A. (2013). *The role of business intelligence in organizational decision-making* (PhD thesis). Copenhagen Business School.

Slim, A., Heileman, G. L., Kozlick, J., & Abdallah, C. T. (2014). Predicting student success based on prior performance. In *Computational Intelligence and Data Mining (CIDM)*. Orlando, FL: IEEE. doi:10.1109/CIDM.2014.7008697

Tunowski, R. (2015). Organization effectiveness and business intelligence systems. Literature Review. *Management and Business Administration. Central Europe*, *23*(4), 55–73.

Turban, E., Sharda, R., & Delen, D. (2010). *Decision support and business intelligence systems* (9th ed.). Upper Saddle River, NJ: Prentice Hall Press.

Uma, K. K., & Sankarasubramanian, R. (2014). Business intelligence system - a survey. *International Journal of Advanced Research in Computer Science and Software Engineering*, *4*(9), 688–691. Retrieved from http://ijarcsse.com/Before_August_2017/docs/papers/Volume_4/9_September2014/V4I9-0372.pdf

Wieder, B., & Ossimitz, M.-L. (2015). The impact of business intelligence on the quality of decision making - a mediation model. *Proceedings of the Conference on Enterprise Information Systems CENTERIS*. 10.1016/j.procs.2015.08.599

Williams, S., & Williams, N. (2003). *The business value of business intelligence* (Vol. 3). Business Intelligence Journal.

Wixom, B., Ariyachandra, T., Douglas, D., Goul, M., Gupta, B., Iyer, L., ... Turetken, O. (2014). The current state of business intelligence in academia: The arrival of big data. *Communications of the Association for Information Systems, 34*, 1–13. doi:10.17705/1CAIS.03401

Wixom, B., & Watson, H. (2010). The BI-based organization. *International Journal of Business Intelligence Research, 1*(1), 13–28. doi:10.4018/jbir.2010071702

Wu &Bartolini. (2007). A service-oriented architecture for business intelligence. *Proceedings of the IEEE International Conference on Service-Oriented Computing and Applications.*

Yadav, S., Bharadwaj, B., & Pal, S. (2012). Data mining applications: A comparative study for predicting student's performance. *International Journal of Innovative Technology and Creative Engineering, 1*(12), 13–19. Retrieved from http://arxiv.org/abs/1202.4815

Zimmermann, J., Brodersen, K. H., Pellet, J., August, E., Buhmann, J. M., & Zurich, E. T. H. (2007). Predicting graduate-level performance from undergraduate achievements. In *Proceedings of the 4th International Conference on Educational Data Mining*, 2–3. Retrieved from http://educationaldatamining. org/EDM2011/wp-content/uploads/proc/edm2011_poster20_Zimmermann.pdf

ADDITIONAL READING

Akhmetov, B., Izbassova, N., & Akhmetov, B. (2012) Developing and customizing university business intelligence cloud in *Proceedings of the International Conference on Cloud Computing Technologies, Applications and Management*, pp. 229–233. 10.1109/ICCCTAM.2012.6488104

Apraxine, D., & Stylianou, E. (2017). Business intelligence in a higher educational institution: the case of University of Nicosia in *the Proceedings of the IEEE Global Engineering Education Conference*, pp. 1735–1746.

Elhassan, I., & Klett, F. (2016). Bridging higher education and market dynamics in a business intelligence framework in *the Proceedings of the 2015 International Conference on Developments in eSystems Engineering*, pp. 198–203.

Fadhil, A. (2015). Implementation issues affecting the business intelligence adoption in public university. *Journal of Engineering and Applied Sciences (Asian Research Publishing Network), 10*, 18061–18069.

Kumaran, S. R., Othman, M. S., & Yusuf, L. M. (2016). Applying theory of constraints (TOC) in business intelligence of higher education: a case study of postgraduates by research program, in *the Proceedings of the International Conference on Science Information Technology*, pp. 147–151.

Magaireah, A. I., Sulaiman, H., & Ali, N. (2017). Theoretical framework of critical success factors (CSFs) for Business Intelligence (BI) System in *the Proceedings of the 8th International Conference on Information Technology*, pp. 455–463.

Rodzi, N. A. H. M., Othman, M. S., & Yusuf, L. M. (2016). Significance of data integration and ETL in business intelligence framework for higher education in *the Proceedings of the 2015 International Conference on Science in Information Technology Big Data Spectrum for Future Information Economy*, pp. 181–186.

Sanchez-Puchol, F., Pastor-Collado, J. A., & Borrell, B. (2017). Towards a unified information systems reference model for higher education institutions. *Procedia Computer Science, 121*, 542–553. doi:10.1016/j.procs.2017.11.072

Sangar, A. B., & Iahad, N. B. A. (2013). Critical factors that affect the success of business intelligence systems (BIS) implementation in an organization. *International Journal of Scientific and Technology Research, 2*, 176–180.

Tulasi, B. (2013). Significance of Big Data and Analytics in Higher Education. *International Journal of Computers and Applications, 68*(14), 21–23. doi:10.5120/11648-7142

Turban, E., Sharda, R., Aronson, J. E., & King, D. (2008). *Business Intelligence: A Managerial Approach*. Pearson/Prentice Hall.

Yeoh, W., & Koronios, A. (2010). Business intelligence systems University of South. *Australia Journal of Computer Information Systems, 50*, 23–32.

Yeoh, W., & Popovič, A. (2016). Extending the understanding of critical success factors for implementing business intelligence systems. *Journal of the Association for Information Science and Technology, 67*(1), 134–147. doi:10.1002/asi.23366

Yusof, A. F., Miskon, S., Ahmad, N., Alias, R. A., Hashim, H., Abdullah, N. S., ... Maarof, M. A. (2015). Implementation issues affecting the business intelligence adoption in public university. *Journal of Engineering and Applied Sciences (Asian Research Publishing Network), 10*.

Zulkefli, N. A., Miskon, S., Hashim, H., Alias, R. A., Abdullah, N. S., Ahmad, N., ... Maarof, M. A. (2015). A business intelligence framework for higher education institutions. *Journal of Engineering and Applied Sciences (Asian Research Publishing Network), 10*.

KEY TERMS AND DEFINITIONS

Big Data: It reflects extremely large data sets that may be analyzed computationally to reveal patterns, trends, and associations, especially relating to human behavior and interactions.

Business Intelligence: BI is an umbrella term that includes the applications, infrastructure and tools, and best practices that enable access to and analysis of information to improve and optimize decisions and performance.

Data Analytics: DA is the process of examining data sets in order to draw conclusions about the information they contain, increasingly with the aid of specialized systems and software.

Decision-Making: It is the process of making choices by identifying a decision, gathering information, and assessing alternative resolutions.

Emerging Economies: An emerging economy reflects the characteristics of a developed market, but does not satisfy standards to be termed a developed market.

Information Management: It is the discipline that analyzes information as an organizational resource, it covers the definitions, uses, value and distribution of all data and information within an organization whether processed by computer or not.

Knowledge Management: It is the efficient handling of information and resources within a commercial organization.

Organizational Effectiveness: It is the concept of how effective an organization is in achieving the outcomes the organization intends to produce.

Chapter 14

Building an Analytics Culture to Boost a Data–Driven Entrepreneur's Business Model

Soraya Sedkaoui
ⓘ https://orcid.org/0000-0002-7134-2871
KM University, Algeria & SRY Consulting Montpellier, France

Mounia Khelfaoui
Khemis Miliana University, Algeria

ABSTRACT

This chapter treats the movement that marks, affects, and transforms any part of business and society. It is about big data that is creating, and the value generating that companies, startups, and entrepreneurs have to derive through sophisticated methods and advanced tools. This chapter suggests that analytics can be of crucial importance for business and entrepreneurial practices if correctly aligned with business process needs and can also lead to significant improvement of their performance and quality of the decisions they make. So, the main purpose of this chapter are exploring why small business, entrepreneur, and startups have to use data analytics and how they can integrate, operationally, analytics methods to extract value and create new opportunities.

INTRODUCTION

When we consider the opportunities offered by big data universe, the power of analytics, algorithm relevance and of what may seem to be revealed by each byte of data, and then the effort involved seems to be doubled to start down into how one can develop the new business model through joining big data analytics arena. In another way, every data byte tells a story and data analytics, in particular, the statistical methods coupled with the development of IT tools (Walwei, 2016), piece together that story's reveal the underlying message (Sedkaoui, 2018a).

DOI: 10.4018/978-1-5225-7277-0.ch014

Many successful entrepreneurs' experiences support that, analytics as a core capability of their startups. These include *Sergey Brin* and *Larry Page* of Google, *Jeff Bezos* of Amazon.com, *Michael Bloomberg* of Bloomberg LP, *Travis Kalanick* and *Garrett Camp* of Uber, *Reed Hastings* of Netflix and more. At this stage, one must wonder '*how they do what they do?*' Somehow, the answer lies in the fact that these experiences have understood the underlying message revealed by the amount volume of data byte available today. They have seen the potential in using analytics not only to differentiate their business models but also to innovate.

With small budgets, limited staff and inexperience, entrepreneurs somehow have to find a way to boost their data-driven project orientation by realizing the potential of big data beyond a promising buzzword. They must pair a vision with a clear profit model if they want to join this arena. Nevertheless, there is a school of thought, which says that "Being entrepreneurial means that an opportunity must be pursued despite the lack of resources, and the ability to leverage external resources is one of the hallmarks of the entrepreneur" (Stevenson & Jarillo, 1990; Stokes & Wilson, 2010).

The challenge, therefore, lies in the ability to extract value from the amount volume of data produced in real-time continuous streams with multiple forms and from multiple sources. In another word, to explore data and uncover secrets from it, we need to find and develop applicable to generate knowledge that can conduct any business project strategies. Therefore, understand the leadership's cognitive is necessary. It helps to determine the factors that can encourage the adoption of new methods as suggested by McAfee and Brynjolfsson (2012) and Ross et al (2013).

Of course, there are multiple ways an entrepreneur can become more data-driven.

By using big data technologies, by exploring the new methods to detect correlations between the quantities of available data, by developing algorithms and tools that can address the variety of data, by optimizing the Business Intelligence process, etc. This provides insights on how they can develop the new business model through the use of IT tools and by providing the ability to analyze data.

That's what this chapter will explore by highlighting the contents and focusing on how to conduct an analytical approach to help entrepreneurs in their business model creation process. Therefore, in this study the following research question will be answered: *How can small businesses drive an analytical approach to get more value out of the available data and optimize their business model in such a way that it will be more frequently used for better conduct their project?*

Through this question, we recall the context of big data, its importance in conducting decision-making, its challenges and the role it plays as a complement to create new opportunities for small enterprise in order to address the different issues.

It is the question posed above that is discussed in the remainder of this chapter, by highlighting it through three sections, a discussion, and a conclusion. The first section discusses the general theoretical background necessary to understand the importance of big data analytics.

The second section addressed to the big data analytics applications. It illustrates its power by showing its wide range of business applications and how it can be applied to generate value and create an oriented-data business model for entrepreneurship. For conduct a data-driven entrepreneur approach, the third section gives key elements to undertake in big data analytics, and how this approach can better guide the business project for innovation by giving the ability to learn from data. Then, the discussion addresses the development of a data culture within business orientations.

So, to be in the context of this book, this chapter pays a particular attention to the role of big data analytics on addressing challenges, and how small business can harness the potential of big data and how the analytics power can help them find creative solutions to the various problems.

WHERE TO START? AN OVERVIEW

As with all innovative areas, it is sometimes difficult to understand what is involved. For this, before going into the thick of the subject and talking only about how data drive entrepreneur's business model process for a small and micro enterprise, this section will cover and discuss the basic concepts that lie behind the big data analytics in order to highlight the importance of working with data. The aim is to introduce and define big data analytics as an immense potential to generate value for businesses. Here is generally what an entrepreneur needs to know to get his feet with big data analytics.

Already! What Is Big Data?

'Data revolution', *'data deluge'*, *'phenomenon'* ... words are diverse to refer to the "big data effect". Analytics use, algorithms application and uncovering the hidden patterns behind the data available today, have excited the business playground. The debates that are emerging during these few years around big data are very similar to those that took place about the "Web" in the early 1990s. After a long and active discussion phase in the literature, big data is entered a phase of use by many companies (Sedkaoui, 2018a). One of the reasons big data has become so popular is the availability of data, which has improved.

Data existing over the time, it is not new, but what makes it so important is the rapid rate and different types in which it is produced in recent times, or what brings us to turn: *"From data to Big data"*. This phenomenon has radically changed the way data are collected, stored and analyzed since it introduces new issues concerning *volume* (how much?), *velocity* (at what speed?) and the *variety* (how diverse?) of data available today. Typically, these three Vs are used to characterize the key properties of big data.

- **Volume:** Refers to the size of the data.
- **Velocity:** Refers to the data provisioning rate and to the necessary time to act on them.
- **Variety:** Refers to the heterogeneity of data acquisition, data representation, and semantic interpretation.

The big data definition can vary significantly from one source to another, but its main characteristics are known. McKinsey (2011) offers their interpretation of what big data is, based on the described 3Vs. The popular definition of big data, which are based on these three properties, is that given by Gartner (2013), which define big data as:

An information asset whose volume is large, velocity is high, and formats are various.

This data comes from social networks, smartphones and other mobile devices, connected objects and IoT sensors (vehicles, medical sensors, surveillance cameras, smartwatch ...) (Sedkaoui, 2018c). Consulting firms (McKinsey, IDC, Gartner ...) see it as a very promising market (27.7 billion $ in 2012, the double in 2016 according to IDC). The challenge for the coming years is to know how to store, exploit and create value, yes! another 'V' of big data.

In addition, storage and processing capabilities are the other major changes in data growth. This is mainly related to the increase of the capacity of storage (see Figure 1) and the computing power.

So, it is no more about the word 'big' now, but how to handle this 'big' of structured, semi-structural and unstructured data, that cannot be managed with traditional tools, and how to deal with its diversity

Figure 1. The growth of storage capacity
Source: Sedkaoui, 2018b

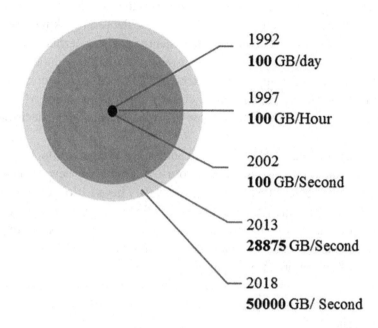

1992
100 GB/day

1997
100 GB/Hour

2002
100 GB/Second

2013
28875 GB/Second

2018
50000 GB/ Second

and velocity to generate value, because nowadays, 'all about value'. What is important is not the size or technique, but how to generate value (analyzes, correlations test, predictions, machine learning algorithms ...).

Understand Data to Derive Knowledge

Nowadays it doesn't take much to convince managers or decision-makers alike of the importance of data for their business activities because most of the business activities are associated with the use, the understanding and the exploiting of data (Sedkaoui, 2018a). Many companies have realized that knowledge is power, and to get this power they have to gather its source, which is data, and make sense of it. This was illustrated by the famous *"knowledge pyramid"* (see Ackoff, 1989), described as a *"knowledge discovery"* where data lays at the base (see Figure 3). The data we produce, as well as other data we accumulate, constitutes a constant source of knowledge.

As a result, data has passed from being a modest and oft-discarded by-product of firms' operations to an active resource with the potential to increase firm performance and economic growth. But, it is important to notice that data available today is very different from data, which existed before. Data is collected from various sources. It can be in different infrastructures, such as cloud, or in different databases, such as rows, columns, or files (Moorthy et al., 2015).

To this structured data, managed in traditional IT applications (ERP, CRM ...) many other data types have been added. These types often called 'unstructured data' or 'semi-structured data', which come from various sources, such as connected objects, social media ...

In addition to these categories, it is also helpful to look at data variety from a company's perspective: internal and external data. Along with capturing data from internal sales information and sensors, companies can also track public responses on Facebook, Twitter, or other social media.

These new types of data may be intended to enrich the types existing before, and from which derive information and then producing knowledge. This idea refers to the knowledge pyramid, which illustrates the importance of data in knowledge creation that improve the decision-making process.

The most important asset of big data lies in the fact that the analysis of this data makes it possible to generate knowledge and create considerable value. However, in traditional models, key-value creation activities can be described using the value chain (Porter, 1985). The value chain concept, primarily geared to the physical world, treats data as a supporting element rather than a source of value itself (Rayport and Sviokla, 1995). But, a correct utilization of those enormous of data in the decision-making process is not easy.

So, the process of decision begins when the top manager has to choose which data to look for, even before starting to collect data. Organizations need to use a structured view of data to improve their decision-making process. To achieve this structured view, they have to collect and store data, perform an analysis, and transform the results into useful and valuable knowledge (Sedkaoui, 2018a).

In fact, the emergence of big data has the potential to influence a company. According to Frizzo-Barker et al., (2016), big data can change the way companies are thinking about data infrastructure, business intelligence, and analytics and information strategy.

By using big data, companies are also able to know more about their business context. McAfee & Brynjolfsson (2012) argue that big data allow companies to improve their decision-making process and therewith their performance.

Data Analytics Power

The new analytical power presents an opportunity to invent and explore new methods, which helps to detect correlations between the quantities of available data. Cukier and Mayer-Schoenberger (2013a; 2013b) see a paradigmatic change in the statistical handling of large data:

Using great volumes of information ... require three profound changes in how we approach data. The first is to collect and use a lot of data rather than settle for small amounts or samples as statisticians have done for well over a century. The second is to shed our preference for highly curated and pristine data and accept messiness: in an increasing number of situations, a bit of inaccuracy can be tolerated, because the benefits of using vastly more data of variable quality outweigh the costs of using smaller amounts of very exact data. Third, in many instances, we will need to give up our quest to discover the cause of things, in return for accepting correlations. With big data, instead of trying to understand precisely why an engine breaks down or why a drug's side effect disappears, researchers can instead collect and analyze massive quantities of information about such events and everything that is associated with them, looking for patterns that might help predict future occurrences. Big data helps answer what, not why, and often that's good enough.

Manyika et al. (2011) argued that:

... there are five broad ways in which using big data can create value. First, big data can unlock significant value by making information transparent and usable at a much higher frequency. Second, as organizations create and store more transactional data in digital form, they can collect more accurate and detailed performance information on everything from product inventories to sick days, and, therefore, expose

variability and boost performance. ... Third, big data allows ever-narrower segmentation of customers and, therefore, much more precisely tailored products or services. Fourth, sophisticated analytics can substantially improve decision-making. Finally, big data can be used to improve the development of the next generation of products and services.

Literature indicates that big data can unlock plenty of new opportunities, and deliver operational and financial value (Ohlhorst, 2013; Morabito, 2015, Foster et al., 2017; McKinsey, 2016).

Big data analytics is considered as an umbrella concept for the data analysis. With the explicit aim of generating value that helps the decision-makers in their strategies. This idea can be formalized using the following definition (Van Barneveld's et al, 2012):

Analytics is the process of developing actionable insight through discovery, modeling and analysis, and interpretation of data.

While:

The idea of *actionable insight* is applied to convey that the objective of analytics is to generate results that directly increase the understanding of those involved in the decision-making process (Cooper, 2012).

Discovery refers to the problem definition and exploratory element of analytics; the identification, collection, and management of relevant data for subsequent and/or concurrent analysis. This discovery stage integrates Cooper (2012) emphasis on a problem definition with what Labrinidis and Jagadish (2012) conceptualize as data management, which includes:

- **Problem Definition:** Identifies what data to collect, and to subsequently begin acquiring it. But, the volume of data manipulated by some companies, especially those related to the Internet, increase considerably. The increasing computerization of all types of processing implies an exponential multiplication of this volume of data, which is now in the order of Petabytes, Exabytes, and Zettabytes. Chen et al, (2012) highlight the multitude of techniques that allow organizations to tap into text, Web, social networks, and sensors, all of which enable the acquisition and monitoring of real-time metrics, feedback, and progress.
- **Data Collection:** The collection and combination of semi-structured and unstructured data require specific technologies, which also have to account for data volume and complexity.
- **Data Management:** Data management involves the storage, cleaning, and processing of the data.

Modeling and analysis are concerned with applying statistical models or other forms of analysis against real-world or simulated data. The middle stage of this categorization involves making sense of the acquired data, to uncover patterns, and to evaluate the resulting conclusions (Tomar et al., 2016).

Interpretation involves making sense of the analysis results of, and subsequently conveying that information in the most comprehensible form onwards to the relevant parties. In another word, making sense of different types of data and generate value from it, results in some form of finding.

The notion of making sense of big data has been expressed in many different ways, including: '*data mining*', '*knowledge extraction*', '*information discovery*', '*data pattern processing*'... Big data analytics is widely used today, due to the conjunction of many factors, such as:

- Data storage costs are constantly decreasing (see the Appendix);

- Increasing computing power;
- An explosion of the amount of information available in digital form;
- This data is largely unstructured and requires different operating techniques than conventional methods.

WHEN BIG DATA CREATE NEW BUSINESS MODELS

Considered, initially, as a way of boosting the analytical strategies of companies, big data is transformed into a way to change their business models. If Facebook, Google, Twitter, LinkedIn, Amazon, Apple, Netflix, Nike, and many other data-driven business models exist, it is thanks to the advance generated by big data and analytics. But, what analytics tools we can use? How have these models been able to draw a profile, especially for small businesses? These are what this section will discuss.

Big Data Applications: Examples

The 'data revolution' has created new business models and investment strategies allowing companies to monetize their existing data and businesses to create new big data solutions. Many companies are increasingly using big data analytics to improve their business. Netflix and Uber are two examples of successful use of the latest analytics technologies (Sedkaoui, 2018a).

Millions of Netflix subscribers generate a lot of data. To analyze this data, this company uses analytical techniques to determine what users will enjoy watching. Netflix's recommendation engine, impressive insight, works through analytics. This company has been able to build predictive models to suggest series that will delight users. It has developed other techniques for enhancing relevant recommendations, which are based on keywords. Subsequently, users receive suggestions based on these keywords, corresponding to the productions they have most appreciated.

In 2015, the message sent by Netflix to its shareholders showed that the big data strategy was paying off. In the first quarter of 2015, 4.9 million new subscribers were registered, compared with four million in the same period in 2014. Similarly, 10 billion hours of content were broadcast. Now, more than 117 million subscribers in the world with around 6 million additional subscribers per quarter worldwide (which refers to more than 8 million in the last quarter of 2017). Then, Netflix net earnings increase in the last quarter of 2017. Thanks to the intelligent use of big data analytics, the influence of Netflix continues to grow. Exported to more than 190 countries, this company continues its personalization work.

By coupling the notion of the sharing economy with big data, the Uber smartphone app connects passengers and drivers with a principle based on big data analytics (*crowdsourcing*). Anyone who is willing to offer his driver services can offer his help easily. During each trip, Uber collects and analyzes data to determine the extent of demand across geographic areas. This allows the company to allocate its resources efficiently. Uber also analyzes the public transport networks in the cities where it operates. By this way, the company can focus primarily on underserved areas.

In addition, Uber has developed algorithms to monitor real-time traffic conditions and travel times. As a result, prices can be adjusted as demand and travel times fluctuate. Then, drivers tend to drive when they are needed most. This pricing method based on big data analytics is patented by Uber. It is called "*surge pricing*". This is an implementation of the "*dynamic pricing*" already commonly used by airlines company and hotel chains to adjust the price on demand in real time through predictive analysis.

Other companies, which are considered as leaders in this field, have developed their strategy basing on big data analytics. The e-commerce giant Amazon recommends products to customers based on their browsing and purchasing habits. Jeff Bezos's company goes further with an artificial intelligence (AI) program based on an algorithm able to design a garment. It is a sort of a fashion creative AI in a way.

In 2016, Amazon represents a larger market than most of the major players in the US market combined. This is impressive, how Amazon gets this success? It is obviously the data. Since its creation in 1994, the company has adopted a culture largely driven by data. Thanks to the knowledge given by the data, the customer gets the right product at the right time, and is satisfied with the image of the logo of Amazon: 'a smile'.

The "ad-tech" companies, such as RocketFuel apply statistical and optimization techniques to determine which banner ads to display. Thus, devices, such as "Fitbit" used for recording and monitoring our physical activities, and their integration with other applications, allow individuals to obtain information on calories burned and food consumed. This allows a creation of new models, which sell this information to insurance companies to better calculate risks (Sedkaoui, 2017).

Many other companies use data analytics. This is the case of NASA, Domino's Pizza or the NFL. Globally, the success of many enterprises (Marr, 2016) is based on the same power: value creation from data.

Data-Driven Business Models (DDMB)

Continuous and rapid changes, the digital revolution, new entrants, innovation ... are all factors that force companies to continually adapt this changing environment that some people call 'VUCA', or: 'volatile', 'uncertain', 'complex' and 'ambiguous'. To survive in this environment, companies must be agile in terms of supply, market, internal organization, income model, etc. Differentiation with competitors is no longer about products or services, but how companies create, deliver and capture value. In other words, the differentiation is about the creation of a new 'Business Model'.

Since the mid-90s and with the advent of Internet startups, the term business model is probably among the most used in the business world, even though it has no clear definition. The concept refers to the way companies do business. Or, how they compete and make profits by using their competencies (De Mauro et al., 2016) and resources to sell goods and services in the market (Zhu & McKelvey, 2013). Drucker (1994) defined the business model as:

what an organization is paid for, what an organization considers being meaningful results (how to make a difference) and where an organization must excel in order to maintain leadership.

By its ability to make the apparent complexity of an organization's business model intelligible, attractive and operational, the model, which is the result of the Swiss's researcher/entrepreneur work (A. Osterwalder), has quickly and widely established itself in the business world. In just a few years, this model becomes the absolute reference in the business model. It is the modelization of the main elements of entrepreneurial activities. It refers to the process through which these activities deliver and capture value. This layout facilitates the description; the definition and the analysis of the interactions of the different parts of the model (see Figure 2).

This model facilitates the global vision of the interactions between the bricks constituting the activity and makes it possible to ask the right questions. What is the promise of the offer, what solution does it bring to the customer's expectation, and besides, to what type of client is activity's value proposition addressed, and how will it be done? Etc.

But, when an entrepreneur starts making more tactical decisions, to develop his business project, data always are helpful. The examples cited before illustrate this best. These companies have carried out a series of successive business model innovations, oriented towards the 'data' and the 'Analytics'.

Being 'data-driven' means making decisions based on data. Traditionally, decision-makers and CEOs make decisions based on the goal they have set. Data-driven companies focus on collecting and efficiently analyzing data and make decisions on that basis. For example, Amazon's decisions are data-based (even the color of the walls was decided by data). Whenever they have an idea, they analyze the data to validate it. Data is a key success factor and companies that successfully use it, will gain in competitiveness.

DDBM puts data at the center of value creation. This importance can be illustrated in different ways, such as analysis, observation of customer behavior, understanding of customer experience, improvement of existing products and services, strategic decision-making, and data marketing. For the last case, data may be the main building block of the company's offer.

Thus, in this category, we will find companies that offer data, whether financial (Bloomberg, Reuters …), economic (Dun & Bradstreet…), or from the social networks (Gnip, DataSift, etc.). This data is aggregated from different sources, generated directly by the company, processed and enriched by various analyzes and highlighted by data access and visualization platforms. As for revenue models, these can be based on a direct sale of data, a license, a subscription or a free provision financed by advertising.

More precisely, among the different big data opportunities, it is possible to identify three broad areas (business model based on big data), in which it creates value and has an impact on companies:

- **Data as a Service:** This first business model is intended for companies that generate a large amount of data, but do not have the means at their disposal to collect or make them in forms that can be analyzed. Many public institutions use this model. Municipalities, for example, generate transportation data, and companies can seize it for their own users.

Figure 2. Business Caneva

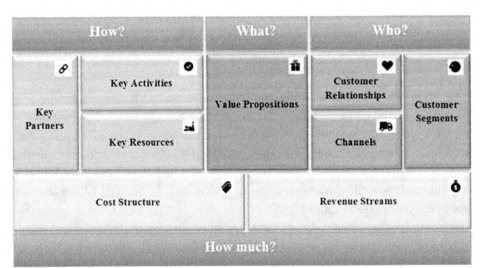

- **Information as a Service:** In this case, the product provides is directly the information obtained from the analysis of the data. Companies that allow their users to monitor their physical activity, such as the number of steps taken during the day, corresponding to this model. Fitbit users, for example, produce the data and they pay for their visualization in graphical form.
- **Recommendation as a Service:** This model is the most lucrative. In this scenario, the product provides is directly a specific recommendation addressed to users of the service to guide their consumption choices. Services like Mint.com offer their users to view their accounts and spending on their different credit cards to get a unified view of their budget. In exchange, Mint allows financial institutions to offer their products in the form of personalized recommendations.

But beyond these well-known business models for which data creates value, there is another category where the data serve as a value creator, notably through the exploitation of big data, without necessarily being present directly in the offer.

In this category we find all companies relying on the use of big data to derive value. For example, we can mention GAFAM or Uber, which uses data related to the location of its clients, its drivers, trips, traffic to determine the price, or Netflix, which uses the collected data about the use of its streaming service to identify themes and concepts of new series, 'House of Cards' is a great example of success.

Globally, the range of different types of DDBM is very wide. Interest in these types of model is recent, there is no current model accurate and shared by all listing the different types of DDBM. Among the most interesting, we can mention:

- The model of Hartmann, Zaki, Feldmann, and Neely (2014);
- The taxonomy of Engelbrecht, Gerlach, and Widjaja (2016).

If big data allows companies to optimize their existing activities, this concept also creates real opportunities to identify and build new ones for small and even micro enterprises.

Key Elements to Conduct a Big Data Project

After defining the target, and taking into account the various business constraints, entrepreneurs will be able to decide the context of their project structure. For example, if they want to develop a detection system of unsubscribing a subscriber to an online service, it will be necessary to define the notion of "the interest" of a subscriber to this online service. As such, they can formulate the following hypothesis: (i) if the customer connects at increasingly spaced intervals, it means that his interest in the online service is weakening; (ii) if the connection sessions to the service become shorter, they can deduce that client begins to lose interest in the online service, etc.

This initial phase focuses on understanding the objectives and requirements of the big data project from a business perspective, and then converting that knowledge into a definition of the data analytics problem. This is to say define the scope of impact and if entrepreneurs are not yet aware to define the goal, they can start with a PoC (Proof of Concept) by using an iterative method, refine their goal as they go along with the results and directions their get from this PoC.

Therefore, to advance in the big data universe and turn data into knowledge entrepreneurs need to define the following key infrastructure elements (Sedkaoui, 2018b):

- **Data Collection:** Depending on the business hypothesis that entrepreneurs would have made on the problem, they will look within for the relevant data that can support the hypothesis.
- **Data Storage:** When entrepreneurs start processing a large amount of data for storage and analysis, or if that data is destined to become a key part of their strategy, they need something else. A distributed system like Hadoop, or cloud-based, might be better suited. In fact, a cloud is an attractive option for most businesses. It is flexible and entrepreneurs do not need physical systems. It also reduces the need for security tools to protect the data. In addition, it is a lot cheaper than investing in dedicated systems and data warehouses.
- **Data Analysis:** Before being able to process data, it will be necessary to prepare that data to make it ready for analysis (this includes remove missing value and outliers). The goal of the data analysis phase is to build a model (solution) able to 'predict' the result of a given problem. But, data analysis is based on technology, which can be grouped corresponding to three types of needs and levels, as summarized in Table 1.

If an entrepreneur is embarking on data analysis, he can start by adopting the first family of tools. The transition from 'beginner' stage to 'standard' or 'expert' (advanced tools) will be done gradually, as the entrepreneur's needs are more specific or the databases grow. The most important thing is to know what an entrepreneur wants to do with this data because that ultimately determines the choice of the technology (Sedkaoui, 2018b).

For entrepreneurs, it is not necessary to proceed directly to the installation of the tools that will integrate the entire value creation chain. It is quite possible to go first with an open source solution, like the Hadoop, Map Reduce, or SaaS, often cheaper, and once the activity has arrived at maturity in big data context, then the entrepreneur can move to more integrated solutions, such as SAS. This kind of software provider also offers flexible solutions that can adapt to the specific needs of its structure.

To begin, it is good to have notions of statistical models and machine learning algorithms. Table 2 classifies the most used algorithms.

- **Data Security:** To optimize the business performance, entrepreneurs must take into account the various threats that affect the data. Developing an accurate view of data and hierarchy allows them to better secure information and provides some agility to better adapt the myriad of rules and regulations that they need to comply with.
- **Data Visualization:** The data visualization intervenes throughout a project on the data to support understanding ((Shafer, 2017). Data visualization allows the final phases to render, explain and highlight the results. The main types of data visualization include dashboards, commercial data

Table 1. Big data technology level

Level	Use case	Tools: Example
Tools for beginners	If entrepreneurs are starting to analyze data	Google Analytics, Google Tag Manager (GTM), Regex101, Excel.
Standard tools	If entrepreneurs have more budgets	Optimizely, Dataiku DSS, Crazyegg, Mixpanel …
Technology for experts	If there is a team dedicated to data analysis and the entrepreneur want to exploit data with very specific needs.	Hadoop, MapReduce, Spark, SQL, Python …

Table 2. Algorithms and their cases of uses

	Algorithm	Learning mode	Problem to be treated
Simple	Simple regression	Supervised	Regression
	Multiple regression	Supervised	Regression
	Naïve Bayes	Supervised	Classification
	Logistic regression	Supervised	Classification
	Hierarchical Classification	Unsupervised	Clustering
	K-means	Unsupervised	Clustering
Complex	Decision tree	Supervised	Classification – Regression
	Random forest	Supervised	Classification – Regression
	Bootstrapping	Supervised	Classification – Regression
	SVM	Supervised	Classification – Regression
	Neural Networks	Supervised	Classification – Regression
	KNN	Supervised	Classification – Regression

visualization platforms, but also simple charts and tables that allow entrepreneurs to communicate ideas quickly. Most small businesses looking to improve their decision-making can rely on simple graphics and visualization tools like word clouds or even Excel.

To better launch a big data project, there are two approaches illustrated in Figure 3:

The bottom-up approach (data-driven approach) goes from the technique to the organization. Entrepreneurs, based on this approach, will first validate the technical choices through a PoC and a case of use that they consider relevant. However, the top-down approach will first impact the organization of the company in order to prepare it to launch big data projects.

Figure 3. Bottom-up and Top-down approaches

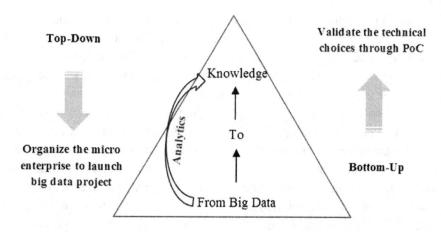

FOR AN ENTREPRENEUR MADE IN DATA

The importance of big data analytics (the *why?*), as with every major innovation, the biggest confusion lies in the exact scope (*what?*), and its implementation (*how?* And *for whom?*). In this context, small businesses or entrepreneurs must open their eyes to data's boundless opportunities. If an entrepreneur wants to be a data-driven, in order to lead his business project idea, so he must adopt a 'data-driven approach'. Better conduct a data-driven approach lies in having a clear analytical objective. In another word, the more the objectives are clear, the more focused and rewarding the analytical approach will be. We can never say it enough: *"there is no good wind for those who don't know where they are going"*. This section shows that there are plenty of things that must be done to become a data-driven innovation or an entrepreneur made in data, in general.

First of All, Learn to Ask Relevant Questions

The data entrepreneur in any field is not necessary a data scientist, developer or statistician, but he is the one who makes data at the center of his business conducting. The data entrepreneur must seek the information where it is not. For that, the most popular way is probably to ask a lot of questions and see what sticks. But it can't be just any questions; it has to be significant questions.

Two essential components are needed to question whether data analytics can or cannot add value to the entrepreneurial project: *"well-defined problem"* and *"data"*.

- **The Definition of the Problem Statement:** Everything in big data analytics begins with a clear problem statement. Determining what type of problem an entrepreneur is facing with, in his business context or ecosystem, will allow the business idea to correctly choose the technique that can be used. The success of an analytics approach cannot be possible without the clarification of what an entrepreneur wants to achieve and what is need to be changed to embrace the advancement that big data entails. This is not just valid in a big data context but in all areas. Small enterprises must clearly define what they want before undertaking anything. This means knowing what they are trying to achieve, what is needed, and why and what level of accuracy is acceptable and actionable. The problem we are trying to solve, by modeling the situation, corresponds to the specific task to be accomplished.
- **Data:** What should be done here is exploring all possible paths to recover the data in order to identify all the variables that affect, directly or indirectly, the phenomenon that interests the project. In another word, how make new opportunities from this data? Which data to select for the analysis? And how apply efficiently analytical techniques to generate value? This kind of question helps the entrepreneur to be able to think critically, in order to improve solutions for business challenges and allow him to understand that, big data opportunities are not in the volume of data but in the digital transformation of business processes. Data is literally the nerve of the era of big data. The data are mostly available but often scattered in several computer tools. An important procedure is to understand the data that will be collected and then analyzed. The idea is that the more we have a good understanding of our data, the better we will be able to use them wisely. This aims to precisely determine where we should look for the data, which data to be analyzed and identify the quality of the data available but also link the data and their meaning from a business perspective.

The growing complexity of the data and business analytics sector and its accelerating dynamics urge entrepreneurs to think and act in an entrepreneurial way. That means understanding what can be done with that available data before exploring it. This includes some basic knowledge about the methods that will be used and the complexities involved. It seems obvious because data is the main raw material of an efficient data analysis process. So, if an entrepreneur doesn't understand the nature of the data related to the problem he is trying to solve, consider that he will not be able to solve it.

So, to understand the context of the target problem, the entrepreneur must play, in some ways, the role of a 'detective'. This can allow him to discover and understand different element related to it and determine the tools he needs to better operate in his ecosystem and derive solutions that allow him to improve innovation. It is, therefore, essential to have at least basic notions of statistics and mathematics to determine the right analysis technique according to the nature of each data.

That means also a significant part of identifying the technologies that will be most relevant for managing the flow of data. For data analytics, preference is given mainly to computer languages, which are standardized for data analysis and information extraction. To meet these information-sharing developments, we need tools across the board to help. We need infrastructure and technologies that accommodate ultrafast data capture and processing. Another key element lies in identifying: Which technology to adopt? Why should entrepreneurs adopt this technology? How about the costs? Etc. Taking into account the growing advanced analytics tools.

Also, it is not only a technological issue that's mater but also, how can you, as an entrepreneur who wants to drive the project idea based on data analysis, transform data to patters. Do you think that to apply analytics techniques or to create a project-oriented on data and analytics you need to have a good command of the different analytics application and how it works? Do you really think that you need to know what is happening behind the analytics scenes?

As a matter of fact, it will be important if you mastery the different analytics tools, but how the algorithm works is not the user's business. It is like when you drive a car without having any idea about its mechanisms because knowledge is different from know-how. That brings us to say that understand data analytics is good but know how to use it is better!

The key lies in an entrepreneur's ability to appreciate the quality and defects of different algorithms. So, he should rather be interested in questions and issues related to the reliability of the results, their value, and their effect on the business context … It must be considered that there is no perfect model, but models that adapt better to situations. In addition, knowing some analytics methods can be a real asset (decision tree, K-means…). Since these different techniques can be directly implemented using the software (SAS, R, Python …) it is not necessary to know how their algorithms work.

The important thing is to understand how they work in general terms and to know which method is most relevant depending on the situation. Select the right method for available data is a very important point.

Big data is opening up a number of new areas for businesses. Products that make data more accessible, that allow analysis and insight development without requiring them to be a statistician, engineer or data analyst are one major opportunity area (Feinleib, 2014).

Asking interesting questions develop your inherent curiosity about data that you are working on. Knowing a little something about everything equips you to understand the context and have the ability to get out the value from data. The key is thinking broadly about how to transform data into a form, which would help to find valuable tendencies and interrelationships.

The following types of questions seem particularly interesting:

- What things might an entrepreneur be able to learn from the data?
- How can he ever hope to understand something he cannot see?
- Which techniques and methods, does he think will prove more accurate?
- How to avoid mistakes and get the best models?
- How can he learn lessons by analyzing available data, and what is he going to do with it?
- How to best use the results of these analyzes?
- What impacts does him expect on the choices to be made?

This kind of questions allow the entrepreneur or small and micro social enterprise to think like a data scientist or be a data scientist, in some ways, to better conduct his project based on data and analytics, that means think about the 'meaningful' of data, so its practice.

Challenges to Take Into Account

As large data sets are currently available from a wealth of different sources, companies are looking to use these resources to promote innovation, customer loyalty and increase operational efficiency. At the same time, they are contested for their end uses, which require a greater capacity to collect, analyze and manage the growing amount of data but also ensure its security. It is to highlight that not merely the existence of large amounts of data that is creating new challenges. Data exploration and analysis turned into a difficult problem in many sectors in the span of big data.

With large and complex data, computation becomes difficult to be handled by the traditional data processing applications which trigger the development of big data applications (Muhtaroglu et al, 2013). If big data are combined with predictive analytics, it produces a challenge for many industries. The combination results in the exploration of these four areas (Inukollu et al, 2014):

- Calculate the risks on large portfolios
- Detect, prevent, and re-audit financial fraud
- Improve delinquent collections
- Execute high-value marketing campaigns

There are many technical challenges that must be addressed to realize the full potential of big data. Warren et al. (2015) state that many companies are unable to apply big data techniques due to limiting factors, such as lack of data, irrelevant or untrustworthy data, or insufficient expertise. The main challenges associated with the development and deployment of big data analytics are:

- **The Heterogeneity of Data Streams:** Dealing with semantic interoperability of diverse data streams requires techniques beyond the homogenization of data formats (Soldatos, 2017). Big data streams tend to be multi-modal and heterogeneous in terms of their formats, semantics, and velocities. Hence, data analytics expose typically variety and veracity. Big data technologies provide the means for dealing with this heterogeneity in the scope of operationalized applications.
- **Data Quality:** The nature of data available can be classified as noisy and incomplete, which creates uncertainty in the scope of the data analytics process. Statistical and probabilistic approaches must be, therefore, employed in order to take into account the noisy nature of data. Also, data can

be typically associated with different reliability, which should be considered in the scope of their integration in an analytical approach.

- **The Real-Time Nature of Big Datasets:** Big data feature high velocities and for several applications must be processed nearly in real-time. Hence, data analytics can greatly benefit from data streaming platforms, which are part of the big data ecosystem. IT advent, Internet and several connected objects provide typically high-velocity data, which however can be in several cases controlled by focusing only on changes in data patterns and reports, rather than dealing with all the observations that stem from connected objects.

- **The Time and Location Dependencies of Big Data:** IoT data come with temporal and spatial information, which is directly associated with their business value in the analytics application context. Hence, data analytics methods must in several cases process data in a timely fashion and from proper locations. Cloud computing techniques (including edge computing architectures) can greatly facilitate the timely processing of data from several locations in the scope of large scale deployments. Note also that the temporal dimensions of big data can serve as a basis for dynamically selecting and filtering streams towards analytics tools for certain timelines and locations.

- **Privacy and Security Sensitivity:** Today, we face new issues in securing and protecting data, which result in new challenging research directions. Some of those challenges arise from increasing privacy concerns with respect to the use of such huge amount of data, and from the need for reconciling privacy with the use of data (Bertino and Ferrari, 2018; Sedkaoui, 2018b). Big data are typically associated with stringent security requirements and privacy sensitivities, especially in the case of IoT applications that involve the collection and processing of personal data. Hence, advanced analytics need to be supported by privacy preservation techniques, such as the anonymization of personal data, as well as techniques for encrypted and secure data storage.

- **Data Bias:** As in the majority of data mining problems, big datasets can lead to biased processing and hence a thorough understanding and scrutiny of both training and test datasets are required prior to their operationalized deployment. Note that the specification and deployment of IoT analytics systems entail techniques similar to those deployed in classical data mining problems, including the understanding and the preparation of data, the testing of the analytics techniques and ultimately the development and deployment of a system that yields the desired performance and efficiency.

Being an entrepreneur is a challenge itself and small businesses must recognize the importance of investing in big data analytics, given its important role as a value generator. But, it may be difficult to practice this kind of analytical techniques coupled with advanced IT tools because it is difficult to secure the funding for several types of needs.

In another word, they are not prepared to fully use the unprecedented amounts of data that they are able to collect for their unique target populations or the business issues they address. Due to capacity constraints, a large part of this challenge lays in the complexity of data collection, data analysis, data security, and how to turn that data into usable information by identifying patterns, exploiting new algorithms, tools and new solutions (value).

Each type of data offers specific benefits and creates specific challenges as we work to extract value. Small enterprises or entrepreneurs, in big data fields, are required to deal with these several issues to be able to seize the full potential of big data. The rise of big data and analytics needs are enabling a new generation of entrepreneurs to embrace opportunities and solve challenges in many fields, a business value included.

Undertake in the Big Data Analytics Domain

Big data is considered a new form of capital in today's marketplace (Mayer-Schönberger & Cukier, 2013a; Satell, 2014), many firms fail to exploit its benefits (Mithas, Lee, Earley, & Murugesan, 2013). For entrepreneurs, it is known that they are unlikely to analyze data on the same scale as large companies like Google, Facebook, Walmart, Twitter, Netflix, Amazon, IBM, and others, due to their limited sources, skills, and IT tools. Yes! It is possible that they are engaging with the free big data tools provided by companies like Google, without forgetting the increase in the prominence of social networks and the fact that engaging with social media which can help generates exposure and traffic for entrepreneurs at a much lower cost than traditional marketing approaches (Schaupp and Belanger, 2014). But, it is to highlight that they are unlikely to have large stores and sophisticated tools to capture, prepare, analyze and manage generated data.

The application of analytics for small and micro enterprises can be divided into three main categories, namely descriptive, predictive and prescriptive analytics.

Descriptive analytics involves using advanced techniques to locate relevant data and identify remarkable patterns in order to better describe and understand what is going on with the subjects in the dataset. Data mining, the computational process of discovering patterns in large datasets involving methods at the intersection of AI, machine learning (ML), statistics and database systems, is accommodated in this category (Sumathi and Sivanandam, 2006).

Descriptive models can give a clear explanation why event behaved, how why certain occurred, but all this already is past perfect. So, entrepreneurs can have a clear vision, based on the past, in the future, on what is more important and how they can function. This appeals predictive models which are seen as a subset of data science (Waller and Fawcett, 2013; Hazen et al, 2014).

Liu and Yang (2017) formalize the way in which a predictive model is made self-organizing via big data. It makes use of available data (several types, created in real-time …), statistical methods, and various algorithms of ML in order to identify the likelihood of future insights based on the past. The built model predicts by answering the question: What is likely to happen?

Predictive analytics use data, statistical algorithms, and ML to predict the likelihood of business trends and financial performance, based on their past behaviors. They bring together several technologies and disciplines, such as statistical analysis, data mining, predictive modeling and ML technology to predict the future of businesses.

Table 3. Data analytics categories

Category	Question	Objective	Example
Descriptive	What happened?	Know the relative position of a client according to predefined criteria	Time clients spent on the Website.
Predictive	What is going to happen?	Anticipate the future, considering what we know from the past	Identify factors that can explain and predict the client' behavior
Prescriptive	What must be done to make this happen?	Achieve a predefined or estimated business objective	Recommendation systems that provide recommendations on products or services ...

With the increasing number of data, computing power and the development of AI software and simple analytical tools uses, many companies can now use predictive analytics. For example, it is possible to anticipate the consequences of a decision or the reactions of customers. Predictive analytics is the act of predicting future events and behaviors present in previously unseen data, using a model built from similar past data (Nyce, 2007; Shmueli, 2011). It has a wide range of applications in different fields, such as finance, education, healthcare, law and more (Sas, 2017; Sedkaoui, 2018a).

In this case, it should be mentioned that the amount of data available is not the problem; the richness of the data, however, is often questionable. This is most certainly required when people want to perform prescriptive analytics. When executed right, this application of mathematical and computational algorithms enables decision-makers to not only look into the future of their own processes and opportunities, but it even presents the best course of action to take for gaining advantages.

The requirements for an accurate and reliable prescriptive analytics outcome are hybrid data, integrated predictions, and prescriptions, taking into account side effects, adaptive ML algorithms and a clear feedback mechanism. Based on the different types of algorithms described in Table 2, the following application cases, which revolve around daily business activities, can explain how to use data analysis.

- **Regression Analysis for Prediction:** This technique can be used to study changes, habits, customer satisfaction levels and other factors related to parameters, such as the budget for an advertising campaign ... Once entrepreneurs change any of these settings, they will have a pretty close idea of what will happen to their user audience.
- **Cluster Analysis to Identify Target Groups:** Cluster analysis makes it possible to identify a group of users (in databases) according to common characteristics. These characteristics can be age, geographical location, occupation, and so on. This is a data analysis technique that is used in marketing to segment the database and to send, for example, some promotion to the right target for a particular product or service (young, retirees, etc.). The combinations of variables are infinite and make the cluster analysis more or less selective depending on the search requirements.
- **Classification Analysis to Identify Spam:** The analytics technique that allows recognizing patterns (recurring patterns) within a database. It is an effective way to make a business strategy more efficient, eliminate redundancy and create optimized sub-archives.
- **Neural Networks to Automate Learning:** This is one of the newest data analytics applications, based on the used machine use for the business actions, and thus the computer that manages the database learns to identify a certain pattern within which are present elements having precise relations between them. The result of this learning is the recognition and memorization of patterns that may be useful, not necessarily immediately but in the future, to decide if the goal is achieved and how. This algorithm can help the entrepreneur to know more precisely about the composition of the target of a product or service for example.

It should be mentioned, that data processing and analysis, in the present day, are brought together under the notion of "Business Intelligence" (BI), due especially to computers' increased processing capabilities.

Small businesses have to expand their efforts to move their small business from using only traditional BI that addresses descriptive analysis (what happened) to advanced analytics, which complements by answering the "why", "what" and "how" as illustrated in Figure 4. Ultimately, 'data science' is inevitable as it can help extract various kinds of knowledge from data.

Clearly, the use of big data analytics and IT tools including clouds will provide numerous opportunities to build an entrepreneur approach that will effectively and efficiently cater to the needs of the various entities. Therefore, it is necessary to include enough resources and finance to support the analytics' uses by entrepreneurs to create value. This investment is essential to reap the full benefits of big data and realize all the envisioned features and capabilities. To help optimize the work and minimize costs of such projects it is recommended to include some of the following activities in the process:

- Understanding first what they can do with big data before they consider adopting it.
- Developing analytics tools to help predict and view possible changes and forecast potential problems. This will help avoid or at least reduce some of the risks involved and also help reduce costs.
- Benefitting from other social enterprises experiences to follow successful models and avoid problematic approaches.
- Benefitting from experts and researchers to research new possibilities for more advanced analytics that suite the project idea and objectives.
- Combining big data with open data. This can help to reach better decisions and optimize various functions.

Therefore, the efforts should concentrate on creating a roadmap for success that covers several stages:

1. Set up the entrepreneur's business issues direction, in the data analytics context, by identifying its mission, vision and strategic and operational objectives.
2. Establish policies, principles, resources and expertise guidelines to control ICT and big data usage.
3. Evaluate and analyze the current situations and the necessary changes and additions to reach the desired result.
4. Identify priorities and use them to determine the most important components and techniques that would offer the greatest business effects with the smallest investment.
5. Realize new innovation opportunities for further development by monitoring current analytics developments and their effects and the arising issues and new requirements.

DISCUSSION: DEVELOP A DATA-DRIVEN CULTURE WITHIN ENTREPRENEURIAL ORIENTATION

Entrepreneurial orientation is defined by Rauch et al, (2009) as *"policies and practices that provide a basis for entrepreneurial decisions and actions"*. Entrepreneurial orientation is another strategic orientation that has been linked to firm performance (Lumpkin & Dess, 1996; Wiklund, 1999; Zahra & Covin, 1995). The most commonly used dimensions of entrepreneurial orientation in the literature are: 'innovativeness', 'risk-taking' and 'proactiveness'.

The two dimensions of entrepreneurial orientation which point to the link between an entrepreneur and big data capabilities are:

- **Innovativeness**: Describes the willingness of the business to introduce novelty technological leadership in developing new processes (Lumpkin and Dess, 2001). Achieving business mission through innovativeness refers to the ability to solve related problems or in effect to create business value. This supports a contention that it will be a key indicator as to whether entrepreneurs will adopt big data analytics.

- **Proactiveness**: Is a forward-looking perspective that suggests that companies with high level of entrepreneurial orientation will be looking to be the first to market capture a particular segment and act in advance in anticipation of future demands (Lumpkin and Dess, 2001). Proactive companies can make use of big data analytics to improve their understanding of their customer and their sector, with the condition that they have access to the right sources of information. It is, therefore, an important element to consider when looking at big data adoption in small enterprises. For example, by retaining the environment, this reflects the tangible and intangible results of breaking patterns, changes in the system, and new discoveries towards process improvement.

The literature suggests that entrepreneurial orientation is a useful lens through which to consider the use of big data analytics in small businesses. And the contention made by McAfee and Brynjolfson (2012) and Ross et al (2013) suggests that a culture of evidence-based decision-making is required for the successful adoption of big data in companies.

There are two ways to transforms data into a valuable contribution to a company (Sedkaoui, 2016):

- Transforming data into information is one of the stages of data value production, which is exploited in order to obtain useful information and to successfully carry out company strategies. This automatically involves database information in company decision-making processes;
- Transforming data into products or processes adds value to companies. This is produced when data analysis must be implemented in the physical world.

It is clear that the ability of entrepreneurs to adopt big data analytics may be understood by looking at their role in the determination of the entrepreneurial culture and how they are deploying their resources to engage with and make use of analytics tools and methods in their field. For them, it is essential to have data, increasingly, many on the environment in which it operates or will operate.

In order to succeed in an analytical approach and boost a big data project, it is necessary to prepare it in advance. To do this, three essential questions must be asked: why, what and how.

- **Why:** The first question to ask is "why? ". In most cases, this question will inevitably occur during the initial briefing with a consultant or client. Many big data projects are launched only because the term big data is in vogue. Many executives board the wagon and begin to approve massive investments of time and money to develop a data platform. Most of the time, this strategy is based entirely on the motive that "everyone is doing it". An in-depth analysis of the goal that an entrepreneur wants to achieve, by accessing this data, as well as an assessment of the investments and expertise that the project needs, are required but too often overlooked in the context of the deployment of a big data strategy.
- **What:** In all sectors, companies are now considering turning the corner on big data and analytics. They recognize in the data a largely untapped source of value creation and an exclusive factor of differentiation. But, many don't know which approach to tackle. What the entrepreneur is trying to do? Does the project want to create an innovative market, or find a new channel that requires information on client interest and future profitability?

Figure 4. Data-driven approach

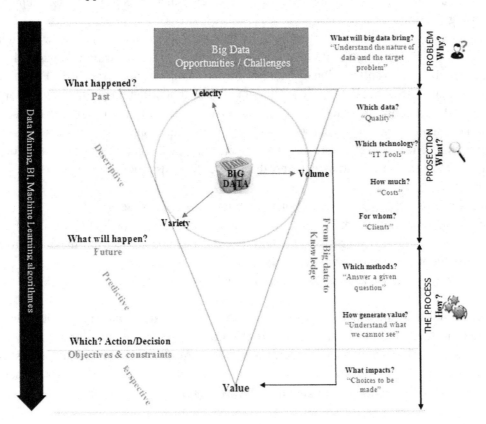

- **How:** While companies do see the great potential that big data analytics can bring to improve their business performance, the reality is that many are struggling to generate value from available data. Gartner (2016) study shows that many big data projects remain blocked and that only 15% have been deployed in production. Examining such failures, it appears that the main factor is in fact not related to the technical dimension, but rather to the processes and human aspects that prove to be as important. Conduct a data-driven project means also to be able, in particular, to answer questions, such as: How can we be sure that big data could help us to create business value? Who should be involved and when? What are the key steps that need to be attentive? Is the project on the right track to succeed? Etc. It is, therefore, essential for data-driven orientation, to ensure:
- **For the Data:** Quality, security, structure …;
- **For the Process:** Well-defined organization, a data-driven culture, its direction …:
- **For Tools:** IT infrastructure, storage, data visualization capability, performance monitoring.

In order to extract value from big data, it must be processed and analyzed in a timely manner, and the results need to be available in such a way as to be able to effect positive change or influence business decisions. It is important to ensure that the project is progressing towards the intended result (see Figure 4). To promote the business innovation process based on data analytics, specific attention will be paid to small enterprises, entrepreneurs, and startups that want engaging in this field. This is important because, it helps to understand their, roles, their needs, the challenges they are dealing with, the business value they can generate, and their position in the innovation ecosystem. Thus, it is needed to address the existing need for theoretical and methodological frameworks, which build on the different elements that iterate in the construction of business innovation and account for its complexity and contextual dimensions (Cajaiba-Santana, 2014).

Big data offers great opportunities but requires significant upstream preparation. To guarantee the success of a project, it is necessary to ask the key questions, find the right answers, and make the most of it. In order to decode the profit of big data, enterprises must continue to innovate and offer a broad popularization of the business changes linked to the advent of the company's digitization. Entrepreneurship is not a new concept by any means, but the way in which entrepreneurs function actually has undergone an astonishing transformation over the last decade.

An entrepreneurial leader has a reputation for being more agile and better at exploiting niche markets than its larger companies. Furthermore, despite constrained resources, they would seem to be ideally suited to take advantage of the opportunities that big data analytics would help identify.

Entrepreneurial in the age of big data, must rely on varied analytical approaches to thought and action to create and implement solutions that are socially, environmentally, and economically sustainable.

Being a data-driven entrepreneur means being at the heart of data valuing and intervene at all stages of the data chain: problem definition, data collection, preparation, modeling and solution creation. An entrepreneur made in data must know how to present and prioritize the results to be used. So, excellent communication skills are needed.

Also, formulate some business questions to develop a method is important, such as: Which sources they use? What data to collect? Why this data? To do what? What answers to expect? How much, should data be processed? Should we do analysis in real time or periodically?

If we take the example of Uber, often cited as a success of big data, the firm does not just capture huge amounts of data from the mobile application used by its drivers and clients. His triumph is based primarily on his ability to collect relevant data to connect clients and service providers. Who needs a car, and where? It is by focusing on these two data that Uber has managed to make taxis obsolete. Uber's case needed to know exactly where the potential clients were to automate the decision-making process when sending the drivers.

For the General Electric case and its software Predix Industrial Internet, the company seeks to know exactly when a machine will fail. The decisions related to the maintenance visit can thus be automated, and the mess related to outages has been removed. For insurers looking to reduce costs, it would be useful to know when a diabetic patient's blood sugar level is dangerously low, to automate intervention decisions and reduce the mess associated with mismanagement of a patient disease.

In Bhopal, India, the Panna Tiger Reserve is using drones (unmanned aerial vehicles) to safeguard against tiger poachers. The data collected has allowed them to improve the efficacy of their efforts and to prove the impact of their activities, thus encouraging greater support and funding for their initiatives.

Also, the Daniel Project, another successful example of using big data analytics, Intel's collaboration with Not Impossible Labs to 3D-print prosthetic arms for a 14-year old war victim. Intel's data competencies contributed significantly to the technological solution. The video of this initiative, shared on social media, captured the hearts and imaginations of consumers across the world and earned Intel more than a half-billion online impressions, an impressive quantification of the intrinsic value of social branding Pascaud (2015).

It is the case of several other examples that highlight the potential of big data for value creation and innovation. For this, small businesses and entrepreneurs must define the important steps to be taken towards this direction. If an entrepreneur knows how and where to look for the right data (smart data), if he can do this by analyzing a lot of information, everything is for the best. But, if he gets there by creating an application directly, it is even better.

It is clear that it is necessary to have a thorough reflection to see the essential elements that constitute the springs of the business activity. New analytics approach in big data age, combines predictive and prescriptive analytics to predict what will happen and how to make it happen. Analytics uses and applications improve the efficiency of the decision-making process and generate value. The difficulty of transforming big data into value or knowledge is related to its complexity, which is growing with the increase of its quantity its velocity and diversification of its types and sources (Sedkaoui, 2017).

Leveraging leading tools and techniques help to manage and extract relevant data from big data. Advanced analytics can range from historical reporting, through to real-time decision support for organizations based on future predictions.

As this chapter has mentioned it before, the future belongs to those who make their relentless approach to tracking data and making adjustments based on their findings. Because data has many things to tell but one must know how to make them talk, by considering algorithms (data analytics techniques) as a recipe, data as ingredients, while the computer (IT tools) is like a mixer that supports a lot of the difficult tasks of an algorithm. It revolves around data, as the digital revolution is continuing, and gives birth to a new concept, a concept made in data in the entrepreneurial' world: "the data entrepreneur".

CONCLUSION

Since the seminal work of Schumpeter (Schumpeter, 1934), entrepreneurship has been regarded as a positive driving force for regional economic growth and development (Birch, 1987; Storey & Johnson, 1987; Reynolds, 1987; Acs & Armington, 2004). Low and MacMillan (1988) emphasized that entrepreneurship is a process that can be undertaken in a variety of contexts. From this point of view, many studies have indeed stressed that contextual conditions, such as education, culture, social support systems, technology, and the presence of human capital, business context and expertise play an important role in the changing conditions for entrepreneurship (Fischer & Nijkamp, 2009).

At the same time, entrepreneurship is becoming more systematic and institutionalized than ever before. Entrepreneurs must develop a new entrepreneurial culture, adjusted to society and based on knowledge, innovation, and involvement of new methods and strategies in entrepreneurial projects. To enable the development of the entrepreneurship field its agenda needs comprehensive adjustments and refocusing on new areas and other factors shaping entrepreneurial ecosystems.

According to Peter Drucker (1970) and K. Knight (1967), Entrepreneurship is about taking a risk.

1. It is the process of creating new values that did not previously exist.
2. It is the practice of starting a new organization, especially new businesses.
3. It involves the creation of new wealth through the implementation of new concepts.

Entrepreneurship is an ancient concept that is both simple and complex at the same time. However, during the few last decades, there are new areas where entrepreneurship is becoming increasingly important. If we look on the history of our society, we will see that it is characterized by the stages of evolutionary change, such as "Agricultural Age", "Industrial Age", "Information Age", and "Technology or Knowledge Age".

At each stage of the development, people have existed, lived and worked together in order to advance the level of technology, improve living conditions, increase the economy, etc. During each age, the entrepreneur is facing many challenges. So, entrepreneurship is not a new concept, what is really 'new' is the way a business project is viewing and attacking by entrepreneurs in the last decade.

Now, many start-up companies are using data as the core enabler for their business and for many it is the fundamental value of their business behind the service they provide.

Big data marks a major turning point in the use of data and is a powerful vehicle for growth and profitability. A comprehensive understanding of a company's data, its potential, and the analytics methods can be a new vector for performance. Big data is a broad term generally referring to very large data collections that impose complications on analytics tools for harnessing and managing such.

Well-chosen and well-implemented methods for data collection and analysis are essential for better understand data. The rise of big data reflects the growing awareness of the 'power' behind data, and of the need to enhance gathering, exploitation, sharing and analyzing that data (Sedkaoui & Monino, 2016). Analytics applications will ensure the proper exploitation of the proliferating volumes of data for a variety of business purposes, involving not only production of simple data-driven insights on operations, but also a prediction of future trends and events.

Big data analytics has become an essential requisite to run most businesses. Though startups and young entrepreneurs, in many fields, might not spend much on big data but definitely need to research, study and follow the trend to take their ventures to heights. Integrating big data analytics can generate many advantages for the entrepreneurs, such as (Sedkaoui, 2018a):

- **Supporting Decision:** As mentioned before, entrepreneurs can make use of the vast amount of data relevant to their particular business. Therefore, they would need to filter the data according to their specific needs and derive meaning from the data that fits them the best. This will not only widen their understanding of their own domain but will also facilitate better decision making, which in turn will improve operational efficiencies.
- **Cost Reduction:** It has been found that big data can be extremely instrumental in augmenting the existing architectures of companies. Additionally, when more accurate decisions are taken, the possibility of incurring losses also gets alleviated. Therefore, with the correct use of analytics startups and entrepreneurs can be successful in cutting down their operational costs, which is typically one of the biggest challenges for every fresh venture.
- **Customer Insights:** The growth of any company depends on how to keep the preferences, likes, tastes ... of their customers into account to design their products and services. Big data analytics can help companies to gain access to the required and relevant information. For example, social media presents a great tool to acquire and assimilate enormous volumes of customer insights and can be used effectively to collect data for this purpose.

- **Open Data Use:** Over the last year there has been an increase in the perceived use of open data by entrepreneurs to build new products and services. Open data, in addition to its potential economic, and creation of new activities also fall within a philosophical choice or ethics. They encrypt collective human behavior, and, therefore, also belong to those we measured these behaviors. The culture of this phenomenon builds on the availability of data to a communication orientation.

So, small businesses are now facing one of the most exciting and critical opportunities: the ability to analyze and value big data for business value creation. These data and the algorithms that can handle them, especially those of artificial intelligence - capable of self-learning - are of great interest to large companies in the technology sector. Their applications are indeed as numerous as they are crucial. For example, it becomes possible to quickly analyze large amounts of medical data, as IBM did with its Watson system. Or, companies have the opportunity to improve their products and make them evolve towards more interactivity as well as towards a more intuitive use, like "smartwatches" at Apple or personal assistants, such as Alexa and Echo at Amazon.

Every entrepreneur will be concerned by the arrival of new powerful tools able to master this previously unstructured data. Analytics widens small enterprises scope as an entity, giving them the ability of doing things they never thought were possible, for example, it offers timely insights, to allow them in making better decisions, about innovation opportunities, it also helps them in asking the right questions and supports them with extracting the right answers as well.

Whether if they understand the potential of big data or not, or if they want to embrace the analytical IT tools or not, build a career in data science or not. One thing is confirmed and cannot be avoided: big data analytics can fundamentally change the way the activities operate. In this context, an entrepreneur can see new opportunities, manage and increase opportunities, by putting the efforts in the right direction, and rationally using his time and energy.

The data revolution continues... And eventually, we will all become interesting by being "an entrepreneur made in data". And, if the *Harvard Business Review* has called the data scientist as "the sexy new job of the 21th century"; then data-driven entrepreneur, who can understand data and have a strong creative streak in order to ask the right questions to get significant value from data, will be the *fashionable* and the *chic* entrepreneur of the century in several domains. So, for entrepreneurs, or for those who want to undertake in the any business sector, for those who have a critical vision towards how generate value or the 'power' from data, prepare yourself to the data revolution age: the age where many underlying messages can be transformed into opportunities in order to help in addressing business challenges.

REFERENCES

Ackoff, R. L. (1989). From data to wisdom. *Journal of Applied Systems Analysis*, *15*, 3–9.

Acs, Z. J., & Armington, C. (2004). Employment growth and entrepreneurial activity in cities. *Regional Studies*, *38*(8), 911–927. doi:10.1080/0034340042000280938

Bertino, E., & Ferrari, E. (2018). Big Data Security and Privacy. In S. Flesca, S. Greco, E. Masciari, & D. Saccà (Eds.), *A Comprehensive Guide Through the Italian Database Research Over the Last 25 Years. Studies in Big Data* (Vol. 31). Cham: Springer. doi:10.1007/978-3-319-61893-7_25

Birch, D. L. (1987). *Job creation in America: How our smallest companies put the most people to work.* New York: The Free Press.

Brynjolfsson, E., & McAfee, A. (2011). *Race Against the Machine: How the Digital Revolution is Accelerating Innovation, Driving Productivity, and Irreversibly Transforming Employment and the Economy.* Lexington, MA: Digital Frontier Press.

Cajaiba-Santana, G. (2014). Social innovation: Moving the field forward. A conceptual framework. *Technological Forecasting and Social Change, 82*, 42–51. doi:10.1016/j.techfore.2013.05.008

Chen, H., Chiang, R. H. L., & Storey, V. C. (2012). Business intelligence and analytics: From big data to big impact. *Management Information Systems Quarterly, 36*(4), 1165–1188. doi:10.2307/41703503

Cooper, A. (2012). What is analytics? Definition and essential characteristics. *CETIS Analytics Series, 1*(5), 1–10.

Cukier, K., & Mayer-Schoenberger, V. (2013b). The Rise of Big Data. *Foreign Affairs, 92*(3), 28–40.

Cukier, K., & Mayer-Schonberger, V. (2013a). *Big Data: A Revolution That Will Transform How We Live, Work and Think.* Boston, MA: Houghton Mifflin Harcourt.

De Mauro, A., Greco, M., Grimaldi, M., & Nobili, G. (2016). Beyond Data Scientists: a Review of Big Data Skills and Job Families. *11th International Forum on Knowledge Assets Dynamics – IFKAD 2016, Towards a New Architecture of Knowledge: Big Data Culture and Creativity.*

Drucker, P. (1970). Entrepreneurship in Business Enterprise. *Journal of Business Policy, 1.*

Drucker, P. (1994). *Innovation and Entrepreneurship: Practice and Principles.* London: Heinemann.

Engelbrecht, A., Gerlach, J., & Widjaja, T. (2016). Understanding the anatomy of Data-driven business models – towards an empirical taxonomy. *European Conference on Information Systems (ECIS), 128.*

Feinleib, D. (2014). *Big Data Bootcamp: What Managers Need to Know to Profit from the Big Data revolution.* Apress. doi:10.1007/978-1-4842-0040-7

Fischer, M. M., & Nijkamp, P. (2009). *Entrepreneurship and regional development.* Working Paper: Serie Research Memoranda. VU University Amsterdam, Faculty of Economics, Business Administration and Econometrics.

Foster, I., Ghani, R., Jarmin, R. S., Kreuer, F., & Lane, J. (2017). *Big Data and Social Science.* Boca Raton, FL: CRC Press.

Frizzo-Barker, J., Chow-White, P. A., Mozafari, M., & Ha, D. (2016). An empirical study of the rise of big data in business scholarship. *International Journal of Information Management, 36*(3), 403–413. doi:10.1016/j.ijinfomgt.2016.01.006

Gartner I. T. Glossary (2013). Retrieved from http://www.gartner.com/it-glossary/big-data/

Gartner. (2016). *Investment in big data is up but fewer organizations plan to invest*. Available at: https://www.gartner.com/newsroom/id/3466117

Hartman, P., Zaki, M., Feildman, N., & Neely, A. (2014). *Big Data for Big Business? A Taxonomy of Data Driven Business Models used by Start-up Firms*. University of Cambridge, Cambridge Service Alliance. Available at: https://cambridgeservicealliance.eng.cam.ac.uk/resources/Downloads/Monthly%20Papers/2014_March_DataDrivenBusinessModels.pdf

Hazen, B. T., Boone, C. A., Ezell, J. D., & Jones Farmer, L. A. (2014). Data quality for data science, predictive analytics and Big Data in supply chain management: An introduction to the problem and suggestions for research and applications. *International Journal of Production Economics*, *154*, 72–80. doi:10.1016/j.ijpe.2014.04.018

Inukollu, V. N., Keshamoni, D. D., Kang, T., & Inukolla, M. (2014). Factors influencing quality of mobile apps: Role o mobile app development life cycle. *International Journal of Software Engineering and Its Applications*, *5*(5), 15–34. doi:10.5121/ijsea.2014.5502

Klein, A. (2017, July). Hard Drive Cost Per Gigabyte. *Backblaze*.

Knight, K. (1967). A descriptive model of the intra-firm innovation process. *The Journal of Business of the University of Chicago*, 40.

Labrinidis, A., & Jagadish, H. V. (2012). Challenges and opportunities with big data. *Proceedings of the VLDB Endowment International Conference on Very Large Data Bases*, *5*(12), 2032–2033. doi:10.14778/2367502.2367572

Liu, G., & Yang, H. (2017). Self-organizing network for variable clustering. *Annals of Operations Research*.

Low, M., & MacMillan, I. (1988). Entrepreneurship: Past research and future challenges. *Journal of Management*, *14*(2), 139–161. doi:10.1177/014920638801400202

Lumpkin, G. T., & Dess, G. G. (1996). Clarifying the entrepreneurial orientation construct and linking it to performance. *Academy of Management Review*, *21*(1), 135–172. doi:10.5465/amr.1996.9602161568

Lumpkin, G. T., & Dess, G. G. (2001). Linking two dimensions of entrepreneurial orientation to firm performance: The moderating role of environment and industry life cycle. *Journal of Business Venturing*, *16*(5), 429–451. doi:10.1016/S0883-9026(00)00048-3

Manyika, J., Chui, M., Brown, B., Bughin, J., Dobbs, R., Roxburgh, C., & Hung Byers, A. (2011). *Big data: The Next Frontier for Innovation, Competition, and Productivity*. Washington, DC: McKinsey Global Institute.

Marr, B. (2016). *Big Data in Practice (Use Cases) - How 45 Successful Companies Used Big Data Analytics to Deliver Extraordinary Results*. Wiley. doi:10.1002/9781119278825

McKinsey Global Institute. (2011). *Big data: The next frontier for innovation, competition, and productivity*. McKinsey Global Institute.

McKinsey Global Institute (2016, December). *The age of analytics: Competing in a Data-driven world*. McKinsey Global Institute.

Mitra, S., Pal, S. K., & Mitra, P. (2002). Data mining in soft computing framework: A survey. *IEEE Transactions on Neural Networks*, *13*(1), 3–14. doi:10.1109/72.977258 PMID:18244404

Moorthy, J., Lahiri, R., Biswas, N., Sanyal, D., Ranjan, J., Nanath, K., & Ghosh, P. (2015). *Big data: Prospects and challenges*. Sage India.

Morabito, V. (2015). *Big data and analytics: strategic and Organizational impacts*. Springer International Publishing. doi:10.1007/978-3-319-10665-6

Muhtaroglu, F. C. P., Demir, S., Obali, M., & Girgin, C. (2013). Business model canvas perspective on big data applications. *Big Data*, *2013*, 32–37.

Nyce, C. (2007). A. Predictive analytics white paper. American Institute for CPCU. *Insurance Institute of America*, 9-10.

Ohlhorst, F. (2013). *Big Data Analytics: Turning Big Data into Big Money*. John Wiley & Sons, Inc.

Pascaud, L. (2015). *Smart data at the heart of Prosocial Brands, Kantar Added Value*. Retrieved from: http://added-value.com/2015/01/23/smart-data-at-the-heart-of-pro-social-brands/

Porter, M. E. (1985). *Competitive Advantage: Creating and Sustaining Superior Performance*. New York: Free Press.

Rauch, A., Wiklund, J., Lumpkin, G. T., & Frese, M. (2009). Entrepreneurial orientation and business performance: An assessement of past research and suggestions for the future. *Entrepreneurship Theory and Practice*, *33*(3), 761–787. doi:10.1111/j.1540-6520.2009.00308.x

Rayport, J. F., & Sviokla, J. J. (1995). Exploiting the Virtual Value Chain. *Harvard Business Review*, *73*(6), 75–85.

Reinsel, D., Gantz, J., & Rydning, J. (2017, April). *Data Age 2025: The Evolution of Data to Life-Critical*. IDC White Paper.

Reynolds, P. D. (1987). New firms: Societal contribution versus survival potential. *Journal of Business Venturing*, *2*(3), 231–246. doi:10.1016/0883-9026(87)90011-5

Ross, J. W., Beath, C. M., & Quaardgas, A. (2013). You may not need big data after all. *Harvard Business Review*, *91*(12), 90–98. PMID:23593770

SAS. (2017). *Predictive Analytics: What it is and why it matters, SAS*. Retrieved from: https://www.sas.com/en_us/insights/analytics/predictive-analytics.html

Satell, G. (2014). Five things managers should know about the big data economy. *Forbes*.

Schaupp, L. C., & Bélanger, F. (2014). The value of social Media for small businesses. *Journal of Information Systems*, *28*(1), 187–207. doi:10.2308/isys-50674

Schumpeter, J. A. (1934). *The theory of economic development: an inquiry into profits, capital, credit, interest, and the business cycle*. New Brunswick, NJ: Transaction Publishers.

Sedkaoui, S. (2017). The Internet, Data Analytics and Big Data. In Internet Economics: Models, Mechanisms and Management (pp. 144-166). Gottinger: eBook Bentham Science Publishers.

Sedkaoui, S. (2018a). *Data analytics and big data.* London: ISTE-Wiley. doi:10.1002/9781119528043

Sedkaoui, S. (2018b). *Big Data Analytics for Entrepreneurial Success.* Hershey, PA: IGI Global.

Sedkaoui, S. (2018c). Statistical and Computational Needs for Big Data Challenges. In A. Al Mazari (Ed.), *Big Data Analytics in HIV/AIDS Research* (pp. 21–53). Hershey, PA: IGI Global. doi:10.4018/978-1-5225-3203-3.ch002

Sedkaoui, S., & Monino, J. L. (2016). *Big data, Open Data and Data Development.* New York: ISTE-Wiley.

Shafer, T. (2017). *Big Data and Data Science.* Elder Research Data Science and Predictive Analytics.

Soldatos, J. (2017). *Building Blocks for IoT Analytics Internet-of-Things Analytics.* River Publishers Series in Signal, Image and Speech Processing.

Stevenson, H. H., & Jarillo, J. C. (1990). A paradigm of entrepreneurship: Entrepreneurial management. *Strategic Management Journal, 11,* 17–27.

Stokes, D., & Wilson, N. (2010). *Small business management and entrepreneurship.* EMEA: Cengage Learning.

Storey, D. J., & Johnson, S. (1987). *Are small firms the answer to unemployment?* Employment Institute.

Sumathi, S., & Sivanandam, S. N. (2006). *Introduction to data mining and its application.* New York: Springer. doi:10.1007/978-3-540-34351-6

Tomar, G. S., Chaudhari, N. S., Bhadoria, R. S., & Deka, G. C. (Eds.). (2016). *The Human Element of Big Data: Issues, Analytics, and Performance.* CRC Press. doi:10.1201/9781315368061

Van Barneveld, A., Arnold, K.E., & Campbell, J.P. (2012). Analytics in higher education: Establishing a common language. *EDUCAUSE Learning Initiative, 1*(1), 1-11.

Waller, M. A., & Fawcett, S. E. (2013). Data science, predictive analytics, and big data: A revolution that will transform supply chain design and management. *Journal of Business Logistics, 34*(2), 77–84. doi:10.1111/jbl.12010

Walwei, U. (2016). Digitalization and structural labor market problems: The case of Germany. *ILO Research Paper, 17,* 1-31.

Warren, J., Donald, J., Moffitt, K. C., & Byrnes, P. (2015). How Big Data Will Change Accounting. *Accounting Horizons, 29*(2), 397–407. doi:10.2308/acch-51069

Wiklund, J. (1999). The sustainability of the entrepreneurial orientation-performance relationship. *Entrepreneurship Theory and Practice, 24*(1), 39–50. doi:10.1177/104225879902400103

Zahra, S. A., & Covin, J. G. (1995). Contextual influences on the corporate entrepreneurship performance relationship: A longitudinal analysis. *Journal of Business Venturing, 10*(1), 43–58. doi:10.1016/0883-9026(94)00004-E

Zhu, Y., & McKelvey, M. (2013). Business models in Big Data in China: Opportunities through sequencing and bioinformatics. In *How Entrepreneurs Do What They Do: Case Studies of Knowledge Intensive Entrepreneurship.* Cheltenham, UK: Edward Elgar Publishers. doi:10.4337/9781781005507.00024

KEY TERMS AND DEFINITIONS

Algorithm: A set of computational rules to be followed to solve a mathematical problem. More recently, the term has been adopted to refer to a process to be followed, often by a computer.

Analytics: Has emerged as a catch-all term for a variety of different business intelligence (BI) and application-related initiatives. For some, it is the process of analyzing information from a particular domain, such as Website analytics. For others, it is applying the breadth of BI capabilities to a specific content area (for example, sales, service, supply chain, and so on). In particular, BI vendors use the "analytics" moniker to differentiate their products from the competition. Increasingly, "analytics" is used to describe statistical and mathematical data analysis that clusters, segments, scores and predicts what scenarios are most likely to happen. Whatever the use cases, "analytics" has moved deeper into the business vernacular. Analytics has garnered a burgeoning interest from business and IT professionals looking to exploit huge mounds of internally generated and externally available data.

Artificial Intelligence: The theory and development of computer systems able to perform tasks that traditionally have required human intelligence.

Big Data: A generic term that designates the massive volume of data that is generated by the increasing use of digital tools and information systems. The term big data is used when the amount of data that an organization has to manage reaches a critical volume that requires new technological approaches in terms of storage, processing, and usage. Volume, velocity, and variety are usually the three criteria used to qualify a database as "big data."

Data Analysis: This is a class of statistical methods that make it possible to process a very large volume of data and identify the most interesting aspects of its structure. Some methods help to extract relations between different sets of data, and thus, draw statistical information that makes it possible to describe the most important information contained in the data in the most succinct manner possible. Other techniques make it possible to group data in order to identify its common denominators clearly, and thereby understand them better.

Entrepreneur: Entrepreneurship is not only an outcome of the ecosystem but also an important input factor since entrepreneurs drive the ecosystem by creating it and keeping it healthy. Drucker believes that what entrepreneurs have in common is not personality traits but a commitment to innovation. For innovation, the entrepreneur must have not only talent, ingenuity, and knowledge but he must also be hardworking, focused and purposeful.

Entrepreneurial: A process, in which opportunities for creating new goods and services are explored, evaluated, and exploited.

Entrepreneurial Activity: Entrepreneurial activity, as an output of the entrepreneurial ecosystem, is considered the process by which individuals create opportunities for innovation. This innovation will eventually lead to a new value in society and this is, therefore, the ultimate outcome of an entrepreneurial ecosystem while entrepreneurial activity is a more intermediary output of the system. This entrepreneurial activity has many manifestations, such as innovative start-ups, high-growth start-ups, and entrepreneurial employees.

Knowledge: It is a type of know-how that makes it possible to transform information into instructions. Knowledge can either be obtained through transmission from those who possess it, or by extraction from experience.

Machine Learning: A method of designing a sequence of actions to solve a problem that optimizes automatically through experience and with limited or no human intervention.

Startups: The first thing that is associated with entrepreneurship is startups. It is necessary to establish its definition in order for it to be used later on in this study. A startup is a human institution designed to create a new product or service under conditions of extreme uncertainty. A startup is also considered as an organization formed to search for a repeatable and scalable business model. The term scalable suggests that the aim of every startup is to grow (and, consequently, to stop being a startup) and into mature to a fully functional company: to an SME.

APPENDIX: COSTS OF STORAGE AND DATA AVAILABILITY (2009-2017)

Figure 5. Costs of storage and data
Source: Reinsel, Gantz and Rydning (2017); Klein (2017)

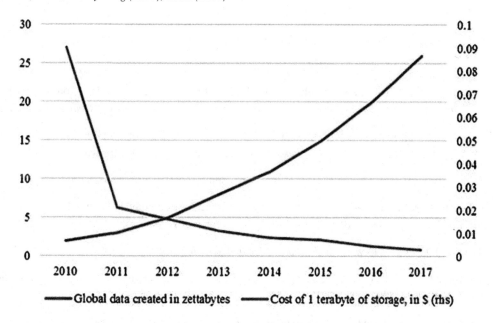

Compilation of References

Abadia, R., Stranieri, A., Quinn, A., & Seifollahi, S. (2011). Real time processing of data from patient biodevices. *Proceedings of the Fourth Australasian Workshop on Health Informatics and Knowledge Management-Volume 120*.

Abdou, H., & Pointon, J. (2011). Credit scoring, statistical techniques and evaluation criteria: A review of the literature. *Intelligent Systems in Accounting, Finance & Management, 18*(2-3), 59–88. doi:10.1002/isaf.325

About us: Splunk Software. (n.d.). Retrieved from https://www.splunk.com/en_us/resources.html

Abramov, J., Sturm, A., & Shoval, P. (2012). Evaluation of the Pattern-based method for Secure Development. *Information and Software Technology, 54*(9), 1029–1043. doi:10.1016/j.infsof.2012.04.001

Ackoff, R. L. (1989). From data to wisdom. *Journal of Applied Systems Analysis, 15*, 3–9.

Acs, Z. J., & Armington, C. (2004). Employment growth and entrepreneurial activity in cities. *Regional Studies, 38*(8), 911–927. doi:10.1080/0034340042000280938

ADA. (2015). Harnessing Big Data to Help Stop Diabetes. *The American Journal of Managed Care, 9*(1), 1–4.

Aggarwal, C. C., & Philip, S. Y. (2007). *A survey of synopsis construction in data streams. In Data Streams* (pp. 169–207). Springer.

Agrawal, N., & Tapaswi, S. (2017). Defense schemes for variants of distributed denial-of-service (DDoS) attacks in cloud computing: A survey. *Information Security Journal: A Global Perspective, 26*(1), 1-13.

Ahmad, A., Hadgkiss, J., & Ruighaver, A. B. (2012). Incident Response Teams–Challenges in Supporting the Organisational Security Function. *Computers & Security, 31*(5), 643–652. doi:10.1016/j.cose.2012.04.001

Ahmad, A., Maynard, S. B., & Park, S. (2014). Information security strategies: Towards an organizational multi-strategy perspective. *Journal of Intelligent Manufacturing, 25*(2), 357–370. doi:10.100710845-012-0683-0

Al-Ameen, M., Liu, J., & Kwak, K. (2012). Security and privacy issues in wireless sensor networks for healthcare applications. *Journal of Medical Systems, 36*(1), 93–101. doi:10.100710916-010-9449-4 PMID:20703745

Al-Janabi, S., Al-Shourbaji, I., Shojafar, M., & Shamshirband, S. (2016). *Survey of main challenges (security and privacy) in wireless body area networks for healthcare applications*. Egyptian Informatics Journal.

Al-Jarrah, O., Yoo, P. D., Muhaidat, S., & Karagiannidis, G. K. (2015). Efficient machine learning for big data: A review. *Big Data Research, 2*(3), 87–93. doi:10.1016/j.bdr.2015.04.001

Allami, R., Stranieri, A., Balasubramanian, V., & Jelinek, H. F. (2016). *ECG Reduction for Wearable Sensor*. Paper presented at the Signal-Image Technology & Internet-Based Systems (SITIS), 2016 12th International Conference on. 10.1109/SITIS.2016.88

Allami, R., Stranieri, A., Balasubramanian, V., & Jelinek, H. F. (2017). A count data model for heart rate variability forecasting and premature ventricular contraction detection. *Signal, Image and Video Processing*, 1–9.

Allianz Global Corporate & Specialty. (2018). *The rise of AI: future perspectives and potential risks.* Retrieved from https://allianz.ru/ru/stuff/Взлет%20искусственного%20интеллекта.pdf

Al-Sarem, M. (2015). Building a decision tree model for academic advising affairs based on the algorithm C4-5. *International Journal of Computer Science Issues*, *12*(5), 33–37.

Amato, F., Mazzocca, N., & Moscato, F. (2018). Model driven design and evaluation of security level in orchestrated cloud services. *Journal of Network and Computer Applications*, *106*, 78–89. doi:10.1016/j.jnca.2017.12.006

Anderson, E., & Choobineh, J. (2008). Enterprise information security strategies. *Computers & Security*, *27*(1-2), 22–29. doi:10.1016/j.cose.2008.03.002

Andress, A. (2003). *Surviving Security: How to Integrate People, Process, and Technology.* Boca Raton, FL: Auerbach Publications. doi:10.1201/9780203501405

Angiuli, O., Blitzstein, J., & Waldo, J. (2015). How to De-Identify Your Data. *Communications of the ACM*, *58*(12), 48–55. doi:10.1145/2814340

Arnott, D., Lizama, F., & Song, Y. (2017). Patterns of business intelligence systems use in organizations. *Decision Support Systems*, *97*, 58–68. doi:10.1016/j.dss.2017.03.005

Arukonda, S., & Sinha, S. (2015). The innocent perpetrators: Reflectors and reflection attacks. *Advanced Computer Science*, *4*, 94–98.

Ashibani, Y., & Mahmoud, Q. H. (2017). Cyber physical systems security: Analysis, challegnes and solutions. *Computers & Security*, *68*, 81–97. doi:10.1016/j.cose.2017.04.005

Asif, R., Merceron, A., & Pathan, M. K. (2015). Predicting student academic performance at degree level: A case study. *Intelligent Systems and Applications*, *1*, 49–61.

Astriim, K. J., & McAvoy, T. J. (1992). Intelligent control. *J. Proc. Cont.*, *2*(3), 115–126. doi:10.1016/0959-1524(92)85001-D

Atteya, H. (2017). *Visualization as a guidance to classification for large datasets.* The American University in Cairo. Retrieved from http://dar.aucegypt.edu/handle/10526/5132

Baars, H., & Kemper, H. G. (2008). Management support with structured and unstructured data—An integrated business intelligence framework. *Information Systems Management*, *25*(2), 132–148. doi:10.1080/10580530801941058

Badola, V. (2015, October 1). *Cloud migration: benefits and risks of migrating to the Cloud.* Retrieved from http://cloudacademy.com/blog/cloud-migration-benefits-risks/

Baker, S. (2018, May 9). *Cambridge Analytica Won't Be Revived Under New Company Name.* Retrieved from Bloomberg: https://www.bloomberg.com/news/articles/2018-05-08/cambridge-analytica-won-t-be-revived-under-new-company-name

Balakrishnan, S. J.-A. (2017). Google Fusion Tables. Encyclopedia of GIS, 788-797.

Balasubramanian Appiah, V. (2012). *Dependability of body area wireless sensor networks in assistive care loop framework (PhD).* University Technology Sydney.

Balasubramanian, V., & Stranieri, A. (2014). *A scalable cloud Platform for Active healthcare monitoring applications.* Paper presented at the e-Learning, e-Management and e-Services (IC3e), 2014 IEEE Conference on. 10.1109/IC3e.2014.7081248

Balasubramanian, V., Hoang, D. B., & Ahmad, N. (2008). *SOAP based Assistive Care Loop using wireless sensor networks.* Paper presented at the IT in Medicine and Education, 2008. ITME 2008. IEEE International Symposium on. 10.1109/ITME.2008.4743897

Balasubramanian, V., Stranieri, A., & Kaur, R. (2015). AppA: assistive patient monitoring cloud platform for active healthcare applications. *Proceedings of the 9th International Conference on Ubiquitous Information Management and Communication.* 10.1145/2701126.2701224

Banker, R., Chang, H., & Kao, Y.-C. (2010). Evaluating Cross-Organizational Impacts of Information Technology – an Empirical Analysis. *European Journal of Information Systems, 19*(2), 153–167. doi:10.1057/ejis.2010.9

Baskerville, R. (2010). Third-Degree Conflicts: Information Warfare. *European Journal of Information Systems, 19*(1), 1–4. doi:10.1057/ejis.2010.2

Baskerville, R., Spagnoletti, P., & Kim, J. (2014). Incident-Centered Information Security: Managing a Strategic Balance between Prevention and Response. *Information & Management, 51*(1), 138–151. doi:10.1016/j.im.2013.11.004

Beare, M. E. (2012). Encyclopedia of Transnational Crime and Justice. Toronto: Academic Press. doi:10.4135/9781452218588

Bellocchio, F., Ferrari, S., Piuri, V., & Borghese, N. (2012). Hierarchical Approach for Multi-scale Support Vector Regression. *IEEE Transactions on Neural Networks and Learning Systems, 23*(9), 1448–1460. doi:10.1109/TNNLS.2012.2205018 PMID:24807928

Benesty, J. C. J. (2009). Pearson Correlation Coefficient. In *Noise Reduction in Speech Processing. Springer Topics in Signal Processing* (Vol. 2). Berlin: Springer. doi:10.1007/978-3-642-00296-0_5

Berberidis, D., Kekatos, V., & Giannakis, G. (2016). Online Censoring for Large-Scale Regressions with Application to Streaming Big Data. *IEEE Transactions on Signal Processing, 64*(15), 3854–3867. doi:10.1109/TSP.2016.2546225 PMID:28042229

Bershadsky, A., Bozhday, A., Evseeva, J., Gudkov, A., & Mkrtchian, V. (2017), Techniques for Adaptive Graphics Applications Synthesis Based on Variability Modeling Technology and Graph Theory. In *Proceedings of CIT&DS 2017,* (pp. 169–179). Springer International Publishing AG. DOI: 10.1007/978-3-319-65551-2_33

Bershadsky, A., Evseeva, J., Bozhday, A., Gudkov, A., & Mkrtchian, V. (2015), Variability modeling in the automated system for authoring intelligent adaptive applications on the basis of three-dimensional graphics. In *Proceedings of CIT&DS 2015* (pp. 149–159). Springer International Publishing AG. DOI: 10.1007/978-3-319-23766-4

Bertino, E., & Ferrari, E. (2018). Big Data Security and Privacy. In S. Flesca, S. Greco, E. Masciari, & D. Saccà (Eds.), *A Comprehensive Guide Through the Italian Database Research Over the Last 25 Years. Studies in Big Data* (Vol. 31). Cham: Springer. doi:10.1007/978-3-319-61893-7_25

Birch, D. L. (1987). *Job creation in America: How our smallest companies put the most people to work.* New York: The Free Press.

Björn Berg, S. G. (n.d.). Retrieved from Qlik Technologies, Inc.: https://www.qlik.com/us/products/qlikview

Blake & Merz. (1998). *UCI repository of machine learning databases.* Academic Press.

Boehmk, B. C. (2016). *Data Wrangling with R.* Springer. doi:10.1007/978-3-319-45599-0

Bojanc, R., Jerman-Blaic, B., & Tekavcic, M. (2012). Managing the Investment in Information Security Technology by Use of a Quantitative Modeling. *Information Processing & Management, 48*(6), 1031–1052. doi:10.1016/j.ipm.2012.01.001

Bojanc, R., & Jerman-Blažic, B. (2012). Quantitative Model for Economic Analyses of Information Security Investment in an Enterprise Information System. *Organizacija*, *45*(6), 276–288. doi:10.2478/v10051-012-0027-z

Bossmann, J. (2016, October 21). *Top 9 ethical issues in artificial intelligence.* Retrieved from https://www.weforum.org/agenda/2016/10/top-10-ethical-issues-in-artificial-intelligence/

Bostrom, N. (2016). *Artificial Intelligence. Stages. Threats Strategies.* Moscow: MIF.

Boutlon, C. (2013). How much Hadoop about nothing. *CIO Journal.* Retrieved from http://blogs.wsj.com/cio/2013/01/25/much-hadoop-about-nothing/

Breen, S., Kofoed, S., Ritchie, D., Dryden, T., Maguire, R., Kearney, N., & Aranda, S. (2017). Remote real-time monitoring for chemotherapy side-effects in patients with blood cancers. *Collegian (Royal College of Nursing, Australia)*, *24*(6), 541–549. doi:10.1016/j.colegn.2016.10.009

Breiman, L. (2001). Random Forests. *Machine Learning*, *45*(1), 5–32. doi:10.1023/A:1010933404324

Breiman, L., Friedman, J., Olshen, R., & Stone, C. (1987). Classification and Regression Trees. *Cytometry*, *8*, 534–535.

Broadbent, A., & Schaffner, C. (2016). Quantum cryptography beyond quantum key distribution. *Designs, Codes and Cryptography*, *78*(1), 351–382. doi:10.100710623-015-0157-4

Broeders, D., Schrijvers, E., Sloot, B., Brakel, R., Hoog, J., & Ballin, E. H. (2017). Big Data and security policies: Towards a framework for regulating the phases of analytics and use of Big Data. *Computer Law & Security Review*, *33*(3), 309–323. doi:10.1016/j.clsr.2017.03.002

Brown, B. (2008). HIPAA Beyond HIPAA: ONCHIT, ONC, AHIC, HITSP, and CCHIT. *Journal of Health Care Compliance*, *10*(41), 1–21.

Brownlee, J. (2011). *Clever Algorithms: Nature-Inspired Programming Recipes.* Morrisville: LuLu.

Brown, S. M., Jones, J., Kuttler, K. G., Keddington, R. K., Allen, T. L., & Haug, P. (2016). Prospective evaluation of an automated method to identify patients with severe sepsis or septic shock in the emergency department. *BMC Emergency Medicine*, *16*(1), 31. doi:10.118612873-016-0095-0 PMID:27549755

Brynjolfsson, E., & McAfee, A. (2011). *Race Against the Machine: How the Digital Revolution is Accelerating Innovation, Driving Productivity, and Irreversibly Transforming Employment and the Economy.* Lexington, MA: Digital Frontier Press.

Burrows, R., & Savage, M. (2014). After the crisis? Big data and the methodological challenges of empirical sociology. *Big Data & Society Journal*, *12*(2), 1–6.

Butler, S. (2018, March 22). Bargain Booze owner Conviviality must raise £125m to halt bankruptcy. *The Guardian.* Retrieved from https://www.theguardian.com/business/2018/mar/21/bargain-booze-owner-conviviality-must-raise-125m-to-halt-bankruptcy

Cajaiba-Santana, G. (2014). Social innovation: Moving the field forward. A conceptual framework. *Technological Forecasting and Social Change*, *82*, 42–51. doi:10.1016/j.techfore.2013.05.008

Campbell, J. P., DeBlois, P. B., & Oblinger, D. G. (2007). Academic analytics: A new tool for a new era. *EDUCAUSE Review*, *42*, 40–57. Retrieved from http://net.educause.edu/ir/library/pdf/ERM0742.pdf

Campbell, K., Gordon, L. A., Loeb, M. P., & Zhou, L. (2003). The Economic Cost of Publicly Announced Information Security Breaches: Empirical Evidence from the Stock Market. *Journal of Computer Security*, *11*(3), 431–448. doi:10.3233/JCS-2003-11308

Caniels, M., & Bakens, R. (2011). The effects of project management information systems on decision making in a multi project environment. *International Journal of Project Management*, 30(2), 162–175.

Cao, B., Zhao, J., Po Yang, Z. L., Liu, X., Kang, X., Yang, S., ... Anvari-Moghaddam, A. (2018). Distributed parallel cooperative coevolutionary multi-objective. *Future Generation Computer Systems*, 82, 256–267. doi:10.1016/j.future.2017.10.015

Carcillo, F., Pozzolo, A. D., Borgne, Y.-A. L., Caelen, O., Mazzer, Y., & Bontempi, G. (2018). SCARFF: A scalable framework for streaming credit card fraud detection with spark. *Information Fusion*, 41, 182–194. doi:10.1016/j.inffus.2017.09.005

Carta, M., & Angst, J. (2016). Screening for bipolar disorders: A public health issue. *Journal of Affective Disorders*, 205, 139–143. doi:10.1016/j.jad.2016.03.072 PMID:27442457

Cass, S. (2018). *The 2017 Top Programming Languages*. Retrieved from https://spectrum.ieee.org/computing/software/the-2017-top-programming-languages

Catley, C., Smith, K., McGregor, C., & Tracy, M. (2009). *Extending CRISP-DM to incorporate temporal data mining of multidimensional medical data streams: A neonatal intensive care unit case study*. Paper presented at the Computer-Based Medical Systems, 2009. CBMS 2009. 22nd IEEE International Symposium on. 10.1109/CBMS.2009.5255394

Centre for Effective Altruism. (2017). *Changes in funding in the AI*. Retrieved from: https://www.centreforeffectivealtruism.org/blog/changes-in-funding-in-the-ai-safety-field/

Cervellera, C., & Macciò, D. (2014). Local Linear Regression for Function Learning: An Analysis Based on Sample Discrepancy. *IEEE Transactions on Neural Networks and Learning Systems*, 25(11), 2086–2098. doi:10.1109/TNNLS.2014.2305193 PMID:25330431

Chaffey, D. (2009). *E-Business and E-Commerce Management: Strategy, Implementation and Practice*. Harlow, UK: Prentice Hall.

Chaffey, D., & White, G. (2011). *Business Information Management* (2nd ed.). Harlow, UK: Prentice Hall.

Chai, S., Kim, M., & Raoc, R. (2011). Firms' information security investment decisions: Stock market evidence of investors' behaviour. *Decision Support Systems*, 50(4), 651–661. doi:10.1016/j.dss.2010.08.017

Chan, M., Estève, D., Fourniols, J.-Y., Escriba, C., & Campo, E. (2012). Smart wearable systems: Current status and future challenges. *Artificial Intelligence in Medicine*, 56(3), 137–156. doi:10.1016/j.artmed.2012.09.003 PMID:23122689

Chapman, P., Clinton, J., Kerber, R., Khabaza, T., Reinartz, T., Shearer, C., & Wirth, R. (2000). *CRISP-DM 1.0 Step-by-step data mining guide*. Academic Press.

Charki, M. H., Josserand, E., & Boukef, N. (2017). The paradoxical effects of legal intervention over unethical information technology use: A rational choice theory perspective. *The Journal of Strategic Information Systems*, 26(1), 58–76. doi:10.1016/j.jsis.2016.07.001

Checkland, P. (1999). *Systems Thinking, Systems Practice*. Chichester, UK: John Wiley & Sons Ltd.

Chen, M., Mao, S., Zhang, Y., & Leung, V. C. (2014). Open issues and outlook in big data. In Big Data: Related Technologies, Challenges and Future Prospects (Vol. 1, pp. 81-89). Springer.

Chen, C. L. P., & Zhang, C. Y. (2014). Data-intensive applications, challenges, techniques and technologies: A survey on big data. *Information Sciences Journal*, 275(1), 314–317. doi:10.1016/j.ins.2014.01.015

Chen, H., Chiang, R., & Storey, V. (2012). Business intelligence and analytics: From big data to big impact. *Management Information Systems Quarterly*, *36*(4), 1165–1188. doi:10.2307/41703503

Chen, H., Ge, L., & Xie, L. A. (2015). User Authentication Scheme Based on Elliptic Curves Cryptography for Wireless Ad Hoc Networks. *Sensors (Basel)*, *15*(7), 17057–17075. doi:10.3390150717057 PMID:26184224

Chen, K., Li, X., & Wang, H. (2015). On the model design of integrated intelligent big data analytics systems. *Industrial Management & Data Systems*, *115*(9), 1666–1682. doi:10.1108/IMDS-03-2015-0086

Chen, L., Jordan, S., Liu, Y.-K., Moody, D., Peralta, R., Perlner, R., & Smith, D. (2016). *Report on Post-Quantum Cryptography*. Gaithersburg, MD: National Institute of Standards and Technology. doi:10.6028/NIST.IR.8105

Cherkassky, V., & Ma, Y. (2002). *Selecting of the Loss Function for Robust Linear Regression*. Academic Press.

Chernyak, L. (2011*). Big Data - a new theory and practice. Open systems*. Retrieved from https://www.osp.ru/os/2011/10/13010990/

Choi, Y., Lee, D., Kim, J., Jung, J., Nam, J., & Won, D. (2014). Security Enhanced User Authentication Protocol for Wireless Sensor Networks Using Elliptic Curves Cryptography. *Sensors (Basel)*, *14*(6), 10081–10106. doi:10.3390140610081 PMID:24919012

Chou, T.-Y., Seng-Cho, T. C., & Tzeng, G.-H. (2006). Evaluating IT/IS Investments: A Fuzzy Multi-Criteria Decision Model Approach. *European Journal of Operational Research*, *173*(3), 1026–1046. doi:10.1016/j.ejor.2005.07.003

Clarke-Sather, A. R., Hutchins, M. J., Zhang, Q., Gershenson, J. K., & Sutherland, J. W. (2011). Development of social, environmental, and economic indicators for a small/medium enterprise. *International Journal of Accounting and Information Management*, *19*(3), 247–266. doi:10.1108/18347641111169250

Collins, S., & McCombie, S. (2012). Stuxnet: The emergence of a new cyber weapon and its implications. *Journal of Policing. Intelligence and Counter Terrorism*, *7*(1), 80–91. doi:10.1080/18335330.2012.653198

Columbus, L. (2016). *Roundup of Analytics, Big Data & BI Forecasts and Market Estimates, 2016, AUG 20*. Retrieved January 16, 2017 from: http://www.forbes.com/sites/louiscolumbus/2016/08/20/roundup-of-analytics-big-data-bi-forecasts-and-market-estimates-2016/#4ea4c90849c5

Cooper, A. (2012). What is analytics? Definition and essential characteristics. *CETIS Analytics Series*, *1*(5), 1–10.

Coronel, C., & Morris, S. (2015). *Database Systems: Design, Implementation, and Management* (11th ed.). Boston: Cengage Learning.

Corporate Governance Codes and Principles. (2012). *Singapore*. Retrieved from http://www.ecgi.org/codes/code.php?code_id=354

Cortell. (2017). *IBM Planning Analytics*. Retrieved July 29, 2018, from http://www.cortell.co.za/our-partners/ibm-planning-analytics/

Côrte-Real, N., Oliveira, T., & Ruivo, P. (2017). Assessing business value of Big Data Analytics in European firms. *Journal of Business Research*, *70*, 379–390. doi:10.1016/j.jbusres.2016.08.011

Couper, M. P. (2013). Is the sky falling? New technology, changing media, and the future of surveys. *Survey Research Methods Journal*, *7*(1), 145–156.

Cox, D., Kartsonaki, C., & Keogh, R. H. (2018). Big data: Some statistical issues. *Statistics & Probability Letters*, *136*, 111–115. doi:10.1016/j.spl.2018.02.015 PMID:29899584

Cristianini, N., & Scholkopf, B. (2002). Support Vector Machines and Kernel Methods: The New Generation of Learning Machines. *AI Magazine, 23*(3), 31–41.

CRM. (2012). Retrieved 1 8, 2013, from Wikipedia: http://en.wikipedia.org/wiki/Customer_relationship_management

Cukier, K., & Mayer-Schoenberger, V. (2013b). The Rise of Big Data. *Foreign Affairs, 92*(3), 28–40.

Cukier, K., & Mayer-Schonberger, V. (2013a). *Big Data: A Revolution That Will Transform How We Live, Work and Think*. Boston, MA: Houghton Mifflin Harcourt.

Da Veiga, A. (2016). Comparing the information security culture of employees who had read the information security policy and those who had not: Illustrated through an empirical study. *Information & Computer Security, 24*(2), 139–151. doi:10.1108/ICS-12-2015-0048

Datoo, S. (2014). Big data: 4 predictions for 2014. *The Guardian*. Retrieved January 20, 2017 from: https://www.theguardian.com/technology/datablog/2014/jan/14/big-data-4-predictions-for-2014

Davenport, T. H., & Harris, J. G. (2006). *Inteligencja analityczna w biznesie: nowa nauka zwyciężania*. Warszawa: MT Biznes. (in Polish)

Davis, C. K. (2014). Viewpoint Beyond Data and Analytics- Why business analytics and big data really matter for modern business organizations. *Communications of the ACM, 57*(8), 39–41. doi:10.1145/2602326

De Mauro, A., Greco, M., Grimaldi, M., & Nobili, G. (2016). Beyond Data Scientists: a Review of Big Data Skills and Job Families. *11th International Forum on Knowledge Assets Dynamics – IFKAD 2016, Towards a New Architecture of Knowledge: Big Data Culture and Creativity*.

de Montjoye, Y.-A., & Pentland, A. S. (2016). Response to Comment on "Unique in the shopping mall: On the reidentifiability of credit card metadata". *Science Journal, 351*(6279), 1274.

De Zwart, M., Humphreys, S., & Van Dissel, B. (2014). Surveillance, big data and democracy: Lessons for Australia from the US and UK. *The University of New South Wales Law Journal, 37*(2), 713–747.

Deep Knowledge Venture's Appoints Intelligent Investment Analysis Software VITAL as Board Member. (2014). Retrieved from: http://www.prweb.com/releases/2014/05/prweb11847458.htm

Delena, D., & Demirkanb, H. (2013). Data, information and analytics as services. *Decision Support Systems, 55*(1), 359–363. doi:10.1016/j.dss.2012.05.044

Department of Communication and the Arts. (2018, February 27). *Future trends in bandwidth demand*. Retrieved from https://www.communications.gov.au/departmental-news/future-trends-bandwidth-demand

Diogo, A. B., & Fernandes, M. M. (2017). Applications of artificial immune systems to computer security: A survey. *Journal of Information Security and Applications, 35*, 138–159. doi:10.1016/j.jisa.2017.06.007

Dong, J., Peng, T., & Zhao, Y. (2010). Automated verification of security pattern compositions. *Information and Software Technology, 52*(3), 274–295. doi:10.1016/j.infsof.2009.10.001

Dor, D., & Elovici, Y. (2016). A Model of the Information Security Investment DecisionMaking Process. *Computers & Security, 63*, 1–13. doi:10.1016/j.cose.2016.09.006

Drucker, P. (1970). Entrepreneurship in Business Enterprise. *Journal of Business Policy*, 1.

Drucker, P. (1994). *Innovation and Entrepreneurship: Practice and Principles*. London: Heinemann.

Duhigg, C. (2014). *The power of habit: Why we do what we do in life and business*. New York: Penguin Random House.

Dur, B. I. (2014). Data visualization and infographics in visual communication design education at the age of information. *Journal of Arts and Humanities*, *5*, 39–50.

Eastin, M. S., Brinson, N. H., Doorey, A., & Wilcox, G. (2016). Living in a big data world: Predicting mobile commerce activity through privacy concerns. *Computers in Human Behavior*, *58*(1), 214–220. doi:10.1016/j.chb.2015.12.050

Ebner, K., Buhnen, T., & Urbach, N. (2014). Think Big with Big Data: Identifying Suitable Big Data Strategies in Corporate Environments. *2014 47th Hawaii International Conference on System Sciences.*

Eggen, A., Hauge, M., Hedenstad, O. E., Lund, K., Legasp, A., Seifert, H., & Simon, P. (2013). *Coalition Networks for Secure Information Sharing (CoNSIS). In MILCOM 2013 - 2013 IEEE Military Communications Conference* (pp. 354–359). San Diego, CA: IEEE. doi:10.1109/MILCOM.2013.68

Eggertsson, T. (2001). Economic behavior and institution. Moscow: Academic Press.

Ekbia, H., Mattioli, M., Kouper, I., Arave, G., Ghazinejad, A., Bowman, T., ... Sugimoto, C. R. (2015). Big data, bigger dilemmas: A critical review. *Journal of the Association for Information Science and Technology*, *66*(8), 1523–1545. doi:10.1002/asi.23294

Elliot, J. A., & Kennedy, D. B. (1988). Estimation and prediction of categorical models in accounting research. *Journal of Accounting Literature*, *7*, 202–242.

Eloff, M. M., & Von Solms, S. H. (2000). Information Security Management: An Approach to Combine Process Certification and Product Evaluation. *Computers & Security*, *19*(8), 698–709. doi:10.1016/S0167-4048(00)08019-6

Elshawi, R., Sakr, S., Talia, D., & Trunfio, P. (2018). Big Data Systems Meet Machine Learning Challenges: Towards Big Data Science as a Service. *Big Data Research*, 1-11.

El-Sherif, H., & El-Sawy, O. (1998). Issue-based decision support systems for the Cabinet of Egypt. *Management Information Systems Quarterly*, *12*(4), 551–569. doi:10.2307/249131

Engelbrecht, A., Gerlach, J., & Widjaja, T. (2016). Understanding the anatomy of Data-driven business models – towards an empirical taxonomy. *European Conference on Information Systems (ECIS), 128.*

Erl, T. (2009). *SOA Design Patterns*. New York: Prentice Hall PTR.

Eubank, N. (2015). *Data Analysis in Python.* Retrieved from http://www.data-analysis-in-python.org/

European Spreadsheet Risks Interest Group (EuSpRIG). (n.d.a). *Horror stories.* Retrieved from http://www.eusprig.org/horror-stories.htm

European Spreadsheet Risks Interest Group (EuSpRIG). (n.d.b). *Welcome.* Retrieved from http://www.eusprig.org/index.htm

Fang, L. (2016, April 14). *The CIA Is Investing in Firms That Mine Your Tweets and Instagram Photos.* Retrieved from The intercept: https://theintercept.com/2016/04/14/in-undisclosed-cia-investments-social-media-mining-looms-large/

Fan, J., Han, F., & Liu, H. (2014). Challenges of Big Data Analysis. *National Science Review Journal*, *1*(1), 293–314. doi:10.1093/nsr/nwt032 PMID:25419469

Feinleib, D. (2014). *Big Data Bootcamp: What Managers Need to Know to Profit from the Big Data revolution.* Apress. doi:10.1007/978-1-4842-0040-7

Fenz, S., Heurix, J., Neubauer, T., & Pechstein, F. (2014). Current challenges in information security risk management. *Information Management & Computer Security*, *22*(5), 410–430. doi:10.1108/IMCS-07-2013-0053

Filkins, B. L., Kim, J. Y., Roberts, B., Armstrong, W., Miller, M. A., Hultner, M. L., ... Steinhubl, S. R. (2016). Privacy and security in the era of digital health: What should translational researchers know and do about it? *American Journal of Translational Research*, 8(3), 1560–1580. PMID:27186282

Financial Reporting Council. (2016). *The UK Corporate Governance Code*. Retrieved from https://www.frc.org.uk/directors/corporate-governance-and-stewardship/uk-corporate-governance-code

Finnie, G. R., & Sun, Z. (2003). R5 model for case-based reasoning. *Knowledge-Based Systems*, 16(1), 59–65. doi:10.1016/S0950-7051(02)00053-9

Fischbacher-Smith, D. (2016). Breaking bad? In search of a (softer) systems view of security ergonomics. *Security Journal*, 29(1), 5–22. doi:10.1057j.2015.41

Fischer, M. M., & Nijkamp, P. (2009). *Entrepreneurship and regional development*. Working Paper: Serie Research Memoranda. VU University Amsterdam, Faculty of Economics, Business Administration and Econometrics.

Fitriana, R., & Djatna, T., & Eriyatno. (2011). Progress in business intelligence system research : A literature review. *International Journal of Basic and Applied Sciences*, 11(3), 96–105.

Flores, W. R., Antonsen, E., & Ekstedt, M. (2014). Information Security Knowledge Sharing in Organizations: Investigating the Effect of Behavioral Information Security Governance and National Culture. *Computers & Security*, 43, 90–110. doi:10.1016/j.cose.2014.03.004

Flowerday, S. V., & Tuyikeze, T. (2016). Information security policy development and implementation: The what, how and who. *Computers & Security*, 61, 169–183. doi:10.1016/j.cose.2016.06.002

Fosso Wamba, S., Gunasekaran, A., & Akter, S. (2016). Big data analytics and firm performance: Effects of dynamic capabilities. *Journal of Business Research*, 70, 356–365. doi:10.1016/j.jbusres.2016.08.009

Foster, I., Ghani, R., Jarmin, R. S., Kreuer, F., & Lane, J. (2017). *Big Data and Social Science*. Boca Raton, FL: CRC Press.

Freund, Y., & Schapire, R. (1999). A Short Introduction to Boosting. *Proceedings of the 16th international joint conference on Artificial intelligence*, 2, 1401-1406.

Friedberg, I., McLaughlin, K., Smith, P., Laverty, D., & Sezer, S. (2016). STPA-SafeSec: Safety and security analysis for cyber-physical systems. *Journal of Information Security and Applications*, 29, 1–12.

Friedman, J. H. (2001). Greedy function approximation: A gradient boosting machine. *Annals of Statistics*, 29(5), 1189–1232. doi:10.1214/aos/1013203451

Friedman, J. H. (2002). Stochastic gradient boosting. *Computational Statistics & Data Analysis*, 38(4), 367–378. doi:10.1016/S0167-9473(01)00065-2

Frizzo-Barker, J., Chow-White, P., Mozafari, M., & Ha, D. (2016). An empirical study of the rise of big data in business Scholarship. *International Journal of Information Management*, 36(3), 403–413. doi:10.1016/j.ijinfomgt.2016.01.006

Fukuyama, F. (1992). *The End of History and the Last Man*. Toronto: Maxwell Macmillan.

Gaidelys, V., & Valodkiene, G. (2011). The Methods of Selecting and Assessing Potential Consumers Used of by Competitive Intelligence. *Inzinerine Ekonomika-Engineering Economics*, 22(2), 196–202.

Gandino, F., Celozzi, C., & Rebaudengo, M. (2017). A Key Management Scheme for Mobile Wireless Sensor Networks. *Applied Sciences*, 7(5), 490. doi:10.3390/app7050490

Gandomi, A., & Haider, M. (2015). Beyond the hype: Big data concepts, methods, and analytics. *International Journal of Information Management, 35*, 137–144.

Gandomi, A., & Haider, M. (2015). Beyond the hype: Big data concepts, methods, and analytics. *International Journal of Information Management, 35*(2), 137–144. doi:10.1016/j.ijinfomgt.2014.10.007

Gandotra, V., Singhal, A., & Bedi, P. (2012). Threat-Oriented Security Framework: A Proactive Approach in Threat Management. *Procedia Technology, 4*, 487–494. doi:10.1016/j.protcy.2012.05.078

Ganeshalingam, S., & Kumar, K. (2001). Detection and prediction of financial distress. *Managerial Finance, 27*(4), 45–55. doi:10.1108/03074350110767132

Gartner I. T. Glossary (2013). Retrieved from http://www.gartner.com/it-glossary/big-data/

Gartner, I. (2005). *Gartner says more than 50 percent of data warehouse projects will have limited acceptance or will be failures through 2007* [Press Release]. Retrieved from https://www.gartner.com/newsroom/id/492112

Gartner, I. (2012). *Gartner says fewer than 30 percent of business intelligence initiatives will align analytic metrics completely with enterprise business drivers by 2014* [Press Release]. Retrieved from https://www.gartner.com/newsroom/id/1891515

Gartner. (2016). *Investment in big data is up but fewer organizations plan to invest.* Available at: https://www.gartner.com/newsroom/id/3466117

Gartner. (n.d.). *Business intelligence (BI).* Retrieved from https://www.gartner.com/it-glossary/business-intelligence-bi

Gentleman, R. I. (n.d.). *About R. Introduction to R.* Retrieved from https://www.r-project.org/

Gey, S., & Nedelec, E. (2005). Model selection for CART regression trees. *IEEE Transactions on Information Theory, 51*(2), 658–670. doi:10.1109/TIT.2004.840903

Gibson, M., Arnott, D., & Jagielska, I. (2004). *Evaluating the intangible benefits of business intelligence: review and research agenda.* Academic Press.

Girolami, M., & Rogers, S. (2006). Variational Bayesian multinomial probit regression with Gaussian process priors. *Neural Computation, 18*(8), 1790–1817. doi:10.1162/neco.2006.18.8.1790

Gkioulos, V., Wangen, G., Katsikas, S. K., Kavallieratos, G., & Kotzanikolaou, P. (2017). Security Awareness of the Digital Natives. *Information, 8*(2), 42. doi:10.3390/info8020042

Gonzalez, H., Halevy, A., Jensen, C. S., Langen, A., Madhavan, J., Shapley, R., & Shen, W. (2010, June). Google fusion tables: data management, integration and collaboration in the cloud. In *Proceedings of the 1st ACM symposium on Cloud computing* (pp. 175-180). ACM. 10.1145/1807128.1807158

Google. (n.d.). *Tutorials.* Retrieved from https://sites.google.com/site/fusiontablestalks/home

Guotai, C., & Zhipeng, Z. (2017). Multi Criteria Credit Rating Model for Small Enterprise Using a Nonparametric Method. *Sustainability, 9*(10), 1834. doi:10.3390u9101834

Guo, Y., Hastie, T., & Tibshirani, R. (2007). Regularized linear discriminant analysis and its application in microarrays. *Biostatistics (Oxford, England), 8*(1), 86–100. doi:10.1093/biostatistics/kxj035 PMID:16603682

Gupta, V., & Singh, J. (2014). A review of data warehousing and business intelligence in different perspective. *International Journal of Computer Science and Information Technologies, 5*(6), 8263–8268.

Habib ur Rehmana, M., Changb, V., Batoolc, A., & Wah, T. (2016). Big data reduction framework for value creation in sustainable enterprises. *International Journal of Information Management, 36*, 917–928.

Hacker's guide to Neural Networks. (n.d.). Retrieved from: https://karpathy.github.io/neuralnets/

Hadžiosmanović, D., Bolzoni, D., & Hartel, P. H. (2012). A log mining approach for process monitoring in SCADA. *International Journal of Information Security, 11*(4), 231–251. doi:10.100710207-012-0163-8

Hair, J. F., Black, W. C., Babin, B. J., Anderson, R. E., & Tatham, R. L. (2006). *Multivariate data analysis* (6th ed.). Upper Saddle River, NJ: Prentice-Hall.

Hajek, P., Olej, V., & Prochazka, O. (2016). Predicting Corporate Credit Ratings Using Content Analysis of Annual Reports – A Naïve Bayesian Network Approach. In S. Feuerriegel & D. Neumann (Eds.), Enterprise Applications, Markets and Services in the Finance Industry (pp 47-61). Springer.

Hall'en, R. (2017). *A Study of Gradient-Based Algorithms*. Mathematical Statistics, Lund University Libraries.

Hamon, M. A., & Quintin, J. (2016). Innate immune memory in mammals. *Seminars in Immunology, 28*(4), 351–358. doi:10.1016/j.smim.2016.05.003 PMID:27264334

Hardy, Q. (2016, December 25). *Why the Computing Cloud Will Keep Growing and Growing*. Retrieved from https://www.nytimes.com/2016/12/25/technology/why-the-computing-cloud-will-keep-growing-and-growing.html?_r=0

Harris, S., & Maymi, F. (2016). *CISSP® All-in-One Exam Guide* (7th ed.). New York: McGraw-Hill Education.

Hartman, P., Zaki, M., Feildman, N., & Neely, A. (2014). *Big Data for Big Business? A Taxonomy of Data Driven Business Models used by Start-up Firms*. University of Cambridge, Cambridge Service Alliance. Available at: https://cambridgeservicealliance.eng.cam.ac.uk/resources/Downloads/Monthly%20Papers/2014_March_DataDrivenBusinessModels.pdf

Haskel, J., & Westlake, S. (2017). *Capitalism without capital*. Moscow: Princeton University Press.

Hausmann, V., Williams, S. P., Hardy, C. A., & Schubert, P. (2014). Enterprise Information Management Readiness: A Survey of Current Issues, Challenges and Strategy. *Procedia Technology, 16*, 42–51. doi:10.1016/j.protcy.2014.10.066

Hazen, B. T., Boone, C. A., Ezell, J. D., & Jones Farmer, L. A. (2014). Data quality for data science, predictive analytics and Big Data in supply chain management: An introduction to the problem and suggestions for research and applications. *International Journal of Production Economics, 154*, 72–80. doi:10.1016/j.ijpe.2014.04.018

Heang, R. (2017). *Literature review of business intelligence*. Academic Press.

He, D., Chen, C., Chan, S., & Bu, J. (2012). Secure and efficient handover authentication based on bilinear pairing functions. *IEEE Transactions on Wireless Communications, 11*(1), 48–53. doi:10.1109/TWC.2011.110811.111240

Henke, N., & Bughin, J. (2016, December). *The Age of Analytics: Competing in a Data Driven World*. McKinsey Global Institute.

Henley, W. E., & Hand, D. J. (1997). Construction of a k-nearest neighbour credit-scoring system. *IMA Journal of Management Mathematics, 8*(4), 305–321. doi:10.1093/imaman/8.4.305

Hiller, J., & Russel, R. (2013). The challenge and imperative of private sector cybersecurity: An international comparison. *Computer Law & Security Review, 29*(3), 236–245. doi:10.1016/j.clsr.2013.03.003

Hjortdal, M. (2011). China's use of cyber warfare: Espionage meets strategic deterrence. *The Journal of Strategic Studies, 4*(2), 1–24.

Hoang, D., & Ruckes, M. (2017). Corporate risk management, product market competition, and disclosure. *Journal of Financial Intermediation, 30*, 107–121. doi:10.1016/j.jfi.2016.07.003

Hoffman, S., & Podgurski, A. (2013). Big Bad Data: Law, Public Health, and Biomedical Databases. *The Journal of Law, Medicine & Ethics, 41*(1), 56–60. doi:10.1111/jlme.12040 PMID:23590742

Hogarth, R. M., & Soyer, E. (2015). Using Simulated Experience to Make Sense of Big Data. *MIT Sloan Management Review, 56*(2), 49–54.

Holsapplea, C., Lee-Postb, A., & Pakath, R. (2014). A unified foundation for business analytics. *Decision Support Systems, 64*, 130–141. doi:10.1016/j.dss.2014.05.013

Hong Kong Corporate Governance: a practical guide a practical guide. (2016). Retrieved from http://www.hkcg2014.com/pdf/hong-kong-corporate-governance-a-practical-guide.pdf

Hong, D., & Hwang, C. (2005). Interval regression analysis using quadratic loss support vector machine. *IEEE Transactions on Fuzzy Systems, 13*(2), 229–237. doi:10.1109/TFUZZ.2004.840133

Hong, J., Kim, J., & Cho, J. (2010). The trend of the security research for the insider cyber threat. *International Journal of Future Generation Communication and Networking, 3*(2), 31–40.

Ho, S. M., Kao, D., & Wu, W.-Y. (2018). Following the breadcrumbs: Timestamp pattern identification for cloud forensics. *Digital Investigation, 24*, 79–94. doi:10.1016/j.diin.2017.12.001

Howarth, F. (2014, September 2). *The Role of Human Error in Successful Security Attacks*. Retrieved from SecurityIntelligence: https://securityintelligence.com/the-role-of-human-error-in-successful-security-attacks/

Howson, C., Sallam, R. L., & Richa, J. L. (2018, Feb 26). *Magic Quadrant for Analytics and Business Intelligence Platforms*. Retrieved Aug 16, 2018, from Gartner: www.gartner.com

Huang, S.-C. (2011). Using Gaussian process based kernel classifiers for credit rating forecasting. *Expert Systems with Applications, 38*(7), 8607–8611. doi:10.1016/j.eswa.2011.01.064

Huang, S.-C., Chuang, P. J., Wu, C. F., & Lai, H. J. (2010). Chaos-based support vector regressions for exchange rate forecasting. *Expert Systems with Applications, 37*(12), 8590–8598. doi:10.1016/j.eswa.2010.06.001

Hu, L., Wang, Z., Han, Q.-L., & Liu, X. (2018). State estimation under false data injection attacks: Security analysis and system protection. *Automatica, 87*, 176–183. doi:10.1016/j.automatica.2017.09.028

IBM. (2013). IBM SPSS Statistics for Windows (21st ed.). International Business Machines Corporation (IBM).

IDC. (2012). *Digital Universe study*. Retrieved January 1, 2017, from: http://www.kdnuggets.com/2012/12/idc-digital-universe-2020.html

IHTSDO. (2018). *SNOMED-CT*. Retrieved from https://www.snomed.org

Imad, B.-H. (2017). Bayesian credit ratings: A random forest alternative approach. *Communications in Statistics. Theory and Methods, 46*(15), 7289–7300. doi:10.1080/03610926.2016.1148730

Inoubli, W., Aridhi, S., Mezni, H., Maddouri, M., & Nguifo, E. M. (2018). An experimental survey on big data frameworks. *Future Generation Computer Systems*, 1–19.

Institute, S. (n.d.). *Products & Solutions A- Z*. Retrieved from SAS/ACCESS® Software: https://www.sas.com

Intelligent Robots Development and Distribution Promotion Act. (2008). Retrieved from http://elaw.klri.re.kr/eng_mobile/viewer.do?hseq=17399&type=part&key=18

Inukollu, V. N., Keshamoni, D. D., Kang, T., & Inukolla, M. (2014). Factors influencing quality of mobile apps: Role o mobile app development life cycle. *International Journal of Software Engineering and Its Applications, 5*(5), 15–34. doi:10.5121/ijsea.2014.5502

Ito, J., & Hui, J. (2017). *Shift*. Moscow: MIF.

Janiesch, C., Matzner, M., & Müller, O. (2012). Beyond process monitoring: A proof-of-concept of event-driven business activity management. *Business Process Management Journal, 18*(4), 625–643. doi:10.1108/14637151211253765

Janis, I. L. (1972). *Victims of groupthink: a psychological study of foreign-policy decisions and fiascoes*. Academic Press.

Janis, I. (1972). *Victims of group-think*. Boston: Houghton Mifflin.

Janssen, M., Van der Voort, H., & Wahyudi, A. (2017). Factors influencing big data decision-making quality. *Journal of Business Research, 70*, 338–345. doi:10.1016/j.jbusres.2016.08.007

Jatoth, C., Gangadharan, G., Fiore, U., & Buyya, R. (2017). QoS-aware Big service composition using MapReduce based evolutionary algorithm with guided mutation. *Future Generation Computer Systems*, 1–11.

Jensen, M., & Meckling, W. (1976). Theory of the firm: Managerial Behavior, Agency costs and Ownership Structure. *Journal of Financial Economics, 3*(4), 305–360. doi:10.1016/0304-405X(76)90026-X

John, G. (2013). *The Age of Artificial Intelligence*. Retrieved from TEDxLondonBusinessSchool: https://www.youtube.com/watch?v=0qOf7SX2CS4

Jones, S. (2017). Corporate bankruptcy prediction: a high dimensional analysis. *Review of Accounting Studies, 22*(3), 1366.

Jones, S., Johnstone, D., & Wilson, R. (2016). Predicting Corporate Bankruptcy: An Evaluation of Alternative Statistical Frameworks. *Journal of Business Finance & Accounting, 44*, 1–2. doi:10.1111/jbfa.12218

Jovanovi, U., Stimec, A., & Vladusi, D. (2015). Big-data analytics: A critical review and some future directions. *International Journal of Business Intelligence and Data Mining, 10*(4), 337–355. doi:10.1504/IJBIDM.2015.072211

Jungwirth, D., & Haluza, D. (2017). Information and communication technology and the future of healthcare: Results of a multi-scenario Delphi survey. *Health Informatics Journal*. doi:10.1177/1460458217704256 PMID:28438103

Kahneman, D. (2014). *Thinking, Fast and Slow*. Moscow: AST.

Kahneman, D., & Tversky, A. (1987). Rational choice and the framing of decisions. *The Journal of Business*, (4), 251–278.

Kakria, P., Tripathi, N., & Kitipawang, P. (2015). A real-time health monitoring system for remote cardiac patients using smartphone and wearable sensors. *International Journal of Telemedicine and Applications, 2015*, 8. doi:10.1155/2015/373474 PMID:26788055

Kalid, N., Zaidan, A. A., Zaidan, B. B., Salman, O. H., Hashim, M., & Muzammil, H. (2018). Based Real Time Remote Health Monitoring Systems: A Review on Patients Prioritization and Related "Big Data" Using Body Sensors information and Communication Technology. *Journal of Medical Systems, 42*(2), 30. doi:10.100710916-017-0883-4 PMID:29288419

Kalra, D., Beale, T., & Heard, S. (2005). The openEHR foundation. *Studies in Health Technology and Informatics, 115*, 153–173. PMID:16160223

Kamel, S. (2008). DSS experience in Africa – cases from Egypt. In Handbook on Decision Support Systems 2. Springer-Verlag.

Kamel, S. (1992). The governorates information and decision support centers project. *Proceedings of the United Nations Seminar on Urban Information Systems and their Applications in Developing Countries*.

Kamel, S. (1993). Decision support in the governorates level in Egypt. *Proceedings of the 4th Information Resources Management Association International Conference (IRMA) on challenges for information management in a world economy*, 390–398.

Kantardzic, M. (2011). *Data Mining: Concepts, Models, Methods, and Algorithms*. Hoboken, NJ: Wiley & IEEE Press. doi:10.1002/9781118029145

Karim, H. V. (2007). *Strategic security management: a risk assessment guide for decision makers*. Amsterdam: Elsevier.

Kauffman, R. J., Srivastava, J., & Vayghan, J. (2012). Business and data analytics: New innovations for the management of e-commerce. *Electronic Commerce Research and Applications*, *11*(2), 85–88. doi:10.1016/j.elerap.2012.01.001

Kerikmäe, D., & Rull, A. (2016). *The Future of Law and eTechnologies*. Springer. doi:10.1007/978-3-319-26896-5

Kesan, P. J., & Hayes, M. C. (2012). Mitigative counterstriking: Self-defense and deterrence in cyberspace. *Harvard Journal of Law & Technology*, *25*(2), 474–529.

Kessel, P. v., Layman, J., Blackmore, J., Burnet, I., & Azuma, Y. (2014). *Insights on governance, risk and compliance: Big data, changing the way businesses compete and operate*. Ernest and Young.

Khana, N., & Al-Yasirib, A. (2016). Identifying Cloud Security Threats to Strengthen Cloud Computing. *Procedia Computer Science*, *94*, 485–490. doi:10.1016/j.procs.2016.08.075

Khan, S., Gani, A., Wahab, A. W. A., Shiraz, M., & Ahmad, I. (2016). Network forensics: Review, taxonomy, and open challenges. *Journal of Network and Computer Applications*, *66*, 214–235. doi:10.1016/j.jnca.2016.03.005

Khemakhem, S., & Boujelbene, Y. (2015). Credit Risk Prediction: A comparative study between discriminant analysis and the neural network approach. *Accounting and Management Information Systems*, *14*(1), 60–78.

Kim, S. H., Wang, Q.-H., & Ullrich, J. B. (2012). A Comparative Study of Cyberattacks. *Communications of the ACM*, *55*(3), 66. doi:10.1145/2093548.2093568

KING IV Report on corporate governance for South Africa. (2016). Retrieved from https://c.ymcdn.com/sites/www.iodsa.co.za/resource/resmgr/king_iv/King_IV_Report/IoDSA_King_IV_Report_-_WebVe.pdf

Klein, A. (2017, July). Hard Drive Cost Per Gigabyte. *Backblaze*.

Klonoff, D. C., Ahn, D., & Drincic, A. (2017). Continuous glucose monitoring: A review of the technology and clinical use. *Diabetes Research and Clinical Practice*, *133*, 178–192. doi:10.1016/j.diabres.2017.08.005 PMID:28965029

Knight, K. (1967). A descriptive model of the intra-firm innovation process. *The Journal of Business of the University of Chicago*, 40.

Kolkowska, E., Karlsson, F., & Hedström, K. (2017). Towards analysing the rationale of information security non-compliance: Devising a Value-Based Compliance analysis method. *The Journal of Strategic Information Systems*, *26*(1), 39–57. doi:10.1016/j.jsis.2016.08.005

Kowalczyk, M., Buxmann, P., & Besier, J. (2013). *Investigating business intelligence and analytics from a decision process perspective: a structured literature review - analytics from a decsion process perspective*. ECIS. Retrieved from http://aisel.aisnet.org/ecis2013_cr/126

Kozhirbayev, Z., & Sinnott, R. O. (2017). A performance comparison of container-based technologies for the Cloud. *Future Generation Computer Systems*, *68*, 175–182. doi:10.1016/j.future.2016.08.025

Krase, H., & Nyatepe-Coo, E. (2012). *Identifying and supporting academically at-risk students in Canadian universities*. Retrieved from http://www.uky.edu/ie/sites/www.uky.edu.ie/files/uploads/BP_Identifying%26 SupportingAcademically At Risk Students . . .pdf

Krombholz, K., Hobel, H., Huber, M., & Weippl, E. (2015). Advanced social engineering attacks. *Journal of Information Security and Applications, 22*, 113–122. doi:10.1016/j.jisa.2014.09.005

Kshetri, N. (2014). Big datas impact on privacy, security and consumer welfare. *Telecommunications Policy, 38*(11), 1134–1145. doi:10.1016/j.telpol.2014.10.002

Kumar, K., & Haynes, J. D. (2003). Forecasting credit ratings using an ANN and statistical techniques. *International Journal of Business Studies, 11*(1), 91-108.

Kumara, B. T., Paik, I., & Zhang, J. (2015). Ontology-Based Workflow Generation for Intelligent Big Data Analytics. In *IEEE International Conference on Web Services*. New York, NY: IEEE. 10.1109/ICWS.2015.72

Kumar, K., & Bhattacharya, S. (2006). Artificial neural network vs linear discriminant analysis in credit ratings forecast. *Review of Accounting and Finance, 5*(3), 216–227. doi:10.1108/14757700610686426

Kurzweil, R. (2005). *The Singularity Is Near*. New York: Viking.

Kuznetsov, E. (2017). The last line of defense of a person is surrendered. *The Platform, 2*, 6-12.

Labrinidis, A., & Jagadish, H. V. (2012). Challenges and opportunities with big data. *Proceedings of the VLDB Endowment International Conference on Very Large Data Bases, 5*(12), 2032–2033. doi:10.14778/2367502.2367572

Lake, P., & Drake, R. (2014). *Information systems management in the big data era*. Springer International Publishing; doi:10.1007/978-3-319-13503-8

Landoll, D. J. (2010). *The security risk assessment handbook: a complete guide for performing security risk assessment* (2nd ed.). New York: CRC Press.

Laney, D. (2001). *3D data management: controlling data volume, velocity, and variety, META Group, Tech. Rep.* Retrieved 10 27, 2015, from http://blogs.gartner.com/doug-laney/files/2012/01/ad949-3D-Data-Management-Controlling-Data-Volume-Velocity-and-Variety.pdf

Laney, D., & Jain, A. (2017, June 20). *100 Data and Analytics Predictions Through*. Retrieved August 04, 2018, from Gartner: https://www.gartner.com/events-na/data-analytics/wp-content/uploads/sites/5/2017/10/Data-and-Analytics-Predictions.pdf

Larson, E. K., & Gray, C. F. (2011). *Project Management: The Managerial Process* (5th ed.). New York: McGraw-Hill.

Lasconjarias, G., & Larsen, J. A. (2015, December 17). *New Research Division Publication - NATO's Response to Hybrid Threats*. Retrieved from NATO Defence college: http://www.ndc.nato.int/download/downloads.php?icode=471

Laudon, K., & Laudon, J. (2014). *Essentials of Management Information Systems*. Boston: Prentice hall.

Lauría, E. J. M., Baron, J. D., Devireddy, M., Sundararaju, V., & Jayaprakash, S. M. (2012). Mining academic data to improve college student retention: an open source perspective. *Proceedings of the Second International Conference on Learning Analytics and Knowledge*, 139–142. 10.1145/2330601.2330637

Lave, J., & Wenger, E. (1998). *Communities of practice*. Academic Press.

Lazer, D. M., Kennedy, R., King, G., & Vespignani, A. (2014). The parable of Google Flu: Traps in big data analysis. *Science Journal, 343*(1), 1203–1205. doi:10.1126cience.1248506 PMID:24626916

Leszczynski, A. (2015). Spatial big data and anxieties of control. *Environment and Planning. D, Society & Space, 33*(6), 965–984. doi:10.1177/0263775815595814

Liao, S.-K., Cai, W.-Q., Handsteiner, J., Liu, B., Yin, J., Zhang, L., ... Pan, J.-W. (2018). Satellite-Relayed Intercontinental Quantum Network. *Physical Review Letters, 120*(3), 030501–030505. doi:10.1103/PhysRevLett.120.030501 PMID:29400544

Liaudanskienel, R., Ustinovicius, L., & Bogdanovicius, A. (2009). Evaluation of Construction Process Safety Solutions Using the TOPSIS Method. *Inzinerine Ekonomika-Engineering Economics, 64*(4), 32–40.

Libert, B. (2013). *Governance 2.0: the future for boards in the age of big data.* Retrieved from https://www.kornferry.com/institute/579-corporate-governance-2-0-the-boardroom-collides-with-the-digital-age

Lichtblau, E., & Weilandaug, N. (2016). Hacker Releases More Democratic Party Files, Renewing Fears of Russian Meddling. *New York Times*, pp. A12-A14.

Li, K. F., Rusk, D., & Song, F. (2013). Predicting student academic performance. *Seventh International Conference on Complex, Intelligent, and Software Intensive Systems Predicting*, 27–33.

Lilley, M., & Frean, M. (2005) Neural Networks: A Replacement for Gaussian Processes? In Intelligent Data Engineering and Automated Learning - IDEAL 2005 (pp. 195-212). Springer. doi:10.1007/11508069_26

Lin, K., Chen, D., & Tsai, W. (2016). Face-Based Heart Rate Signal Decomposition and Evaluation Using Multiple Linear Regression. *IEEE Sensors Journal, 16*(5), 1351–1360. doi:10.1109/JSEN.2015.2500032

Linkletter, C., Bingham, D., Hengartner, N., Higdon, D., & Ye, K. Q. (2006). Variable selection for Gaussian process models in computer experiments. *Technometrics, 48*(4), 478–490. doi:10.1198/004017006000000228

Lin, S., Huang, R., & Chiueh, T. (1998). A tunable Gaussian/square function computation circuit for analog neural networks. *IEEE Transactions on Circuits and Systems. 2, Analog and Digital Signal Processing, 45*(3), 441–446. doi:10.1109/82.664259

Lin, Z., Lin, D., & Pei, D. (2017). Practical construction of ring LFSRs and ring FCSRs with low diffusion delay for hardware cryptographic applications. *Cryptography and Communications, 9*(4), 431–440. doi:10.100712095-016-0183-8

Liu, G., & Yang, H. (2017). Self-organizing network for variable clustering. *Annals of Operations Research.*

Loch, K., Straub, S., & Kamel, S. (2003). Diffusing the internet in the Arab world: The role of social norms and technological culturation. *IEEE Transactions on Engineering Management, 50*(1), 45–63. doi:10.1109/TEM.2002.808257

Lohr, S. (2012, February 11). The Age of Big Data. *The New York Times*, pp. 1-5.

Lord, N. (2017, February 28). *Social Engineering Attacks: Common Techniques & How to Prevent an Attack.* Retrieved from Digital Guardian: https://digitalguardian.com/blog/social-engineering-attacks-common-techniques-how-prevent-attack

Low, M., & MacMillan, I. (1988). Entrepreneurship: Past research and future challenges. *Journal of Management, 14*(2), 139–161. doi:10.1177/014920638801400202

Lowry, P. B., & Wilson, D. (2016). Creating agile organizations through IT: The influence of internal IT service perceptions on IT service quality and IT agility. *The Journal of Strategic Information Systems, 25*(3), 211–226. doi:10.1016/j.jsis.2016.05.002

Ludoslaw, D., & Remigiusz, L. (2013). Methodological aspects and case studies of business intelligence application tools in knowledge management as corporations' strategy development. *Proceedings of the Management, Knowledge and Learning International Conference*, 1461–1468.

Luhn, H. P. (1958). A Business intelligence system. *IBM Journal of Research and Development*, *2*(4), 314–319. doi:10.1147/rd.24.0314

Lumpkin, G. T., & Dess, G. G. (1996). Clarifying the entrepreneurial orientation construct and linking it to performance. *Academy of Management Review*, *21*(1), 135–172. doi:10.5465/amr.1996.9602161568

Lumpkin, G. T., & Dess, G. G. (2001). Linking two dimensions of entrepreneurial orientation to firm performance: The moderating role of environment and industry life cycle. *Journal of Business Venturing*, *16*(5), 429–451. doi:10.1016/S0883-9026(00)00048-3

Lusher, S. J., McGuire, R., van Schaik, R. C., Nicholson, C. D., & de Vlieg, J. (2014). Data-driven medicinal chemistry in the era of big data. *Drug Discovery Today*, *19*(7), 859–868. doi:10.1016/j.drudis.2013.12.004 PMID:24361338

Malatras, A., Geneiatakis, D., & Vakalis, I. (2016). On the efficiency of user identification: A system-based approach. *International Journal of Information Security*, *15*(1), 1–19.

Malerba, D., Esposito, F., Ceci, M., & Appice, A. (2004). Top-down induction of model trees with regression and splitting nodes. *IEEE Transactions on Pattern Analysis and Machine Intelligence*, *26*(5), 612–625. doi:10.1109/TPAMI.2004.1273937 PMID:15460282

Management Sciences in the Modern World. (2018). Book of reports of Scientific-Practical conference: Financial University under the Government of the Russian Federation. Saint-Petersburg: Publishing house "Real Economy".

Manyika, J., Chui, M., Brown, B., Bughin, J., Dobbs, R., Roxburgh, C., & Hung Byers, A. (2011). *Big data: The Next Frontier for Innovation, Competition, and Productivity*. Washington, DC: McKinsey Global Institute.

Marr, B. (2016). *Big Data in Practice (Use Cases) - How 45 Successful Companies Used Big Data Analytics to Deliver Extraordinary Results*. Wiley. doi:10.1002/9781119278825

Martin, A., Raponi, S., Combe, T., & Pietro, R. D. (2018). Docker ecosystem – Vulnerability Analysis. *Computer Communications*, *122*, 30–43. doi:10.1016/j.comcom.2018.03.011

Martinez-Caro, J.-M., Aledo-Hernandez, A.-J., Guillen-Perez, A., Sanchez-Iborra, R., & Cano, M.-D. (2018). A Comparative Study of Web Content Management Systems. *Information*, *9*(2), 27. doi:10.3390/info9020027

Mateos, G., Bazerque, J., & Giannakis, G. (2010). Distributed Sparse Linear Regression. *IEEE Transactions on Signal Processing*, *58*(10), 5262–5276. doi:10.1109/TSP.2010.2055862

Matney, S. A., Settergren, T., Carrington, J. M., Richesson, R. L., Sheide, A., & Westra, B. L. (2017). Standardizing Physiologic Assessment Data to Enable Big Data Analytics. *Western Journal of Nursing Research*, *39*(1), 63–77. doi:10.1177/0193945916659471 PMID:27435084

McAfee, A., & Brynjolfsson, E. (2012). Big data: The management revolution. *Harvard Business Review*, (October): 61–68. PMID:23074865

McKinsey Global Institute (2016, December). *The age of analytics: Competing in a Data-driven world*. McKinsey Global Institute.

McKinsey Global Institute. (2011). *Big data: The next frontier for innovation, competition, and productivity*. McKinsey Global Institute.

McKinsey Global Institute. (2017). *A future that works: automation, employment, and productivity, US*. Retrieved from https://www.mckinsey.com/~/media/mckinsey/featured%20insights/Digital%20Disruption/Harnessing%20automation%20for%20a%20future%20that%20works/MGI-A-future-that-works-Executive-summary.ashx

McKinsey. (2011, May). *Big data: The next frontier for innovation, competition, and productivity.* Retrieved from McKinsey Global Institute: http://www.mckinsey.com/business-functions/business-technology/our-insights/big-data-the-next-frontier-for-innovation

McQuade, S. (2006). *Understanding and Managing Cybercrime.* Boston: Allyn & Bacon.

Mendling, J. (2018). Blockchains for Business Process Management - Challenges and Opportunities. *ACM Trans. Manag. Inform. Syst., 9.*

Merton, R. K. (1949). *Social theory and social structure.* New York: Free Press.

Microsoft. (n.d.b). *Power Pivot: Powerful data analysis and data modeling in Excel.* Retrieved from https://support.office.com/en-us/article/Power-Pivot-Powerful-data-analysis-and-data-modeling-in-Excel-A9C2C6E2-CC49-4976-A7D7-40896795D045

Mikalef, P., Pappas, I. O., Krogstie, J., & Giannakos, M. (2017). Big data analytics capabilities: A systematic literature review and research agenda. *Information Systems and e-Business Management,* 1–32. doi:10.100710257-017-0362-y

Milovidov, V.D. (2017). Corporate governance 2.0: Evolution of the system of corporate relations in digital society. *Problems of the National Strategy, 4*(43), 171-189.

Mintzberg, G., Raisinghani, D., & Théoret, A. (1976). The Structure of "Unstructured" Decision Processes. *Administrative Science Quarterly, 21*(2), 246–275. doi:10.2307/2392045

Mitra, S., Pal, S. K., & Mitra, P. (2002). Data mining in soft computing framework: A survey. *IEEE Transactions on Neural Networks, 13*(1), 3–14. doi:10.1109/72.977258 PMID:18244404

MITSloan & BCG. (2017). *Global executive study. Reshaping Business With AI.* Retrieved from https://sloanreview.mit.edu/projects/reshaping-business-with-artificial-intelligence/

Mittelman, J. H. (2011). Global (in) security: The confluence of intelligence and will. *Global Change, Peace & Security, 23*(2), 135–139. doi:10.1080/14781158.2011.580954

Miyamoto, M. (2014). Credit risk assessment for a small bank by using a multinomial logistic regression model. *International Journal of Finance and Accounting, 3*(5), 327–334.

Mkrttchian, V., & Aleshina, E. (2017i). Tolerance as Reflection of Sliding Mode in Psychology. In Sliding Mode in Intellectual Control and Communication: Emerging Research and Opportunities (pp. 91–99). Hershey, PA: IGI Global/ doi:10.4018/978-1-5225-2292-8.ch009

Mkrttchian, V., & Stephanova, G. (2013). Training of Avatar Moderator in Sliding Mode Control Environment for Virtual Project Management. In Enterprise Resource Planning: Concepts, Methodologies, Tools, and Applications (pp. 1376-1405). Hershey, PA: IGI Global. Doi:10.4018/978-1-4666-4153-2.ch074

Mkrttchian, V., Kataev, M., Hwang, W., Bedi, S., & Fedotova, A. (2016). Using Plug-Avatars "hhh" Technology Education as Service-Oriented Virtual Learning Environment in Sliding Mode. In Leadership and Personnel Management: Concepts, Methodologies, Tools, and Applications (pp. 890-902). Hershey, PA: IGI Global. Doi:10.4018/978-1-4666-9624-2.ch039

Mkrttchian, V. (2011). Use 'hhh" technology in transformative models of online education. In G. Kurubacak & T. Vokan Yuzer (Eds.), *Handbook of research on transformative online education and liberation: Models for social equality* (pp. 340–351). Hershey, PA: IGI Global. doi:10.4018/978-1-60960-046-4.ch018

Mkrttchian, V. (2012). Avatar manager and student reflective conversations as the base for describing meta-communication model. In G. Kurubacak, T. Vokan Yuzer, & U. Demiray (Eds.), *Meta-communication for reflective online conversations: Models for distance education* (pp. 340–351). Hershey, PA: IGI Global. doi:10.4018/978-1-61350-071-2.ch005

Mkrttchian, V., & Aleshina, E. (2017). *Sliding Mode in Intellectual Control and Communication: Emerging Research and Opportunities*. Hershey, PA: IGI Global. doi:10.4018/978-1-5225-2292-8

Mkrttchian, V., & Aleshina, E. (2017a). The Sliding Mode Technique and Technology (SM T&T) According to Vardan Mkrttchian in Intellectual Control(IC). In *Sliding Mode in Intellectual Control and Communication: Emerging Research and Opportunities* (pp. 1–9). Hershey, PA: IGI Global. doi:10.4018/978-1-5225-2292-8.ch001

Mkrttchian, V., & Aleshina, E. (2017b). Sliding Mode in Virtual Communications. In *Sliding Mode in Intellectual Control and Communication: Emerging Research and Opportunities* (pp. 10–21). Hershey, PA: IGI Global. doi:10.4018/978-1-5225-2292-8.ch002

Mkrttchian, V., & Aleshina, E. (2017c). Sliding Mode in Real Communication. In *Sliding Mode in Intellectual Control and Communication: Emerging Research and Opportunities* (pp. 22–29). Hershey, PA: IGI Global. doi:10.4018/978-1-5225-2292-8.ch003

Mkrttchian, V., & Aleshina, E. (2017d). Digital Control Models of Continuous Education of Persons with Disabilities Act (IDEA) and Agents in Sliding Mode. In *Sliding Mode in Intellectual Control and Communication: Emerging Research and Opportunities* (pp. 31–62). Hershey, PA: IGI Global. doi:10.4018/978-1-5225-2292-8.ch004

Mkrttchian, V., & Aleshina, E. (2017e). Terms of Adaptive Organization of the Educational Process of Persons with Disabilities with the Use of Open and Distance Learning Technologies (Open and Distance Learning – ODL). In *Sliding Mode in Intellectual Control and Communication: Emerging Research and Opportunities* (pp. 63–69). Hershey, PA: IGI Global. doi:10.4018/978-1-5225-2292-8.ch005

Mkrttchian, V., & Aleshina, E. (2017f). Providing Quality Education for Persons With Disabilities Through the Implementation of Individual Educational Programs Managed by the Intelligent Agents in the Sliding Mode. In *Sliding Mode in Intellectual Control and Communication: Emerging Research and Opportunities* (pp. 70–76). Hershey, PA: IGI Global. doi:10.4018/978-1-5225-2292-8.ch006

Mkrttchian, V., & Aleshina, E. (2017g). Regulation of Discourse in Accordance With the Speech Regulation Factors Creating Conditions for Adaptability to the Situation. In *Sliding Mode in Intellectual Control and Communication: Emerging Research and Opportunities* (pp. 77–85). Hershey, PA: IGI Global. doi:10.4018/978-1-5225-2292-8.ch007

Mkrttchian, V., & Aleshina, E. (2017h). Complex Social, Medical, Psychological, and Educational Support for People with Disability Act (IDEA). In *Sliding Mode in Intellectual Control and Communication: Emerging Research and Opportunities* (pp. 86–90). Hershey, PA: IGI Global. doi:10.4018/978-1-5225-2292-8.ch008

Mkrttchian, V., Amirov, D., & Belyanina, L. (2017). Optimizing an Online Learning Course Using Automatic Curating in Sliding Mode. In N. Ostashewski, J. Howell, & M. Cleveland-Innes (Eds.), *Optimizing K-12 Education through Online and Blended Learning* (pp. 213–224). Hershey, PA: IGI Global. doi:10.4018/978-1-5225-0507-5.ch011

Mkrttchian, V., Aysmontas, B., Uddin, M., Andreev, A., & Vorovchenko, N. (2015). The Academic views from Moscow Universities of the Cyber U-Learning on the Future of Distance Education at Russia and Ukraine. In G. Eby & T. Vokan Yuzer (Eds.), *Identification, Evaluation, and Perceptions of Distance Education Experts* (pp. 32–45). Hershey, PA: IGI Global. doi:10.4018/978-1-4666-8119-4.ch003

Mkrttchian, V., Bershadsky, A., Bozhday, A., & Fionova, L. (2015). Model in SM of DEE Based on Service Oriented Interactions at Dynamic Software Product Lines. In G. Eby & T. Vokan Yuzer (Eds.), *Identification, Evaluation, and Perceptions of Distance Education Experts* (pp. 230–247). Hershey, PA: IGI Global. doi:10.4018/978-1-4666-8119-4.ch014

Mkrttchian, V., Kataev, M., Hwang, W., Bedi, S., & Fedotova, A. (2014). Using Plug-Avatars "hhh" Technology Education as Service-Oriented Virtual Learning Environment in Sliding Mode. In G. Eby & T. Vokan Yuzer (Eds.), *Emerging Priorities and Trends in Distance Education: Communication, Pedagogy, and Technology*. Hershey, PA: IGI Global. doi:10.4018/978-1-4666-5162-3.ch004

Mkrttchian, V., & Stephanova, G. (2013). Training of Avatar Moderator in Sliding Mode Control. In G. Eby & T. Vokan Yuzer (Eds.), *Project Management Approaches for Online Learning Design* (pp. 175–203). Hershey, PA: IGI Global. doi:10.4018/978-1-4666-2830-4.ch009

Mohamed, H., & Robert, P. (2010). *Dynamic Tree Algorithms.* arXiv:0809.3577 [math.PR]

Mohammed, F., Ibrahim, O., & Ithnin, N. (2016). Factors influencing cloud computing adoption for e-government implementation in developing countries: Instrument development. *Journal of Systems and Information Technology*, *18*(3), 297–327. doi:10.1108/JSIT-01-2016-0001

Molotnikov, A. E. (2017). *The forth industrial revolution and modern understanding of corporate business forms. Business law. N 2* (pp. 3–16). Moscow: Lawyer.

Mood, D. (2016, February 24). *Post-Quantum Cryptography: NIST plan for the future.* Retrieved from pqcrypto2016.jp: https://pqcrypto2016.jp/data/pqc2016_nist_announcement.pdf

Moody's Investor service. (2017). *Moody's rating system in brief.* Retrieved from https://www.moodys.com/sites/products/ProductAttachments/Moody's%20Rating%20System.pdf

Moorthy, J., Lahiri, R., Biswas, N., Sanyal, D., Ranjan, J., Nanath, K., & Ghosh, P. (2015). *Big data: Prospects and challenges.* Sage India.

Morabito, V. (2015). *Big data and analytics: strategic and Organizational impacts.* Springer International Publishing. doi:10.1007/978-3-319-10665-6

Möslein, F. (2017). Robots in the Boardroom: AI and Corporate Law. *Research Handbook on the Law of Artificial Intelligence*, 10-15.

Mourad, A., Laverdiere, M.-A., & Debbabi, M. (2008). An aspect-oriented approach for the systematic security hardening of code. *Computers & Security*, *27*(3-4), 101–114. doi:10.1016/j.cose.2008.04.003

Moutinho, L., Rita, P., & Li, S. (2006). Strategic diagnostics and management decision making: A hybrid knowledge-based approach. *Intell. Sys. Acc. Fin. Mgmt*, *14*(3), 129–155. doi:10.1002/isaf.281

Muhtaroglu, F. C. P., Demir, S., Obali, M., & Girgin, C. (2013). Business model canvas perspective on big data applications. *Big Data*, *2013*, 32–37.

Mumtaz, H., Alshayeb, M., Mahmood, S., & Niazi, M. (2018). An empirical study to improve software security through the application of code refactoring. *Information and Software Technology*, *96*, 112–125. doi:10.1016/j.infsof.2017.11.010

Nagy, H. M., Aly, W. M., & Hegazy, O. F. (2013). An educational data mining system for advising higher education students. *International Journal of Computer, Electrical, Automation Control and Information Engineering*, *7*(10), 622–626.

National Research Council. (2013). *Frontiers in Massive Data Analysis.* Washington, DC: The National Research Press.

Negash, S. (2004). Business intelligence. *Communications of the Association for Information Systems, 13*, 177–195. doi:10.17705/1CAIS.01315

Negnevitsky, M. (2011). *Artificial intelligence: a guide to intelligent systems*. Harlow, UK: Addison Wesley/Pearson.

New Generation of Artificial Intelligence Development Plan. (2017). Retrieved from https://chinacopyrightandmedia. wordpress.com/2017/07/20/a-next-generation-artificial-intelligence-development-plan/

New Scientist. (2007). *South Korea creates ethical code for righteous robots*. Retrieved from https://www.newscientist. com/article/dn11334-south-korea-creates-ethical-code-for-righteous-robots/

Nikishova, M. I. (2018). *Application of AI technologies in the system of corporate governance* (Unpublished PhD thesis). Financial University under the Government of the Russian Federation, Russia, Moscow.

NIST. (2015). *Reports on Computer Systems Technology 1500-5. Big Data Public Working Group*. Gaithersburg, MD: National Institute of Standards and Technology.

NIST. (2017, March 1). *Cybersecurity Framework Overview*. Retrieved from NIST: https://www.nist.gov/file/354081

Nofal, M. I., & Yusof, Z. M. (2013). Integration of business intelligence and enterprise resource planning within organizations. *Procedia Technology, 11*, 658–665. doi:10.1016/j.protcy.2013.12.242

NVP. (2017). *Big Data Executive Survey*. Retrieved from http://newvantage.com/wp-content/uploads/2017/01/Big-Data-Executive-Survey-2017-Executive-Summary.pdf

Nyce, C. (2007). A. Predictive analytics white paper. American Institute for CPCU. *Insurance Institute of America*, 9-10.

OECD. (2015). *G20/OECD Principles of Corporate Governance*. Retrieved from http://www.oecd.org/daf/ca/principles-corporate-governance.htm

Ohlhorst, F. (2013). *Big Data Analytics: Turning Big Data into Big Money*. John Wiley & Sons, Inc.

Ohm, P. (2010). Broken promises of privacy: Responding to the surprising failure of anonymization. *UCLA Law Review Journal, 57*(1), 1701–1818.

Okamoto, T., & Takashima, K. (2015). Achieving short ciphertexts or short secret-keys for adaptively secure general inner-product encryption. *Designs, Codes and Cryptography, 77*(2), 725–771. doi:10.100710623-015-0131-1

openEHR. (2018). *Clinical Knowledge Manager*. Retrieved from http://openehr.org/ckm/

Osuna, E., Freund, R., & Girosi, F. (1997). An Improved Training Algorithm for Support Vector Machines. *Proceedings of the IEEE Signal Processing Society Workshop on Neural Networks for Signal Processing VII*, 276-285. 10.1109/NNSP.1997.622408

Panko, R. (1998). What we know about spreadsheet errors. *Journal of Organizational and End User Computing, 10*(2), 15–21. doi:10.4018/joeuc.1998040102

Pascaud, L. (2015). *Smart data at the heart of Prosocial Brands, Kantar Added Value*. Retrieved from: http://added-value. com/2015/01/23/smart-data-at-the-heart-of-pro-social-brands/

Passalis, N., & Tefas, A. (2018). Learning bag-of-embedded-words representations for textual information retrieval. *Pattern Recognition, 81*, 254–267. doi:10.1016/j.patcog.2018.04.008

Pasta, D. (2009). *Learning When to Be Discrete: Continuous vs. Categorical Predictors*. San Francisco, CA: ICON Clinical Research.

Pat Hanrahan, C. C. (n.d.). *Combine, shape, and clean your data for analysis with Tableau Prep*. Retrieved from https://www.tableau.com/products/prep

Patel, N., & Upadhyay, S. (2012). Study of Various Decision Tree Pruning Methods with their Empirical Comparison in WEKA. *International Journal of Computers and Applications*, *60*(12), 20–25. doi:10.5120/9744-4304

Pearson, Y. (2017). *The interview for the Mail.ru company*. Retrieved from https://hi-tech.mail.ru/review/ian-pearson/

Pekka Pääkkönen, D. P. (2015). Reference Architecture and Classification of Technologies, Products and Services for Big Data Systems. *Big Data Research*, *2*(4), 166–186. doi:10.1016/j.bdr.2015.01.001

Peltier, T. R. (2010). *Information security risk analysis* (3rd ed.). New York: CRC Press, Auerbach Publications.

Pettey, C., & van der Meulen, R. (2018, April 25). *Gartner Says Global Artificial Intelligence Business Value to Reach $1.2 Trillion in 2018*. Retrieved August 04, 2018, from Gartner: https://www.gartner.com/newsroom/id/3872933

Plauger, P. J. (1993). *Programming on purpose: Essays on software design*. Englewood Cliffs, NJ: Prentice Hall.

Policy Department Citizens' Rights and Constitutional Affairs. (2016). *European Civil Law Rules in Robotics*. Retrieved from http://www.europarl.europa.eu/RegData/etudes/STUD/2016/571379/IPOL_STU(2016)571379_EN.pdf

Popovič, A., Vukšić, V. B., & Bach, M. P. (2013). Supporting performance management with business process management and business intelligence: A case analysis of integration and orchestration. *International Journal of Information Management*, *33*(4), 613–619. doi:10.1016/j.ijinfomgt.2013.03.008

Porter, M. E. (1985). *Competitive Advantage: Creating and Sustaining Superior Performance*. New York: Free Press.

Powell, S. G., & Baker, K. R. (2004). *Management science: The art of modeling with spreadsheets*. Hoboken, NJ: Wiley.

Prabhakaran, S. (2017). *Top 50 ggplot2 Visualizations - The Master List*. Retrieved from r-statistics.co: http://r-statistics.co/Top50-Ggplot2-Visualizations-MasterList-R-Code.html

Pratt, M. (2017). *7 keys to a successful business intelligence strategy*. Retrieved August 1, 2018, from https://www.cio.com/article/2437838/business-intelligence/7-keys-to-a-successful-business-intelligence-strategy.html

Pressman, R., & Maxim, B. (2014). *Software engineering: A practitioner's approach*. Boston: McGraw-Hill.

Principles of Corporate Governance. (2016). Retrieved from https://businessroundtable.org/sites/default/files/Principles-of-Corporate-Governance-2016.pdf

Prokopenya, V. (2018). *Truths, half-truths and lies about artificial intelligence*. The European Financial Review. Available http://www.europeanfinancialreview.com/?p=25629

Provost, F., & Fawcett, T. (2013). *Data science for business*. Sebastopol, CA: O'Reilly Media.

PWC. (2017a). *Annual corporate directors survey*. Retrieved from https://www.pwc.com/us/en/governance-insights-center/annual-corporate-directors-survey.html

PWC. (2017b). *CEO Pulse*. Retrieved from https://www.pwc.com/gx/en/ceo-agenda/pulse.html

PWC. (2017c). *The acceleration of innovative development*. Retrieved from https://www.pwc.ru/ru/assets/pdf/artificial-intelligence-realizations-rus.pdf

Qin, B., Huang, J., Wang, Q., Luo, X., Liang, B., & Shi, W. (2017). Cecoin: A decentralized PKI mitigating MitM attacks. *Future Generation Computer Systems*, 1–11.

Quinn, A., Stranieri, A., Yearwood, J., Hafen, G., & Jelinek, H. F. (2008). AWSum-Combining Classification with Knowledge Aquisition. *Int. J. Software and Informatics*, *2*(2), 199–214.

R, P. R. (n.d.). *Understanding statistics in the behavioral sciences*. Cengage Learning.

Raffensperger, J. F. (2001). New guidelines for spreadsheets. *Proceedings of the European Spreadsheet Risks Information Group (EuSpRIG)*, 61-76.

Ragini, J. R., Anand, P. R., & Bhaskar, V. (2018). Big data analytics for disaster response and recovery through sentiment analysi. *International Journal of Information Management*, *42*, 13–24. doi:10.1016/j.ijinfomgt.2018.05.004

Raisinghani, M. S. (2004). *Business intelligence in the digital economy : opportunities, limitations, and risks*. Hershey, PA : Idea Group Pub. Retrieved from http://services.igi-global.com/resolvedoi/resolve.aspx?doi=10.4018/978-1-59140-206-0

Rauch, A., Wiklund, J., Lumpkin, G. T., & Frese, M. (2009). Entrepreneurial orientation and business performance: An assessment of past research and suggestions for the future. *Entrepreneurship Theory and Practice*, *33*(3), 761–787. doi:10.1111/j.1540-6520.2009.00308.x

Rawlings, J., Pantula, S., & Dickey, D. (1998). *Applied Regression Analysis: A Research Tool*. Springer. doi:10.1007/b98890

Rayport, J. F., & Sviokla, J. J. (1995). Exploiting the Virtual Value Chain. *Harvard Business Review*, *73*(6), 75–85.

Reinsel, D., Gantz, J., & Rydning, J. (2017, April). *Data Age 2025: The Evolution of Data to Life-Critical*. IDC White Paper.

Renaud, K., Flowerday, S., Warkentin, M., Cockshott, P., & Orgeron, C. (2018). Is the responsibilization of the cyber security risk reasonable and judicious? *Computers & Security*, *78*, 198–211. doi:10.1016/j.cose.2018.06.006

Renwick, S. L., & Martin, K. M. (2017). Practical Architectures for Deployment of Searchable Encryption in a Cloud Environment. *Cryptography*, *1*(3), 19. doi:10.3390/cryptography1030019

Reynolds, P. D. (1987). New firms: Societal contribution versus survival potential. *Journal of Business Venturing*, *2*(3), 231–246. doi:10.1016/0883-9026(87)90011-5

Rizk, N., & Kamel, S. (2013). ICT and building a knowledge society in Egypt. *International Journal of Knowledge Management*, *9*(1), 1–20. doi:10.4018/jkm.2013010101

Robbins, S., Bergman, R., Stagg, I., & Coulter, M. (2012). *Management 6*. Frenchs Forest: Pearson Australia.

Robles-Bykbaev, V., Quisi-Peralta, D., López-Nores, M., Gil-Solla, A., & García-Duque, J. (2016). *SPELTA-Miner: An expert system based on data mining and multilabel classification to design therapy plans for communication disorders*. Paper presented at the Control, Decision and Information Technologies (CoDIT), 2016 International Conference on.

Romero, C., & Ventura, S. (2010). Educational data mining: A review of the state-of-the-art. *Transactions on Systems. Man and Cybernetics - Part C: Applications and Reviews*, *40*(6), 601–618. doi:10.1109/TSMCC.2010.2053532

Ross, J. W., Beath, C. M., & Quaardgas, A. (2013). You may not need big data after all. *Harvard Business Review*, *91*(12), 90–98. PMID:23593770

Ross, R., Viscuso, P., Guissanie, G., Dempsey, K., & Riddle, M. (2016). *Protecting Controlled Unclassified Information in Nonfederal Systems*. Gaithersburg, MD: National Institute of Standards and Technology. doi:10.6028/NIST.SP.800-171r1

Rothstein, M. A. (2015). Ethical Issues in Big Data Health Research: Currents in Contemporary Bioethics. *The Journal of Law, Medicine & Ethics*, *43*(2), 425–429. doi:10.1111/jlme.12258 PMID:26242964

Rouhani, S., Asgari, S., & Mirhosseini, S. (2012). Business intelligence concepts and approaches. *American Journal of Scientific Research*, *50*, 62–75.

Russell, S., & Norvig, P. (2010). *Artificial Intelligence: A Modern Approach* (3rd ed.). Prentice Hall.

Russian dialogue of cultures and civilizations - mutual enrichment. (n.d.). Retrieved from http://svop.ru/проекты/lectorium/17025/.

Ruževičius, J., & Gedminaitė, A. (2007). Business Information Quality and its Assessment. *Inzinerine Ekonomika-Engineering Economics, 52*(2), 18–25.

Salleh, K. A., & Janczewski, L. (2016). Technical, organizational and environmental security and privacy issues of big data: A literature review. *Procedia Computer Science Journal, 100*(1), 19–28. doi:10.1016/j.procs.2016.09.119

Sanila, S., Subramanian, D. V., & Sathyalakshmi, S. (2018). Real-Time Mining Techniques: A Big Data Perspective for a Smart Future. *Indian Journal of Science and Technology, 10*(42), 1–7. doi:10.17485/ijst/2017/v10i42/120344

Sapsford, R., & Jupp, V. (Eds.). (2006). *Data collection and analysis*. Sage. doi:10.4135/9781849208802

SAS. (2017). *Predictive Analytics: What it is and why it matters, SAS*. Retrieved from: https://www.sas.com/en_us/insights/analytics/predictive-analytics.html

Sá-Soares, F., Soares, D., & Arnaud, J. (2014). Towards a Theory of Information Systems Outsourcing Risk. *Procedia Technology, 16*, 623–637. doi:10.1016/j.protcy.2014.10.011

Satell, G. (2014). Five things managers should know about the big data economy. *Forbes*.

Schalkoff, R. J. (2011). *Intelligent Systems: Principles, Paradigms, and Pragmatics*. Boston: Jones and Bartlett Publishers.

Schaupp, L. C., & Bélanger, F. (2014). The value of social Media for small businesses. *Journal of Information Systems, 28*(1), 187–207. doi:10.2308/isys-50674

Schloeffel, P., Beale, T., Hayworth, G., Heard, S., & Leslie, H. (2006). The relationship between CEN 13606, HL7, and openEHR. *HIC 2006 and HINZ 2006: Proceedings, 24*.

Schneider, G. (2011). *Electronic Commerce* (9th ed.). Course Technology.

Schumpeter, J. A. (1934). *The theory of economic development: an inquiry into profits, capital, credit, interest, and the business cycle*. New Brunswick, NJ: Transaction Publishers.

Schwab, K. (2016). *The Fourth industrial Revolution*. Moscow: Publishing house.

Sedkaoui, S. (2017). The Internet, Data Analytics and Big Data. In Internet Economics: Models, Mechanisms and Management (pp. 144-166). Gottinger: eBook Bentham Science Publishers.

Sedkaoui, S. (2018a). *Data analytics and big data*. London: ISTE-Wiley. doi:10.1002/9781119528043

Sedkaoui, S. (2018b). *Big Data Analytics for Entrepreneurial Success*. Hershey, PA: IGI Global.

Sedkaoui, S. (2018c). Statistical and Computational Needs for Big Data Challenges. In A. Al Mazari (Ed.), *Big Data Analytics in HIV/AIDS Research* (pp. 21–53). Hershey, PA: IGI Global. doi:10.4018/978-1-5225-3203-3.ch002

Sedkaoui, S., & Monino, J. L. (2016). *Big data, Open Data and Data Development*. New York: ISTE-Wiley.

Sewell, M. (2008). *Structural Risk Minimization*. Technical Report: Department of Computer Science, University College London. Retrieved from http://www.svms.org/srm/

Shafer, T. (2017). *Big Data and Data Science*. Elder Research Data Science and Predictive Analytics.

Shamala, P., Ahmad, R., Zolait, A. H., & Sahib, S. (2015). Collective information structure model for Information Security Risk Assessment (ISRA). *Journal of Systems and Information Technology, 17*(2), 193–219. doi:10.1108/JSIT-02-2015-0013

Shao, Y., Li, C., Gu, J., Zhang, J., & Luo, Y. (2018). Efficient jobs scheduling approach for big data applications. *Computers & Industrial Engineering, 117*, 249–261. doi:10.1016/j.cie.2018.02.006

Sharma, C. S. (2016). *Securing Cyberspace: International and Asian Perspectives*. New Delhi: Pentagon Press.

Sharma, V., Stranieri, A., Ugon, J., Vamplew, P., & Martin, L. (2017). An Agile Group Aware Process beyond CRISP-DM: A Hospital Data Mining Case Study. *Proceedings of the International Conference on Compute and Data Analysis*. 10.1145/3093241.3093273

Shatnawi, R., Qlthebyan, Q., Ghalib, B., & Al-Maolegi, M. (2014). *Building a smart academic advising system using association rule mining*. arXiv:1407.1807

Shearer, C. (2000). The CRISP-DM model: The new blueprint for data mining. *Journal of Data Warehousing, 5*(4), 13–22.

Shen, Y., & Zhang, Y. (2014). Transmission protocol for secure big data in two-hop wireless networks with cooperative jamming. *Information Sciences, 281*(1), 201–210. doi:10.1016/j.ins.2014.05.037

Shimmer. (2018). Retrieved from http://www.shimmersensing.com/products/shimmer3-ecg-sensor#specifications-tab

Shin, D. (2016). Demystifying big data: Anatomy of big data developmental process. *Telecommunications Policy, 40*(9), 837–854. doi:10.1016/j.telpol.2015.03.007

Shollo, A. (2013). *The role of business intelligence in organizational decision-making* (PhD thesis). Copenhagen Business School.

Shrivastavaa, S., Sharmab, A., & Shrivastavac, D. (2015). An Approach for QoS Based Fault Reconfiguration in Service. *Procedia Computer Science, 46*, 766–773. doi:10.1016/j.procs.2015.02.145

Shull, F. (2014). The True Cost of Mobility? *IEEE Software, 31*(2), 5–9. doi:10.1109/MS.2014.47

Singer, W. P., & Friedman, A. (2014). *Cyber Security and Cyber War: What Everyone Needs to Know*. New York: Oxford University Press.

Singh, H. (2015, August 24). *8 Best Practices for Executing a Successful Big Data Analytics Strategy*. Retrieved May 1, 2016, from https://www.linkedin.com/pulse/8-best-practices-executing-successful-big-data-analytics-singh

Singh, A., & Chatterjee, K. (2017). Cloud security issues and challenges: A survey. *Journal of Network and Computer Applications, 79*, 88–115. doi:10.1016/j.jnca.2016.11.027

Singh, A., & Fhom, H. C. S. (2017). Restricted usage of anonymous credentials in vehicular ad hoc networks for misbehavior detection. *International Journal of Information Security, 16*(2), 195–201. doi:10.100710207-016-0328-y

Sitton, M., & Reich, Y. (2016). Enterprise Systems Engineering for Better Operational Interoperability. *Systems Engineering*.

Slim, A., Heileman, G. L., Kozlick, J., & Abdallah, C. T. (2014). Predicting student success based on prior performance. In *Computational Intelligence and Data Mining (CIDM)*. Orlando, FL: IEEE. doi:10.1109/CIDM.2014.7008697

SmartVision. (n.d.). *CRSP-DM*. Retrieved from http://crisp-dm.eu

Smith, D. (2005). Dancing with the mysterious forces of chaos: Issues around complexity, knowledge and the management of uncertainty. *Clinician in Management*, (3/4), 115–123.

Smith, S. (1992). Towards an intelligent planning system. *International Journal of Project Management, 10*(4), 213–218. doi:10.1016/0263-7863(92)90080-S

Smola, A., & Schölkopf, B. (1998). *A Tutorial on Support Vector Regression NeuroCOLT Technical Report.* NC-TR-98-030, Royal Holloway College, University of London, UK.

Soini, M., Nummela, J., Oksa, P., Ukkonen, L., & Sydänheimo, L. (2008). Wireless body area network for hip rehabilitation system. *Ubiquitous Computing and Communication Journal, 3*(5), 42–48.

Soldatos, J. (2017). *Building Blocks for IoT Analytics Internet-of-Things Analytics.* River Publishers Series in Signal, Image and Speech Processing.

Soomro, Z., Hussain Shah, A. M., & Ahmed, J. (2016). Information security management needs more holistic approach: A literature review. *International Journal of Information Management, 36*(2), 215–225. doi:10.1016/j.ijinfomgt.2015.11.009

Soros, G. (2013). Fallibility, reflexivity, and the human uncertainty principle. *Journal of Economic Methodology, 20*(4), 309–329. doi:10.1080/1350178X.2013.859415

Springer, S., & Deutsch, G. (1983). Left brain, Right brain. Moscow: Mir.

Standard & Poor's. (2016, October 12). *Standard & Poor's History.* Retrieved from https://www.isin.net/standard-poors/

Steenackers, A., & Goovaerts, M. J. (1989). A credit scoring model for personal loans. *Insurance, Mathematics & Economics, 8*(1), 31–34. doi:10.1016/0167-6687(89)90044-9

Stepanova, M., & Thomas, L. C. (2001). PHAB scores: Proportional hazards analysis. *The Journal of the Operational Research Society, 52*(9), 1007–1016. doi:10.1057/palgrave.jors.2601189

Stepchenko, D., & Voronova, I. (2015). Assessment of Risk Function Using Analytical Network Process. *Inzinerine Ekonomika-Engineering Economics, 26*(3), 264–271.

Stevenson, H. H., & Jarillo, J. C. (1990). A paradigm of entrepreneurship: Entrepreneurial management. *Strategic Management Journal, 11*, 17–27.

Stewart, J. M., Tittel, E., & Chapple, M. (2005). *CISSP: Certified Information Systems Security Professional Study Guide* (3rd ed.). San Francisco: Sybex.

Stokes, D., & Wilson, N. (2010). *Small business management and entrepreneurship.* EMEA: Cengage Learning.

Storey, D. J., & Johnson, S. (1987). *Are small firms the answer to unemployment?* Employment Institute.

Storey, V. C., & Song, I. Y. (2017). Big data technologies and management: What conceptual modeling can do. *Data & Knowledge Engineering, 108*, 50–67. doi:10.1016/j.datak.2017.01.001

Strang, K. D., & Alamieyeseigha, S. (2017). What and Where Are the Risks of International Terrorist Attacks. In Violence and Society: Breakthroughs in Research and Practice. IGI Global. doi:10.4018/978-1-5225-0988-2.ch026

Strang, K. D. (2012). Logistic planning with nonlinear goal programming models in spreadsheets. *International Journal of Applied Logistics, 2*(4), 1–14. doi:10.4018/jal.2012100101

Strang, K. D. (2013). Homeowner behavioral intent to evacuate after flood warnings. *International Journal of Risk and Contingency Management, 2*(3), 1–28. doi:10.4018/ijrcm.2013070101

Strang, K. D. (2015a). Exploring the relationship between global terrorist ideology and attack methodology. *Risk Management Journal, 17*(2), 65–90. doi:10.1057/rm.2015.8

Strang, K. D. (2015b). *Palgrave Handbook of Research Design in Business and Management*. New York: Palgrave Macmillan. doi:10.1057/9781137484956

Strang, K. D., & Alamieyeseigha, S. (2015). What and where are the risks of international terrorist attacks: A descriptive study of the evidence. *International Journal of Risk and Contingency Management, 4*(1), 1–18. doi:10.4018/ijrcm.2015010101

Strang, K. D., & Sun, Z. (2016). Analyzing relationships in terrorism big data using Hadoop and statistics. *Journal of Computer Information Systems, 56*(5), 55–65.

Strang, K. D., & Sun, Z. (2017). Scholarly big data body of knowledge: What is the status of privacy and security? *Annals of Data Science, 4*(1), 1–17. doi:10.100740745-016-0096-6

Stranieri, A., & Yearwood, J. (2012). The Case for a Re-Use of Community Reasoning. In J. Yearwood & A. Stranieri (Eds.), *Approaches for Community Decision Making and Collective Reasoning* (pp. 237–249). IGI Global.

StrategyandPart of the PWC. (2018). *Review of the global venture market and the most advanced technologies, new business models.* Retrieved from https://www.strategyand.pwc.com/media/file/Next-Big-Thing_RU.pdf

Sumathi, S., & Sivanandam, S. N. (2006). *Introduction to data mining and its application.* New York: Springer. doi:10.1007/978-3-540-34351-6

Sun, J., Sun, Z., Li, Y., & Zhao, S. (2012). A Strategic Model of Trust Management in Web Services. *Physics Procedia, 24*(B), 1560-1566.

Sun, Z., & Firmin, S. (2012). A strategic perspective on management intelligent systems. In Management Intelligent Systems, AISC 171 (pp. 3-14). Springer. doi:10.1007/978-3-642-30864-2_1

Sun, Z., & Yearwood, J. (2014). A theoretical foundation of demand-driven web services. In Z. Sun, & J. Yearwood (Eds.), Demand-Driven Web Services: Theory, Technologies, and Applications (pp. 1-25). IGI-Global. doi:10.4018/978-1-4666-5884-4.ch001

Sun, Z., Sun, J., & Meredith, G. (2012). Customer Decision Making in Web Services with an Integrated P6 Model. *Physics Procedia, 24*(B), 1553-1559.

Sun, Z. (2016). A Framework for Developing Management Intelligent Systems. *International Journal of Systems and Service-Oriented Engineering, 6*(1), 37–53. doi:10.4018/IJSSOE.2016010103

Sun, Z. (2018). 10 Bigs: Big Data and Its Ten Big Characteristics. *PNG UoT BAIS, 3*(1), 1–10. doi:10.13140/RG.2.2.31449.62566

Sun, Z., & Finnie, G. (2004). *Intelligent Techniques in E-Commerce: A Case-based Reasoning Perspective.* Berlin: Springer-Verlag. doi:10.1007/978-3-540-40003-5

Sun, Z., & Finnie, G. (2005). *Experience management in knowledge management. LNAI 3681* (pp. 979–986). Berlin: Springer-Verlag.

Sun, Z., Strang, K. D., & Li, R. (2016). Ten bigs of big data: A multidisciplinary framework. *Proceedings of 10th ACM International Conference on Research and Practical Issues of Enterprise Information Systems (CONFENIS 2016), 1,* 550-661.

Sun, Z., Strang, K., & Yearwood, J. (2014). *Analytics service oriented architecture for enterprise information systems. In Proceedings of iiWAS2014* (pp. 506–518). Hanoi: ACM. doi:10.1145/2684200.2684358

Sun, Z., Sun, L., & Strang, K. (2018). Big Data Analytics Services for Enhancing Business Intelligence. *Journal of Computer Information Systems, 58*(2), 162–169. doi:10.1080/08874417.2016.1220239

Sun, Z., & Wang, P. (2017). Big Data, Analytics and Intelligence: An Editorial Perspective. *Journal of New Mathematics and Natural Computation, 13*(2), 75–81. doi:10.1142/S179300571702001X

Sun, Z., Zou, H., & Strang, K. (2015). *Big Data Analytics as a Service for Business Intelligence. In LNCS 9373* (pp. 200–211). Berlin: Springer.

Su, Y., Gao, X., Li, X., & Tao, D. (2012). Multivariate Multilinear Regression. *IEEE Transactions on Systems, Man, and Cybernetics. Part B, Cybernetics, 42*(6), 1560–1573. doi:10.1109/TSMCB.2012.2195171 PMID:22677310

Sveen, F., Torres, J., & Sarriegi, J. (2009). Blind Information Security Strategy. *International Journal of Critical Infrastructure Protection, 2*(3), 95–109. doi:10.1016/j.ijcip.2009.07.003

Sweller, J. (2010). Element interactivity and intrinsic, extraneous, and germane cognitive load. *Educational Psychology Review, 22*(2), 123–138. doi:10.100710648-010-9128-5

Swetapadma, A., & Yadav, A. (2017). A Novel Decision Tree Regression-Based Fault Distance Estimation Scheme for Transmission Lines. *IEEE Transactions on Power Delivery, 32*(1), 234–245. doi:10.1109/TPWRD.2016.2598553

Swire, P. (2013). Finding the best of the imperfect alternatives for privacy, health it, and cybersecurity. *Wisconsin Law Review,* (2): 649–669.

Tableau. (2015). *Top 8 Trends for 2016: Big Data.* Retrieved from www.tableau.com/Big-Data

Tao, M., Zuo, J., Liu, Z., Castiglione, A., & Palmieri, F. (2018). Multi-layer cloud architectural model and ontology-based security service framework for IoT-based smart homes. *Future Generation Computer Systems, 78,* 1040–1051. doi:10.1016/j.future.2016.11.011

Terry, G. R. (1968). *Principles of Management* (5th ed.). Homewood, IL: Richard D. Irwin, Inc.

Terry, N. (2015). Navigating the Incoherence of Big Data Reform Proposals. *The Journal of Law, Medicine & Ethics, 43*(1), 44–47. doi:10.1111/jlme.12214 PMID:25846163

The Civil Law Rules on Robotics. (2016). Retrieved from http://www.europarl.europa.eu/RegData/etudes/STUD/2016/571379/IPOL_STU(2016)571379_EN.pdf

The Dutch Corporate Governance Code. (2016). Retrieved from https://www.mccg.nl/?page=3779

The State University of Management. (2017). *Proceedings from the 1st scientific-practical Conference Step into the future: AI and digital economy.* Moscow: Author.

Thierauf, R. J. (1982). *Decision Support Systems for Effective Planning and Control: A Case Study Approach.* Englewood Cliffs, NJ: Prentice Hall.

Thilo, F. J., Hürlimann, B., Hahn, S., Bilger, S., Schols, J. M., & Halfens, R. J. (2016). Involvement of older people in the development of fall detection systems: A scoping review. *BMC Geriatrics, 16*(1), 42. doi:10.118612877-016-0216-3 PMID:26869259

Thorpe, J. H., & Gray, E. A. (2015). Law and the Public's Health: Big data and public health - navigating privacy laws to maximize potential. *Public Health Reports, 130*(2), 171–175. doi:10.1177/003335491513000211 PMID:25729109

Tiago, O., Manoj, T., & Espadanal, M. (2014). Assessing the determinants of cloud computing adoption: An analysis of the manufacturing and services sectors. *Information & Management, 51*(5), 497–510. doi:10.1016/j.im.2014.03.006

TIOBE The software Quality Company. (2018, June). Retrieved from https://www.tiobe.com/tiobe-index/

Toffler, E. (2004). *The third wave.* Moscow: AST.

Tomar, G. S., Chaudhari, N. S., Bhadoria, R. S., & Deka, G. C. (Eds.). (2016). *The Human Element of Big Data: Issues, Analytics, and Performance.* CRC Press. doi:10.1201/9781315368061

Tropina, T., & Callanan, C. (2015). *Self- and Co-regulation in Cybercrime, Cybersecurity and National Security.* New York: Springer International Publishing. doi:10.1007/978-3-319-16447-2

Tsai, C., Lai, C., Chao, H., & Vasilakos, A. (2015). Big data analytics: A survey. *Journal of Big Data, 2*(1), 31–62. doi:10.118640537-015-0030-3 PMID:26191487

Tu, C. Z., Yuan, Y., Archer, N., & Connelly, C. E. (2018). Strategic value alignment for information security management: A critical success factor analysis. *Information & Computer Security, 26*(2), 150–170. doi:10.1108/ICS-06-2017-0042

Tunowski, R. (2015). Organization effectiveness and business intelligence systems. Literature Review. *Management and Business Administration. Central Europe, 23*(4), 55–73.

Turban, E., Sharda, R., & Delen, D. (2010). *Decision support and business intelligence systems* (9th ed.). Upper Saddle River, NJ: Prentice Hall Press.

Turban, E., & Volonino, L. (2011). *Information Technology for Management: Improving Performance in the Digital Economy* (8th ed.). Hoboken, NJ: John Wiley & Sons.

Turing, A. (1950). Computing Machinery and Intelligence. *Mind, 49*(236), 433–460. doi:10.1093/mind/LIX.236.433

Tutton, J. (2010). Incident Response and Compliance: A Case Study of the Recent Attacks. *Information Security Technical Report, 15*(4), 145–149. doi:10.1016/j.istr.2011.02.001

Uma, K. K., & Sankarasubramanian, R. (2014). Business intelligence system - a survey. *International Journal of Advanced Research in Computer Science and Software Engineering, 4*(9), 688–691. Retrieved from http://ijarcsse.com/Before_August_2017/docs/papers/Volume_4/9_September2014/V4I9-0372.pdf

Umam, A. (n.d.). *Ardian Umam Blog.* Retrieved from https://ardianumam.wordpress.com/tag/regression/ArdianUmam Blog.

Urban, T. (2015). *The AI Revolution: The Road to Superintelligence.* Retrieved from https://waitbutwhy.com/2015/01/artificial-intelligence-revolution-1.html

US Department of Defence. (2015, June). *2015 - The National Military Strategy of the United States of America.* Retrieved from Aquisition Community Connection: http://www.jcs.mil/Portals/36/Documents/Publications/2015_National_Military_Strategy.pdf

US-CERT. (2017, January 24). *Critical Infrastructure Cyber Community Voluntary Program.* Retrieved from US-CERT: https://www.us-cert.gov/ccubedvp

Vaidhyanathan, S., & Bulock, C. (2014). Knowledge and Dignity in the Era of Big Data. *The Serials Librarian, 66*(1-4), 49–64. doi:10.1080/0361526X.2014.879805

Vajjhala, N. R., & Strang, K. D. (2017). Measuring organizational-fit through socio-cultural big data. *Journal of New Mathematics and Natural Computation, 13*(2), 1–17.

Vajjhala, N. R., Strang, K. D., & Sun, Z. (2015). Statistical modeling and visualizing of open big data using a terrorism case study. *Open Big Data Conference,* 489-496. 10.1109/FiCloud.2015.15

Van Barneveld, A., Arnold, K.E., & Campbell, J.P. (2012). Analytics in higher education: Establishing a common language. *EDUCAUSE Learning Initiative, 1*(1), 1-11.

van der Aalst, W. M. P., ter Hofstede, A. H. M., & Weske, M. (2003). Business process management: A survey. In W.M.P van der Aalst, & M. Weske (Eds.), Business Process Management. Lecture Notes in Computer Science (vol. 2678). Berlin: Springer. doi:10.1007/3-540-44895-0_1

Van Halteren, A., Bults, R., Wac, K., Konstantas, D., Widya, I., Dokovsky, N., ... Herzog, R. (2004). Mobile patient monitoring: The mobihealth system. *The Journal on Information Technology in Healthcare, 2*(5), 365–373.

Van Laerhoven, K., Lo, B. P., Ng, J. W., Thiemjarus, S., King, R., Kwan, S., ... Needham, P. (2004). Medical healthcare monitoring with wearable and implantable sensors. *Proc. of the 3rd International Workshop on Ubiquitous Computing for Healthcare Applications.*

van Loenen, B., Kulk, S., & Ploeger, H. (2016). Data protection legislation: A very hungry caterpillar: The case of mapping data in the European Union. *Government Information Quarterly, 33*(2), 338–345. doi:10.1016/j.giq.2016.04.002

Van Merriënboer, J. J. G., & Krammer, H. P. (1987). Instructional strategies and tactics for the design of introductory computer programming courses in high school. *Instructional Science, 16*(3), 251–285. doi:10.1007/BF00120253

van Otterlo, M. (2014). Automated experimentation in Walden 3.0: The next step in profiling, predicting, control and surveillance. *Surveillance & Society, 12*(2), 255–272. doi:10.24908s.v12i2.4600

Vapnik, V. (1998). *Statistical Learning Theory*. New York: Wiley-Interscience Publication.

Vardi, M. Y. (2016). The Moral Imperative of Artificial Intelligence. *Communications of the ACM, 59*(5), 5. doi:10.1145/2903530

Varian, H. R. (2014). Big data: New tricks for econometrics. *The Journal of Economic Perspectives, 28*(2), 3–27. doi:10.1257/jep.28.2.3

Venkatasubramanian, K., Deng, G., Mukherjee, T., Quintero, J., Annamalai, V., & Gupta, S. K. (2005). Ayushman: A wireless sensor network based health monitoring infrastructure and testbed. *Proceedings of the First IEEE international conference on Distributed Computing in Sensor Systems.* 10.1007/11502593_39

Vermeulen, E. P. (2015). *Corporate Governance in a Networked Age*. Tilburg Law School Legal Studies Research Paper Series No. 16/2015.

Villaronga, E. F., Kieseberg, P., & Li, T. (2018). Humans forget, machines remember: Artificial intelligence and the Right to Be Forgotten. *Computer Law & Security Review, 34*(2), 304–313. doi:10.1016/j.clsr.2017.08.007

Vinge, V. (1993). *The Coming Technological Singularity*. Retrieved from http://www.accelerating.org/articles/coming-techsingularity.html

Visser W. (2008). CSR 2.0: The new era of corporate sustainability and responsibility. *CSR International Inspiration Series, 1,* 1-2.

Walkenbach, J. (2002). *Microsoft Excel 2000 power programming with VBA*. Foster City, CA: IDC Books.

Walkenbach, J. (2010). *Microsoft Excel 2010 power programming with VBA*. Hoboken, NJ: Wiley. doi:10.1002/9781118257616

Waller, M. A., & Fawcett, S. E. (2013). Data science, predictive analytics, and big data: A revolution that will transform supply chain design and management. *Journal of Business Logistics, 34*(2), 77–84. doi:10.1111/jbl.12010

Walwei, U. (2016). Digitalization and structural labor market problems: The case of Germany. *ILO Research Paper*, *17*, 1-31.

Wamba, S. F., Akter, S., Edwards, A., Chopin, G., & Gnanzou, D. (2015). How 'big data' can make big impact: Findings from a systematic review and a longitudinal case study. *International Journal of Production Economics*, *165*, 234–246. doi:10.1016/j.ijpe.2014.12.031

Wang, F.-Y. (2012). A big-data perspective on AI: Newton, Merton, and Analytics Intelligence. *IEEE Intelligent Systems*, *27*(5), 2-4.

Wang, H., Jiang, X., & Kambourakis, G. (2015). Special issue on Security, Privacy and Trust in network-based Big Data. *Information Sciences*, *318*(1), 48–50. doi:10.1016/j.ins.2015.05.040

Wang, J.-N., Du, J., Chiu, Y.-L., & Li, J. (2018). Dynamic effects of customer experience levels on durable product satisfaction: Price and popularity moderation. *Electronic Commerce Research and Applications*, *28*, 16–29. doi:10.1016/j.elerap.2018.01.002

Wang, W., & Hu, L. (2014). A secure and efficient handover authentication protocol for wireless networks. *Journal of Sensors*, *14*(7), 11379–11394. doi:10.3390140711379 PMID:24971471

Wang, Y., Kung, L., & Byrd, T. A. (2018). Big data analytics: Understanding its capabilities and potential benefits for healthcare organizations. *Technological Forecasting and Social Change*, *126*, 3–13. doi:10.1016/j.techfore.2015.12.019

Ward, J. C. (2014). Oncology Reimbursement in the Era of Personalized Medicine and Big Data. *Journal of Oncology Practice / American Society of Clinical Oncology*, *10*(2), 83–86. doi:10.1200/JOP.2014.001308 PMID:24633283

Warren, J., Donald, J., Moffitt, K. C., & Byrnes, P. (2015). How Big Data Will Change Accounting. *Accounting Horizons*, *29*(2), 397–407. doi:10.2308/acch-51069

Watson, H. J. (2014). Tutorial: Big Data Analytics: Concepts, Technologies, and Applications. *Communications of the Association for Information Systems*, *34*, 65. doi:10.17705/1CAIS.03465

Weiss, R., & Zgorski, L.-J. (2012, March 29). *Obama Administration Unveils "Big Data" Initiative: Announces $200 Million in New R&D Investments*. Retrieved from http://www.cccblog.org/2012/03/29/obama-administration-unveils-200m-big-data-rd-initiative

Wheatley, M. (2016). *Wikibon forecasts Big Data market to hit $92.2B by 2026*. Retrieved January 1, 2017, from: http://siliconangle.com/blog/2016/03/30/wikibon-forecasts-big-data-market-to-hit-92-2bn-by-2026/

Wickham, H., Francois, R., Henry, L., & Müller, K. (2015). dplyr: A grammar of data manipulation. *R package version 0.4, 3*.

Wickham, H. (2014). Tidy data. *Journal of Statistical Software*, *59*(10), 1–23. doi:10.18637/jss.v059.i10 PMID:26917999

Wieder, B., & Ossimitz, M.-L. (2015). The impact of business intelligence on the quality of decision making - a mediation model. *Proceedings of the Conference on Enterprise Information Systems CENTERIS*. 10.1016/j.procs.2015.08.599

Wikipedia. (2018, July 26). *List of virtual communities with more than 100 million active users*. Retrieved July 27, 2017, from https://en.wikipedia.org/wiki/List_of_virtual_communities_with_more_than_100_million_active_users

Wiklund, J. (1999). The sustainability of the entrepreneurial orientation-performance relationship. *Entrepreneurship Theory and Practice*, *24*(1), 39–50. doi:10.1177/104225879902400103

Willems, E. (2011). Cyber-terrorism in the process industry. *Computer Fraud & Security*, *3*(3), 16–19. doi:10.1016/S1361-3723(11)70032-X

Williams, S., & Williams, N. (2003). *The business value of business intelligence* (Vol. 3). Business Intelligence Journal.

Winkler, I. (2010). *Justifying IT Security – Managing Risk & Keeping your network Secure.* Qualys Inc.

Wittenbaum, G. M. (2000). The bias toward discussing shared information: Why are high-status group members immune. *Communication Research, 27*(3), 379–401. doi:10.1177/009365000027003005

Wixom, B., Ariyachandra, T., Douglas, D., Goul, M., Gupta, B., Iyer, L., ... Turetken, O. (2014). The current state of business intelligence in academia: The arrival of big data. *Communications of the Association for Information Systems, 34*, 1–13. doi:10.17705/1CAIS.03401

Wixom, B., & Watson, H. (2010). The BI-based organization. *International Journal of Business Intelligence Research, 1*(1), 13–28. doi:10.4018/jbir.2010071702

World Economic Forum & Accenture. (2017). *Digital Transformation Initiative.* Retrieved from https://www.accenture.com/t20170411T120304Z__w__/us-en/_acnmedia/Accenture/Conversion-Assets/WEF/PDF/Accenture-DTI-executive-summary.pdf

Wu &Bartolini. (2007). A service-oriented architecture for business intelligence. *Proceedings of the IEEE International Conference on Service-Oriented Computing and Applications.*

Wu, H.-C., & Wu, Y.-T. (2016). Evaluating credit rating prediction by using the KMV model and random forest. *Kybernetes, 45*(10), 1637–1651. doi:10.1108/K-12-2014-0285

Xu, R., Chen, Y., Blasch, E., & Chen, G. (2018). BlendCAC: A Smart Contract Enabled Decentralized Capability-Based Access Control Mechanism for the IoT. *Computers, 7*(3), 39. doi:10.3390/computers7030039

Yadav, S., Bharadwaj, B., & Pal, S. (2012). Data mining applications: A comparative study for predicting student's performance. *International Journal of Innovative Technology and Creative Engineering, 1*(12), 13–19. Retrieved from http://arxiv.org/abs/1202.4815

Yang, C. N., Wu, C. C., & Wang, D. S. (2014). A discussion on the relationship between probabilistic visual cryptography and random grid. *Information Sciences, 278*, 141–173. doi:10.1016/j.ins.2014.03.033

Yar, M. (2006). *Cybercrime and Society.* London: Sage.

Yearwood, J., & Stranieri, A. (2010). *Technologies for Supporting Reasoning Communities and Collaborative Decision Making: Cooperative Approaches: Cooperative Approaches.* IGI Global.

Yeow, A., Soh, C., & Hansen, R. (2018). Aligning with new digital strategy: A dynamic capabilities approach. *The Journal of Strategic Information Systems, 27*(1), 43–58. doi:10.1016/j.jsis.2017.09.001

Yobas, M. B., & Crook, J. N. (2000). Credit scoring using neural and evolutionary techniques. *IMA Journal of Management Mathematics, 11*(2), 111–125. doi:10.1093/imaman/11.2.111

Zaharia, M. H. (2014). Generalized Demand-Driven Web Services. In Z. Sun, & J. Yearwood (Eds.), Handbook of Research on Demand-Driven Web Services: Theory, Technologies, and Applications (pp. 102-134). IGI Global. doi:10.4018/978-1-4666-5884-4.ch005

Zaharia, M. H. (2016). A Paradigm Shift in Cyberspace Security. In B. A. Hamid & R. Arabnia (Eds.), Emerging Trends in ICT Security (pp. 443-451). Morgan Kaufmann.

Zahra, S. A., & Covin, J. G. (1995). Contextual influences on the corporate entrepreneurship performance relationship: A longitudinal analysis. *Journal of Business Venturing, 10*(1), 43–58. doi:10.1016/0883-9026(94)00004-E

Zhang, P., Zhou, M., & Fortino, G. (2018). Security and trust issues in Fog computing: A survey. *Future Generation Computer Systems*, *88*, 16–27. doi:10.1016/j.future.2018.05.008

Zhang, W., Du, Y., Yoshida, T., Wang, Q., & Li, X. (2018). SamEn-SVR: Using sample entropy and support vector regression for bug number prediction. *IET Software*, *12*(3), 183–189. doi:10.1049/iet-sen.2017.0168

Zhong, R. Y., Huang, G. Q., Lan, S., Dai, Q. Y., Chen, X., & Zhang, T. (2015). A big data approach for logistics trajectory discovery from RFID-enabled production data. *International Journal of Production Economics*, *165*(1), 260–272. doi:10.1016/j.ijpe.2015.02.014

Zhu, Y., & McKelvey, M. (2013). Business models in Big Data in China: Opportunities through sequencing and bioinformatics. In *How Entrepreneurs Do What They Do: Case Studies of Knowledge Intensive Entrepreneurship*. Cheltenham, UK: Edward Elgar Publishers. doi:10.4337/9781781005507.00024

Zhu, Z., Barnette, R. K., Fussell, K. M., Michael Rodriguez, R., Canonico, A., & Light, R. W. (2005). Continuous oxygen monitoring—A better way to prescribe long-term oxygen therapy. *Respiratory Medicine*, *99*(11), 1386–1392. doi:10.1016/j.rmed.2005.03.010 PMID:15878655

Zikopoulos, P., Eaton, C., DeRoos, D., Deutsch, T., & Lapis, G. (2011). *Understanding Big Data: Analytics for Enterprise Class Hadoop and Streaming Data*. McGraw-Hill Osborne Media.

Zimmermann, J., Brodersen, K. H., Pellet, J., August, E., Buhmann, J. M., & Zurich, E. T. H. (2007). Predicting graduate-level performance from undergraduate achievements. In *Proceedings of the 4th International Conference on Educational Data Mining*, 2–3. Retrieved from http://educationaldatamining.org/EDM2011/wp-content/uploads/proc/edm2011_poster20_Zimmermann.pdf

Ziwen, S., Yuhui, L., & Li, T. (2018). Attack localization task allocation in wireless sensor networks based on multi-objective binary particle swarm optimization. *Journal of Network and Computer Applications*, *112*, 29–40. doi:10.1016/j.jnca.2018.03.023

About the Contributors

Zhaohao Sun graduated from Bond University Australia, University of Ballarat, Brandenburg Technical University Cottbus (TU Cottbus), Germany and Hebei University, China with PhD, Graduate Cert. of Edu., MSc (Dipl.-Math.), MSc, and BSc respectively. Dr Sun is currently a full professor of Information Technology, Head of Department of Business Studies, PNG University of Technology, Director of Research Centre of Big Data Analytics and Intelligent Systems (BAIS). He is also an adjunct professor of the Federation University Australia, chair professor of Hebei University of Science & Technology, adjunct professor of Hebei Normal University. He has 5 books and 140+ refereed research paper publications, completed 20+ research grants, supported by from the Chinese Government, German Government, Australian Government, USA Government and PNG Government, and lectured 45+ different courses for undergraduate and postgraduate students of IT, IS, CS and EMBA in universities of Australia, China and PNG. He is an editor and/or associate editor of five international journals. His research has appeared in Journal of Computer Information Systems, Intelligent Journal of Intelligent Systems, Information Sciences, Knowledge-Based Systems, etc. His current research interests include big data, big data analytics, artificial intelligence, business intelligence, multiagent systems, intelligent systems. He is a senior member of ACS, and a member MAIS and MIEEE.

* * *

Nabeel Al-Qirim is a passionate teacher and a developer of different Information Systems, Business, Innovation & Entrepreneurship courses at both undergraduate and graduate levels (i.e., Knowledge management, E-Business, Strategic IS, E-Government, IT Governance, E-Governance, etc.). He is also a keen researcher (h-index 17) and his research interests covered different Information systems topics, Innovation & Entrepreneurship and IT-education/pedagogy and mostly related to investigating the adoption and diffusion of different technologies in different contexts using both qualitative (case studies, focus group) and quantitative (surveys) methods. He authored one research book and co-authored another and co-edited three books in the area of Small to Medium-Sized Enterprises (SMEs) and E-Commerce. He published more than 100 research papers in refereed and highly-impact international outlets (i.e., PACIS, AMCIS, ECIS, IFIP, BLED, EM, Computer & Education, ECRA, Medical Informatics, Telemedicine and eHealth, etc.). He lead/participated in several panels, workshops, conferences and journal's special-issues. He is also a member in leading academic and professional associations (IEEE senior member, ACM, AIS) and in the editorial advisory board of several journals (JIKM, IJCEC, JECO, BPMJ, IJNOV, IDI,

IJCA). He is involved in the community through participating in different academic and non-academic committees. Dr Al-Qirim is in academia (UAEU, Auckland University of Technology) since 1999 and before that he worked for 10 years in the IT industry as Business&IT consultant (1989-1998). This professional experience has shaped his teaching and research in terms of methodology and approach.

Heba Atteya has always found inspiration in working with data and finding its underlying hidden patterns. She believes that data-informed decision-making is what every institution need to compete in this highly competitive market. Heba completed her MSc in Computer Science at The American University in Cairo (AUC) in Spring 2017 in the topic of visualizing large datasets. She earned her bachelor of science in Information Systems with honors in 2010 and joined AUC as a full-time staff member since 2011. She has maintained a successful record of achievements at AUC, which qualified her for the position of the Business Intelligence and Data Analytics Director in 2017 founding and overseeing the development of the AUC datawarehouse with the mission of supporting informed-decision making at all levels; strategic, operational and tactical. Prior to that she was a research assistant from 2015 to 2017 and a business analyst from 2011 to 2015.

Venki Balasubramanian specialises in Body Area Wireless Sensor Network for remote healthcare monitoring research. His research opened up new research area in measuring time critical applications. He is a pioneer in building (pilot) remote healthcare monitoring applications for pregnant women. His research on dependability measure using BAWSN has seen as emerging research area in the field of eHealth. In recent years he has focused particularly on cloud computing, electronic medical records and in the application of body area wireless sensor networks for assistive care.

Ritwik Bandyopdahyay is a B.Tech student at School Of Computer Engineering, KIIT University, Bhubaneswar, Odisha, India.

Paul Blayney joined the Accounting Discipline at the University of Sydney following his first academic position at the University of Technology in Lae, Papua New Guinea. Prior to his academic career he completed his chartered accounting training with a "Big 8" public accounting firm in Calgary, Canada. Paul received his PhD doctorate in 2013 from the School of Education at the University of New South Wales with submission of his doctoral thesis "application of cognitive load theory to the design of learning tasks and instruction in accounting".

Sowmyarani C. N. is currently working as Associate Professor in Rashtreeya Vidyalaya College of Engineering Computer Science and Engg at Bangalore. She possesses an M.E. postgraduate degree from UVCE, Bangalore University and possess Ph.D degree in Computer science and Engineering at RVCE Research center from Visvesvaraya Technological University.

Veena Gadad is an Assistant Professor for the Department of Computer Science and Engineering, RVCE Bengaluru. She is also pursuing a Ph.D in the area of Privacy Preserving Data Publishing.

Leyla Gamidullaeva is a Doctoral Candidate for a PhD in Economics and is an Associate professor at the Department of Management and Economic Security of Penza State University. L. Gamidullaeva has authored over 200 refereed publications. She is the author of over ten books in innovation management, economic development, networking approach. She also has authored more than 150 articles published in various conference proceedings and journals.

Adrian Gepp is a recent recipient of the American Accounting Association Best Dissertation Award in the Forensic Accounting Section. Adrian uses big data and predictive modelling to reveal unique insights about problems of economic and social importance. Adrian's research spans fraud detection, quantifying advertising effectiveness, health analytics, fintech, business failure prediction and workplace design. Adrian has received multiple external grants to support my research. In addition to researching as an inaugural member of Bond University's Centre for Actuarial and Financial Big Data Analytics, Adrian manages the industry relationships. Adrian has also presented research at numerous corporate education events and has organised several of these events.

Sourish Ghosh is a B.Tech student in School Of Computer Engineering, KIIT University, Bhubaneswar, Odisha, India.

Ana Maria Ifrim is teaching at the Titu Maiorescu University. She is the author of 2 books and over 15 articles for various national and international conferences.

Sherif Kamel is the dean of the school of business at the American University in Cairo. Previously, he served as the senior advisor for strategic planning to the president of the university (2016-2017) and vice president of the university for information management (2015-2016). During his first spell as dean (2009-2014), the school achieved triple crown accreditation, introduced the Executive MBA, the master of science in finance, established the Center for Entrepreneurship and Innovation and the university's accelerator, the Venture Lab, to foster entrepreneurial activities and to encourage interactions between entrepreneurs, students, faculty, and members of the community becoming Egypt's primary university-based incubator. Moreover, the MBA program ranked top by Forbes Middle East and executive education open enrolment ranked 68th by the FT. Kamel was associate dean for executive education (2008-2009) where he established the International Executive Education Institute and was director of the school's executive education (2002-2008). Before joining AUC, he led several training and professional institutes of the Cabinet of Egypt Information and Decision Support Center (1989-2001). Kamel is an Eisenhower Fellow. He is a board member of the American Chamber of Commerce in Egypt and Education for Employment Egypt. He was a board member of the World Bank Knowledge Advisory Commission (2012-2014) and a founding member of the Internet Society of Egypt (1996). Kamel holds a Ph.D. in information systems from London School of Economics and Political Science, an MBA, a BA in business administration and an MA in Islamic art and architecture from the American University in Cairo. His research and teaching interests include management of information technology, information technology transfer to developing nations, organizational transformation, electronic business, decision support systems and entrepreneurship. His work is broadly published IS and management journals and books. He is the editor of three books; E-Strategies for Technological Diffusion and Adoption: National

ICT Approaches for Socioeconomic Development (2010), Electronic Business in Developing Countries: Challenges and Opportunities (2005) and Managing Globally with Information Technology (2003). Kamel is an advocate of diversity, empowerment, inclusion and using a bottom-up leadership approach.

Mounia Khelfaoui, PhD, Senior Lecturer (HDR), Department of Economics, Khemis Miliana University, Algeria; Researcher at Organizational Development and Innovation Laboratory, University of Khemis Miliana, Algeria.

Kuldeep Kumar did his Ph D. from University of Kent at Canterbury and is currently Professor and Head of Economics and Statistics Department in the Faculty of Business at Bond University. He has taught at the Indian Institute of Management, Lucknow and National University of Singapore before joining Bond University, Gold Coast, Australia in 1993. Dr Kumar has published more than 110 research papers in the international refereed journals/conference proceedings, eleven chapters in the books, 25 book reviews for Royal Statistical Society besides presenting papers in more than hundred seminars and conferences. He has been Key note speaker and Chaired sessions in several conferences. He has also edited a special issue of Managerial Finance journal besides several conference proceedings. His current research interests are in the areas of bankruptcy prediction, financial fraud detection, forensic accounting and higher education. Dr Kumar is Fellow of Royal Statistical Society since 1984 and a chartered statistician. Recently he was awarded the status of Chartered Scientist by the Science Council of United Kingdom.

Mikhail Kuznetsov has more than 15 years of experience in investment and management consulting, working in one of the largest financial development institutions - IFC, World Bank Group. More than 10 years of experience in the Board of Directors in huge and middle-sized companies in finance, energetic, transport, food sectors. Founder of the National Association of Corporate Directors (more than 400 participants, 25 cities). Member of the Expert Committee on Corporate Governance under Federal Agency for State Property Management, Central Bank of the Russian Federation. Phd, MBA lector at RANEPA (Russian Presidential Academy of National Economy and Public Administration under the President of the Russian Federation), and MSU (Lomonosov Moscow State University), author of 3 books and more than 30 articles about corporate governance and strategic management.

Iman Megahed is the Chief Strategy and Institutional Effectiveness Officer at the American University in Cairo (AUC). In her current role, she manages multiple data and analytics functions including institutional research, data governance, business intelligence, data warehouse management, and analytics as well as other key institutional effectiveness functions including assessment, strategic planning, accreditation and business process improvement. Previously she held a number of positions in University IT where she was responsible for project managing leading ERP implementations. She founded an office for Online Student Services which applied web services and portal technology to enhance student services. She also held the position of, Executive Director of Data Analytics and Institutional Research, where she led the establishment of the Business Intelligence function at AUC. With a successful track record in administrative positions in Higher Education since 1992, Iman has accumulated an extensive and unique blend of skills. This skill set ranges from pure technical expertise, a strong sense of service, results-oriented management style, effective project management skills and profound understanding of institutional effectiveness and informed based decision making. Iman earned her Ph.D. in Organizational Behavior from Cairo University and her MBA and BS in Computer Science with honors from The American University in Cairo.

Indivar Mishra is a B.Tech student in School Of Computer Engineering, KIIT University, Bhubaneswar, Odisha, India.

Vardan Mkrttchian received his Doctorate of Sciences (Engineering) in Control Systems from Lomonosov Moscow State University (former USSR). Dr. Vardan Mkrttchian taught for undergraduate and graduate student's courses of control system, information sciences and technology, at the Astrakhan State University (Russian Federation), where he was is the Professor of the Information Systems (www.aspu.ru) six years. Now he is full professor in CAD department of Penza State University (www.pnzgu.ru). He is currently chief executive of HHH University, Australia and team leader of the international academics (www.hhhuniversity.com). He also serves as executive director of the HHH Technology Incorporation. Professor Vardan Mkrttchian has authored over 400 refereed publications. He is the author of over twenty books published of IGI Global, included ten books indexed of SCOPUS in IT, Control System, Digital Economy, and Education Technology. He is also has authored more than 200 articles published in various conference proceedings and journals.

Maria Nikishova is of Corporate Governance practice in The Center for Corporate Development Topcompetence and head of the Annual research "The National Corporate Governance Index" in Russia. Nikishova is also an Author and Editor in chief of the media on corporate governance Corpshark.ru. Postgraduate student of the Financial University under the Government of the Russian Federation. Ms. Nikishova specializes in digital business transformation and IT Governance. Author of more than 15 articles about corporate governance and digital technologies.

Ibrahim Oba is teaching at the Titu Maiorescu University. She is the author of 3 books, over 20 articles to various national and international conferences.

Ionica Oncioiu holds a Ph.D. in economy and accounting. Her research interests include the development of SMEs innovation, Project Management, Accounting Information Systems, Asset Management and E-Commerce Marketing. She has had more than 10 years of experience in this area and has published 10 text books and more than 70 papers in scholarly peer reviewed international journals, also authoring eight books.

Svetlana V. Panasenko is Head of department of trade policy in Plekhanov Russian university of economics, Moscow, Russia.

Anca Gabriela Petrescu is teaching at the University Valahia. The whole period was marked of academic activities, coordination of scientific publications, courses, textbooks and scientific research. She is the author of 5 books, over 50 articles to various national and international conferences.

Iman Raeesi Vanani is a PhD Graduate in Systems Management, School of Management, University of Tehran. He is currently an assistant professor in Allameh Tabataba'i University. He received his MSc in Information Technology Management from School of Management, University of Tehran and his BA in Public Administration from Allameh Tabataba'i University. His research interests include Data Science, Advanced Analytics, Business Intelligence, Data Mining, Enterprise Resource Planning, and Big Data Management. He has published many conceptual and practical research papers in various international journals, conference proceedings, and books including International Journal of Hospitality Management, Neural Computing and Applications, The IUP Journal of Knowledge Management, Intelligent Engineering Informatics, Iranian Management Vision Journal, Iranian Journal of Science and Technology Policy, Journal of Information Technology and Sciences, Information Science Reference Publications, and other international and Iranian journals, Books and conferences.

Kamel Rouibah is a Full Professor of information systems, College of Business Administration (CBA), Kuwait University. He holds a PhD in Information Systems from Ecole Polytechnique of Grenoble, France. Before joining CBA, he worked at the Faculty of Technology Management at Eindhoven (Netherlands) and Institut National de la Recherche Scientifique (France). His research interests include Design of Information Systems, Management Information Systems, Engineering Data Management, Workflow Management, Information System and Information Technology Acceptance, diffusion, and satisfaction. He has authored/coauthored over 50 research publications in peer-reviewed reputed journals and conference proceedings. He was involved in several European projects. His publications appeared in several leading journals: Journal of Strategic Information System, Electronic Commerce Research and Applications, International Journal of Information Management, IT & People, Journal of Global Information Management, Computers in Human Behavior, Computers in Industry; Information Management & Computer Security, International Journal of Computer Integrated Manufacturing; Robotics & Computer Integrated Manufacturing Journal; Journal of Decision System; Journal of Engineering Design, International Journal of Handheld Computing Research, Telematics and Informatics, and International Journal for E-Adoption. He has received the excellence younger researcher award from Kuwait University for the academic year 2001/2002 and the distingguised research in 2017. Dr Rouibah is an Associate Editor of AJIS, JECO and has directed many funded research projects, and has served as the program committee member of various international conferences (Australasian Conference of Information Systems-ACIS, Information System Development-ISD; ACM Symposium on Applied Computing on e-Business Applications; IADIS, etc.) and reviewer for various international journals (IT & People, Journal of Global Information Management, Industrial Management & Data System, Journal of Electronic Commerce in Organization, International Journal of e-Adoption, International Journal of Computer Integrated Manufacturing, International Journal of Production Research, The Australasian Journal of Information System, Arab Journal of Administrative Sciences, Journal of Global Information Technology Management, Asian Academy of management Journal, Information Management & Computer Security, Communication of the IIMA.). Dr Rouibah sits on the Editorial Board of several IS journals: Journal of Global Information Management; Journal of Electronic Commerce in Organizations (JECO); International Journal of e-Adoption; The Australasian Journal of Information System, International Journal of Handheld Computing Research, International Journal of Advanced Pervasive and Ubiquitous Computing (IJAPUC). He is the co-editor of "Emerging markets and e-commerce in developing economies" book. He has taught many information systems courses in France, Netherlands, and Kuwait.

Saeid Sadeghi Darvazeh is a Ph.D. student in industrial management from Allameh Tabataba'i University, Tehran, Iran. He has presented his works at several international conferences, and has published in various academic journals. He has published more than 10 papers in journals such as the Journal of Urban Economics and Management, Management Research in Iran, and Journal of Industrial Management. His research interests include the areas of logistics and supply chain management, big data analytics, and multi criteria decision making. He is reviewer of Journal of Urban Economics and Management.

Soraya Sedkaoui is a Senior Lecturer at Khemis Miliana University (Algeria) and Data Analyst at SRY Consulting (Montpellier, France), with more than 10 years of Teaching, Training, Research and Consultation experience in econometrics, statistics, big data analytics and machine learning. She earned her PhD in Economic Analysis and HDR (habilitation) in Economic and Applied Statistics. Dr. Sedkaoui was working as a Researcher at TRIS laboratory, University of Montpellier, France (2011-2016). Her science-oriented research experience and interests are in the areas of big data, Computer Science and the development of algorithms and models for business applications and problems. Dr. Sedkaoui's prior books and research has been published in several refereed editions and journals.

Mohamed Adel Serhani is currently an Associate Professor, College of Information Technology, U.A.E University, Al Ain, U.A.E. He is also an Adjunct faculty in CIISE, Concordia University, Canada. He holds a Ph.D. in Computer Engineering from Concordia University in 2006, and MSc. in Software Engineering from University of Montreal, Canada in 2002. His research interests include: Cloud for data intensive e-health applications, and services; SLA enforcement in Cloud Data centers, and Big Data value chain, Cloud federation and monitoring, Non-invasive Smart health monitoring; management of communities of Web services; and Web services applications and security. He has a large experience earned throughout his involvement and management of different R&D projects. He served on several organizing and Technical Program Committees and he was the program Co-chair of the IEEE conference on Innovations in Information Technology (IIT´13), Chair of IEEE Workshop on Web service (IWCMC´13), Chair of IEEE workshop on Web, Mobile, and Cloud Services (IWCMC´12), and Co-chair of International Workshop on Wireless Sensor Networks and their Applications (NDT´12). He has published more than 100 refereed publications including conferences, journals, a book, and book chapters.

Kenneth Strang has more than 260 mostly-sole-authored scholarly publications. He is a professor who teaches and supervises undergraduate, graduate and doctoral students across five disciplines: business administration, management information systems, marketing/consumer behavior, supply chain management and economics/statistics. Ken has a doctorate in project management (operations research), an MBA (strategic management), a BSBA (marketing), an AAS (IT) all with summa cum laude/honors plus he is an internationally licensed Project Management Professional (PMI, USA), a Certified Network Administrator (Novell, USA), a Certified Research Professional (IIPMR, USA), a Fellow Life Management Institute with distinction (LOMA, USA) and a Certified Procurement Professional (IIPMR, USA). Dr. Strang has lifetime grants over $7 million+, and he has won several honors including a Behavior Energy Climate Change Fellowship from the American Council for an Energy-Efficient Economy, the Emerald Literati award and Duke of Edinborough community service medal, along with several presidential citations. He is the Editor-in-Chief of a peer reviewed journal and Associate-Editor at others.

Andrew Stranieri is an associate professor and researcher in the Centre for Informatics and Applied Optimisation at Federation University Australia. His research in health informatics spans data mining in health, complementary and alternative medicine informatics, telemedicine and intelligent decision support systems. He is the author of over 150 peer reviewed journal and conference articles and has published two books.

Aleena Swetapadma works as assistant professor in KIIT University, India.

Mark Wallis has completed his Honours from the Bond University Business School in Actuarial Science in 2017. Mark completed his Bachelor degree in Actuarial Science from Bond University, Australia in 2016. As a researcher he is primarily interested in the development of financial trading systems, data mining, optimization and other complex real-world problem domains. Mark currently serves as a data scientist in Melbourne.

Mihai Horia Zaharia is currently an associate professor at the Computer Engineering department from "Gheorghe Asachi" Technical University. He received a Ph.D. in Computer Science from the same university in 2002. The research interest areas are related to distributed systems, parallel computer architecture, computer networks security, design patterns, microprocessor applications, decision support systems, distributed artificial intelligence, social networks, social modeling, psychology and mobile computing/internet of things, internet of things, organizational evaluation. He received several research grants from The National University Research Council of Romania as director. Also it was involved in some European projects from Leonardo or FP7 frameworks as technical director. He published over 70 papers as author or coauthor in national or international publications. Also he published as author or as coauthor eight books at national level.

Index

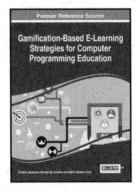

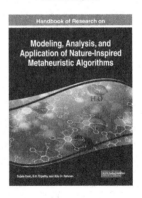

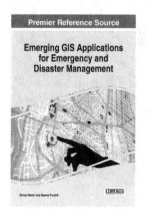
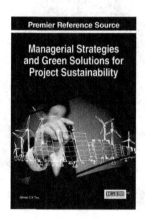

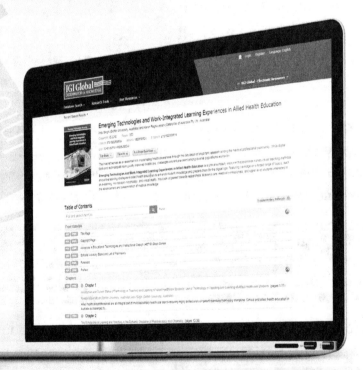

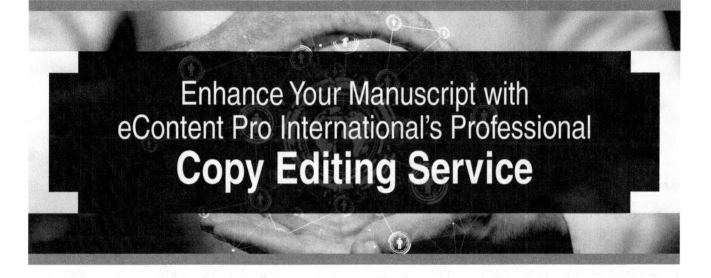

Printed in the United States
By Bookmasters